INDIGENOUS LIFE AROUND THE GREAT LAKES

MIDWEST ARCHAEOLOGICAL PERSPECTIVES
William Lovis, *series editor*

The American Midcontinent, stretching from the Appalachians to the Great Plains, and from the boreal forests of Canada to the Gulf of Mexico, is home to a rich and deep multiethnic past that even after 150 years of exploration continues to fascinate scholars and the public alike. Beginning with colonization by the first Native American big game hunters, through the origins of domestic food production and construction of the largest earthen monuments in North America, and ultimately the entry of multiple colonial empires and their varying interactions with native populations, the story of the region is an exciting one of changing cultural and environmental interactions and adaptive strategies. The diverse environments that characterize the region have fostered a multiplicity of solutions to the problem of survival, ranging from complex sedentary agriculturally intensive societies to those with highly refined seasonal resource strategies keyed to timed movement and social flexibility.

To explore this region from new and different vantage points the Midwest Archaeological Conference Inc. and the University of Notre Dame Press are pleased to launch the Midwest Archaeological Perspectives series, a unique collaborative book series intended for a broad range of professional and interested lay audiences. The books published in Midwest Archaeological Perspectives will be the most compelling and current works of archaeological narrative and insight for the region, with a temporal scope encompassing the span of human use of the region from the first colonizing Paleoindian cultures to the more recent historical past. The series will explore both old questions tackled from new perspectives, and new and interesting questions arising from the deployment of cutting-edge theory and method.

INDIGENOUS LIFE AROUND THE GREAT LAKES

War, Climate, and Culture

RICHARD W. EDWARDS IV

University of Notre Dame Press
Notre Dame, Indiana

 *Midwest Archaeological Conference, Inc.*

University of Notre Dame Press
Notre Dame, Indiana 46556
undpress.nd.edu

Copyright © 2020 by the University of Notre Dame

All Rights Reserved

Published in the United States of America

Library of Congress Control Number: 2020940878

ISBN: 978-0-268-10817-5 (Hardback)
ISBN: 978-0-268-10818-2 (Paperback)
ISBN: 978-0-268-10820-5 (WebPDF)
ISBN 978-0-268-10819-9 (Epub)

For Jacob, Emily, Mason, Connor, and Bradley

CONTENTS

	List of Figures	ix
	List of Tables	xi
	Preface	xiii
	Acknowledgments	xv
	Introduction	1
ONE	Culture History and Archaeological Background	13
TWO	Risk Management and Other Theoretical Considerations	49
THREE	Methods and Methodology	75
FOUR	Results of Macrobotanical Data Collection	83
FIVE	Results of Isotopic Data Collection	95
SIX	The Koshkonong Diet	115
SEVEN	Regional Dietary Trends	125
EIGHT	Understanding the Implications of Agriculture	159

NINE	Risk Management in Oneota Economies	171
TEN	Assessing the Relationship between Agriculture and Political Complexity in the Midcontinent	201
ELEVEN	Conclusions	211
	Appendix A: Macrobotanical Data	217
	Appendix B: CSA Isotopic Data	239
	References Cited	243
	Index	281

FIGURES

Figure I.1   Location of localities and sites discussed in the text   3
Figure 1.1. Regional chronology of Upper and Middle Mississippian Localities   19
Figure 1.2. Location of Oneota village sites in the Koshkonong Locality   27
Figure 1.3. Map of archaeological excavations at the Crescent Bay Hunt Club   28
Figure 1.4. Map of archaeological excavations at the Koshkonong Creek Village   30
Figure 1.5. Radiocarbon chronology of the Koshkonong Locality   31
Figure 2.1. Modern flooded agricultural fields in Jefferson County, Wisconsin   58
Figure 2.2. Diagram of theoretical model   60
Figure 2.3. List of theoretical expectations   64
Figure 2.4. Map of Koshkonong Locality sites relative to neighboring sites   73
Figure 4.1. Box plot of Crescent Bay Hunt Club macrobotanical remains   84
Figure 4.2. Box plot of Koshkonong Creek Village macrobotanical remains   84
Figure 4.3. Box plot of maize and maize kernel densities (count) from Koshkonong sites   86
Figure 4.4. Box plot of maize and maize kernel densities (weight) from Koshkonong sites   86

Figure 4.5.	Box plot of cultigen densities (count) from Koshkonong sites 87	
Figure 4.6.	Principal components analysis: CBHC vs. KCV 88	
Figure 4.7.	Principal components analysis: Early vs. Late 89	
Figure 4.8.	Principal components analysis: Wigwam vs. longhouse 93	
Figure 5.1.	Box plot of aggregated $\delta^{13}C$ values: Eastern and Western Upper Mississippian groups 103	
Figure 5.2.	Box plot of aggregated $\delta^{13}C$ values: Early and late Oneota groups 104	
Figure 5.3.	Box plot of aggregated $\delta^{13}C$ values: Early and late Upper Mississippian groups 104	
Figure 5.4.	Box plot $\delta^{13}C$ values among archaeological cultures and regions 105	
Figure 5.5.	Box plot $\delta^{15}N$ values: Archaeological cultures and regions 111	
Figure 5.6.	Box plot $\delta^{15}N$ values: Early and Late Prehistoric Upper Mississippian 113	
Figure 5.7.	Box plot $\delta^{15}N$ values: Eastern and Western Upper Mississippian 113	
Figure 6.1.	Caloric contributions of food sources to modeled diets 119	
Figure 7.1.	Principal components analysis: Interregional analysis, first and second principal components 148	
Figure 7.2.	Principal components analysis: Interregional analysis, second and third principal components 149	
Figure 8.1.	Digging sticks produced from faunal elements 167	
Figure 9.1.	Modeled mean temperatures for January and July in Fort Atkinson, Wisconsin 172	
Figure 9.2.	Modeled available water, Fort Atkinson, Milwaukee, and Horicon, Wisconsin 173	
Figure 9.3.	Examples of bioarchaeological evidence of violent trauma in the Koshkonong Locality 175	
Figure 9.4.	Maize kernel-to-cupule ratio through time in the Koshkonong Locality 180	
Figure 10.1.	People-plant interactions within the domestication continuum 208	

TABLES

Table 1.1. Markers of osteological violence and type of violence   23

Table 1.2. Radiocarbon dates from the Koshkonong Locality   32

Table 1.3. Calibrated radiocarbon dates from comparative sites   37

Table 2.1. List of potential aggregated resources in Wisconsin northern Illinois   67

Table 3.1. List of primary macrobotanical samples in analysis   77

Table 3.2. List of sites for comparative analysis   78

Table 4.1. Structure function: Seasonal and functional criteria   92

Table 4.2. Structure function: Presence of seasonal and functional criteria in structure types   92

Table 5.1. Aggregated comparative isotopic data   96

Table 5.2. Canine bone isotopic results   99

Table 5.3. Canine bone AMS results   100

Table 5.4. Summary data for human and dog stable isotope data ($\delta^{13}C$)   106

Table 5.5. Summary data for human and dog stable isotope data ($\delta^{15}N$)   112

Table 6.1. Modern nutritional data of four sources known in the prehistoric Koshkonong diet   118

Table 6.2. Total calorie and protein contributions of each food source in the models   120

Table 6.3. Koshkonong Locality diversity indices   124

Table 7.1. $\delta^{13}C$ and macrobotanical density data for all comparative and study sites   126

Table 7.2. Diversity indices of all comparative and study sites   127

Table 7.3. Ubiquity values of taxa categories for all comparative and study sites   128

Table 7.4. Presence of fruit genera by locality   129

Table 7.5. Distribution of "other seeds"   130

Table 7.6. Comparison of cultigens in western Wisconsin and Koshkonong Locality sites   134

Table 8.1. List of agricultural sites in the Koshkonong Locality   161

Table 9.1. Summary data of excavation and feature count and size for study sites   181

Table 9.2. List of common responses to raiding present in the Koshkonong Locality   185

Table 9.3. Maize kernel-to-cupule ratio through time   197

PREFACE

MIDWEST ARCHAEOLOGICAL PERSPECTIVES: A PARTNERSHIP BETWEEN THE MIDWEST ARCHAEOLOGICAL CONFERENCE INC. AND THE UNIVERSITY OF NOTRE DAME PRESS

The inauguration of a new archaeological monograph series is an exciting enterprise for our community, and it is therefore with tremendous pride that we present this first volume in Midwest Archaeological Perspectives (MAP), a joint publishing venture of the University of Notre Dame Press and the Midwest Archaeological Conference (MAC) Inc. Monograph-length works in archaeology have dwindled in number over the past decade or more, for numerous reasons not competing well against high-level refereed journal articles. This dilemma has been especially true for the Midwest and the Midcontinent at large. Yet many topics require platforms that allow for the development and articulation of complex arguments, more fulsome explanations, and the presentation of more substantial supporting data. It is precisely this niche at which MAP is directed, with the fundamental goals of the series being to explore the region from new and different vantage points and to attract and reach both professional and interested lay audiences with innovative and leading-edge research on the archaeology of the Midwest and the Midcontinent. As envisioned, there are two paths available to authors for publication in MAP.

Launched in 2017, the collaborative enterprise between the University of Notre Dame and MAC Inc. is linked to an annual dissertation competition and the offer of a contract to publish a modified version of the dissertation as a book through the press. Selection of the winning dissertation is made by the editor and editorial board of MAP. Eligible dissertations must have been completed and dated in the three years preceding the year of the award.

The current volume, by Richard W. Edwards IV, is the first recipient of the dissertation prize, which was announced in 2018. Edwards tackles some very large problems in the research he presents here, and he tackles them in many interesting ways that go beyond a monolithic argument to a vantage point that relies on multiple strands of independent evidence to allow for strong inference. While the crux of Edwards's work is the longstanding question of the role of (corn) agriculture in the late precontact (ca. AD 1000–1450) western Great Lakes, it is the way that he deploys both traditional and nontraditional scientific methods that make his approach appealing, as well as the way in which those results are applied to social issues of significance. The empirical forte of Edwards's presentation relies on the analysis of macrobotanical remains—the traditional array of preserved identifiable plant parts such as seeds and nuts—coupled with dietary isotopes ($\delta^{13}C$ and $\delta^{15}N$) from dog skeletons, in this case used as proxies or replacements for similar analyses of human remains, which allow for reconstruction of dietary reliance on different foodstuffs but particularly maize. Edwards terms this the canine surrogacy approach, or CSA. The research proceeds to use these data in a risk management framework to assess degrees of local stress and decision making, local trends toward complexity, and degrees of cooperative interregional interaction. Edwards's multiple contributions of powerful complementary data sets, theoretical and problem orientations, and comparative regional framework make a compelling story of late precontact lifeways from a novel vantage point. We are pleased to present his work as our inaugural volume.

William Lovis

ACKNOWLEDGMENTS

I am indebted to a great many people and organizations without whose help this book would not have been possible. First and foremost, I want to thank my committee. Their insights and collective knowledge have allowed me to pursue this research in a directed fashion, have helped me understand the complex array of cultural processes at work, and have provided me with hands-on and real-world experience. In particular, I would like to thank Robert Jeske, my committee chair, and Robert Sasso. Bob Sasso helped steer me into archaeology as an undergraduate and has continued to act as a friend and mentor. He is the person who made me realize that archaeology was not only an option for me, but my calling, and he is the reason I decided to go to graduate school at the University of Wisconsin at Milwaukee (UWM).

As a friend and mentor, Bob Jeske has been the driving force in my professional development. As my adviser, he has literally read every conference paper, article draft, grant application, and thesis and dissertation chapter that I have written. For both our sakes, I do not want to know how many pages or hours that amounts to. His regular and detailed feedback has improved not only my writing style, but my research focus. He has provided me with more opportunities than I can count and has shaped my views and skills as an archaeologist. Last but far from least, our "Oneota Fluid Dynamics" sessions at County Claire, Bar Louie, and elsewhere have helped me understand and appreciate the archaeology of Oneota and the Midwest as a whole. My other committee members have been invaluable resources. Jean Hudson's expertise in human behavior and subsistence was critical. Her keen eye with animal bones made the CSA portion of my research possible. The impact of her encyclopedic knowledge of resources and citations cannot be overstated. Finally, I want to thank Pat Richards and Brian Nicholls for their comments, advice, support, and training over the course of my graduate career. Both have helped me in countless ways since I was a master's degree student.

Many other faculty and staff members at UWM have also been helpful. I would like to thank J. Patrick Gray for his statistical insights, John Richards for advice and perspectives on Middle Mississippians, Seth Schneider for his ceramic and Oneota knowledge and his personal support of me and my research, and Jenny Picard for her advice on seeds and resources. As a whole, the Department of Anthropology at UWM has provided me with significant support, by providing funding through the Preliminary Dissertation Grant and by nominating me for the Distinguished Dissertator Fellowship. Both of these sources of funding made my research possible. Finally, the resources of the Archaeology Research Laboratory were indispensable.

I also acknowledge the financial support of the National Science Foundation (NSF). The NSF's Dissertation Improvement Grant (Grant #1640364) provided the funding for the isotopic tests and AMS assays of the dog remains. In addition to samples from UWM, the Wisconsin Historical Society, the Milwaukee Public Museum, and the Mississippi Valley Archaeology Center at University of Wisconsin at La Crosse provided dog samples for analysis. In particular I would like to thank Angela Glasker (WHS), Dawn Scher-Thomae (MPM), Claudia Jacobson (MPM), Connie Arzigian (MVAC), and Jim Theler (MVAC) for their assistance in obtaining the samples and navigating the bureaucratic process of obtaining permissions.

I would like to thank Katie Egan-Bruhy, not only for training me to identify seeds, but also for her patience while doing so, her analytical advice, and her willingness to provide a critical eye for my identifications. She and Commonwealth Heritage Group have been very generous, sharing published resources as well as raw data. Without this, there would be very limited comparison for my data sets.

I also owe a great debt to the landowners of our Koshkonong sites and the larger Busseyville community. In particular, I would like to thank Greg Weisensel and family for letting me regularly dig giant holes in the middle of the crops and for other support, such as backfilling the holes when our work was finished. The members of the Crescent Bay Hunt Club have provided tremendous support. Kevin Schmeling has also been very helpful.

His knowledge of the local archaeology and the people in the community has helped us know not only where to dig but also who to talk to. This has made our research in the region, and KCV in particular, possible.

Finally, I would like to thank my personal support network: my friends and family. My family have always been my strongest supporters. For as long as I can remember, my parents have pushed me to follow my dreams, pursue my passions, and receive an education. And they have listened without complaint when I drone on about my research. Because of this encouragement, I became part of the first generation in my family to go to college and the first to earn a PhD. I am equally indebted to my sister Sara, who has been a rock, an inspiration, and when necessary a staunch defender. Jacob, Emily, Mason, and Connor have all been inspirations; I hope that through my successes you'll see that it's okay to follow whatever dreams you have. Anything is possible when you have inspiration, persistence, and a good support system.

There are too many friends and colleagues to thank individually, but I do need to thank several. Brendan and Kim, thank you for your constant support and for providing a southern refuge from Milwaukee whenever I needed it. Lara, Alexis, and Natalie, thank you for your support and reading all my work. To the many other friends who have been there for me, you know who you are, and I thank you! Finally, I need to thank the Franklin Starbucks and the Glendale Bar Louie: the combination of caffeine, beer, and a place to be other than my apartment allowed me to write this tome.

Introduction

The turn of the eleventh century AD marks the beginning of monumental cultural shifts in the North American Midcontinent (see, e.g., Brown 1965; Emerson 1999; Fowler 1978; Gibbon 1982; Griffin 1952, 1967; Hall 1962; Jeske 1992; McKern 1945; Overstreet 1981; Pauketat 1994). Across the region, people began to aggregate on the landscape, thereby creating new and larger social groups. In turn, these groups developed new cultural practices for creating and maintaining social cohesion and for providing life's necessities, such as food, shelter, and raw materials. In the process, old political relationships were reconfigured, and a new social landscape was created (see Richards and Jeske 2002). One of the few ubiquitous shifts was the wholesale adoption of maize (e.g., Bender, Baerreis, and Steventon 1981; Brown 1982; Emerson, Hedman, and Simon 2005; Emerson et al. 2010; Fritz 1992; Gallagher and Arzigian 1994; Kelly 1992; Pratt 1994; Simon 2014). Along the length of the Mississippi River, people shifted from economies based on small-scale gardening, hunting, and gathering to full-scale agriculture. Around the world, such agricultural transitions are often accompanied by a roughly simultaneous growth of social inequality, hierarchically oriented political structures, and the centralization of political authority.

Essentially, in most places around the world the development of agriculture is intrinsically connected to the foundations of life as we know it today. This is also true for many groups in the Midcontinent. The development of the hierarchical Middle Mississippian polities saw the rise of cities ruled by elites throughout much of southeastern and midcontinental North America (e.g., Fowler 1978; Hall 1991; Pauketat 1994). The site of Cahokia in present-day Illinois marks the pinnacle of this phenomenon in eastern North America. At its height, Cahokia was larger than many contemporaneous cities in Europe and held a prominent position in regional politics, trade, and religion (Hall 1991; Pauketat and Lopinot 1997). However, groups in Wisconsin and northern Illinois aggregated and adopted maize, yet maintained egalitarian traditions and did not experience the rise of inequity (e.g., Emerson, Hedman, and Simon 2005). These northern groups are known to archaeologists broadly as Upper Mississippians (Griffin 1960, 1967; Hall 1962; McKern 1945). For decades, archaeologists had minimal data that could be used to infer the importance of maize in Upper Mississippian economies (Brown 1982). Without data to the contrary, most archaeologists assumed that Upper Mississippian societies followed the common global trend: the people in these groups were not truly agriculturalists but rather incorporated small to modest amounts of maize in a diverse diet. However, recent data obtained through new techniques suggest that members of at least some Upper Mississippian groups were consuming as much maize as their Middle Mississippian contemporaries (Emerson, Hedman, and Simon 2005; Emerson et al. 2010; Pratt 1994), and this finding has given archaeologists reason to question long-held assumptions about Upper Mississippian economies and the relationship between maize and social hierarchies in the Midcontinent.

Scholars have also questioned why people began to aggregate on the landscape, adopt maize agriculture, and create strikingly different material culture from their ancestors, most notably new pottery types (Gibbon 1982; Green 2014; Overstreet 1997, 1998; Richards and Jeske 2002; Theler and Boszhardt 2000, 2006). These questions become even more important if the rise of agriculture is independent of hierarchical political development. The region known as the Koshkonong Locality, situated in southeastern Wisconsin, was home to an early group of Upper Mississippians and provides an ideal location for an in-depth examination of the social and political developments that began in the eleventh century (fig. I.1). In this project, I address three primary research questions: (1) What was the significance of maize in Upper Mississippian societies? (2) What is the relationship between the development of agriculture and social hierarchies in the Midcontinent? (3) How and why was agriculture incorporated into Upper Mississippian subsistence systems? I approach these questions from

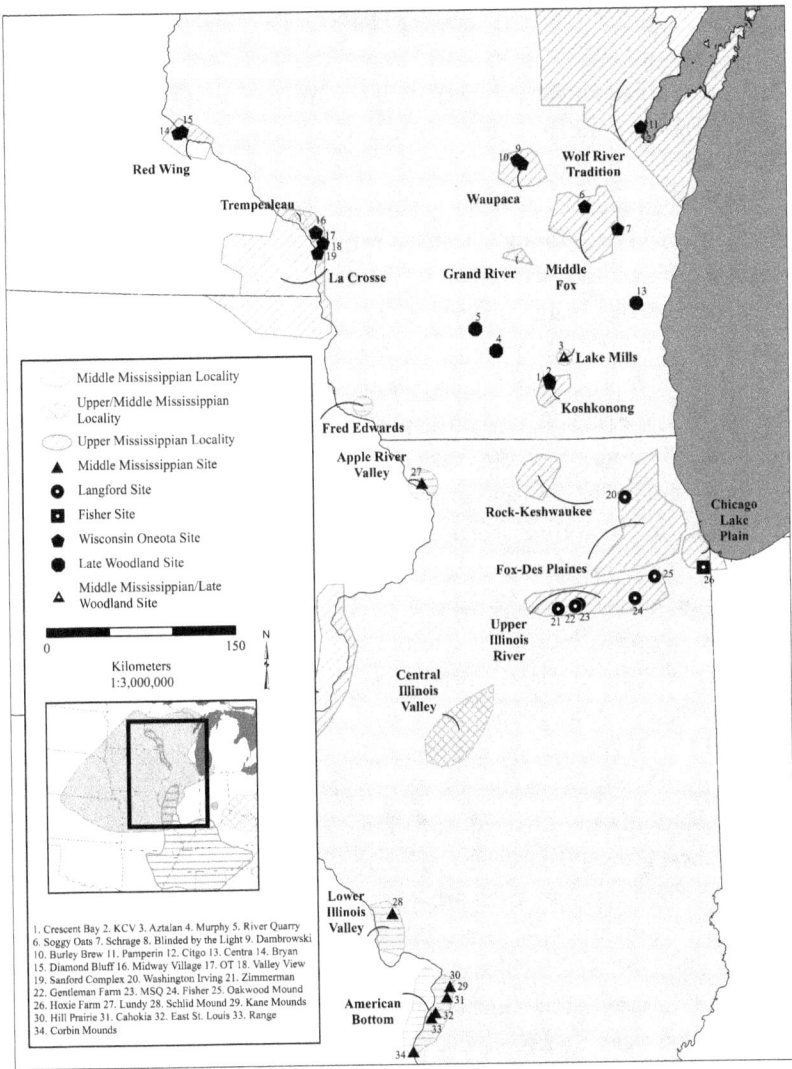

Figure I.1. Location of localities and sites discussed in the text

an essentially functional perspective, trying to determine what benefits were gained by adopting maize and indirectly the wholesale reorganization of daily life, social relationships, and virtually every social structure. I approach these questions through the lens of risk management, using the Koshkonong Locality as a case study and reference point for the broader regional analysis.

MISSISSIPPIANS

The term "Mississippian" has been used in numerous ways by various scholars. Without modifiers, the term technically refers to either Upper or Middle Mississippians, though it is often used as shorthand to refer to Middle Mississippian sites or lifeways. Middle Mississippian polities almost invariably are thought to have exhibited greater levels of political organization and population sizes. "Upper Mississippian" is a broad term that incorporates many different archaeological cultures (Griffin 1967; McKern 1945). For the purposes of this research, it is used to refer to a subset of three interrelated archaeological cultures, Wisconsin Oneota, Langford, and Fisher. A more in-depth discussion follows in chapter 1, but for now it is sufficient to note that each of these terms refers to groups with generally similar lifeways and material culture that lived in Wisconsin and northeastern Illinois from at least the eleventh to the fifteenth century AD. It is important to note that none of these terms should be conflated with a tribe or other real-world social group. Rather, each term likely includes multiple groups with distinct identities and social traditions but that cannot be reliably distinguished with archaeological data.

The relationship between Middle Mississippians, Upper Mississippians, and Late Woodland groups (those that continued traditional practices from before AD 1000) has been a source of continued debate among scholars (see Richards and Jeske 2002; Salkin 2000). The degree of interaction among these groups and the relative influence on one another's political and social developments have been debated for decades, with few signs of abating (e.g., Boszhardt 2004; Green 2014; Overstreet 1998; Theler and Boszhardt 2000, 2006). Much of the disagreement stems from regional variation and the attempt by some researchers to apply their localized findings on a regional scale. Therefore, while my focus is on the Koshkonong Locality, I contextualize it at multiple scales: intralocal, interlocal, and regional.

SOCIAL AND ENVIRONMENTAL CLIMATE OF THE WESTERN GREAT LAKES

Currently, the relationship between the Koshkonong Locality, its immediate non-Oneota neighbors (i.e., occupants of contemporaneous Aztalan and Late Woodland sites), and other Oneota localities is unclear (Richards and Jeske 2002). On a local scale, the use of shell tempering and vessel morphology distinguishes the Koshkonong potters from their Late Woodland neighbors (e.g., Hall 1962; McKern 1945; Richards and Jeske 2002; Schneider 2015), and vessel paste and morphology distinguish them from their Middle Mississippian neighbors at Aztalan (e.g., Hall 1962; Richards 1992; Richards and Jeske 2002; Schneider 2015).

Schneider's (2015) ceramic analysis indicates that Koshkonong groups were part of a larger Oneota social network. Schneider has demonstrated that the Koshkonong Oneota pottery recipes and styles are connected with trends in the Waupaca and Grand River Localities to the north. However, the residents of the Koshkonong Locality were at the edge of this network. Their pottery styles were distinct from these northern groups, and Koshkonong potters went out of their way to distinguish themselves by embellishing many of their pots with a grooved paddle surface treatment. Carpiaux (2018; Carpiaux and Edwards 2017) suggests that this trend may increase through time, which could indicate the entrenchment of a local identity. The development of a distinct local identity within the Oneota world is supported by multiple lines of evidence, such as lithic procurement patterns (Sterner 2012, 2018; Wilson 2016), and appears to be the norm across Oneota localities in Wisconsin (e.g., O'Gorman 2010, 589). The absence of Woodland or Middle Mississippian pottery at Crescent Bay (Schneider 2015) and the Koshkonong Creek Village (Carpiaux 2018) is striking given the proximity of Aztalan and Late Woodland sites to the locality. While the ceramics and lithics at Koshkonong sites are indicative of isolation, the burial record suggests some degree of interaction with neighbors, albeit violent. Several individuals at Koshkonong sites exhibit evidence of trauma and violent death, possibly from raiding or other forms of intergroup violence (Jeske 2014). If violence, or the threat of violence, was perceived as severe, it could have significantly altered the way that the Koshkonong residents moved about the landscape, procured food, and interacted with their neighbors (sensu Keeley 2016; Milner 1992; Pauketat 2009; Tung 2012).

The social stressors present in the Koshkonong Locality provide an important opportunity to gauge their impact on group organization, subsistence practices, and other cultural traits. However, these social factors were not the only stressors within the locality. A transition from relatively warm and wet to cold and dry climatic conditions shortly after the archaeological appearance of Oneota artifacts could also have created significant environmental stresses (Baerreis and Bryson 1965; Baerreis, Bryson, and Kutzbach 1976; McEnaney and Bryson 2005). Both social and environmental factors would have posed significant risks to the residents of the Koshkonong Locality and likely would have elicited very different responses (Hart 1993).

EVALUATING RISK MANAGEMENT IN ONEOTA SOCIETIES

Given the combination of social and environmental conditions facing Oneota groups, we can expect that they made efforts to minimize their exposure to risk. Given the primacy of people's need for food and the level of impact social and environmental stresses would have on the subsistence base, examinations of food procurement practices should elucidate their stress responses (e.g., Milner 2007; VanDerwarker and Wilson 2016). Multiple lines of evidence identify the Oneota subsistence system's risk responses. First, macrobotanical data provide broad archaeological signatures for subsistence practices (see Hastorf and Popper 1988). Second, isotopic ($\delta^{13}C$ and $\delta^{15}N$) data more directly measure food consumption patterns (see Ambrose 1987). Together, the two lines of evidence can demonstrate what foods were eaten and, in the case of maize, in what proportions (e.g., Hart 1993; Halstead and O'Shea 1989b). These data should display different patterns depending on the sources of risk, the chosen strategies to mitigate the risk, and the social institutions administering them.

A model of Oneota subsistence under social and environmental stress is presented based on models developed by Winterhalder and Goland (1997) and using assumptions of risk aversion as defined and described by numerous authors (e.g., Cashdan 1990a; Halstead and O'Shea 1989a; Hart 1990, 1993; Kipnis 2002; Marston 2011; Scarry 2003; Stone and Downum 1999; Winterhalder 1986, 1990). Risk management strategies are generally divided into five types: diversification, mobility, storage, exchange, and intensification. These strategies are neither mutually exclusive nor fully compatible, and the most appropriate strategy depends on the sources of risk and internal social factors.

Exclusively environmental risks are usually best mitigated by increased mobility and increasing diet breadth (e.g., diversification). Social risks (e.g., threat of attack) in the Great Lakes region are usually best mitigated by intensification and decreased mobility (Hart 1993). Under the correct circumstances, highly aggregated resources (such as large bison herds) may allow for high mobility and defensibility. However, risks are rarely single sourced, and therefore the most appropriate strategies are often nuanced and locally dependent (e.g., Hart 1990). Furthermore, because it is people who employ such strategies, the decisions to undertake them must be administered through social structures. Therefore, the strategies also create real-world repercussions; risk management strategies both shape and are shaped by social institutions (Halstead and O'Shea 1989b; O'Shea 1989). For example, groups that wish to exercise mobility must either have large territories or negotiate access to or through their neighbor's land. Such negotiations often take place through particular lineages (e.g., the Bear Clan among the Ho Chunk) (see, e.g., Radin 1923). Situations of significant need may affect the traditional balance of power, and overuse of such systems may strain existing relationships.

Basic Expectations

In the models presented, for socially risky environments, Koshkonong residents should choose to reduce mobility and intensify agricultural pursuits. As groups invest in particular locations and move less, resource depression is expected and should force further intensification of agricultural resources and/or locally available aggregated resources. Such resources can feed sizable populations, and agricultural output can be artificially increased through greater investment if additional food is required. In such cases, more land can be cleared and planted, crops can be grown more densely, or more productive plant varieties can be grown. Such agricultural intensification leaves material signatures in the archaeological record that can be detected.

If environmental factors are the most significant, then the models predict Koshkonong residents should increase mobility and agricultural products should be a minor component of the diet. Wild resources should be ranked highly, though the types will depend on the nature of the risk (e.g., local vs. regional and continuous vs. discontinuous). Environmental risks, particularly local ones, should magnify the importance of exchange with other groups. However, regular violence should reorient exchange; a risk of attack should reduce the number of opportunities for trade (though not necessarily reduce the total volume), and military alliances are likely to become embedded in the system. Trading partners may be valued not only for the foods they can supply, but the military aid they can offer.

To assess the nature of the risk management systems, the risks themselves, and thereby the overall political and physical landscape the Koshkonong residents were living in, this study relies on three primary lines of evidence. I assess the nature of the Koshkonong diet through both macrobotanical evidence (macroscopic charred plant remains) and stable isotope analysis of bones. The macrobotanical data provide specific information about what plants were regularly used and which ones were likely important, but they cannot reveal how important the various resources were. The isotopic data quantify the importance of maize and meat in the diet but cannot directly inform on other aspects of the diet. Together, these two lines of evidence provide a relatively clear picture of the diet in the Koshkonong Locality.

By joining the data sets, it is possible to make inferences concerning access to resources relative to use, degree of movement within and beyond the locality, and intersite interaction. And from there, it is possible to interpret aspects of the social, political, and environmental contexts that resulted in the decisions behind the choices that led to the establishment of the economic system that generated the material culture.

Several statistical measures are used to analyze the data, including principal components analysis (PCA), traditional statistical tests (e.g., Mann Whitney U, Chi-Square), and traditional measures of macrobotanical assemblages (e.g., diversity indices). These types of statistical tests allow for multiscalar analysis of the largely nonparametric paleobotanical and isotopic data sets (Marston 2014; Smith 2014). By applying a combination of social and economic theory with these powerful statistical analyses on robust regional data sets, it is possible not only to identify, but to assess important trends and anomalies. The theoretical approach allows for an interpretive framework that is both systematic and flexible. The risk management approach must account for flexibility because human behavior is expected to vary based on the social and environmental conditions. Using such a system allows for inferences about both sets of conditions, social and environmental (Hart 1993). It is through these environmentally specific inferences that we begin to assess and understand cultural responses. Because each group is situated in a distinct social and environmental context, it is necessary to recognize intergroup variation while not obscuring similarities or shared traits among groups.

INTERPRETING THE ONEOTA ECONOMY

This book has three chapters that provide essential background information. Two chapters address the relevant data collected for this analysis, and five chapters discuss the data analysis and its implications. Chapter 1 describes the culture history and archaeology of the region. In this chapter, I discuss what Oneota is and how it relates to other Upper, Middle, and non-Mississippian societies. I also provide a thorough background on the Koshkonong Locality and the primary study sites, the Crescent Bay Hunt Club (CBHC, 47JE904) and the Koshkonong Creek Village (KCV, 47JE379). It also provides basic descriptions of comparative sites used to contextualize the primary data set.

Chapter 2 describes the theoretical underpinnings of the analysis. I draw heavily from Halstead and O'Shea's (1989a, 1989b) seminal work on risk management theory for my basic theoretical orientation. This perspective is augmented by Marston's (2012) research on agricultural-specific risk management strategies. Finally, I draw heavily from both Hart (1990, 1993) and Winterhalder and Goland (1997) to establish my expectations within the risk management framework. In the western Great Lakes, groups should reduce mobility and increase their reliance on maize and other cultivated resources if under significant threat of attack.

Chapter 3 discusses the methods and methodologies I implemented in my analysis. This includes a discussion of the specific analytical methods used to identify and evaluate the macrobotanical and isotopic data. It also includes a discussion of the canine surrogacy approach (CSA), which justifies my use of dog, rather than human, remains to determine maize and meat consumption levels.

Chapter 4 describes the results of the macrobotanical analysis. It begins by addressing the basic patterns identified at each site. Both the KCV and CBHC data sets indicate that maize is a highly ranked resource. It is the densest and most ubiquitous resource at both sites. Wild rice, chenopodium, and acorn were also highly ranked floral resources. Some variation between sites' samples was noted, but overall the residents of both sites appear to be following a similar culinary tradition. Few changes were noted through time; perhaps most significant is the decline of acorn and the corresponding increase in wild rice utilization.

Chapter 5 describes the results of the isotopic data. Because the sample size is limited, it also contextualizes the data obtained for this book in relation to previously published human and dog isotopic data from Upper Mississippian, Middle Mississippian, and Late Woodland societies in Illinois, Wisconsin, and Minnesota (Edwards, Jeske, and Coltrain 2017; Emerson, Hedman, and Simon 2005; Emerson et al. 2010; Pratt 1994). The data indicate that residents of eastern and early sites (i.e., Koshkonong and Langford sites) consumed statistically more maize than those at later and western sites (i.e., La Crosse sites), with early western sites (i.e., Red Wing sites) holding an intermediate position. Upper Mississippian groups consumed more maize than Late Woodland groups and were statistically indistinguishable from the overall Middle Mississippian pattern.

Chapter 6 focuses on interpreting the overall subsistence patterns within the Koshkonong Locality. It begins by addressing Brown's (1982) question, "What kind of economy did the Oneota have?" This chapter pulls together all lines of evidence to classify the level of agricultural reliance and dietary focus in the Koshkonong sample. It also uses a novel approach to combine the isotopic and macrobotanical data to model the caloric importance of particular resources. All indications point to the Koshkonong Oneota people as being highly reliant on maize-based agriculture. The long-standing notion that Oneota groups, by definition, had a diversified diet is erroneous.

Chapter 7 serves to contextualize the Koshkonong data within a larger cultural framework. It compares the patterns identified in the previous chapters with published data from Upper Mississippian sites in seven other localities, Middle Mississippian sites in two localities, and five Late Woodland sites, representing both recognized groups (i.e., collared and non-collared ware producers) (e.g., Salkin 2000). The chapter focuses on how the Koshkonong diet is similar to and different from its contemporaneous neighbors. In particular, it explores regional and cultural variation in cuisines, localized adaptations, degree of agricultural reliance, and diet breadth. It appears that in terms of agricultural reliance, Koshkonong may trend higher than some other sites but is not unique. In fact, it is likely that maize agriculture is a hallmark of Oneota lifeways—with the possible exception of far northern groups. However, there is no single Oneota economy. Each locality has distinct local dietary traditions.

Chapter 8 addresses the implications of the Koshkonong diet for the people within the locality. It focuses on the tasks that the chosen subsistence system would have generated. It also addresses the impact such choices would have on the seasonal scheduling of labor. It is likely that these shifts would have served to increase the labor load of women and that men's responsibilities became less attached to subsistence tasks. These changes would have affected the ways that people obtained status and interacted with one another. The changes also would have affected the seasonal scheduling of labor tasks. Spring would have necessitated substantial labor investments to prepare and plant fields. Likewise, fall harvests would have been more labor-intensive relative to earlier time periods.

Chapter 9 ties together the data from the previous chapters to identify which risk management strategies were used among the Koshkonong Oneota. It then addresses the social and political implications of such a system, in particular, levels of social and political strife, environmental instability, and the impact of such risks on the social connections of people within the Koshkonong Locality. The data indicate that the Koshkonong system was focused on mitigating social risks. All lines of evidence are indicative of a social system that would allow people to remain on or near the main village sites. The landscape data not only indicate that the residents did stay close to home but also that the locations of the villages were intentionally chosen for their defensibility as well as their economic potential.

Chapter 10 addresses the final research question concerning the relationship between agriculture and the development of complex and hierarchical political systems in the Midcontinent. It addresses the question of what agriculture is—that is, which Late Prehistoric groups should be considered agricultural—and what that means for its role in the development of social inequality. Regardless of which definition is used, the Upper Mississippian groups all qualify as agricultural. This finding stands in contrast to the Middle Mississippian groups, which developed along starkly different cultural trajectories.

Chapter 11 draws the book to a close by discussing the overall conclusions. It also highlights the implications of this research and identifies important areas for future research. The Late Prehistoric was a time of significant social and environmental instability. This, in turn, led to the development of a risky landscape across the western Great Lakes. The growing risk of violent encounters forced a shift in political relationships, diets, and overall lifeways. These changes have long been noted in material culture and settlement patterns as indicators of the rise of Mississippian cultures.

ONE

Culture History and
Archaeological Background

As the term is used today, "Upper Mississippian" typically includes sites and artifact assemblages labeled by archaeologists as Oneota, Langford, Oliver, and Fort Ancient. The term is regularly applied to sites ranging from Ohio to the Plains. This study is primarily concerned with the eastern extent of Oneota and with Langford and does not directly examine the eastern groups (Fort Ancient and Oliver). Oneota is an Upper Mississippian material culture manifestation present throughout much of the western Great Lakes and eastern Plains regions during the Late Prehistoric (Brown 1965; Hall 1962; Overstreet 1997) (see fig. I.1). The term "Oneota" was coined by Keyes (1929) to refer to sites and assemblages in the Oneota River valley (now known as the Upper Iowa River) of Iowa. More specifically, he used it to differentiate sites with shell-tempered ceramics from those with the more ubiquitous grit-tempered Woodland sherds. Early researchers noted that a suite of other material culture often accompanies Oneota ceramics.

Researchers throughout the northern Midcontinent quickly began using the term to refer to sites with similarly shell-tempered ceramics that were not consistent with Cahokia-style vessels (McKern 1945). At a 1935 conference, archaeologists formally defined the "Oneota Aspect" of the Upper Mississippian Archaeological Culture to include the three foci in northern Illinois, two foci exclusively in Wisconsin, and the Orr focus (which included southwestern Wisconsin, Iowa, and Minnesota) while acknowledging that there were also materials far to the west that were likely connected to Oneota (Griffin 1937). McKern (1931) argued that the Oneota Aspect also included triangular arrowheads (typically Madison Points) and snub-nosed scrapers. Brown (1965, 113) described Oneota as the "dominant stylistic complex in the Prairie Peninsula." Similar related cultural manifestations have been noted, primarily in northern Wisconsin, with related artifact styles and generally similar lifeways but with different combinations of grit- and shell-tempered ceramics.

Today, Oneota is often recognized not just as a particular assemblage, but one representing a similar suite of lifeways. These lifeways are generally described as being focused on a mixed foraging and agricultural or horticultural economy that included a diverse suite of resources including maize, Eastern Agricultural Complex (EAC) plants (e.g., sunflower and chenopodium), wetland flora and fauna, large mammals, and fish (e.g., Brown 1982). Given this large geographic range, significant variation is present across space. Therefore, Oneota cannot practically be discussed as a whole and is usually treated on a regional basis (Logan 1998; Overstreet 1997). However, even regional treatments of Oneota can obscure significant variation in subsistence, settlement, social organization, and so on (Jeske and Edwards 2015). Failure to acknowledge inter- and intraregional variation has been a source of several debates in the literature. In Wisconsin, debates have most notably been related to chronology (e.g., Boszhardt 1998, 2004; Overstreet 2001). As a result, several scholars have called for recognizing that each Oneota locality has its own history and unique, though not totally independent, cultural trajectory (e.g., Edwards and Jeske 2015; Jeske and Edwards 2015). In recognition of this pattern, general trends are initially discussed, followed by more detailed regional descriptions.

RELEVANT REGIONAL EXPRESSIONS

Oneota sites are not evenly distributed across the landscape (see fig. I.1). Rather, the sites are clustered into what are known as localities (Hall 1962; McKern 1945; Overstreet 1997, 2000). The landscapes separating the localities appear to have been unoccupied—at least by Mississippian (Upper or Middle) sites (Richards and Jeske 2002). Sites within these localities are often seen as more tightly connected to each other than to sites in other localities (Gibbon 1972a; McKern 1945; O'Gorman 2010), though the degree to which localities vary is not clear (Jeske and Edwards 2015; Jeske et al. 2016; Schneider 2015). Due to a lack of fine-scale comparative data, many researchers have often focused on regional differences. In Wisconsin, we can see two broad divisions (e.g., Egan-Bruhy 2014; Henning 1998a, 1998b; McKern 1945; Overstreet 1997)—Eastern and Western—with at least three subregions in eastern Wisconsin: northern, central, and southern (e.g., Jeske and Edwards 2015).

Eastern Wisconsin Oneota

Oneota research in eastern Wisconsin has a long history, dating to the early twentieth century (Gibbon 1972a; Hall 1962; McKern 1931, 1945). The Grand River area was among the first to be studied (Jeske 1927), followed soon after by sites near Lake Winnebago (McKern 1945) and Lake Koshkonong (Hall 1962). Further localities have been identified in the Green Bay–Door Peninsula region (Mason 1966), Waupaca (Hamilton et al. 2010), and northeastern Wisconsin (Buckmaster 1979). Southern ceramic assemblages are dominated by shell tempering (Hall 1962; McKern 1931, 1945; Schneider 2015). Assemblages from northern sites are known as Mero, including those on the Door Peninsula, and tend to have both grit- and shell-tempered ceramics (Mason 1966; Overstreet 2009). Several lines of evidence suggest that there are significant differences among localities, in terms of ceramics, diet, raw material acquisition patterns, and political relationships (Edwards and Jeske 2015; Jeske et al. 2016; Schneider 2015). Most localities appear to be occupied starting around AD 1050 but are abandoned by AD 1400. The Lake Winnebago region is the one exception; it may have been occupied until AD 1600 (see Jeske et al. 2016; Overstreet 1997).

Western Wisconsin

There are two primary localities in western Wisconsin; Red Wing/Lake Pepin and La Crosse. The Red Wing Locality extends across the Mississippi River into Minnesota and has a long history of research (for a discussion of the history of research in the region, see Gibbon and Dobbs 1991; Rodell 1991). It appears that the area was possibly occupied by both Oneota and Middle Mississippian groups (Gibbon and Dobbs 1991; Lawshe 1947; Maxwell 1950). Oneota groups resided in the locality from approximately AD 1000 to 1400 (Schirmer 2002, table 1.3).

The primary Oneota occupation of the La Crosse terrace began around AD 1300, and the region was abandoned shortly after AD 1600 (Boszhardt 1989). Boszhardt (1994) divided the chronology into three phases, Brice Prairie (AD 1300–1400), Pammel Creek (AD 1400–1500), and Valley View (AD 1500–1625). The Pammel Creek phase marks an apparent large-scale migration to the La Crosse region; the density of post–AD 1400 sites is significant and suggests that the area was a major population center.

Illinois Oneota–Upper Mississippian

The situation in northern Illinois is more complicated. Researchers have long postulated that there were at least two separate contemporaneous Upper Mississippian groups: Langford and Fisher. Huber is a third Upper Mississippian tradition in the region but is later in time. It may represent the cultural descendant of Fisher (Bluhm and Liss 1961; Brown 1990). However, Emerson et al. (2015) argue that the two groups are not related.

McKern (1943) noted that both Langford and Fisher vessel types were similar to the Grand River Focus Oneota ceramics in Wisconsin. Fisher sites can still be identified by unique aspects of ceramic assemblages. These unique characteristics include a combination of shell tempering with a distinct set of decorative motifs and surface treatments (e.g., cord marking) (Faulkner 1972; Griffin 1946, 1948; Langford 1927). Fisher territory largely coincided with Langford; however, site placement was distinct, indicating that each group had different criteria for habitation placement (e.g., Jeske 1989). Fisher sites are common occurrences on terraces overlooking large rivers (e.g., the Illinois River) but rarely extend into the smaller river valleys. In general, Fisher sites are placed in locations with access to arable floodplain soils (Jeske 1989). Excavations at large sites (e.g., Hoxie Farm) indicate that Fisher site occupants relied heavily on wild resources and cultivated plants, including EAC cultigens (e.g., Jackson and Emerson 2013).

Mafic grit-tempered globular vessels with everted rims characterize Langford tradition assemblages (Bird 1997; Brown 1961; Faulkner 1972;

Fowler 1940; Griffin 1948). Langford sites are ubiquitous in northern Illinois river valleys, including the Kishwaukee, Lower Rock, Upper Illinois, Fox, Des Plaines, and DuPage (Bird 1997; Birmingham 1975; Brown 1961; Fowler 1940; Hart and Jeske 1987; Jeske 1989, 2003b; Jeske and Hart 1988). Smaller Langford sites are also found in remote upland settings, providing access to a different suite of resources (Jeske 1989, 2003b). Langford groups appear to rely on a diverse suite of foods, with maize and wild starchy seeds apparently among the most important floral resources (Egan 1988; Egan-Bruhy and Nelson 2013; Simon 1999). Isotopic evidence suggests that maize may have been an equally important dietary contributor to Langford groups as it was for Middle Mississippians (Emerson, Hedman, and Simon 2005).

ORIGINS

The reason for the sudden arrival of Oneota material culture at approximately AD 1050–1100 is unclear. Numerous researchers have postulated explanations; however, to date no published work is widely accepted or sufficiently accounts for regional variation. For decades, many scholars have suspected that Middle Mississippians, from Cahokia in particular, may have played a significant role—an idea still popular today with many scholars (e.g., Green 2014). Griffin (1960) initially felt that Oneota represented Middle Mississippians who had moved north and after the onset of the Little Ice Age devolved into Oneota when they could no longer support large aggregated populations. When radiocarbon data discounted this possibility, numerous alternate theories were devised.

Overstreet (1989, 1995) has also argued for a nonlocal origin of Oneota groups, whereas Gibbon (1972a) has argued that Oneota groups represent local Late Woodland populations that fused in reaction to the more organized Middle Mississippians on their southern flank. Many authors have made similar related arguments—that contact with Middle Mississippians and some driving factor led Late Woodland groups to adopt new practices that we call Oneota or Langford (Emerson 1999; Fowler 1940; Jeske 1990). Theler and Boszhardt (2000, 2006) have argued that Mississippian influence, increased population pressures, and declining deer populations were the catalysts for the shift of western Late Woodland populations.

Green (2014) argues that the shift occurred after Mississippian religious proselytizing. Emerson (1999) has argued that the increased military threat of Middle Mississippians caused desperate Late Woodland groups in northern Illinois to unify into Langford through a process of tribalization. While these Middle Mississippian–centered hypotheses may reflect the events in some localities, they lack broad explanatory power as they do not fit the data across the Oneota landscape.

Following regional arguments made by many researchers (e.g., Brown 1982), Jeske and Edwards (2015; Edwards and Jeske 2015) illustrate that there is insufficient time for Middle Mississippians to have affected such a change in the local Late Woodland population in the area around the Koshkonong Locality. Moreover, Richards and Jeske (2002) show the coeval nature of Middle Mississippian, Oneota, and Late Woodland groups in Wisconsin. The earliest evidence of Middle Mississippians in the region occurs after the Oneota groups were already established. Furthermore, there is no indication of any significant interaction between Lake Koshkonong Oneota groups and Aztalan despite the short distance between them (see also Overstreet 1995, 60). Given the variation among localities, it is likely that no single answer will fully or sufficiently explain the origins of all Oneota.

CHRONOLOGY

Several Oneota chronologies have been suggested (e.g., Hall 1962; Gibbon 1972a, 1986; Overstreet 1997); however, recent data have called into question their broad-scale applicability. Therefore, I use a simplified early versus late system that is divided at AD 1400, when a big shift in Oneota lifeways occurred (Jeske et al. 2016). Jeske et al. (2016) argue that the beginning of the fifteenth century AD marks a reorganization of political boundaries and overall social organization (fig. 1.1). Formerly disparate groups spread across the landscape were either pulled or pushed together. At roughly the same time, we see the abandonment of the Koshkonong, Waupaca, and Grand River Localities in Wisconsin. Other areas of the state may also have been abandoned; however, we lack sufficient chronological clarity in several areas, particularly in northern Wisconsin. We also see the disappearance of Langford ceramics in northern Illinois shortly after AD 1400 (Bird 1997; Jeske 1990, 2000b; Strezewski, Hedman, and Emerson 2012) and the replacement of Fisher ceramics with Huber, though it is unclear if the Fisher-to-

Culture History and Archaeological Background 19

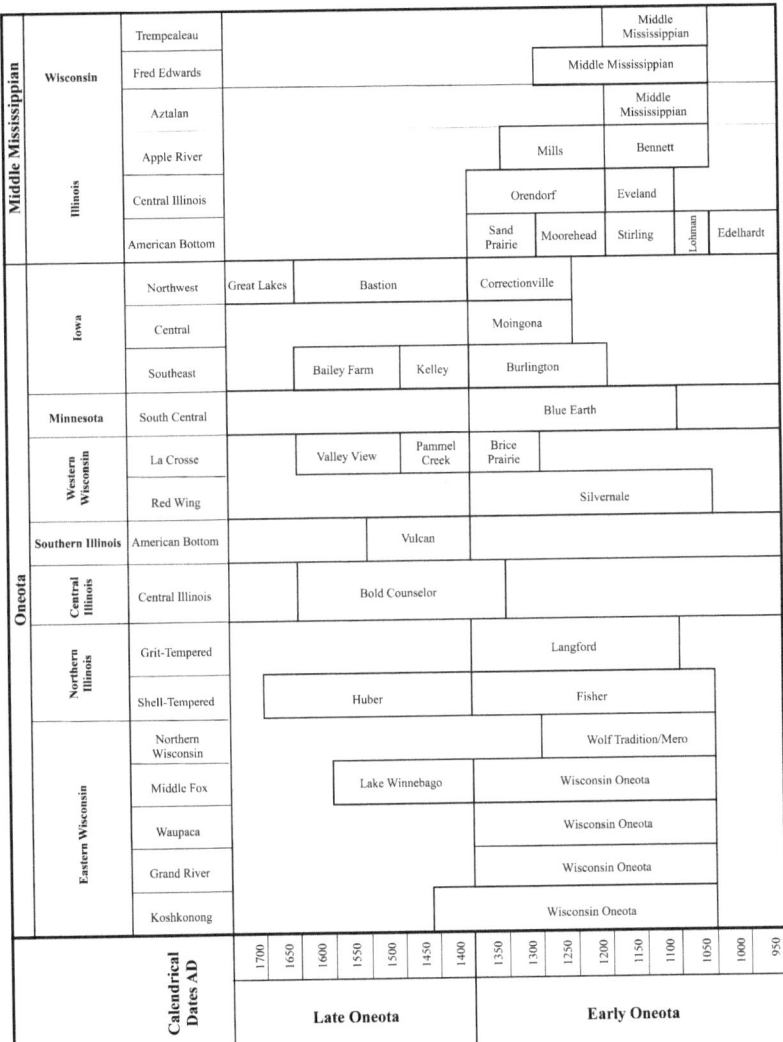

Figure 1.1. Regional chronology of Upper and Middle Mississippian localities in the study region (after Schneider 2015)

Huber replacement represents an in situ transition (Brown 1990; Faulkner 1972) or a population replacement (Emerson and Emerson 2015). Many authors have noted a significant increase in the number and density of sites in the Lake Winnebago–Middle Fox and La Crosse terrace regions (e.g., Overstreet 1997), suggesting that groups began to aggregate in these two locations, in addition to the Huber groups in the Chicago area.

It appears that no Oneota locality, from the Upper Illinois River valley north into Wisconsin, was unaffected by changes that occurred around AD 1400 (see fig. 1.1). Therefore, when referring to chronologies intended for a wide geographic focus, an early (pre–AD 1400) and late (post–AD 1400) dichotomy seems most appropriate (Jeske et al. 2016). However, it is also important to realize that localities were, to varying extents, isolated and independent (Edwards and Jeske 2015; Gibbon 1972a; Jeske et al. 2015; Jeske et al. 2016; O'Gorman 2010). Therefore, we should expect to see changes within some localities that are not reflected in others. Thus, the early/late dichotomy is relevant only for large-scale analyses. Internal chronologies for each locality need to be locally defined, such as those proposed by Boszhardt (1994) for La Crosse and Schirmer (2017) for Red Wing. These chronologies need to account for the effects of local historical trajectories and interactions among groups. In sum, given that fine-grained analyses are now possible and increasingly available, broad generalizations about Oneota lifeways through time and space have limited explanatory value.

SUBSISTENCE

Brown (1982) argued that Oneota subsistence practices were diversified, relying on domesticated plants, wetland resources, and hunting. He also argued that the subsistence systems were highly flexible and adapted to the local conditions. Hart made a similar point about the agricultural systems.

> The relationship between climate, population density, and agricultural management indicates that Oneota agricultural production should not be thought of as a unitary phenomenon. Population densities and climatic variables were not constant throughout the upper Midwest during the Mississippian period. It follows from microeconomic theory that there should be regional and even local variation in agricultural production as a result of varying population density and climatic conditions. (Hart 1990, 575)

While Brown's (1982) arguments were made prior to most flotation-based paleoethnobotanical analyses, his general arguments are still generally thought to hold true. An examination of faunal materials from western Wisconsin indicates that aquatic resources were a vital aspect of the diet. Theler

(Arzigian et al. 1994; Arzigian et al. 1989; Theler 1989, 1994) has regularly argued for the importance of fish and mollusks in the Oneota diet. Tubbs and O'Gorman (2005) have estimated the relative dietary contribution of faunal resources and suggest that fish and mollusks provided from 55% to 75% of the faunal assemblages. Wetland plants were also important. In northern localities, wild rice (*Zizania* sp.) appears to have played a notable role in the Oneota diet (Arzigian 2000; Egan-Bruhy 2014; Hunter 2002), while aquatic tubers were more important to Langford groups in northern Illinois, though their dietary contribution was likely limited (Egan-Bruhy and Nelson 2013). I refer to wild rice as *Zizania* sp. because there is debate among botanists about the historic ranges of the two extant species: *Zizania aquatica* and *Zizania palustris*. Today, Wisconsin is in the range of both plants. There is nothing to suggest a difference in economic potential between the two.

Some degree of a farming base for Oneota groups is unquestioned. While there appears to be considerable variability in the reliance on domesticates such as maize (*Zea mays*), beans (*Phaseolus vulgaris*), and squash (Cucurbitaceae), all major Oneota habitation sites appear to rely on maize, if not all three, to a high degree (Egan-Bruhy 2014; Egan-Bruhy and Nelson 2013; Jeske et al. 2016; Simon 2014). The high rate of scapulae hoes in La Crosse and Lake Winnebago–Middle Fox noted by numerous researchers (e.g., Gallagher and Arzigian 1994; Gallagher and Sasso 1987; Jeske 1989; Overstreet 1997; Sasso 2014) is also suggestive of the great importance of agriculture. The presence of bison scapulae, which were apparently acquired at significant cost through trade and/or during long-distance hunting trips to the Plains, helps underscore the effort invested in agricultural pursuits (Gallagher and Arzigian 1994; Sasso 2014; Theler 1989). Isotopic analyses taken from human remains at several Langford burial sites also suggest a high reliance on maize, consistent with many Middle Mississippian groups (Emerson et al. 2010).

Hunting, the third of Brown's (1982) criteria, also still appears to have provided a significant component of the Oneota diet. La Crosse terrace sites indicate a heavy reliance on white-tailed deer (*Odocoileus virginianus*) in the subsistence system (Theler 1989; Tubbs and O'Gorman 2005). Deer and elk (*Cervus elaphus*) were likely of vital importance in the Koshkonong Locality, providing as much as 70% of the faunal diet. The full faunal analysis from the Koshkonong Locality was completed very recently (McTavish 2019), after this analysis was finished, so I primarily rely on the preliminary studies (Agnew et al. 2016; Edwards 2013; Hunter 2002; Jeske et al. 2016;

Picard and McTavish 2015; Van de Pas, McTavish, and Klemmer 2015). Northern Illinois groups also appear to have a had strong focus on upland-game hunting (Emerson 1999; Hunter 2002; Jeske 2002, 2003b; McTavish 2015). The diversified nature of Oneota subsistence has often been interpreted as a risk management strategy (Gallagher and Arzigian 1994). By focusing on a wide array of resources, failure in one can be easily mitigated by increased use of others (Halstead and O'Shea 1989b; O'Shea 1989). However, this idea has generally been used as a heuristic device and has rarely been tested in any rigorous sense. In some areas, it has been noted that there is a strong emphasis on local resource acquisition (Edwards and Jeske 2015; McTavish 2015) and that it may be part of a defensive strategy to minimize the risk of ambushes from opposing groups (Milner 1992, 2007). This can be seen in the extreme in northern Illinois, where there was a high degree of resource processing (e.g., marrow extraction and use of bone as fuel) at several sites—notably Washington Irving, Robinson Reserve (McTavish 2015), La Salle County Home (Cross and Jeske 1988; Martin 2002), and Hoxie Farm (Martin 2013).

INTERGROUP VIOLENCE IN ONEOTA SOCIETIES

In the past twenty-five years, increased attention has been paid to the effects of intergroup violence in shaping Oneota lifeways. Some of the best early evidence comes from the Central Illinois River valley, where expanding Oneota groups came into conflict (Milner 1992; Milner, Anderson, and Smith 1991). Milner and colleagues (1991) note that at Norris Farms #36, the high rate of violent encounters is consistent with a raiding style of warfare, where small groups would enter enemy territory and lay in wait for the opportunity to ambush a small group as they went about their daily routines away from the village. Approximately 16% of the cemetery population shows evidence of violent death (table 1.1). When children are excluded, that number rises to roughly 30% of the cemetery population. More than 42% of those who died violently appear to have survived a previous attack only to have been killed in a subsequent encounter. An additional 2% of the total cemetery population survived attacks and eventually died from apparently nonviolent causes. Elsewhere, Milner (2005) makes clear that the skeletal evidence underrepresents the actual number of

Table 1.1. Markers of osteological violence and associated type of violence presented by Milner et al. 1991

Osteological Markers	Nonviolent Incident	Interpersonal Violence	Intergroup Violence
Perimortem blunt-force trauma (e.g., cranial impact)	x	x	x
Perimortem trauma consistent with defensive injury (e.g., forearms)		x	x
Perimortem sharp-force trauma		x	x
Projectile point embedded in bone		x	x
Trophy taking/mutilation (e.g., removal of hands, scalping)			x
Scavenger gnaw marks (i.e., away from site ambush led to scavenging)			x
Mass graves			x
Male-to-female ratio relatively even*			x

* Consistent with raiding-style intergroup conflict.

war-related deaths, as not all wounds will have an impact on bone (e.g., arrow wounds to the stomach). Therefore, the estimate that 30% of the population died from enemy attacks should be considered conservative.

This high rate of warfare does not appear to be an isolated occurrence. A comparative study along the western margins of Lake Winnebago showed similar levels of violence in central Wisconsin (Karsten 2015). Karsten (2015) analyzed 126 individuals from six sites and found that 21% showed evidence of violent deaths. The proportion rises to roughly 30% when children are excluded. He concluded that a similar pattern of violence was likely occurring in the Middle Fox Locality as at Norris Farms #36. Jeske (2014) notes that many individuals within the Koshkonong Locality also suffered violent deaths. However, because of small sample sizes and because most human remains have been recovered as isolated finds, there is less demographic detail. Human remains recovered from Upper Mississippian sites in northern Illinois also regularly show evidence of intergroup violence (e.g., Berres 2001; Emerson et al. 2010; Fowler 1940; Jackson and Emerson 2013; Jeske 2003a; Langford 1927), as do many in Iowa (Benn 1995).

The data show that throughout much if not all of Oneota history, warfare was a significant fact of life. Everyone would have known someone who was killed in a raid. Cultural practices to ameliorate raiding's effects would have been required. Milner (2007, 199) argues that groups facing this type of threat would have had to "modify subsistence practices or move to safer, but less productive, places." Anyone leaving the safety of the village could potentially be at risk, requiring shifts in group size (both village and work party), composition, and range.

Groups would leave the protection of the village less often. When they did, they would do so in larger numbers and would be less likely to travel long distances. This would almost certainly reduce productivity. Except with the most aggregated resources, large groups would be less efficient at exploiting resources, particularly if a portion of the group is focused on their defense rather than resource acquisition. Leaving the site less often may preclude groups from accessing certain wild resources while they are most viable and increase the opportunity for competing animals to obtain a larger portion of the yield. Finally, fewer and shorter trips will restrict the range of resources (see Chacon and Mendoza 2007; Keeley 1996; Maschner and Reedy-Maschner 1998; Rice and LeBlanc 2001). VanDerwarker and Wilson (2016) have illustrated that groups living in the Central Illinois River valley were forced to restrict their hunting ranges and reduce foraging forays. Meanwhile, these groups were unable to offset the reduction in food, thereby increasing the likelihood of food shortages. These issues would be exacerbated if stored foods or agricultural fields were also destroyed in an attack (Milner, Anderson, and Smith 1991).

HISTORICAL CONNECTIONS

The disappearance of Oneota groups is also a point of contention. Several different tribes have been suggested as the descendants of Oneota. Most suggested connections are to Chiwere-Siouan-speaking groups (Griffin 1937; McKern 1945; Springer and Witkowski 1982). In eastern Wisconsin, many archaeologists think that the Ho Chunk (historically known as the Winnebago) are the most likely descendants (Hall 1993, 1995; Overstreet 1993; Richards 1993). Ho Chunk oral tradition places them in Wisconsin from the beginning of time; historically, they were the first group contacted by the French in Wisconsin, and they identify themselves as the descendants of the Effigy Mound builders (Radin 1923). Their long-documented history in the region has given scholars good reason to associate Ho Chunk and Oneota peoples; however, the lack of historical components on Oneota sites creates a gap between the historic and prehistoric groups that cannot be easily explained (Mason 1993). Overstreet (2009) has also suggested that the Menominee, a group native to northern Wisconsin, may be the descendants of the northern Mero groups, though these sites also lack a clear transition or overlap between historic and prehistoric components.

No clear connection has been made for Huber ceramics in northern Illinois, although Cremin (1996) makes a case for a Potawatomi connection. The Potawatomi are native to southern Lake Michigan, where Berrien ware is commonly found. Berrien ware is extremely similar to Huber ware (Cremin 1996). Danner pottery, which appears similar to Fort Ancient styles from Ohio (Brown 1990), is clearly associated with the historic Illini occupations at both the Illiniwek Village site in Missouri (Grantham 1993) and the Zimmerman site, also referred to as the Grand Village of the Kaskaskia (Brown 1961; Brown 1975) and the Grand Village of the Illinois (Stelle et al. 1993). Zimmerman is on the northern bank of the Illinois River, across from Starved Rock in the Upper Illinois River valley (Park 2010; Stelle et al. 1993). In the west, archaeologists have had better success connecting prehistoric Oneota groups to historically known tribes: in Iowa, for example, the Ioway have been linked to Orr Phase Oneota sites (Wedel 1959, 1976, 1981, 1986).

DETAILED DESCRIPTIONS OF PRIMARY STUDY SITES

History of Archaeological Research in the Koshkonong Locality

Since the mid-twentieth century, the Koshkonong Locality has intermittently been a hub of Oneota research. In the late 1950s Robert Hall (1962) began excavations at the Carcajou Point site; he used the ceramic assemblage to define Oneota ceramics and chronology. In 1968 David Baerreis led a University of Wisconsin–Madison (UW–Madison) field-based course at the Crescent Bay Hunt Club, though the results were never formally published (Gibbon n.d.). Janet Spector (1975) did her dissertation work at the Crab Apple Point site; however, her research was focused on the historical component. In the 1980s and 1990s, Lynne Goldstein's Southeast Wisconsin Archaeological Program conducted several surveys as part of the Crawfish Rock Archaeological Project, relocating multiple sites and identifying several new ones (e.g., Rodell 1984). In 1998 Robert Jeske began a biennial field school through UWM's Program in Midwestern Archaeology. The field school conducted excavations and surveys at several sites in the region, though most work has been conducted at the Crescent Bay, Schmeling, and Koshkonong Creek Village sites.

Previous research has suggested that the Koshkonong Oneota groups chose village location based on many factors, but economics was consistently ranked high (Edwards 2010; Hunter 2002). Oneota sites throughout Wisconsin, Minnesota, Iowa, and Illinois were typically placed with access to preferential resources, though the exact pattern is unique from locality to locality (Dobbs and Shane 1982; Gallagher and Stevenson 1982; Michalik 1982; Tiffany 1982). Koshkonong sites were primarily placed in a middle ground, between two diverse sets of resources: in one direction, upland resources and arable land; wetland and aquatic resources in the other (Edwards 2010). Furthermore, the sites were placed on high ground overlooking the aquatic resources (fig. 1.2).

The Crescent Bay Hunt Club. The Crescent Bay Hunt Club was first excavated by David Baerreis and students from the University of Wisconsin–Madison during a limited project in fall 1968. Through the course of investigations, they excavated several pit features and uncovered a structure similar to the dome-shaped wigwams (hereafter referred to as wigwams) reported historically throughout the western Great Lakes (Gibbon n.d.). The University of Wisconsin–Milwaukee field school, under the direction of Robert Jeske, returned to excavate the site in 1998. Jeske conducted ten field school seasons there through 2017 (Jeske 2000a, 2003a, 2010; Jeske et al. 2015; Jeske, Foley Winkler, and Lambert 2003; Jeske et al. 2013; Jeske et al 2017). These excavations uncovered more than one hundred pit features and six additional structures (Jeske et al. 2015; Moss 2010; Sterner-Miller 2014). In total, three types of structures have been identified (fig. 1.3). Three rectangular wigwam structures, including the one from 1968, have been uncovered. They have double wall construction and average about 20 m^2 (Jeske 2010; Moss 2010). Three longhouses were also identified at the site. These structures were built using the post-in-trench construction technique. Only one longhouse structure has been sufficiently excavated to accurately estimate size: 140 m^2. Radiocarbon dates suggest that they are contemporaneous with the wigwam structures (Jeske 2010; Jeske et al. 2017; Moss 2010). Features in and near the longhouses contained buds, indicating that the longhouses may have been used in the winter (Edwards and Pater 2011; see also ch. 4). The third structure type was identified in 2014. This structure consists of a half-meter-deep basin, with posts placed

Culture History and Archaeological Background 27

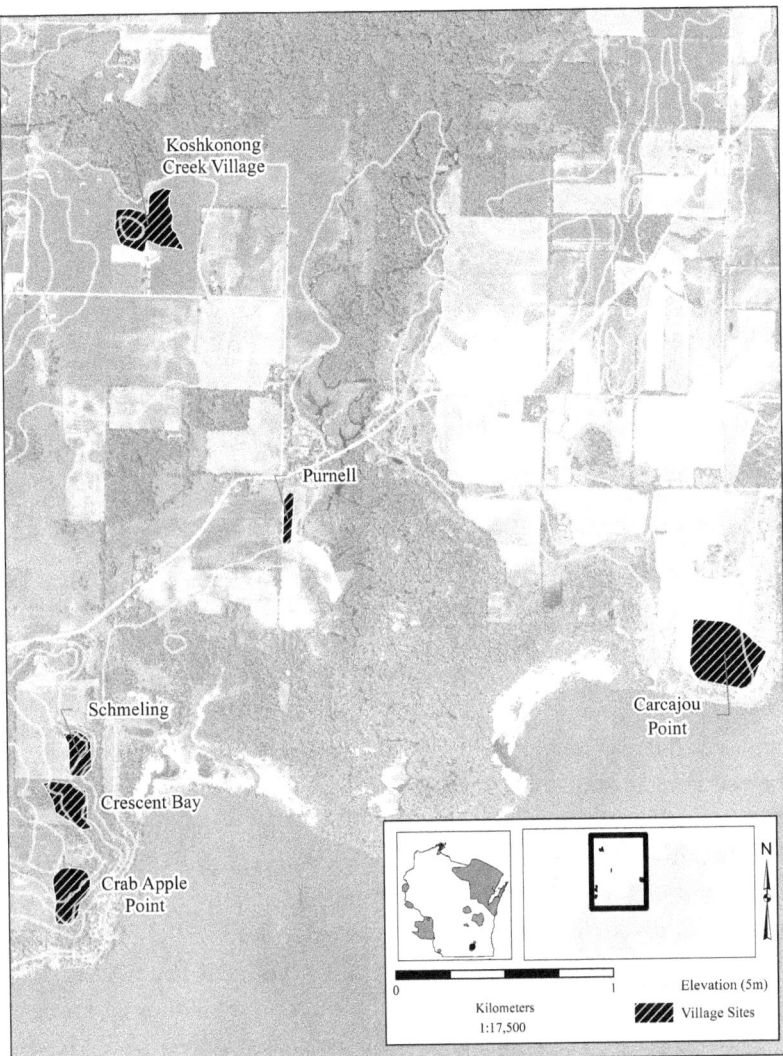

Figure 1.2. Locations of Oneota village sites in the Koshkonong Locality

on a ledge around the margin. The entire basin measured approximately 5 m² and is too small to be a house structure; its function remains unclear, and analysis is still under way (Jeske et al. 2015; Sterner-Miller 2014).

The site appears to have been occupied throughout the year (Edwards and Pater 2011), in contrast to many villages in the La Crosse terrace (Sasso 1989), where separate summer and winter villages seem to be the norm, or

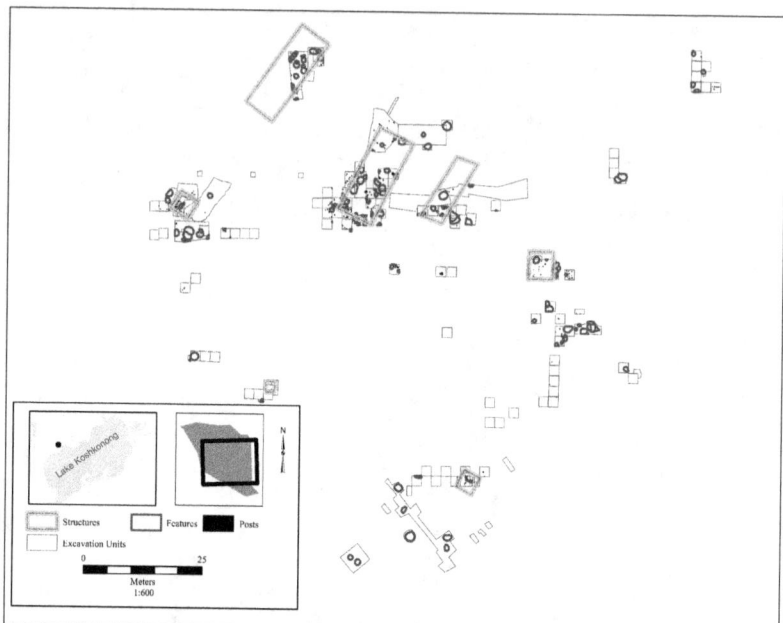

Figure 1.3. Map of archaeological excavations at the Crescent Bay Hunt Club

northern Illinois (Jeske 1989, 1990, 2000a), where many villages appear to be multiseasonal but not necessarily year-round. Faunal evidence suggests that animal food sources were highly diversified but that mammals were relied on more heavily than any other single source; fish also constituted a significant proportion of the diet (Edwards 2013; Van de Pas, McTavish, and Klemmer 2015). Previous floral analyses by Jean Nelson, Lee Olsen, and the author, under the supervision of Kathryn Egan-Bruhy, were conducted on several features from the site. These analyses all showed a similar subsistence pattern—one that included an emphasis on three plants, maize, wild rice, and chenopodium, but also included other EAC plants and an array of wild resources that included nuts, berries, and aquatic plants (Edwards and Pater 2011; Egan-Bruhy 2001a; Olsen 2003).

Environmental reconstructions of the region have allowed for the subsistence data to be contextualized (Edwards 2010; Hunter 2002; Jeske and Edwards 2012). This diversified subsistence strategy fits well with its location in the landscape (Edwards 2010). The site sits atop an 8 m ridge overlooking what would have been extensive wetlands to the east—providing easy access to aquatic and wetland resources. Most of the arable land and upland hunting grounds were to the west of the site.

Koshkonong Creek Village. The Koshkonong Creek Village was first identified by Stout and Skavlem (1908) but was not the subject of professional research for many decades. Skavlem identified the site based on the dense scatterings of refuse present in the plowed fields, including large amounts of ceramics and freshwater mussel shell. Stout and Skavlem also noted that there were several mounds in the immediate vicinity of the village and that human remains had been recovered by the landowner, which C. E. Brown (1909) notes are associated with the village. In 1987, the Southeast Wisconsin Archaeological Program surveyed the area, though those researchers referred to it as the Twin Knolls (Musil 1987). The walkover survey identified the site as primarily Oneota; most ceramics were shell tempered, though a minority of the materials appeared to be Woodland or older.

Beginning in 2008, field schools under the direction of Robert Jeske began research at the site. In 2008 a walkover survey relocated and expanded the boundaries, identified two large artifact concentrations, and confirmed the Oneota occupation at the site (Cowell, Scheutz, and Schneider 2008). In 2010 additional survey work located the north and east boundaries of the site, and four units were placed in the Woodland portion of the site along the bluff overlooking the creek. A modest concentration of Late Woodland ceramics and projectile points was recovered, but no features were identified (Pater, Edwards, and Spott 2010). Beginning in 2012, biennial excavations began in the Oneota portion of the site. Between 2012 and 2017, a total of 88 m^2 were excavated, and portions of both longhouse- and wigwam-style structures have been identified. Approximately twenty-five pit features have been excavated (Edwards 2014a; Edwards and Spott 2012; Jeske et al. 2015; Jeske et al. 2013) (fig. 1.4).

Environmental reconstruction suggests that the site was placed atypically for the locality (Edwards 2010). While most sites were situated along the lake and its associated wetlands, KCV was placed inland along Koshkonong Creek. The site's residents had significantly less access to the wetland and aquatic resources than their regional neighbors. However, they had greater access to arable land and upland resources. Preliminary faunal analyses indicate that different food procurement strategies were used at KCV and CBHC: a different suite of fish were exploited, and large

Figure 1.4. Map of archaeological excavations at the Koshkonong Creek Village

mammals made up a much higher proportion of the overall diet (Agnew et al. 2016; Edwards and McTavish 2012; McTavish and Edwards 2014; Van de Pas, McTavish, and Klemmer 2015). No prior floral analyses have been conducted at the site.

Regional Chronology. Radiocarbon assays from the two sites indicate that they were both occupied from approximately AD 1050 to 1400

Culture History and Archaeological Background 31

Figure 1.5. Radiocarbon chronology of the Koshkonong Locality (calibrated 2σ)

(table 1.2; fig. 1.5). Dates from Schmeling and Carcajou Point align with the assays from KCV and CBHC, indicating that the Oneota occupation of the locality lasted from the eleventh through the fifteenth century AD. However, the error ranges of the radiocarbon dates make it impossible to determine if the sites were all occupied simultaneously or consecutively.

Table 1.2. Radiocarbon dates from the Koshkonong Locality. All dates calibrated with Calib 700.

Site	Context	Material	Age BP	Error Term	1σ	%	2σ	%	Reference
KCV	F12-06 zL	Bean	520	20	1410–1427	100	1399–1438	100	Edwards 2016
CBHC	F04-14 Z2	Maize/Nut	530	40	1329–1340 1369–1434	17 83	1312–1359 1387–1444	30 70	Richards and Jeske 2015
CBHC	F12-53	Maize Cob	580	15	1322–1347 1392–1403	72 28	1314–1357 1388–1409	68 32	Jeske et al. 2017
KCV	F12-06 zB	Residue	605	20	1307–1328 1341–1362 1385–1395	41 40 19	1299–1370 1380–1403	78 22	Edwards 2014
CBHC	F04-14 z6	Residue	590	40	1310–1360 1387–1405	73 27	1296–1415	100	Richards and Jeske 2015
KCV	F14-29 zb	Residue	610	30	1302–1328 1341–1367 1382–1395	40 40 20	1296–1403	100	Edwards 2016
CBHC	F00-06	Maize/Nut	600	40	1306–1363 1385–1400	79 21	1294–1411	100	Richards and Jeske 2015
CBHC	F00-11	Maize/Nut	600	70	1300–1368 1381–1406	74 26	1279–1432	100	Richards and Jeske 2015
CBHC	F00-26	Maize/Nut	620	80	1294–1333 1337–1398	39 61	1262–1438	100	Richards and Jeske 2015
Carcajou	F15	Wood	660	80	1275–1327 1342–1395	50 50	1222–1423	100	Richards, Richards, and Nicholls 1998
CBHC	F02-01	Residue	690	15	1280–1292	100	1275–1299 1370–1380	93 7	Richards and Jeske 2015

Table 1.2. Radiocarbon dates from the Koshkonong Locality. All dates calibrated with Calib 700. (*cont.*)

Site	Context	Material	Age BP	Error Term	1σ	%	2σ	%	Reference
CBHC	F0-14	Residue	700	20	1277–1290	100	1269–1299 1370–1379	95 5	Richards and Jeske 2015
Carcajou	F12	Wood	700	70	1255–1318 1352–1390	65 35	1195–1195 1206–1410	<1 99	Richards, Richards, and Nicholls 1998
CBHC	F00-21	Maize/Nut	720	40	1257–1297 1375–1375	99 1	1222–1308 1361–1386	89 11	Richards and Jeske 2015
CBHC	F04-35	Residue	745	20	1264–1278	100	1247–1286	100	Richards and Jeske 2015
KCV	F14-29	Residue	740	25	1263–1281	100	1226–1232 1244–1290	2 98	Edwards 2016
CBHC	F04-14	Residue	730	40	1254–1296	100	1218–1304 1365–1384	94 6	Richards and Jeske 2015
Schmeling		Residue	765	15	1257–1273	100	1224–1234 1242–1278	6 94	Richards and Jeske 2015
CBHC	F10-29	Residue	765	15	1257–1273	100	1224–1234 1242–1278	6 94	Jeske 2010
CBHC	F02-40	Residue	750	40	1227–1231 1245–1284	6 94	1208–1298 1371–1378	99 1	Richards and Jeske 2015
CBHC	F04-03	Residue	785	15	1225–1232 1224–1264	21 79	1222–1269	100	Richards and Jeske 2015
SCH		Residue	785	20	1224–1234 1242–1265	28 72	1220–1271	100	Richards and Jeske 2015
CBHC	F68-01	Wood	760	50	1224–1280	100	1166–1299 1370–1379	98 1	Bender, Baerreis, and Steventon 1970

Table 1.2. Radiocarbon dates from the Koshkonong Locality. All dates calibrated with Calib 700. (*cont.*)

Site	Context	Material	Age BP	Error Term	1σ	%	2σ	%	Reference
CBHC	F10-98	Residue	795	15	1224–1235 1241–1259	37 63	1219–1265	100	Richards and Jeske 2015
CBHC	F68-06	Wood	780	50	1217–1277	100	1159–1293	100	Bender, Baerreis, and Steventon 1970
CBHC	F06-63	Residue	800	40	1213–1268	100	1166–1277	100	Richards and Jeske 2015
CBHC	F68-10	Wood	800	50	1192–1197 1205–1272	4 95	1055–1076 1153–1287	2 98	Bender, Baerreis, and Steventon 1970
CBHC	F68-26	Wood	810	50	1189–1266	100	1051–1082 1128–1133 1151–1284	4 1 95	Bender, Baerreis, and Steventon 1970
CBHC	F10-14	Dog bone	854	21	1169–1177 1181–1214	20 80	1156–1228 1231–1247	96 5	Appendix B
CBHC	F10-11	Dog bone	856	24	1168–1216	100	1058–1065 1066–1074 1154–1252	1 1 98	Appendix B
CBHC	F04-14	Residue	880	40	1050–1082 1128–1135 1151–1216	27 5 68	1037–1225 1234–1243	98 2	Richards and Jeske 2015
Carcajou	—	Wood	890	80	1043–1103 1118–1216	38 61	1016–1271	100	Hall 1960
CBHC	F04-15	Residue	920	40	1043–1104 1118–1158	60 40	1026–1192 1197–1205	98 2	Richards and Jeske 2015

Table 1.2. Radiocarbon dates from the Koshkonong Locality. All dates calibrated with Calib 700. (*cont.*)

Site	Context	Material	Age BP	Error Term	1σ	%	2σ	%	Reference
KCV	F12-01	Residue	1000	20	999–1001 1013–1035	3 97	989–1044 1100–1119 1144–1145	93 6 0	Edwards and Spott 2012
Crab Apple	Oneota Feature	Wood	980	55	999–1002 1012–1053 1079–1152	1 38 61	909–911 969–1190 1198–1203	<1 99 <1	Spector 1975
CBHC	F04-22	Residue	990	20	1016–1040 1110–1115	92 8	994–1047 1089–1122 1139–1148	78 19 3	Richards and Jeske 2015
Carcajou	F17	Wood	990	250	777–791 804–842 860–1259	3 7 90	581–1428	100	Hall 1960
Carcajou	F5	Wood	1010	70	969–1053 1079–1152	60 40	887–1190 1199–1202	99 <1	Richards et al. 1998
Carcajou	F8	Wood	1020	80	900–921 950–1051 1082–1128 1134–1151	9 61 22 8	778–790 810–810 826–840 863–1211	1 <1 1 98	Richards et al. 1998
Carcajou		Wood	1020	250	771–1224 1239–1240	99 1	557–1415	100	Hall 1960
Carcajou		Wood	1520	250	237–731 735–769	95 5	-4–1018	99	Hall 1960

DESCRIPTIONS OF COMPARATIVE SITES

This section provides the essential background information for the comparative sites, including those with comparative paleoethnobotanical data and those where dog isotopic data were collected. The section discusses sites based on their archaeological culture and is subdivided by regions or localities.

Upper Mississippian Sites

The sites in this category are both the most numerous and the most geographically diverse. A total of twenty comparative sites across three states and nine localities compose this category (table 1.3). These sites also include the full time span of Oneota, from around AD 1050 to 1650.

Middle Fox Locality Sites. The Schrage (47FD581) and Soggy Oats (47WN595) sites are the comparative sites from the Middle Fox Locality (see fig. I.1). Schrage (Schneider and Richards 2010), excavated in 2009, is located on the east side of Lake Winnebago. Excavations were restricted to the modern extent of U.S. Highway 151. In total, 86 pit features were identified and excavated. Based on the density of features and the density of the materials they contained, the site has been interpreted as a village site. Calibrated AMS dates range from AD 1000 to 1380. The site appears to have been occupied year-round based on the flora (Egan-Bruhy 2010a).

Egan-Bruhy at Commonwealth Cultural Resources Group (CCRG) (now Commonwealth Heritage Group) conducted the floral analysis. Thirty-five samples from 29 features were analyzed. The analytical methods match those used in this project (described in ch. 3). The results indicate that the population was highly reliant on maize, which was highly ubiquitous (present in 89% of samples) and present in moderate densities (16 ct./10 liters). The high proportion of cupules, glumes, and cob fragments indicates that maize was heavily processed on site and may have been intentionally used as a fuel source. Nuts were apparently a major secondary resource. Nuts were present in 51% of samples and were identified in high densities (53 ct./10 liters). Grains were also cultivated as a secondary resource, including chenopodium (*Chenopodium* sp.), barnyard grass (*Echinochloa* sp.), and wild rice (*Zizania* sp.).

Table 1.3. Calibrated (2σ) radiocarbon dates from comparative sites (calibrated with Calib 700)

Locality	Site Name	Site Number	Occupation Range*	References
Middle Fox	Schrage	47FD581	AD 1000–1380	Schneider and Richards 2010; Egan-Bruhy 2010a
	Soggy Oats	47WN595		Egan-Bruhy 2001b
Waupaca	Blinded by the Light	47PT191	AD 950–1350	Hamilton et al. 2010; Egan-Bruhy 2010b
	Dambrowski	47PT160	AD 1000–1400	
	Burley Brew	47PT159	AD 950–1350	
Green Bay	Citgo	47BR460	**	Egan-Bruhy 2012
	Pamperin Park	47BR389	**	Egan-Bruhy 2012
Red Wing	Bryan	21GD004	AD 1020–1440	Schirmer 2002
	Diamond Bluff	47PI002	AD 1020–1450	Rodell 1997
La Crosse	Tremaine	47LC095	AD 1275–1650	O'Gorman 1995
	OT	47LC262	AD 1320–1650	O'Gorman 1993
	Filler	47LC149	AD 1420–1650	O'Gorman 1994
	Pammel Creek	47LC061	AD 1290–1640	Arzigian 1989; Arzigian et al. 1989; Boszhardt 1989
	Valley View	47LC034	AD 1020–1650	Stevenson 1994; Stevenson 1985
	Sanford District	47LC394	AD 1040–1440	Arzigian et al. 1994; Holtz-Leith 2006, 2011
Northeastern Illinois (Langford and Fisher)	Fisher	11WI5	AD 1045–1400	Emerson, Jeske, and Calentine 2006; Griffin 1948; Parmalee 1962; Strezewski 2006
	Zimmerman	11LS13	AD 1050–1385	Brown 1961; Egan 1993; Jeske and Hart 1988
	Washington Irving	11K52	AD 1110–1440	Jeske 2000b; Richards and Jeske 2015
	Hoxie Farm	11CK4	AD 1220–1620	Brown and O'Brien 1990; Jackson and Emerson 2013

Soggy Oats is a much smaller site, with only five features identified (Egan-Bruhy 2001b). Three of the pit features are interpreted as hearths or roasting pits. A single storage pit and a post mold were also identified. The site has been interpreted as a fall nut-processing camp. Egan-Bruhy used the same analytical methods as those used in this project to analyze the flora. The sample indicates that maize was an important aspect of the diet, even at camp sites. It was found in two of the four pit features. Squash was also present in the sample. Nutshell was found in three of the four pit features, as well as a sampled post mold. Little barley and chenopodium were also found at the site. Nutshell was generally present in moderate densities, though Feature 8 contained significantly greater amounts. Despite the site's short occupation, the general dietary patterns are similar to Schrage's. Overall, the assemblage is less diverse, though it appears maize was a major component of the diet in the locality regardless of the situation. At Soggy Oats, it is not known if maize was brought as a provision or if there were dispersed agricultural fields near the processing site. Given the six-to-one ratio of maize cupule/cob fragments to kernels, it is possible that the site also served as a maize field processing location. The site does show less diversity of seeds, which is understandable considering the short-term nature of its occupation.

Waupaca Locality Sites. Three sites from the Waupaca Locality were chosen for comparison. Burley Brew (47PT159), Dambrowski (47PT160), and Blinded by the Light (BBTL, 47PT191) are all interpreted as Oneota villages that were occupied from the eleventh through the fourteenth century AD (see fig. I.1). The sites were all excavated by the Museum Archaeology Program of the Wisconsin Historical Society as part of the U.S. Highway 10 project. Therefore, the areas excavated were limited to the construction areas and may not be fully representative of the large sites (Hamilton et al. 2010).

Each of the sites is located near the Waupaca and Tomorrow Rivers in Portage County, southeast of present-day Stevens Point. Despite their general proximity, the sites appear to have been differentially placed on the landscape. BBTL, the easternmost site, is roughly 2.5 km north of the river valley, on relatively low ground (20–30 ft. lower than the adjacent bluff) and is immediately adjacent to an intermittent stream (Hamilton et al. 2010, 3–5). Dambrowski is immediately adjacent to the Waupaca River, on high ground, overlooking the river valley. The site is close to the river on three sides; it is largely within the inside curve of an oxbow. Whereas

BBTL occupies the lowest land in the immediate vicinity of the site, Dambrowski occupies nearly the highest. Immediately to the east, a hill overlooks the site, and the village sat 10 to 12 m above the river (Hamilton et al. 2010, 6–7). Burley Brew, the westernmost site, is less than 2 km from Dambrowski. The site is multicomponent and covers a large area, both along and inland from the Waupaca River. Much of the site is on relatively flat ground (Hamilton et al. 2010, 29–30).

The floral analysis at all three of the sites was completed by Egan-Bruhy (2010b) using the same methods as this project. The Burley Brew assemblage included 10 samples, each from a different feature, for a total 126 liters. Blinded by the Light contained 58 samples from 39 features for a total of 408 liters. The floral assemblages from all three sites support warm-season occupation of the villages, from late spring through early fall. Blinded by the Light and Dambrowski also contain buds, indicating they were also occupied during the cold seasons and were likely occupied year-round. The lack of cold season indicators at Burley Brew may represent actual seasonal differences or may be sampling bias.

Green Bay Locality Sites. The Citgo and Pamperin Park sites are both located in mainland Wisconsin near the west shore of Green Bay, across from the Door Peninsula (see fig. I.1). The sites are along the north shore of the Suamico River. The two sites are separated by less than 500 m. Pamperin Park directly overlooked the river (Egan-Bruhy 2012); Citgo was slightly farther inland, approximately 200 m from the river. Egan-Bruhy conducted the analysis for the Citgo site, using comparable methods. A total of seven contexts from three features totaling 25 liters of sediment were analyzed from the Oneota component of the site. The bulk of the assemblages (excluding wood and bark charcoal) is nutshell. Given the large number of aquatic tubers, the site was likely occupied during the late spring, perhaps longer (Egan-Bruhy, pers. comm.). The relatively high importance of nutshell supports cold season occupation, with nuts used as a buffer resource to get through the winter.

Pamperin Park was occupied from Early Woodland through Oneota. The density and permanence of the site are ambiguous. According to Egan-Bruhy (2012, 1), "The Late Woodland and Oneota occupations appear to be longer-term occupations characteristic of village sites, although interestingly the range of resources represented suggests a seasonal occupation."

Jean Nelson conducted the floral analysis under the supervision of Egan-Bruhy using methods comparable to those in this analysis. Approximately 270 liters of sediment from 28 Oneota features were analyzed. The presence of buds and the overall floral assemblage are consistent with cold season occupation of the site. Maize does not appear to be a significant component of the diet, as it is found in low ubiquities and densities. Nutshell is found in much higher densities and ubiquities, which indicates that nuts were an important aspect of the winter diet at the site and perhaps in the region as a whole (Egan-Bruhy 2012).

Red Wing Locality. The Red Wing Locality occupies both sides of the Mississippi River, between present-day Minneapolis and La Crosse where the Cannon and Trimbelle Rivers join the Mississippi (see fig. I.1). Numerous Oneota sites have been identified in the region, including seven notably large Oneota villages (Dobbs 1984; Fleming 2009; Gibbon and Dobbs 1991; Schirmer 2002). Sites in the region generally date between AD 1000 and 1450 (Schirmer 2002, 56, table 1.3). Most if not all the major villages were likely occupied simultaneously (Fleming 2009, 151; Rodell 1997, 34). Village sites are generally located atop glacial outwash terraces and are often associated with large mound complexes. Fleming (2009) argues that although they were interconnected, villages separated by the Mississippi River were less connected with one another than with villages on the same side. He attributes the differences in connectedness to distinct resource catchments and different trade networks. Essentially, each site was more connected with trade networks on its own side of the river (i.e., east/Wisconsin side for Diamond Bluff and west/Minnesota side for Bryan), and its resource catchment rarely crossed the Mississippi River.

Two village sites from Red Wing were chosen for comparison because they had comparable data sets. The Bryan site, on the west side of the Mississippi, includes comparative floral analysis conducted by Schirmer (2002) and human isotopic data (Pratt 1994). Schirmer's methods were generally similar to those used in this analysis. The site has a long history of excavation and is the most thoroughly investigated site in the locality (Schirmer 2002, 129). It sits atop a terrace overlooking the Cannon River and includes an associated mound complex. The village covered approximately 8 h. Diamond Bluff (also referred to as Mero I), a large village on the east side of the river, includes two sets of dog remains (Alex n.d.), which were sampled and submitted for isotopic analysis. The site sits atop the north end of a large terrace and, like Bryan, is associated with many mounds. Also like Bryan, the site has a long excavation history (Rodell 1997).

La Crosse Locality. The La Crosse Locality contains a dense concentration of Oneota sites that primarily postdate AD 1200 (Boszhardt 1994; Overstreet 1997). The site settlement system in this region is multilayered and dynamic, consisting of seasonal villages of multiple sizes and associated hamlets, mortuary sites, and logistical camps (Sasso 1989). The primary comparative sites, Tremaine, Filler, and OT (see fig. I.1), are part of what is commonly referred to as the Tremaine Complex, as the sites are in close proximity to one another near Halfway Creek (O'Gorman 1994). The Museum Archaeology Program, under the direction of Jodie O'Gorman, excavated each of the sites (O'Gorman 1995). Multiple researchers conducted the floral analyses but all used the Illinois Department of Transportation method designed by Wagner and are comparable to the methods used in this project (Hunter and Berg 1993). Generally, most of the sites were occupied toward the end, or after, the Koshkonong Locality occupation. The earliest of the three sites is Tremaine, which appears to have been first occupied between AD 1300 and 1400. The site was most heavily occupied between AD 1400 and 1500, with evidence of a minor occupation after AD 1500 (O'Gorman 1995). The bulk of the OT occupation was also during the Valley View phase, primarily in the early AD 1400s, with portions of the site occupied in the early to mid-1600s (O'Gorman 1993). The Filler site was occupied the latest, after AD 1600 (O'Gorman 1994).

A total of eight dog bone samples from four La Crosse area sites were selected for isotopic analysis. Two were from the previously described OT site and were recovered from O'Gorman's (1993) excavations in two different levels of Feature 3. Samples were obtained from the Wisconsin Historical Society with the assistance of Angela Glasker. Two dog mandibles were obtained from the Valley View site, one from Pammel Creek and one from the Sanford Archaeological Complex (generally near or within the Gunderson site).

The Pammel Creek site was excavated several times, but the Mississippi Valley Archaeological Center (MVAC) conducted the most significant excavations, in the 1980s. These excavations uncovered a large portion of the site, including numerous pits, houses, and other features from the fifteenth-century AD village site (Arzigian and Boszhardt 1989). Using the radiocarbon dates and ceramics, Boszhardt (1989) argues that the site was primarily occupied in the first half of the fifteenth century AD. Arzigian and Boszhardt (1989, 33) argue that the site occupation was "relatively short-term." The exact size of the site is unclear, but it is at least 2.5 h. The site is named for the artificial creek it abuts and is within 1 km of the Mississippi River and its associated wetlands (Arzigian and Boszhardt 1989). The site shows definitive evidence of occupation from late spring through early fall (Arzigian et al. 1989).

The floral remains from the site were analyzed by Arzigian (1989); however, the domesticates (e.g., maize) were not quantified in the same manner used in this analysis and were not included in the macrobotanical comparison. Radiocarbon dates from the site range between AD 1280 and 1640, but most have large two-sigma ranges, making it difficult to narrow the range with radiocarbon dates alone. Permission to do destructive testing on dog remains from the site was granted by MVAC. James Theler identified the single dog from the site. Theler removed a sample from the mandible, with the assistance of myself and Constance Arzigian. The sample was then sent to the University of Utah for isotopic analysis.

The Valley View site overlooks the La Crosse River, about 6.5 km northeast of its confluence with the Mississippi River (Stevenson 1994, 237). The site was excavated by MVAC as a cultural resource management project and the University of Wisconsin–La Crosse as a field school. The bulk of the occupation was between AD 1500 and 1600; however, a small number of early radiocarbon assays have been obtained that range from AD 1020 to 1330. These early dates are generally discarded as erroneous because they are earlier than all other previously reported Oneota dates in the region and the ceramics were consistent with a later-dated assemblage (Stevenson 1994) based on the La Crosse ceramic chronology (Boszhardt 1994). Theler identified a total of two dog mandibles. Like Pammel Creek, MVAC gave permission for the destruction of the mandibles. Samples were removed in La Crosse prior to being sent to Utah for isotopic analysis.

The Sanford Archaeological District is in southern La Crosse, within the city boundaries. Because of the density of modern occupation, numerous construction projects have required periodic archaeological investigations, most notably by MVAC. They found a large-scale Oneota occupation dating roughly between AD 1300 and 1500 (Holtz-Leith 2006,

2011). Much of the Sanford Archaeological District is atop a terrace, running from the base of large bluffs to the east of the site and overlooking the Mississippi River to the west (Holtz-Leith 2011). During the 1999 excavations of the Seventh Street Project, dog remains were identified in Feature 37 (Holtz-Leigh 2006). One mandible was selected for analysis. Two additional dogs were identified from the 1991 excavations in Features 59 and 516 (Arzigian et al. 1994), and dog bones from these burials were used for this analysis. Identification, sampling, and permissions for both samples are the same as described for Pammel Creek.

Illinois Sites. Comparative floral material was used from three Upper Mississippian sites in northern Illinois (see fig. I.1), and comparative dog remains were identified from one additional Upper Mississippian northern Illinois site. These sites span nearly the entire geographic range of Upper Mississippian in northern Illinois and include sites from the Fox–Des Plaines (Washington Irving), Chicago Lake Plain (Hoxie Farm), and Upper Illinois River Localities (Fisher and Zimmerman). The only major habitation area without any comparative sites is the Rock/Kishwaukee Locality. The sites also encompass both archaeological cultures present in the region that were contemporaneous with the Oneota occupation of the Koshkonong Locality, Fisher and Langford.

The Washington Irving site sits on a terrace overlooking Jelkes Creek, a tributary of the Fox River. The site boundary covers approximately 4 h (Jeske 1990, 2000). The site was noted by an American expedition that crossed the region in 1817 and again by the General Land Office (GLO) surveyor in 1838 (Jeske 1990). The explorers described likely earth lodges, while the GLO surveyor simply noted the presence of mounds. Excavations conducted by a field school under the direction of Jeske confirmed that these were not mounds but the remnants of earth lodges. A series of 13 radiocarbon assays date the site between cal. AD 1000 and 1440 (Jeske 1990; Richards and Jeske 2015).

The site is normally described as multiseasonal, with direct evidence of occupation for spring through fall (Jeske 1990, 2000). The insulated nature of the earth lodges would have been ideal for winter heating, so it is likely that the site was occupied year-round (R. Jeske, pers. comm.). Floral remains from 35 features excavated in 1984–85 were examined by Egan-Bruhy using methods comparable to those in this project.

Two sites from the Upper Illinois River valley were included in the analysis. The Zimmerman site was used for its comparative floral data. The Fisher site has dog remains for isotopic testing as well as previously published human isotopic data (Emerson et al. 2010). Zimmerman is a multicomponent site with a long history of archaeological investigation, dating to 1947 (Brown 1961, 1975; Jeske and Hart 1988). The site extends over a mile on a terrace along the northern banks of the Illinois River; however, the various components are largely separated via horizontal stratigraphy (Brown 1961). The prehistoric components include Late Woodland and Langford; the historic Danner component is associated with the Illini village first encountered by Marquette and Jolliet in 1673, and it is the Illini village to which Marquette returned to found the Mission of the Immaculate Conception in 1675 (Brown 1961).

While the historic Illini occupation has been a major focus of investigations (Brown 1961; Brown 1975), its late prehistoric Langford occupation is of relevance for this research (Brown 1961; Jeske and Hart 1988). The site is located near many other important sites in the Upper Illinois River valley, including Material Service Quarry (MSQ) and Gentleman Farm, among others (Brown 1967; Brown and O'Brien 1990; Emerson et al. 2010). The floral materials all come from the Langford component of the site, located in Grid D (Brown 1961). Five of the twelve samples come from Northwestern University excavations conducted in 1987 under a grant from the National Park Service (Jeske and Hart 1988). The remainder comes from 1991 field school excavations, under the direction of James A. Brown (unpublished). Egan-Bruhy conducted both analyses using methods comparable to those used in this analysis (Egan 1993a; Jeske and Hart 1988).

The Fisher site was first excavated by George Langford (1927) in the early twentieth century and has been subjected to intermittent, yet considerable, archaeological research (Emerson, Jeske, and Calentine 2006; Griffin 1946, 1948; Horner 1947; Langford 1927; Parmalee 1962; Strezewski 2006). The site is multicomponent and was occupied by Langford and Fisher groups sequentially (Griffin 1946, 1948). It is located atop a roughly 10 m high terrace overlooking the Des Plaines River, near the confluence of the Des Plaines and Kankakee Rivers, which forms the headwaters of the Illinois River (Langford 1927). In total, 50 houses and 12 burial mounds have been identified; many of them have been excavated and analyzed (Griffin 1948). The sample from the site includes bones from two definitive dogs and one potential dog that I previously analyzed (Edwards, Jeske, and Coltrain 2017), as well as human bones analyzed isotopically by the Illinois State Archaeological Survey that provide greater understanding of the dietary range at the site (Emerson et al. 2010). The site is contemporaneous with the Oneota occupation of Koshkonong (Edwards, Jeske, and Coltrain 2017; Emerson, Jeske, and Calentine 2006).

The Hoxie Farm site has a long history of archaeological inquiry (e.g., Brown and O'Brien 1990; Jackson 2017; Jackson and Emerson 2013). It overlooks the Little Calumet River southeast of modern-day Chicago. The area surrounding the site was reported to have included a mixture of wetlands, forests, and prairies (Meyer 1952) (see fig. I.1). Marshes were abundant east of the site, prairie to the south (Brown and O'Brien 1990). Recent radiocarbon assays from the site range from the thirteenth through the seventeenth century (Jackson and Emerson 2013) and include both Fisher and Huber components (Brown and O'Brien 1990; Jackson and Emerson 2013). The Fisher component, excavated by the Illinois Transportation Archaeological Research Program (ITARP) uncovered a significant portion of a large prehistoric fortified village (Jackson and Emerson 2013). Nelson and Egan-Bruhy (2013) conducted the floral analysis of 31 features, totaling more than 500 liters, using methods comparable to this analysis. Feature types include hearths, earth ovens, and trash pits. The Illinois State Archaeological Survey (ISAS, formerly ITARP) recently completed analysis of a larger portion of the site, including Fisher and Huber components (Jackson 2017). Their analyses included both radiocarbon and dietary isotopes; however, 20 of 43 samples were rejected for different reasons. Given the high failure rate, these materials are not included in this analysis.

All the Langford and Fisher sites in this study appear to have been occupied year-round based on house type; all appear to be villages and to have been occupied (or reoccupied) for a length of time similar to that of the Koshkonong sites. The combined data sets are geographically representative of three distinct localities, covering most of the Upper Mississippian territory in northeastern Illinois. They also include both distinct archaeological cultures that were present in the region concurrent with the Koshkonong occupation.

Late Woodland

Several Late Woodland sites were selected to provide comparative data (see fig. I.1). To fully contextualize the Koshkonong subsistence strategy, both collared and non-collared ware sites in southeastern Wisconsin were sought. However, there are relatively few sites with macrobotanical or isotopic data available.

Two non-collared ware sites were selected, one with macrobotanical data and one with isotopic data. Nitschke Mounds, an Effigy Mound site, is in Dodge County near the Horicon Marsh (Kaufmann 2005) and was first excavated by W. C. McKern (1930). A bone from a single dog burial, from Mound 21, was subjected to isotopic testing and has been previously reported (Edwards, Jeske, and Coltrain 2017).

Centra 53/54 (Centra) is a small habitation site located in Washington County. CCRG excavated this multicomponent site as part of a Phase III mitigation. The limited excavations identified both Late Archaic and Late Woodland components (Egan 1993b). The site is clearly Late Woodland, but the two rim sherds make precise identification difficult. Neither of the identified rims contained collars. The identifiable body sherds were of the Madison type, often associated with non-collared ware sites; however, Late Woodland sites with both pottery types have been noted (Clauter 2003, 2012). The site was situated in a diverse environment near the Milwaukee River; multiple swamps, lakes, and other wetlands were present in the immediate vicinity of the habitation. The single radiocarbon assay, taken from wood charcoal, indicates that the site was occupied contemporaneously with the Koshkonong Locality (2σ range: cal. AD 1300–1625). The floral analysis of eight units, including two definitive features, was conducted by Egan-Bruhy using comparable methods. There are few indicators of seasonality, and Egan-Bruhy argues that the assemblage, with very low densities, is not inconsistent with winter storage (Egan 1993b, 45). However, the bulk of the identified plants are available in summer and early fall (e.g., blackberry [*Rubus* sp.], knotweed [*Polygonum* sp.]). Therefore, I tentatively identify this site as a low-intensity non-collared ware warm season occupation.

Two collared ware camps were also used for comparison. Murphy and River Quarry were both excavated by the Museum Archaeology Program. The sites are multicomponent but include a substantial Late Woodland occupation, denoted by the presence of collared ceramic vessels. Radiocarbon dates from Murphy span from cal. AD 400 to 1300. River Quarry dates are more constrained, between cal. AD 1000 and 1300. Both sites are contemporaneous with Koshkonong. Both sites are in Dane County, but Murphy is adjacent to a wetland near Lake Mendota. River Quarry is near the Wisconsin River (Hawley 2011). Floral analysis was conducted by Egan-Bruhy using comparable methods. Both faunal and floral data clearly indicate fall through winter occupation of the sites (Hawley 2011, 286).

Middle Mississippian

Two Middle Mississippian sites were chosen for comparison to Koshkonong. The first, Aztalan (see fig. I.1), has been excavated for decades, starting with Barrett (1933) in the early twentieth century. Aztalan is in Jefferson County, along the banks of the Crawfish River. The Crawfish is a tributary of the Rock, and Aztalan is only 25 km upriver from the Koshkonong sites (Richards and Jeske 2002, 34). The site has been occupied since the Paleoindian period (Goldstein and Richards 1991; Sampson 2008), but it is best known as a large Late Woodland site occupied by Middle Mississippians (e.g., Barrett 1933; Goldstein and Richards 1991; Richards 1992). Zych (2013) has argued that the manner in which the northeast mound was constructed and associated ceremonies indicate a creolization or merging of a Mississippian group from the American Bottom and a local Late Woodland group that was already living at the site. The site was heavily fortified with a palisade, built with substantial posts (Barrett 1933; Birmingham and Goldstein 2005; Goldstein and Freeman 1997). Recent radiocarbon dates make clear that the Middle Mississippian occupation occurred between around AD 1100 and 1250 (Richards and Jeske 2002).

Picard (2013) analyzed the paleoethnobotanical data from the site. Her data set contains samples from two different field seasons and from before and after the arrival of the Middle Mississippians and the subsequent restructuring of the site. Picard's methods were the same as those used in this research. However, the Late Woodland samples from the 1984 field season do not have associated soil volumes, making them incomparable to other sites. However, the Middle Mississippian occupation samples are directly comparable to other sites in this project. Also, the Aztalan Late Woodland data can still be used for diversity indices as they are based on raw counts rather than density.

Lundy is the other Middle Mississippian site. Located in the Apple River valley of northwestern Illinois, the site is approximately 1.2 h in area and has been excavated intermittently since the 1980s (Emerson, Millhouse, and Schroeder 2007, 1–5). The site is situated above the Apple River, just north of its confluence with the Mississippi River, and its Mississippian occupation ranges from AD 1100 to 1350 (Emerson, Millhouse, and Schroeder 2007, 11–12). Botanical analysis of samples from Center for American Archaeology excavations was conducted by the Illinois State Museum on behalf of the Illinois State Archaeological Survey. The methods used were broadly comparable to my own. The results of the analysis were published in a comprehensive interpretation and overview of the site (Emerson, Millhouse, and Schroeder 2007).

TWO

Risk Management and
Other Theoretical Considerations

Cultural and environmental instability instills the risk of failure in all subsistence systems (see, e.g., Kipnis 2002). When insufficient food is obtained for the entire population, some level of starvation and death follows. However, through cultural adaptations, humans make efforts to mitigate and buffer against such occurrences and embed these practices in several cultural systems beyond just subsistence (Cashdan 1990a; Halstead and O'Shea 1989b; Winterhalder 1986). Halstead and O'Shea (1989b) argue that the study of these cultural constructions can inform on an array of anthropological questions, from the functional, about the nature of economic systems, to questions concerning long-term cultural change.

The sources and the nature of variation in food productivity are important factors to consider. Predictability, scale, and the severity of variation are of particular importance. Following Halstead and O'Shea's (1989b) definitions, "predictability" refers to the ability of prehistoric groups to foresee variation in productivity or output accurately. For example, winter in temperate climates is predictable. Anyone living in a temperate climate knows that there will be certain times of the year when low temperatures and snow make plant resources scarce and when many animals migrate or hibernate and the remaining ones become leaner. Furthermore, most tasks become more difficult (transportation increases with snowfall, larger amounts of firewood are needed for heating purposes, etc.). While the exact time line may vary from year to year, the overall pattern is well known and easily predicted. In regions like Wisconsin, regardless of severity, winter will be a lean time. While the severity may vary, the same general plan of provisioning food and firewood will generally hold true. The best way to survive winter is to already have all the resources you need before it starts. However, the success of these plans is often determined by the level of productivity during the warmer seasons and typically must be bolstered by winter hunts, ice fishing, and other activities. These buffering actions are subject to unpredictable weather events, like storms or atypical temperatures. Some form of these events can occur year-round.

These other factors are less predictable. For example, droughts or blizzards occur with little warning, which makes planning for them difficult. Taking steps to mitigate drought every year may be a costly endeavor. If so, it is less likely that everyone in a group would be willing to maintain the costly behavior after several good years or during years when other unpredictable events necessitate alternate actions. Furthermore, the severity and scale of a drought may vary from event to event. While droughts may be relatively unpredictable, in many regions they can be expected to occur during at least a few years each decade. If a particularly bad drought (extremely dry, extremely long, or both) occurs, typical mitigation tactics may not be successful. Furthermore, the range of areas affected can vary from event to event. A drought may extend over an entire region, or it may affect a much smaller area. The scale will greatly affect the range of viable mitigation options. Each source of variation has its own parameters for scale, severity, and predictability. Hailstorms, for example, are extremely unpredictable, highly variable in severity, and tend to be very localized in their effects. The result, regardless of steps taken, is that food returns will not be consistent annually. Since in any given year the final food yields cannot be predicted, it is essential for all groups to attempt to employ mechanisms that will reduce the overall likelihood of food scarcity most effectively. Since different threats may require contradictory strategies, there is often no way to know if the appropriate strategy was used until it is too late. Risk buffering strategies are essentially wagers. Like any form of gambling, understanding the probability of various outcomes is key (Cancian 1980; Cashdan 1990a; Fleisher 1990; Gladwin 1980; Halstead and O'Shea 1989b).

Risks can be divided into two types based on their source: social (typically threat of warfare) and environmental (long-term: climate shifts;

short-term: unexpected weather patterns or seasonal variation) (Hart 1993). These two types of risks are usually mitigated by opposing strategies. Environmental stress can be mitigated through mobility; people can move to an area less affected by the current conditions or expand their range so that they can access resources that are less affected. Both forms of mobility tend to reduce the importance of agriculture because people are less capable of investing in the landscape (Jones 2005), whereas the threat of warfare tends to increase it. As outside groups become more threatening, pulling in to a defendable territory and intensifying agriculture can allow the population to remain relatively safe and fed (Hart 1990, 1993). Marston (2011) makes a similar argument: agricultural groups tend to focus on one of two primary strategies, diversification and intensification.

Hart (1993) points out that many strategies can operate in conjunction with each other to bolster their effect. For example, modifications to local kin networks (Minnis 1985) and regional alliance and trading networks (O'Shea 1989) together can have a stronger effect than either alone. The greater the risk, the more likely it is that larger networks of people will be included (Minnis 1985). However, for the trade networks to be beneficial, a high degree of environmental complexity is needed. If trading partners are facing the same issues because they are in the same environmental contexts, trade will be ineffective (Halstead and O'Shea 1989a). By understanding which risk management techniques are used, it is possible to make inferences about the social and physical environments, and perhaps better understand the nature of social relationships, both those creating and those mitigating risks.

DEFINING RISK

"Risk," as used by archaeologists, often refers to the potential for loss (Marston 2010, 2011). For example, each year agricultural groups face the potential for an early frost, a hailstorm, or numerous other events that kill crops before they can be harvested. Economists and ecologists typically use the term "risk" to refer to the probability of particular return rates or the variance of the yields (Fleisher 1990). For example, resource A has a mean return rate of X and a variance of Y. When a known diet and risk levels are compared to the required intake levels, it can be predicted how often the whole diet or individual aspects of the diet will produce insufficient returns (e.g., Cashdan 1990a; Fitzhugh 2001; Fleisher 1990; Stephens and Charnov 1982). Studies in risk management often look at these predicted return rates and measure the effects of various diet modifications or other risk buffering mechanisms (e.g., Byers et al. 2016 on storage; Goland 1993 on field scattering; Scarry 1993 on crop diversification; Kuznar 2002; Winterhalder 1986 on food sharing).

GENERAL RISK MANAGEMENT TECHNIQUES

There are a wide array of social structures in which risk management strategies can be manifested. The techniques chosen are dependent on the specific cultural, economic, and environmental contexts of a given society (e.g., Halstead and O'Shea 1989b; Hart 1993). Halstead and O'Shea (1989b) divide strategies into four categories: mobility, diversity, storage, and exchange. Marston (2011) divides them into two broad categories: intensification and diversification. In this second system, storage is considered a means of temporal diversification and mobility is related to the degree of intensification.

Mobility

"Mobility" refers to the ability of groups to move away from areas where natural resources are insufficient (see Wendrich and Barnard 2008). If resources become depressed in a region, in many circumstances human groups may choose to move to a new area where resource depression is either not present or present to a lower degree. The source of resource depression and the extent of the move will determine its efficacy. Localized issues may not require a long-distance relocation to completely mitigate the issue. However, if large-scale problems arise, such as regionwide droughts, it may not be possible to move out of the affected area. In these cases, it is necessary to either move to the location that is least affected or move on a regular basis as resources become depleted. Mobility can be significantly constrained by a variety of social, economic, and environmental factors. Generally, mobility works best for groups with small populations, with nonstored resources, and in regions with low population densities, easily traversed terrain, and sufficiently dispersed resources (Binford 1980). Cultivated fields are not portable, so mobility generally works best for foraging societies.

Diversity

In some situations, it makes more sense to widen the resource base—to expand the diet breadth rather than, or in conjunction with, increased mobility (e.g., Colson 1979; Kaiser and Voytek 1983; Morrison et al. 1996; Scarry 1993). If the resources typically exploited by a group are less available, it may make more sense to exploit a wider array of resources in a given region than move to a new area. The nature of the shortage and of the available resources will affect the utility and character of diversification. For example, if drought is the root cause of the shortfall, it is likely that all plants and animals will be affected to varying degrees. Depending on the suite of resources available, groups may choose to focus on a narrow range of drought-resistant resources (relatively narrow diet breadth), on a wide array of resources over a large geographic area (relatively wide diet breadth), or some combination of the two.

Diversity and mobility can work well together (Halstead and O'Shea 1989a). In some cases, diversification may require increased mobility (or the reverse may be true). For example, relatively sedentary groups may need to set up camps in new locations to acquire new resources. Also, if a group moves to a new territory, or a different portion of their territory, high-ranked resources may be in lower abundance or densities, requiring the use of other resources to offset the loss.

Storage

In situations where resources are abundant but only for a limited time, it may make sense to preserve them for future use, essentially increasing the available food diversity at that future time (e.g., Kaplan, Hill, and Hurtado 1990, Kuijt 2009; Low 1990; O'Shea 1989). The portion of the food gathered but not needed immediately can be curated. However, storage is not without costs. Food usually requires labor to prepare it for storage (e.g., drying of wild rice, smoking of meat). Storage facilities must be constructed, requiring additional labor and material inputs. The stored food must then be guarded from any number of factors that could destroy it. For example, pests (e.g., rodents or insects), moisture, raiders (both human and nonhuman animals such as raccoons) that may wish to steal some or all of the stored food, and fire (natural, intentional, and accidental) can destroy stored food resources. Relying on stored food is both a means to mitigate risk and a source of risk itself. Ideally, however, it is easier to predict and prevent loss during storage than during other situations (e.g., interannual crop yields).

Storage and high mobility are not usually complementary, though there are strategies that can incorporate both (e.g., partial group or seasonal mobility). Storage facilities are rarely transportable. Therefore, relocation of habitation sites becomes a greater labor investment if new storage pits, corncribs, or other structures need to be rebuilt at the new village location. The contents of the pits also need to be relocated, so either the extensive storage facilities must be moved at great expense and increased potential for loss or the stored food must be left at the old location. The latter would mark wasted energy and resource expenditures for the initial acquisition of the food, and it would temporarily increase subsistence risk until the lost food can be replaced. In situations where food is readily and regularly available, this may not be a significant risk, but for agricultural groups in temperate climates, the long duration between harvests means that supplemental resources may be taxed until the next harvest if stored surplus is lost or reduced during relocation.

Sedentism is usually more compatible with storage and can allow for part of the group to remain mobile while other parts can remain with the stored resources. Extractive camps (e.g., for hunting, fishing, wild ricing) can be established away from the main village. The food resources can then be brought to the main village for final processing and consumption and/or storage. Resources that are not immediately available around sites can be added to the diet (potentially allowing for the incorporation of diversification), and surpluses can be saved and used during lean times. Because the resources need to be transported anyway, the costs of using the strategies together are minimized while at least some degree of risk reduction is gained from each activity (see Byers et al. 2016; Winterhalder, Lu, and Tucker 1999).

Exchange

The final category under consideration is exchange. Exchange includes any type of interaction in which one group obtains needed items from another. Exchange may incorporate elements of mobility and diversification if it requires travel beyond the normal range and if it includes the procurement of items not typically found in the diet. When Halstead and O'Shea (1989b) discuss exchange, they describe it in reciprocal terms, which includes trade among allies (positive reciprocity) but also raiding and/or stealing as a form of negative reciprocity.

Positive Reciprocity. When groups have insufficient food, they may turn to neighbors with whom they have a positive relationship as a potential solution (Halstead and O'Shea 1989b). If the neighbors are not also facing shortages, they may be able to provide some level of subsistence support. As is the nature of any reciprocal relationship, there is some expectation that the debt will be repaid at some date in the future. In some cases, the relationship is relatively informal and occurs on an as-needed basis. However, because the timing of resource depletion is not usually predictable, nor is it necessarily equitable, these exchange networks often include some form of regular exchange or a ceremonial aspect that encourages each group to invest in the relationship with the other. That way, each group has some regular expected contributions, the debts are continually cycling, and both groups are invested in maintaining the relationship even during a long string of good years (see also Hames 1990; Kaplan, Hill, and Hurtado 1990; Smith and Boyd 1990; Winterhalder 1986).

Food Sharing. In addition to intergroup exchange, individuals or subgroups within any group may engage in reciprocal exchanges for food. This can include many of the advantages of both diversification and mobility without actually changing the resources or territories targeted. However, its utility depends greatly on the structure of the group and the nature of resource and landownership. If members of a given society have access to discontinuous resource patches, spread across a wide territory, then they will likely be able to access different types of resources (diversification), which may be differentially affected by the various sources of variability (mobility). Historically and ethnographically, foraging groups are far more likely to engage in this reciprocal behavior than are food producers (Gurven 2004, 2006; Kaplan and Hill 1985; Kaplan, Hill, and Hurtado 1990; Winterhalder 1990; Winterhalder and Goland 1997).

Negative Reciprocity. Rather than ask for food from a neighbor, there are situations in which it may prove advantageous to simply take it. In this situation, wherein one group obtains something for relatively no cost from another, it is, by definition, a form of negative reciprocity. A successful attack on an enemy village may be able to provide considerable quantities of food. But there are several caveats that must be considered. For example, if the opposing group does not utilize storage facilities, then the amount of food that may be obtained from this method is limited to what is collected for immediate use. Also, because food is usually stored in the habitation sections of sites, it is normally defended relatively heavily. The more heavily defended the stores, the greater the cost of procurement. If the storage facilities are hidden, for example, in underground pits, or otherwise difficult to access, the cost increase is magnified. It may also be possible to attack work parties and take what food they have on hand either from collection or brought from the habitation for meals. This introduces the challenge of finding and successfully attacking a mobile target while remaining undetected. Finally, it may be possible to raid the sources of the food itself (e.g., fields, hunting grounds), but this will require some familiarity with enemy territory and runs the risk of accidental discovery (for examples of negative reciprocity, see Garnsey and Morris 1989; O'Shea 1989).

One additional consideration is that once the attack has been made (or the attacking force is otherwise discovered) the enemy is alerted to your presence. To be successful, it requires you to evade the enemy and retreat to friendly territory while carrying the stolen food. Regardless of success, a raid on an enemy may spur retaliatory attacks. Even if no such attack ever comes, your group must allocate resources to defensive activities, leading to yet further costs. Under most circumstances, raiding strictly to minimize risk does not make sense. However, because risk management is rarely the sole purpose of raiding, nor does raiding exist in a social vacuum, it was employed in many circumstances.

AGRICULTURAL RISK MANAGEMENT STRATEGIES

Agricultural risk management strategies fall under the same categories described above, but the specific strategies employed are often distinct from hunter-gatherer techniques (Marston 2010). Because archaeologists only see disarticulated fragments of the risk management systems, the "challenge ... lies in identifying the material products of risk-management systems, recovering those material remains and then quantifying them in such a way as to relate them directly to a particular risk management strategy" (Marston 2010, 120) To surmount this challenge, it is necessary to have a firm understanding of the social and physical environment, the resources necessary to sustain the group under study, and the variety of factors that can affect subsistence choices. While understanding the effects of these multiple physical and social constraints on human behavior is difficult, doing so has the potential to inform us about subsistence choices and may elucidate aspects of other social structures that may explain changes through time.

While the basic goals remain the same, there are several strategies and concerns related specifically to agriculturists that do not apply to foragers. The differences tend to revolve around two factors. First, agricultural societies are highly reliant on one or more types of plants that provide food relatively few times per year (in northern latitudes, usually once); and second, foraging societies often rely on a wide array of resources that provide food on a regular basis (Marston 2010). Typically, the foraging interval is shorter than the harvest interval for crops, so failure or loss can be replaced or mitigated more quickly. Furthermore, agriculturalists usually rely on fewer plant taxa, and those taxa are more spatially aggregated. This makes them more vulnerable to predation, damage, or disease (Winterhalder and Goland 1997).

Agriculture-Specific Techniques

Marston (2011) divides agricultural diversification into three categories: spatial, temporal, and crop diversity. Temporal diversification is storage and works essentially the same way for agricultural and foraging groups. However, large surpluses associated with agriculture may magnify the number and/or size of storage facilities. Spatial diversification in agricultural settings is usually achieved by field scattering. By varying field locations and placing fields in different microecological contexts, it may be possible to avoid total crop failure from small-scale threats such as localized storms (O'Shea 1989). Field scattering can also mitigate the effects of larger-scale threats. For example, in dry years, fields in low areas or having wetter soils may outperform those in better-drained or higher fields. The reverse is true in wet years. Because farmers do not know what the upcoming year will bring, planting in multiple locations can act as an insurance policy, but it

Figure 2.1. Photograph of modern flooded agricultural fields in Jefferson County, Wisconsin, west of Crescent Bay Hunt Club. Photo by author

comes with a cost—primarily in terms of increased labor and time while moving people, equipment, and food between and among fields (Gallagher and Sasso 1987; Goland 1993; McCloskey 1972, 1991; Winterhalder 1990; Winterhalder and Goland 1997). Today, many farmers continue to plant in both high and low areas so that they can be prepared for a wider array of weather events. For example, in summer 2017, heavy rains in the study area killed many of the crops in low-lying fields (fig. 2.1), but the crops on high ground survived. By planting in both areas, the farmers ensured that at least a portion of their harvest would survive despite not knowing how much rain would fall.

The final form of agricultural diversification includes increasing the number or varieties of agricultural crops. Multi- or intercropping maize with other plants, particularly squash and beans, has been proven beneficial (Gallagher 1992; Hart 2008; Monaghan, Schilling, and Parker 2014; Mt. Pleasant 2010; Mt. Pleasant and Burt 2010; Scarry 1993). Distinct varieties of a single taxon will perform differently under varying circumstances. As Doolittle (2000, 138) points out, different varieties of cultigens or domesticates have different growth characteristics and requirements. The different types of plants represent different levels of risk and different potential uses. Hurt (1987, 33) writes that "Huron primarily raised flint corn, which matured in one hundred days, and flour corn, which ripened within 130 days." By varying the types planted, it may be possible to decrease the risk of crop failure (Hart 1999). While cob row numbers do not directly correlate with maize varieties, they can act as a proxy (Bird 1970; Cutler and Blake 1969; Fritz 1992; Goette et al. 1990; King 1994). Analysis of the number of domesticated taxa and the number of maize varieties can serve as a measure of agricultural diversity (Marston, Guedes, and Warriner 2014).

Increasing the consumption of wild resources can also diversify the diet. For a resource to be a sufficient supplement or buffer for a high-yield domesticate like maize, it must meet several criteria (O'Shea 1989b): (1) it must be storable; (2) it must occur in sufficiently dense patches to be exploited with the necessary efficiency; (3) its harvesting (or hunting, etc.) should not conflict with the agricultural labor; and (4) its abundance should be based on factors independent of the agricultural output. That is, any environmental factors that may depress maize output should not significantly affect the availability of the buffer resource. O'Shea (1989) identifies fish and, to a lesser degree, wild rice as ethnohistoric examples of buffer resources. If a buffering option is chosen to replace significant quantities of crops in lean years, then increased storage capacity must also be available, or it must be continuously available for harvest or collection.

Marston (2011, 196) argues that overproduction is the primary outcome of agricultural intensification. However, it is difficult to identify overproduction in archaeological contexts because it consists of producing more of the same. Marston suggests that it can most easily be seen in increased storage facilities and vessels. However, clear chronologies for features, known use lengths, and population densities are necessary to determine a storage baseline.

Risk and Uncertainty

Winterhalder and Goland (1997) use a combination of theoretical orientations and approaches to explain the adoption of domesticated plants. They use the Eastern Woodlands as an example and describe the pathways to adoption that various domesticates could take. Their theoretical framework for plant domestication sets up a series of testable hypotheses about how people will react under certain circumstances and the potential ramifications of these actions. Thus it would establish a plausible explanation for a series of social changes witnessed in the Late Prehistoric Great Lakes and how the continued use of maize could affect inter- and intragroup dynamics.

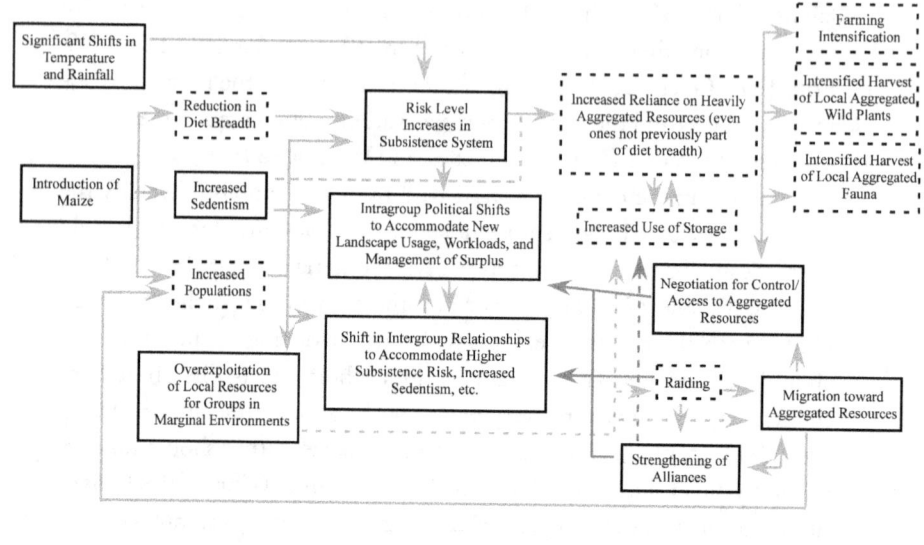

Figure 2.2. Diagram of the theoretical model developed for this study

Their model suggests that during the Woodland, anthropogenic modification to the landscape would necessarily increase. Subsequently, resource abundance would become increasingly dependent on human intervention. However, prior to around AD 800 or 900, when maize became economically important, the suite of cultigens was not capable of feeding the entire population, at least not more efficiently and reliably than maintaining wild resources in the diet. The adoption of maize as a highly ranked resource would allow for significant population growth and/or aggregation, thereby setting in motion a series of social changes. If food is consistently plentiful, then drastic changes may not ensue. However, in the temperate climates of the western Great Lakes, environmental instability would not allow for perpetual good harvests. Therefore, risk management systems were essential to survival, but they could have caused systemic changes to settlement systems, intragroup politics, and intergroup relationships (fig. 2.2).

EXPECTATIONS

The shift from the Late Woodland to Upper Mississippian settlement subsistence system would have set in motion several shifts in intragroup organization. Some would have happened immediately. Others would have a slower onset. As small changes accumulate, they create further changes down the line. The move to larger villages, with more sedentary populations, requires different systems of organization. There are more mouths to feed, more houses, more garbage, and more opinions about how things should be done or more requests for those who have influence. Mobility is also reduced. If a person decides things are not going satisfactorily, it becomes harder to pick up and leave once they have invested significant time, energy, and resources in planting. Therefore, new mechanisms to manage disputes may be necessary.

The shift to an agricultural economy has labor demands different from those of a foraging economy. Shifts in the size, distribution, and timing of work parties are required. Maize agriculture of the terminal Late Woodland and Mississippian periods would need intensive labor investments, particularly by women. Some scholars have argued that this may have led to an alteration in the ways that gendered labor was valued (e.g., Benn 1995; Hollinger and Benn 1995). Unfortunately, many of these shifts are difficult to identify archaeologically. However, it is possible to identify shifts in subsistence strategies, food processing, and so on, and from there, it is possible to make inferences about some correlated human actions. Using Winterhalder and Goland's (1997) model, further informed through a broader lens of risk management, we can test hypotheses to determine which behaviors, relationships, or strategies were in use by the Koshkonong Oneota population.

First, it is necessary to test the primary ideas on which the model is built. Maize has long been inferred to have been a major component of the diet, but we need to answer several major questions.

(1) *What was the nature of the diet in the Koshkonong locality?*
    (a) How important was maize to the diet?
    (b) How diversified was the diet, and what taxa did it include?
(2) *How does the subsistence system in Koshkonong differ from those of other groups (Upper and Middle Mississippian, Late Woodland)?*

Understanding the nature of the Koshkonong system allows for comparisons with other contemporaneous groups (Late Woodland, Middle Mississippian, Oneota). The nature of any similarities or differences and any potential exchange can also help determine what sorts of stresses groups were under. Regional stresses (e.g., widespread drought) should have different outcomes from local ones (e.g., hailstorms). Also, such relative data are essential for determining how broad or focused the Koshkonong subsistence system was. Once we have answers for the first questions, we can begin to apply the data to the model by asking:

(3) *What risk management strategies were used in the Koshkonong Locality?*
   (a) Can we see risk management strategies that work with the natural environment?
   (b) Can we see risk management strategies that work with the social environment?

According to Pearsall (2009, 611), to understand the role and implications of agriculture, it is essential to look not just at sites, but at the physical and social landscape. Furthermore, Halstead and O'Shea (1989b, 38) argue that risk management strategies were "interrelated, such that changes in any one component altered the role and other strategies in the mediating episodes of stress. The aggregate result of such compounded alterations was directional or evolutionary change, which transformed the social matrix in which decisions were made and through which further responses were affected." Because these changes were made through and mitigated by social actions and decisions of people, it is through this lens that it is possible to gain a better understanding of the social fabric underlying the economic activities that are archaeologically visible. Finally, with an informed understanding of the social mechanisms responsible for agricultural production and the degree of agricultural reliance we can begin to revisit a very old question:

(4) *What are the relationships between the development of agriculture and complex social structures, social hierarchies, and institutions?*

There is a frequently cited relationship between intense (or intense and specialized) agriculture and social stratification and complexity that has historical (Buckland 1878; Morgan 1877; Tylor 1881), global (Bar-Yosef 2000; Bender 1978; Childe 2003; Drennan and Quattrin 1995; Price 1995), and local (Benn 1989; Gallagher and Arzigian 1994; Griffin 1967; Jeske 1992; Kelly 1992; Lopinot 1992, 1994; Mueller and Stephens 1991) roots. In recent decades, the ubiquity and thereby necessity of this relationship has been called into question (e.g., Price 1995, 2003; Price and Bar-Yosef 2011; Smith 2001). This data set provides an ideal means of testing the assumption and bringing the Eastern Woodlands into the larger anthropological debate.

ASSESSING RISK MANAGEMENT STRATEGIES

To begin to test the model, assumptions and inferences must be made explicit and expectations must be tested (fig. 2.3). First, reliance on maize can be best established using multiple lines of evidence, including macrobotanical and isotopic data. Once reliance on maize has been confirmed, it is necessary to measure how it was integrated into the subsistence system. Each of the groups that relied on maize had increased subsistence risk.

Regardless of probability, a harvest will eventually fail as a result of environmental or outside social factors. It is difficult to replace a substantial portion of any system, so a failure of maize puts the whole system at risk. If groups live in less than optimal locations, the loss is even harder to replace. If an area does not have access to substantial supplementary aggregated resources, self-reliance in famine years may be impossible. If poor harvests last for many years, the problem becomes exacerbated.

Therefore, it is necessary for maize agricultural groups to have or develop mechanisms to reduce risk of catastrophic failure. Using the heuristic framework provided by Halstead and O'Shea (1989b), we can expect groups to intensify, diversify, increase mobility, increase use of storage facilities, and engage in exchange (positive and negative). Each of these strategies should have archaeologically visible signatures. The model also allows for extrapolating potential secondary outcomes based on the employment (or lack) of various strategies. The following sections provide a description of how we might test the various expectations of the model and their potential ramifications using floral data. When floral data are unavailable, a discussion of other data is provided.

| **Maize & Sedentism** | Maize dependent groups should exhibit greater sedentism |

If True - Subsistence settlement systems should reflect longer-term occupations
- Longer or more seasons of occupation
- Larger and/or more durable structures
- Increased use of storage
- Increased reliance of logistical mobility - Reduced residential mobility

If False - Subsistence settlement should look the same based on the metrics above

| **Diet Breadth Decrease** | Groups that use maize will have a reduced diet breadth |

If True - Maize dependent groups will exhibit lower diversity indices than comprable non-collared ware Late Woodland sites

If False - Maize dependent groups will exhibit equal or greater diversity indices than comprable non-collared ware Late Woodland sites

| **Climate-Based Risks** | Shifting climate increases instability |

If **climate** only/primary source of risk then groups should turn to non-agricultural resources and increase mobility (increase in dietary diversity)

If climate is not a risk/minor risk (**social risks** are primary factor) then simple agricultural systems should be relied on heavily (homogenous systems)

If a **combination** of climate/social risk factors then increased reliance on agriculture with a simultaneous diversification of agricultural system

| **Resource Depletion** | Increased population levels, increased social stress, or a combination will lead to a focus on local resources and the depletion of some high-ranked wild resources |

If False - no dietary shifts through time will be noted
If True - high-ranked wild resources will
- Decrease in importance
- Eventually fall out of diet breadth

Those most likely to **decrease or drop** are
- Those with slower regeneration times - such resources would be over exploited and not be present in sufficient quantities to maintain significant use and/or have greater variance - reliance on such plants would increase risk factors - removing it from diet breadth or demoting its ranking would increase stability - except in years when more stable measures are/have failed

| **Aggregated Resources** | Increased risk in system leads to further decrease in diet breadth and focus on aggregated resources |

If True - then expect one or more of the following
- Decreased diversity indices in later contexts
- Increased reliance on agricultural remains
- Increased reliance on wild rice, goosefoot, or other local cultigens
- Decrease in high variance resources

If False - then no shift in subsistence strategies through time

| **Intergroup Interaction** | Alliance networks are strengthened - relationships with foes deteriorate |

If True - one or more of the following should be evident
- Evidence of intergroup violence
- Construction of defensive structures
- Increased trade or interaction among groups
- Aggregation of allied groups together on landscape

Figure 2.3. List of theoretical expectations

Intensification

Intensification is one option for managing risk in the Koshkonong Locality (Gallagher and Arzigian 1994; Keegan and Butler 1987; Marston 2011). The easiest means to identify the intensification of any single resource is to see its density or ubiquity increase through time. Minor shifts may be difficult to see, but any large-scale efforts at intensification should be visible in this manner. Agricultural intensification does not only have to be growing more of something; greater investments of labor, for example, the construction of ridged fields, to ensure that the same number of plants survive is another form of intensification (Gallagher and Arzigian 1994). Two agricultural sites have been identified in the Koshkonong Locality, Loge Bay (47JE087) and Messemer (47JE092). Both agricultural sites were described as garden beds (Stout and Skavlem 1908); however, it is unclear if either site is associated with the Oneota occupation. To date, it is unknown if there are other forms of agricultural intensification in the locality (e.g., technological).

Diversification

Intensification can help groups overproduce food, which allows surpluses to last longer. However, if an entire harvest in a given year is lost, so too is any intended surplus. Therefore, intensification is still risky if it is not coupled with diversification or some other risk management strategy (e.g., storing surplus sufficient for a number of years). If the risks are sufficiently great, several forms of agricultural diversification may be needed.

Field Scattering. Because most agricultural fields have not survived, it is impossible to directly test the expectation that Koshkonong groups would have diversified field location. Indeed, Doolittle (2000, 162) describes the act of looking for nonridged agricultural fields as akin to looking for the proverbial needle in the haystack. While corn hills and ridged fields have been identified archaeologically in a few cases, such as the now buried but still extant corn hills at Carroll University in Waukesha, Wisconsin (Sasso, pers. comm., 1998), at Sand Lake (Gallagher et al. 1987), and at the Garden Bed and Kletzsch Park sites (Benchley et al. 1979; McKern 1930), they are few and far between (Doolittle 2000, 162–64). However, indirect indicators may be present. Examination of the locations of sites relative to soil types, topography, and so on can be used to infer possible locations of fields and their potential for variation (Doolittle 2000, 165).

Diet Breadth. According to Winterhalder and Goland (1997) and O'Shea (1989), aggregated wild resources can act as ideal resources to buffer against agricultural loss. Prehistorically, there were numerous aggregated resources available throughout Wisconsin that may have served this function (table 2.1). However, their utility may be locally and temporally dependent; therefore, their ability to buffer a poor maize harvest depends on their local conditions, their nutritional value, and the amount of maize being replaced. Ideally, the food will have a fast renewal rate; that is, its population will rebound quickly after heavy exploitation. For example, wild rice has very specific habitat requirements (Vennum 1988); it was only abundant in select locations. If conditions are consistently right, it will provide significant quantities of food year after year. Historically, wild rice harvests failed roughly every four years. So it may have been an option for groups with access to significant stands. However, it was not necessarily a widely available resource. Elk, which form small sex-based herds most of the year and large herds of over one hundred animals in the winter would have been a large aggregated resource. However, the slow reproduction rate of large mammals could lead to significant resource depletion in a relatively short time. Therefore, elk may have been a short-term buffer but would be risky to rely on as a primary supplement (Keene 1981). Furthermore, under heavy predation, elk reproduction rates decrease, making elk unreliable long-term primary resources (Winnie 2007).

Lake Koshkonong was known historically as a productive source of wild rice. In the mid-1800s, it was said to look like more like a meadow than a lake because this aquatic grass was so prevalent (Lapham 1855). Previous research on Koshkonong Oneota subsistence has identified wild rice as a highly ubiquitous and dense food resource (Edwards and Pater 2011; Egan-Bruhy 2001a). While wild rice is prone to periodic failures, it produces large quantities of food in good years, and the factors that reduce productivity typically occur in the spring, giving groups sufficient time to focus on other resources (Vennum 1988). This food source is also particularly attractive because of its availability. It is generally available before the main harvest of maize, and it is available for several weeks, which means that harvest timing has some measure of flexibility (Jenks 1901; Vennum

Table 2.1. List of potential aggregated resources in Wisconsin and northern Illinois

Resource Type	Example	Habitat	Availability	Source
Nuts	Acorn, walnut	Forest (dense)/ savannah (less)	August–October (species dependent)	Keene 1981
Wild rice	n/a	Shallow water	Late August to early September	Jenks 1901 Vennum 1988
Spawning fish	Walleye, sturgeon	Lakes, rivers, streams	Variable	Becker 1983 Theler 1989
Bush fruits	Raspberry, grape	Forest/savannah (especially edges)	Midsummer to fall	Keene 1981
Tubers	Wild leek, cattail	Wet environments	Early spring to late fall	Curtis 1959 Keene 1981
Weedy seeds/ greens	Goosefoot/ amaranth	Disturbed habitats	Spring to late fall	Keene 1981
Herd mammals	Elk, deer, bison	Forest edge, forest edge prairies	Most aggregated in winter	Keene 1981
Migrating birds/ waterfowl	Passenger pigeon, duck	Forest (pigeon) Lakes/wetlands (waterfowl)	Late spring to early fall	Keene 1981

1988). Given these characteristics, it is expected that wild rice should increase in importance through time.

Southeastern Wisconsin was home to large tracts of oak and hickory forests and savannahs (Brink 1835; Burnham 1836; Miller 1833). Acorn, hickory, and walnut were widely available in this environment. Nuts are typically good sources of both calories and nutrients; however, they are subject to significant variation in annual productivity that is difficult to predict (Gardner 1997; Keene 1981). Furthermore, nuts are typically available for shorter periods than wild rice. They also are more likely to be eaten by other animals before humans can acquire them if significant steps to curb the rodent population are not taken. Finally, many species of acorn and walnut are available around the same time that large amounts of labor would be needed for harvesting and processing maize and other agricultural outputs or wild rice. Previous research at Oneota sites in the Koshkonong Locality supports nuts as an important resource, particularly acorn (Egan-Bruhy 2001a, 2014). Nuts are expected to be an important buffer resource; however, as time goes on, they will most consistently be used as a backup rather than a primary component of the diet.

Weedy Seeds. Weedy seeds may have been a highly aggregated resource, but they were also already an important aspect of the Late Woodland diet (Stevenson et al. 1997). According to the Winterhalder and Goland (1997) model, these plants are likely to decrease in dietary rank, and some may even be dropped from the diet all together. Of the starchy and oily seeds previously identified at the Crescent Bay Hunt Club, only goosefoot has been identified as a significant part of the diet (Edwards and Pater 2011; Egan-Bruhy 2001a; Olsen 2003). Olsen (2003) identified wild and domesticated variants, though they could have been grown together in managed garden plots. Based on the model, *Chenopodium* should be less important at Oneota sites than at Late Woodland sites, and its importance should decrease slightly over time as groups intensify use of other resources (e.g., density may remain constant, but maize, wild rice, or other aggregated resources will become more important as these aggregated resources become a greater focus of the diet).

Fruits. Bush fruits (sensu Keene 1981) offer a relatively productive source of food. They are relatively dense and are found most prolifically at the edges of forests, which were common in the savannah-dominated environment around Lake Koshkonong (Edwards 2010). However, it is unlikely that berries could have been acquired in sufficient quantities to serve as a primary resource for large, aggregated, and sedentary populations. Historical accounts indicate that berries were combined with animal fat and bone grease to make pemmican, an important traveling food and stored resource (Gilmore 1919; Hodge 1910). Pemmican is not likely to show up in the archaeological record of Wisconsin. I predict that berries will be a minor aspect of the Koshkonong Oneota assemblages.

Tubers. Keene (1981) identified tubers as one of the most abundant and productive resources in Michigan's Lower Peninsula. However, tubers rarely preserve archaeologically; therefore, regardless of their dietary importance, it is unlikely that they will account for a significant amount of the Koshkonong Oneota floral assemblage.

Faunal Resources. The variation in faunal resources is beyond the scope of this analysis. Previous studies have shown that both large mammals and fish were significant resources (Agnew et al. 2016; Edwards 2013; Edwards and McTavish 2012; Hunter 2002; McTavish 2013; Van de Pas, McTavish, and Klemmer 2015). Deer, bison, and elk have all been identified from CBHC and KCV. While deer may not be an aggregated resource for most of the year, they yard up, or form larger groups, in the winter and become an aggregated resource. They are also attracted to agricultural fields, so garden-side hunting both protects crops and artificially aggregates deer. Keene (1981) notes that fish are often most productive per area in smaller bodies of water, and many species (e.g., walleye, various panfish) aggregate while spawning. Lake Koshkonong and the Rock River and its tributaries provide a great deal of surface area that should be highly productive. The concentration of Oneota sites along Koshkonong Lake and Koshkonong Creek (Edwards 2010) fits well with the inference that groups would move to areas with significant access to such aggregated resources.

Crop Diversification. Crop diversification may be manifested in several ways. Distinct varieties of maize have different growth characteristics and survive in different situations (Hart 1999; Hurt 1987). Maize varieties are most easily visible archaeologically through cob row numbers (Cutler and Blake 1969; Scarry 1993). In addition to maize, numerous species of agricultural resources are expected. Previous research has identified squash (Egan-Bruhy 2001a), as well as cultigens like goosefoot (Olsen 2003).

Exchange, Warfare, and Mobility

Depending on the proportional importance of maize, access to aggregated resources as buffers may have been as important to the settlement subsistence system as access to arable land. The more these resources were available, the more stability was inherent in the system. So long as stability is maintained, there would not be subsistence pressures to relocate. If resources are not available locally, a group can either move to where they are or send work parties to obtain them. However, the threat of attack can force people to remain close to home, where defenses are available (Milner 2007; VanDerwarker and Wilson 2016).

In theory, mobility should be relatively easy to identify archaeologically. Sites with short occupation spans were likely occupied by people who employed a highly mobile strategy. However, it is often difficult to determine if a site was continuously occupied or returned to on a regular basis, and the error range for radiocarbon dates is too wide to differentiate. Furthermore, the radiocarbon issue makes it difficult to use the number of sites in a region. A region may have many sites because of greater mobility, or there may have been a larger contemporaneous population occupying multiple sites in the area simultaneously. Hart (1993) argues that mobility is unlikely for groups under physical threat. Given the proximity of Aztalan and Late Woodland sites to Koshkonong, this does not seem to be a likely option in Koshkonong if there were hostilities among the various archaeological groups.

Within the Eastern Woodlands, the resource base makes combining the strategies of aggregation and mobility difficult. In regions such as the Plains, where there are large aggregated migratory resources (e.g., bison), the relationship between sedentism and defense may be different. For example, bison can provide a resource base for a large population and can be acquired by large cooperative hunting groups, allowing the hunters to maintain safety in numbers. Furthermore, bison hunting does not require the group to remain in the same location for large portions of the year. In southeastern Wisconsin, no analogous resources exist. To be efficiently gathered, either most wild plants must be obtained in small groups or their locations are so aggregated that guaranteed access to the resource would encourage increased sedentism. Without a consistent presence in the area, it would be difficult to prevent other groups from laying claim to the resource. Animal resources in the Eastern Woodlands are also unlikely to allow for effective group aggregation with high mobility. For example, many fish aggregate for spawning, but this occurs at predictable times and locations. While collection of these fish may feed a large aggregated population for that time, once the fish disperse, it is difficult to maintain large population densities without the use of other aggregated resources. Historically, to the north of the study area, the Chippewa aggregated during spawning season and dispersed into smaller groups afterward (Densmore 1979; Nesper 2002).

If there is evidence of considerable mobility, then the threat of warfare was likely either minimal or less significant than the risk of remaining sedentary. If there is evidence of restricted mobility, then the threat, or perceived threat, of attack must have been significant. The more mobility was restricted, the greater the threat must have been. There is no way to quantitatively measure mobility, but qualitative assessment of the numbers and types of sites in a settlement system, the defensibility of sites, and the general character of a settlement system can be used to estimate the relative degree of each threat.

The interaction among neighboring groups is subject to change once one group's buffering mechanisms fail. When mobility increases the chance of groups competing for territory also increases, particularly if more than one group is on the move. In southeastern Wisconsin, the Late Woodland groups using non-collared ware ceramics are often thought to have been particularly mobile, while Late Woodland groups using collared ware ceramics and Oneota groups are thought to have primarily used other strategies, though it is unclear to what extent (e.g., Overstreet 1997; Stevenson et al. 1997). It is also unclear how much competition for land existed among or within archaeological cultures. Smith (2011) has argued that during earlier Archaic and Woodland times, populations were not sufficiently dense to push groups to domesticate plants, suggesting that pressures other than population led to domestication. Population sizes in Late Woodland and Mississippian times are also unknown, making it difficult to assess competition for land.

Trade is another option to mitigate resource failure that would not require population movement. However, trade can be difficult to identify. Exchange of food items would be difficult if not impossible to see archaeologically (Minnis 1985). The food itself and any associated bags or baskets are unlikely to have survived. If any did survive, it would be nearly impossible to differentiate the imported from local foods. Ceramic containers are more likely to survive. However, it is difficult to distinguish undecorated Oneota vessels, so interlocality exchange is difficult to identify without petrographic analysis. Trade between archaeological cultures (e.g., Late Woodland and Oneota) should be easier to identify stylistically, particularly if ceramics were included in the exchange. In such cases, the reasons for and the type of exchange are still unknown. Other items may also be exchanged during trade expeditions, some of which may be more easily identified as nonlocal (e.g., copper, galena, food).

While testing is beyond the scope of this project, there is another important aspect to exchange that must be considered. Historically, before groups could trade with one another, members of the two trading parties were often expected to engage in some type of ceremonial activity to formalize the relationship, often becoming fictive kin, for example, as argued for the Calumet Ceremony (Hall 1997). It is not known how far back in time these ceremonies extend. While they are not easily seen archaeologically, these ceremonies would require a shared set of symbols that allow both groups to identify and acknowledge that the other party accepted the shared rights and responsibilities.

While a single exchange or ceremonial occasion may be beyond our ability to identify, recurring use of the ceremony should show a patterned use of the shared or at least overlapping sets of symbols on one or more media. If these relationships were or became important, then we can expect that they may have been incorporated into more mundane items as well. Schneider's (2015) ceramic analysis of the Waupaca, Grand River, and Koshkonong assemblages shows that there was some degree of communication and shared symbolism among the localities. There are also shared, albeit fewer, symbols between Koshkonong and northern Illinois groups. Pozza (2016, 2019) has shown that many of the same symbols used on ceramics were used in copper. And Overstreet (1997) has argued that there is a shift in ceramic decorations, from mostly undecorated to mostly decorated, after 1300. For now, an argument can be made that people within the multiple Oneota localities were connected through ceremonies—religious and/or cosmological—and the importance of the ceremonies may have increased over time. The symbolic similarities may have been a means of signaling membership in a larger shared network (sensu Hart et al. 2016; Hall 1962; Schneider 2015).

We must also consider exchange among or between different archaeological cultures. Edwards and Jeske (2015) have examined the evidence for interaction between Aztalan and Koshkonong sites and found it lacking. Overstreet (1997) has suggested that any such interaction was likely confrontational and not cooperative. In addition, there are several Late Woodland sites around present-day Madison, Wisconsin, that contain small numbers of Oneota sherds (Haas, Picard, and Jones 2017). While it is unclear why there are few Oneota vessels at otherwise Late Woodland sites, exchange cannot be ruled out at this time (fig. 2.4).

Previously, intergroup violence has been noted within the study area. The best data from the Midwest indicate that warfare took the form of cyclical violence, in which one group raids another, followed by retaliation (Keeley 2016; Milner 2005, 2007; Milner, Anderson, and Smith 1991; Strezewski 2006; VanDerwarker and Wilson 2016). In this process, neighbors become blood enemies as cyclical raiding turns minor disputes into large, long-standing feuds. In the process, crops are destroyed; farmers, hunters, and foragers are killed; and it becomes more difficult to leave

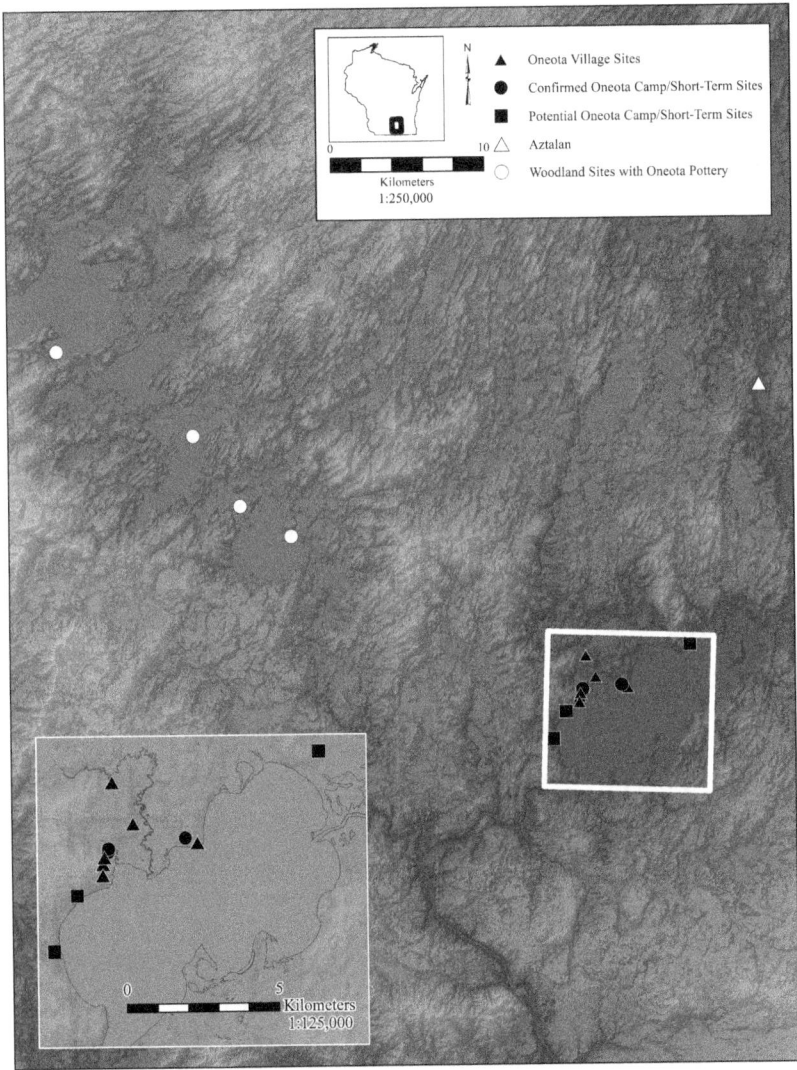

Figure 2.4. Map of Koshkonong Locality sites relative to neighboring contemporaneous archaeological sites

settlements to obtain food (Milner 2007; VanDerwarker and Wilson 2016). Violence does not necessarily have to occur regularly to affect people's behavior. Sasso (1989) notes that the mere perception of a threat is necessary for people to take extensive actions, like building stockades or palisades for defense. Ethnographers have recorded the investment of substantial amounts of time, energy, and raw materials in defense when a threat is perceived. For example, among the Dani of Highland New Guinea, men spent a large portion of their time building and repairing defensive structures (e.g., watchtowers) and weaponry (bows and spears). Even more time was spent manning defenses. On a typical day, men generally stood guard while women worked the agricultural fields, cared for the pigs, and tended to children. This does not account for the time men spent on the ritual and religious aspects of war that would not necessarily leave a clear material trace (Gardner and Heider 1969; Heider 1996). As Winterhalder and Goland (1997) argue, non-normative risks are often better predictors of human behavior. And as Hart (1990, 1993) notes, these social stresses tend to push people into reducing mobility while intensifying agricultural production to supplement the resources lost while reducing active catchments.

THREE

Methods and Methodology

What people deem fit to eat, how they choose to prepare and eat it, and with whom they share it are all part of a cultural code. What is required in order to answer the perplexing questions is a research strategy that considers these codes.

—Wilma Wetterstrom, "Cognitive Systems, Food Patterns, and Paleoethnobotany"

PALEOETHNOBOTANICAL SAMPLING STRATEGY

A total of 41 contexts from 16 features at the Koshkonong Creek Village and Crescent Bay Hunt Club sites were examined for this project. Both sites contain dated cultural deposits near structures, with a similar suite of morphological shapes. Both sites were excavated using the same procedures; therefore, field sampling bias should not affect the results of the analysis. The AMS samples taken from burned food residues scraped from ceramic vessels, or from individual maize or nutshells associated with vessels, provide relatively tight control for context and confidence in the chronology.

The samples from CBHC consist of eight cylindrical pits and five basin features. From the features, twenty-two zones (distinct portions of features identified based on a combination of soil color, texture, etc.) were selected for examination (table 3.1). In total, they represent over 3,700 liters of floated sediment. Features were chosen from across the site and in association with several different house structures. Commonwealth Heritage Group previously analyzed three full and two partial features. I analyzed the remainder. Three features from KCV were chosen, representing nineteen zones. The samples totaled 1,100 liters of floated sediment. Prior to this research, no floral analysis had been conducted.

Samples were chosen to control for both inter- and intrasite variation. Care was taken to find samples that represent both the early and late Oneota occupations at the sites, allowing for comparison of changes through time. Samples from associations with different types of structures were also chosen. At CBHC, samples near Longhouse 1 and Wigwams 2 and 3 were chosen to examine household variation. Two features (F04-03 and F10-14) are in the southeast corner of the site and may be part of a ritual area. F10-14 has a dog burial that appears to be a ritual deposition (Edwards 2014b). Adjacent to the feature is a shallow basin with a dog skull and a bear skull and articulated deer leg bones, which are an uncommon combination of features and remains. The feature is near one of the human burials at the site. F04-03 is only 3 m from the dog burial; while it may not be associated with any ritual activity, neither is it associated with any identified house structures at the site. All samples from KCV came from the 2012 field season because the 2014 and 2017 materials were not floated when the analysis began. Because all the 2012 units were in the same excavation block, all the features appear to be associated with the same structure type (Edwards and Spott 2012).

In addition to chronological and household variation, feature morphology was considered. Moss (2010) suggests that cylindrical pits and basins were used for different functions. Therefore, both feature types were selected for the assemblage. Furthermore, whenever possible, both basins and cylindrical pits were selected from early and late wigwam and longhouse contexts.

Comparative Sites

To determine how Koshkonong foodways compare to regional subsistence systems, several sites with comparable data sets were chosen (table 3.2).

Table 3.1. List of primary macrobotanical samples in study (gray cells: fully analyzed prior to project; bold outlined cells: partially analyzed prior to project)

Feature Number	Feature Shape	Liters of FLOT Sorted	Number of Zones Sorted	Chronology	Structure Association	Known Seasonal Association
Crescent Bay Hunt Club						
F00-11	Cylinder	430.5	2	Late	Longhouse 1	Winter
F00-26	Cylinder	189.5	1	Late	Longhouse 1	Winter
F02-25	Basin	57	1	Unknown	Longhouse 1	Unknown
F04-03	Cylinder	27	1	Middle	No structure	Unknown
F04-11	Basin	499	1	Unknown	House 3	Unknown
F04-14	Cylinder	201	6	Mixed	House 2	Unknown
F04-15	Cylinder	279	2	Early	House 2	Unknown
F04-22	Cylinder	950	1	Early	Longhouse 1	Winter
F06-63	Cylinder	210	3	Early	House 2	Unknown
F10-14	Cylinder	300	1	Unknown	No structure	Unknown
F10-19	Basin	110	1	Unknown	House 3	Unknown
F10-29	Basin	375	1	Middle	House 3	Unknown
F10-98	Basin	88	1	Middle	House 3	Unknown
Koshkonong Creek Village						
F12-01	Cylinder	410	5	Early	House 1	Unknown
F12-06	Cylinder	615.5	13	Late	House 1	Unknown
F12-26	Basin	79	1	Unknown	House 1	Unknown

Table 3.2. List of sites for comparative analysis

Site Name	Site Number	Archaeological Culture	Locality	Reference
Centra 53/54	47WT189	Late Woodland: Non-Collared Ware	Central Wisconsin	Egan 1993b
River Quarry	47DA768	Late Woodland: Collared Ware	Central Wisconsin	Egan-Bruhy 2009
Murphy	47DA736	Late Woodland: Collared Ware	Central Wisconsin	Egan-Bruhy 2009
KCV	47JE379	Oneota	Koshkonong	This book
CBHC	47JE904	Oneota	Koshkonong	This book
Tremaine	47LC095	Oneota	La Crosse	O'Gorman 1995
OT	47LC262	Oneota	La Crosse	O'Gorman 1993
Filler	47LC149	Oneota	La Crosse	O'Gorman 1994
Citgo	47BR460	Oneota	Green Bay	Egan-Bruhy, pers. comm.
Pamperin Park	47BR245	Oneota	Green Bay	Egan-Bruhy 2012
Schrage	47FD581	Oneota	Middle Fox	Egan-Bruhy 2010a
Soggy Oats	47WN595	Oneota	Middle Fox	Egan-Bruhy, pers. comm.
Dambrowski	47PT160	Oneota	Waupaca	Egan-Bruhy 2010b
Blinded by the Light	47PT191	Oneota	Waupaca	Egan-Bruhy 2010b
Burley Brew	47PT159	Oneota	Waupaca	Egan-Bruhy 2010b
Washington Irving	11K052	Langford	Fox/Des Plaines	Jeske 2000
Zimmerman	11LS013	Langford	Upper Illinois	Egan 1993a
Hoxie Farm	11CK004	Fisher	Chicago Lake Plains	Egan-Bruhy and Nelson 2013
Aztalan	47JE001	Middle Mississippian	Southeastern Wisconsin	Picard 2013
Lundy	11JD140	Middle Mississippian	Apple River	Emerson, Millhouse, and oeder et al. 2007

Sites were chosen to compare Upper Mississippian sites across space and to compare different archaeological cultures (e.g., Lake Koshkonong Oneota vs. Aztalan). Sites analyzed with comparable methods were selected for analysis; most were analyzed by Egan-Bruhy or people she had trained. Non-collared ware sites with paleoethnobotanical data are few, so only one was chosen for comparison.

THE CANINE SURROGACY APPROACH AND ISOTOPIC ANALYSIS METHODS

Because it is difficult to determine the relative importance of any particular plant in the subsistence system or the proportion of the diet provided by plants relative to meat, nonpaleoethnobotanical methods were sought. Isotopic analyses of human remains have been used in the Midwest to gain insight into these topics (Ambrose 1987; Ambrose, Buikstra, and Krueger 2003; Bender, Baerreis, and Steventon 1981; Emerson, Hedman, and Simon 2005; Emerson et al. 2010; Hedman, Hargrave, and Ambrose 2002; Lynott et al. 1986; Schurr 1998).

Depending on the method of photosynthesis (C_3 or C_4), plants absorb differing proportions of ^{12}C and ^{13}C, known as $\delta^{13}C$. These differences are detectable using stable carbon isotope analysis. As plants are consumed, these values transfer through the food chain predictably (Burton and Koch 1999; Katzenberg 1993). Samples taken from the bone collagen of adult humans represent a weighted average of long-term diet since the carbon in human bone collagen turns over slowly, requiring approximately thirty years to replace existing carbon with an equivalent amount of new carbon (Harkness and Walton 1972; Libby et al. 1964; Stenhouse and Baxter 1977, 1979). Because maize is the only C4 plant to play a significant role in the prehistoric Great Lakes diets, $\delta^{13}C$ analysis provides an ideal means of tracking the use and importance of maize among Late Prehistoric populations (Bender, Baerreis, and Steventon 1981).

Analyses of nitrogen isotopes have been used to identify an animal's trophic level. The higher the animal's position in the food chain, the greater its $\delta^{15}N$ values, the ratio of ^{15}N to ^{14}N (Ambrose and DeNiro 1986; Schoeller 1999). For archaeologists, $\delta^{15}N$ analyses are ideally suited for estimating the dietary contribution of hunting to the diet (Ambrose 1987; Ambrose and Norr 1993; Bochrens et al. 2006).

While these studies normally rely on the analysis of human remains, there are often ethical (Walker 2008) or legal issues (e.g., Native American Graves Protection and Repatriation Act; Wisconsin burial law §157.70) that limit such testing. In cases where human remains are unavailable for testing, archaeologists have begun using dog remains as a proxy (Cannon, Schwarcz, and Knyf 1999; Guiry 2012, 2013). The use of dogs as proxies is known as the canine surrogacy approach and has been proven effective at forager and agricultural sites around the world (Guiry 2012). CSA applications have been used as a proxy for human diets (Burleigh and Brothwell 1978) and for tracking human movement on the landscape (Clutton-Brock and Noe-Nygaard 1990; Fischer et al. 2007; Noe-Nygaard 1988). CSA analyses are based on the premise that dogs have a unique bond with humans (Morey 2006). This bond leads to human populations feeding dogs a suite of foods similar to their own, such as scraps and food by-products (Guiry 2012, 2013; White et al. 2001, 2004). In addition, the dogs regularly consumed human feces. The similar diet is reflected in the similarity of dog and human bone chemistry (Allitt, Stewart, and Messner 2008; Cannon, Schwarcz, and Knyf 1999; Katzenberg 1989; White et al. 2004).

Tankersley and Koster (2009) have demonstrated that CSA is applicable in Ohio, and Edwards, Jeske, and Coltrain (2017) have done so for the western Great Lakes. The applicability of CSA is assessed by comparing dog bone isotopes to associated human samples. For dogs, $\delta^{13}C$ values are often within the range of the human values, and dog $\delta^{15}N$ values often trail human values slightly (about 0.5‰). The discrepancy between human and dog $\delta^{15}N$ values is often attributed to human consumption of dog meat (for a full discussion, see Guiry 2012, 2013).

EVALUATION OF RESEARCH QUESTIONS

(1) *What was the nature of the diet in the Koshkonong Locality?*

The nature of the diet can be defined based on two variables: its position on the horticultural to agricultural continuum; and its position on the diverse to focused continuum. Before it is possible to determine the value of either variable, it is necessary to identify which resources were most important. This can be achieved with the macrobotanical assemblage, to a degree, by assessing density values (Marston 2014; Miller 1988) and ubiquity indices (Marston 2014; Minnis 1985; Popper 1988; Wright 2010). The more often a resource is used, the greater the chance it will be exposed to fire and the more specimens will be preserved.

The role of agricultural plants needs to be assessed in relation to wild resources. While the ubiquity and density values are a good starting point, they cannot answer the whole picture. Issues of differential preservation make it difficult to clearly and quantifiably rank resources (Ford 1979; Fuller, Stevens, and McClatchie 2014; Gallagher 2014; Pearsall 1988, 2010; Popper 1988). This is why it is essential to use the stable isotopes as well. The $\delta^{13}C$ can approximate maize's importance, though it cannot directly measure the significance of other resources. The $\delta^{15}N$ provides an indication of the importance of meat in the diet. When all three lines of evidence are used in conjunction, inferences about the nature of the diet can be made.

It is also important to identify variation within the locality. This can first be achieved by examining the macrobotanical assemblages of the two sites. Which resources are present and absent? Are they present in similar diversities and ubiquities? If there is variation, what explains it? Is it a matter of differences in site location and access to environmental niches (see Edwards 2010)? Or can it be better explained by seasonal, social, or functional differences?

To assess the diversity or focus of the diet, several measures are used. The first is taxonomic richness, or number of species used (Lyman 2008). However, this measure gives us only one part of the picture as a diet can be focused on one resource but still include small amounts of many other resources. Therefore, diversity indices are used to combine the taxonomic richness with the proportional importance of each resource (Lyman 2008; Marston 2014; Peres 2010; Popper 1988; VanDerwarker 2010). The Shannon (Pearsall 1983; Popper 1988; VanDerwarker 2010) and Simpson's (Lyman 2008; Marston 2014) indices have a long history of use in paleoethnobotany and zooarchaeology. However, these values are useful only when compared to values from other sites. So they can be useful for determining if one site is considerably more focused than the other but will be of most use in answering the second research question, below.

Finally, a series of principal components analyses (PCA) (Gauch 1982; Greenacre 1984; Pearsall 2010; Shennan 1997; Smith 2014; ter Braak 1995) is used to mine the data for patterns. PCA is useful because it is a multivariate method that can find patterns not readily apparent in the data or with univariate methods. It is used to look for differences between sites, time periods, and depositional contexts.

(2) How does the subsistence system in Koshkonong differ from those of other groups?

This question is approached using techniques similar to those used to compare KCV and CBHC. The overall macrobotanical assemblage is assessed: What resources are used in which localities? Which resources are most important? How important are agricultural resources, and how focused (or diversified) is the diet? If each group appears to be using the same resources in the same manner, then it is unlikely that each locality is using a truly locally adapted diet. However, if there is variation in agricultural reliance—which plants are used (agricultural or nonagricultural) or how those resources are ranked—then an argument can be made for a locally adapted diet. Diversity indices, isotope values, density measures, and ubiquity indices play important roles in assessing this question.

(3) What risk management strategies were used in the Koshkonong Locality?

To answer this question, it is first necessary to address its four components. First, does the Koshkonong diet shift through time as predicted by the model (see ch. 2)? This assessment includes comparison within the locality and with Late Woodland sites. For intralocality comparisons, Mann Whitney U tests are used to compare early and late components. If the model is correct, agricultural and aggregated resources should be statistically distinct between early and late contexts. Then specific risk management strategies can be assessed. Storage is assessed by examining feature quantity, size, and morphology. Evidence of other risk management strategies is examined using human osteological data (evidence of intergroup violence) and site distribution data (as evidence of group mobility) and will reference ceramic analyses (on evidence for interaction, see Carpiaux 2018; Schneider 2015).

(4) What are the relationships between agriculture and cultural complexity?

This question is assessed through statistical comparison of Upper and Middle Mississippian $\delta^{13}C$ values. Human and dog samples from Illinois, Wisconsin, and Minnesota Upper Mississippian sites are combined. Upper and Middle Mississippian values are compared using Mann Whitney U tests. Traditional approaches suggest that Middle Mississippian values should be higher than and statistically distinct from the Upper Mississippian values.

FOUR

Results of Macrobotanical Data Collection

At KCV and CBHC, 41 contexts in 16 features totaling over 4,800 liters of sediment were analyzed (see appendix A). Initial examination of the data sets shows generally similar patterns (figs. 4.1, 4.2). Both sites were occupied year-round; samples from both sites contain food plants that grew between spring and autumn, as well as tree buds, which grow in late winter and early spring. Furthermore, the residents relied on maize-based agriculture, accompanied by squash, with beans added in late contexts. At both sites, maize is the densest and most ubiquitous plant, located in every feature. Agricultural output was supplemented with a variety of plants; however, wild rice and acorns were the most significant nonagricultural food resources. Other than maize, no other plants were found in comparable densities or ubiquities. Chenopodium and hickory were also used to moderate degrees. Small amounts of fruits, tubers, and other wild resources were also identified to lesser and varying degrees.

To determine if the diets at the two sites differed significantly, the assemblages were subjected to a series of statistical tests (univariate Mann Whitney U and multivariate PCA). Together, the two sets of statistical analyses indicate that the diet at the two sites was generally very similar. The PCA could not differentiate the two sites, but it did identify important trends in the data. The univariate analyses found few statistical differences between the two sites' assemblages.

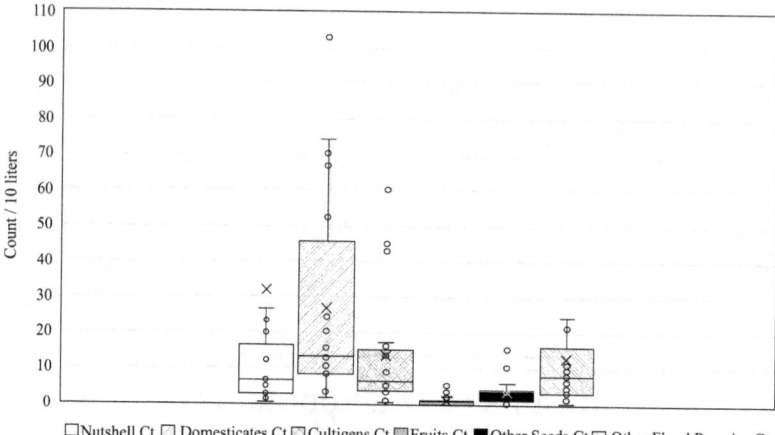

Figure 4.1. Box plot of Crescent Bay Hunt Club macrobotanical remains (count/10 liters)

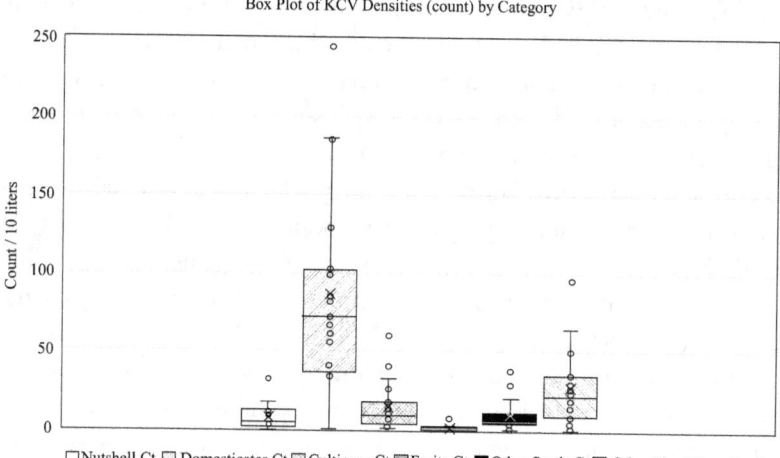

Figure 4.2. Box plot of Koshkonong Creek Village macrobotanical remains (count/10 liters)

Though maize was the focus of subsistence at both sites, it seems to be more important at KCV, where maize kernels were found in greater densities (figs. 4.3, 4.4). The assemblages also indicated a difference in the way maize was processed. At KCV, there was a higher ratio of kernels to cupules than at CBHC, indicating (1) that residents at CBHC were more likely than the residents at KCV to process maize on the site, (2) that they used a different technique to remove the kernels from the cobs, or (3) that they disposed of the cob remains in a fashion that was more likely to preserve them. A final possibility is that the larger number of features at CBHC provides a more complete picture of the local processing and/or refuse patterns and the high ratio at KCV reflects sampling bias. At this point, it is not possible to distinguish among these various scenarios.

Chenopodium was also a major component of the CBCH assemblage, accounting for a substantial portion of the overall seeds. The plant has previously been identified as one of the most ubiquitous and densest floral resources at CBHC (Edwards and Pater 2011; Edwards 2016; Jeske et al. 2016). However, based on raw count, density, and ubiquity values, the KCV assemblage contains only small amounts of the seed. The total density at CBHC is roughly five times greater than at KCV and the average density is more than one and a half times greater at CBHC (fig. 4.5). Despite the proximity of CBHC to Lake Koshkonong, this trend does not extend to wild rice. Somewhat surprisingly, the aquatic plant was found at both sites in statistically indistinguishable densities. It appears either that wild rice was sufficiently ingrained in the local subsistence regimen that people at KCV were willing to travel a little farther to harvest or trade for the plant or that Koshkonong Creek and its associated wetlands provided an adequate habitat for it to grow in sufficient numbers to fulfill the needs of the site residents.

Environmental reconstructions indicate the area around KCV was more heavily wooded than that around CBHC. Therefore, if nuts were exploited opportunistically or proportional to their availability, it would not be unexpected for the residents at KCV to have used nuts to a greater degree than those at CBHC. Oak and hickory were the dominant trees noted in the General Land Office survey notes (Brink 1835; Burnham 1836; Miller 1833), so acorn and hickory would have been readily available. However, deforestation for firewood, clearance of agricultural lands, and burning to maintain a savannah environment (Wagner 2003) may have reduced the

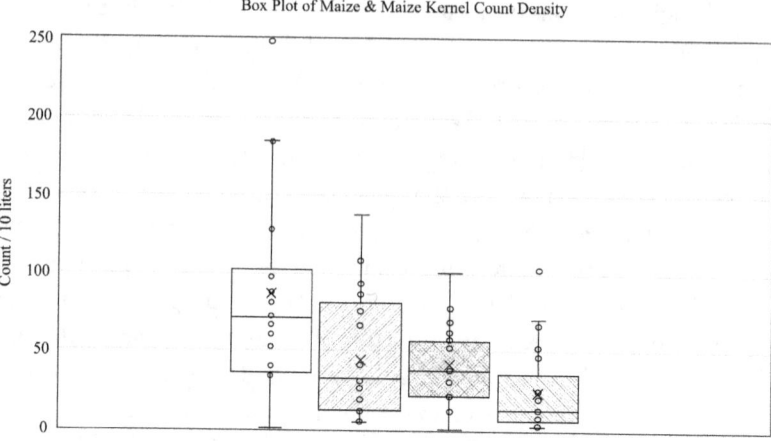

Figure 4.3. Box plot of maize and maize kernel densities (count/10 liters) from Koshkonong sites

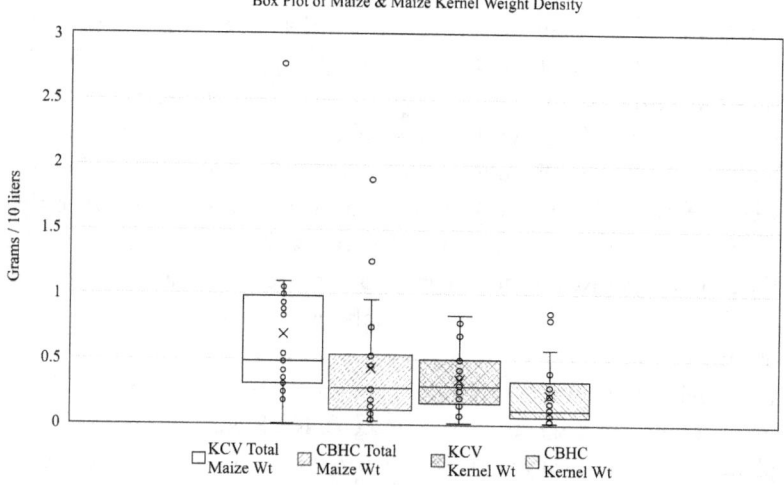

Figure 4.4. Box plot of maize and maize kernel densities (grams/10 liters) from Koshkonong sites

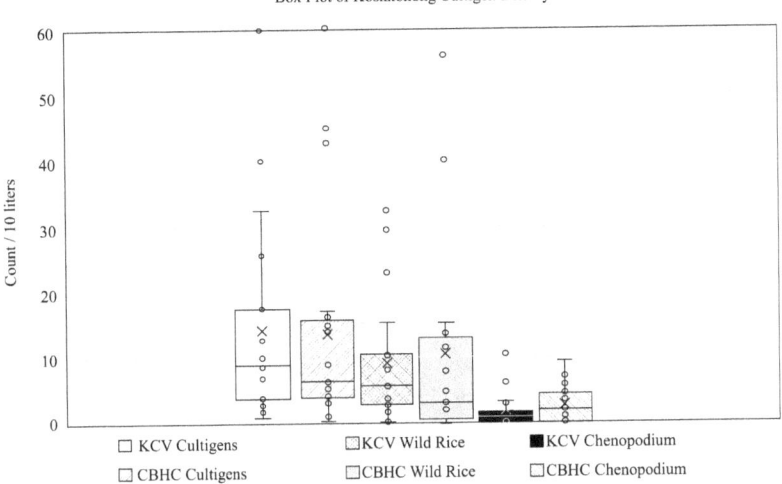

Figure 4.5. Box plot of cultigen densities (count/10 liters) from Koshkonong sites

nut-bearing trees in the sites' vicinities. Acorn is found in significant densities at both sites. Walnut and hickory were also commonly identified, though in far lower quantities. As with wild rice, environmental differences do not appear to have had a significant impact on the diet. The data indicate that there is no statistical difference in the amount of nutshells at the two sites.

Given the high density of shell fragments at both sites, it appears that nuts, particularly acorns, were a significant resource for their residents. Density and ubiquity numbers suggest that it may have been the most important resource after maize. However, because nutshell is a waste product from processing the nuts and other seeds represent the edible portions of the foods, it is likely that the relative importance of acorn is somewhat inflated. However, that acorn is found in roughly 80% of the contexts at both sites should not be overlooked.

RELATIONSHIPS AMONG RESOURCES

While the PCA could not distinguish the two sites, it was able to identify important intrasite variation and relationships among different types of

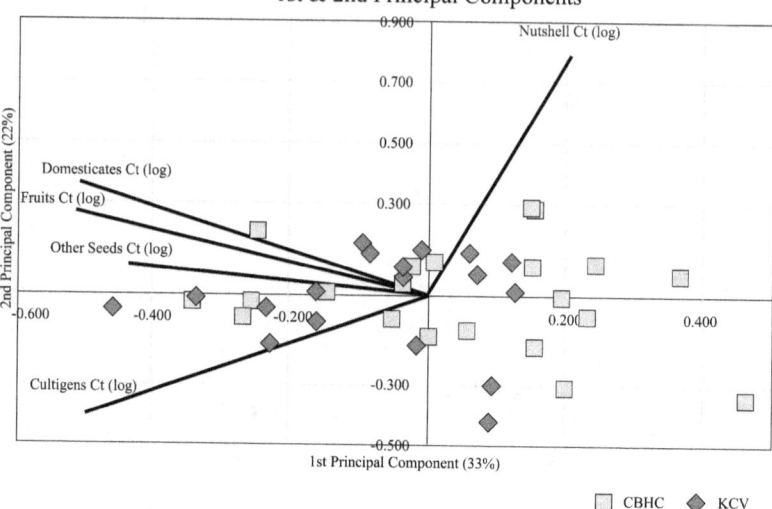

Figure 4.6. Principal components analysis: CBHC vs. KCV—first and second principal components

food resources. The first principal component separates contexts that have disproportionately high densities of nutshells relative to everything else (fig. 4.6). The second principal component primarily highlights contexts with different relative proportions of nutshells and cultigens. So in figure 4.6, above, contexts with large amounts of nutshells trend toward the right of the graph, and those with few nutshells are at the left. Those with a high ratio of cultigens to nuts trend near the bottom of the graph, and those with a high ratio of nuts to cultigens are at the top.

This information is important for several reasons. First, the high degree of overlap between CBHC and KCV supports the results of the univariate analysis. On a resource-by-resource basis, and as a whole, the floral assemblages from the two sites are very similar. Second, I argue that PCA can help identify methods to cope with scarcity. Here, nuts apparently were very important. Typically, when nutshell densities are high, other types of plants are in low densities (first principal component). Furthermore, cultigens and nuts are inversely correlated, so nutshell densities tend to be low when cultigens are most dense, and vice versa (second principal component).

I posit that nuts acted as a safety net: when harvests failed, nuts could be procured in large numbers and could act as insurance against starvation.

Results of Macrobotanical Data Collection

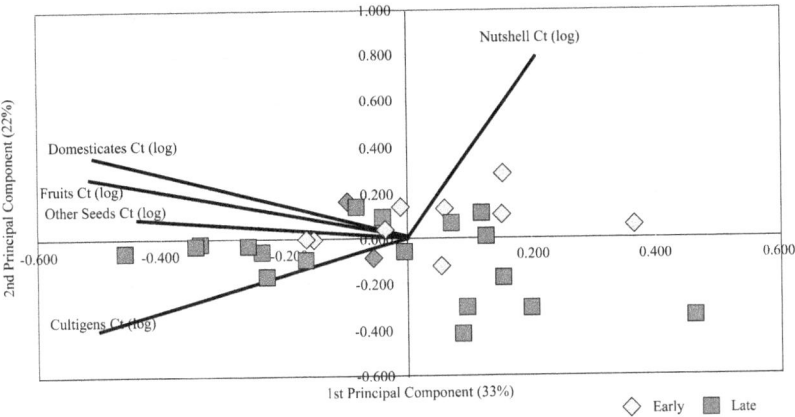

Figure 4.7. Principal components analysis: Early vs. late—first and second principal components

Both principal components support this inference. Under normal circumstances, maize was the primary food resource, but cultigens and wild resources, including nuts, were procured (negative PC1 value, positive PC2 value). In some cases, cultigens were favored instead of nuts (negative PC1 and PC2 values). When maize production levels were low, labor was shifted to nut collecting (positive PC1 and PC2 values). In some contexts, there were few plant remains identified overall (positive PC1 values, negative PC2 values). However, the AMS data suggest that the use of nuts as a buffer resource was temporary.

TEMPORAL SHIFTS

The only two significant temporal shifts identified were a decrease in nutshell use, particularly acorn, and an increase in wild rice densities and ubiquities. The univariate analysis indicates that wild rice consumption increased from early to late contexts (pre– vs. post–AD 1200), while nut consumption decreased. This is what PC2 detected. When the PCA values are resymbolized to show chronology instead of sites (fig. 4.7), essentially all the contexts with low PC2 values (i.e., more wild rice than nuts) are late (post–AD 1200). In general, late contexts are either closely associated with cultigens but not nuts or they are not associated with any variable (positive PC1, negative PC2), indicating that overall densities of plant remains were low (these features are almost exclusively associated with longhouses; see discussion below).

In short, during the early occupation, nuts were often collected at the cost of cultigens (PC2). It appears that acorn was likely a buffer resource during the first half of the Oneota occupation of the Koshkonong Locality and may have been exploited more heavily when maize harvests were poor (PC1). In later contexts, wild rice appears to take over the buffering role that was performed by nuts before AD 1200. In early contexts, wild rice densities were moderate and relatively consistent. In later contexts, the density of wild rice was significantly higher, though more variable. In many contexts, it was positively correlated with non-nutshell densities (positive PC1 and PC2 values), indicating that it was not usually necessary for the foragers to reduce the collection of fruits and other seeds when wild rice harvests were plentiful. Note that most of the values on the left side of the graph stay near the x-axis, indicating that as their cultigen levels rose, nutshell decreased but with minimal impact to other resources.

No other significant dietary changes were identified. Maize, chenopodium, and fruit density values all remained stable through time. This is moderately surprising given that by circa AD 1200 the social landscape was shifting significantly. Aztalan was abandoned, as were most if not all of the Late Woodland sites in southern Wisconsin. The Oneota residents at Koshkonong initially lived in a crowded environment, but by AD 1200, only the residents of Koshkonong Oneota sites remained, which appears to have had a minimal impact on their diet.

EXPLORING STRUCTURE FUNCTIONS

The final facet of the paleoethnobotanical assemblage examined was structure function at CBHC. Two different structure types have been identified at Crescent Bay (see ch. 1 for a fuller description). To date, it is not clear what if any functional distinction exists. An initial examination of the data suggests that there may have been seasonal differences in use, as Moss (2010) argued. With the presence of buds, longhouses were likely used in the cold season and wigwams were likely used throughout much of the year. However, closer examination of the data indicates that the assemblages are significantly different on almost every level. These differences suggest that there was likely a functional difference.

If two structure types were used in the same manner (i.e., both habitation structures used throughout the year), then their assemblages should be very similar. However, if there are seasonal or functional differences between longhouses and wigwams, then we should expect to have differences in the floral assemblages (table 4.1). For example, the presence of buds is a good indicator of cold season use, as they normally form during late winter or early spring. However, their absence does not necessarily indicate warm season occupation. Violets (*Viola* sp.) bloom in the spring, so the presence of their seeds is a good indicator of cold season occupation. While nuts, maize, wild rice, aquatic tubers, and many other plants are harvested in the fall, they can be stored, so it is difficult to use them as seasonal indicators. Cold temperatures in winter require heating of structures. This need, in addition to the normal cooking and other domestic activities, will produce wood charcoal in greater densities than warm season occupations. Therefore, if the structures have the same function but differences in seasons of occupation, then there should be a greater density of wood charcoal in the winter structures.

If the structures have different functional uses, then we can expect differences in floral assemblages that are distinct from seasonal indicators (table 4.2). The main distinction should be evident in food refuse. As the locus of domestic activities, habitation structures should have relatively high densities of a wide array of food remains. The presence of significant amounts of food remains does not guarantee that they were used as habitations, as some special-purpose structures may have been associated with communal food consumption (e.g., clan lodges, ceremonial structures). However, food remains in low densities or absent from features is inconsistent with habitation structures.

When the data are examined, the overall densities of floral materials appear to be the biggest difference. Features associated with wigwams tend to have the densest food refuse and charcoal; those associated with longhouses do not. This distinction is likely related to a functional difference in the structures. If the densities associated with wigwams are typical of domestic refuse, then it does not seem likely that the longhouses were used as

Table 4.1. Structure function: Seasonal and functional criteria

Seasonal Criteria for Habitation Structures	Warm Season	Cold Season
Buds		X
Wood charcoal (high density)	X	X
Wood charcoal (low density)	X	
Violet (*Viola* sp.)		X
Functional Criteria	**Habitation**	**Nonhabitation**
Food refuse (high density)	X	
Food refuse (low density)		X

Table 4.2. Structure function: Presence of seasonal and functional criteria in structure types

Seasonal Criteria for Habitation Structures	Wigwam	Longhouse
Buds		X
Wood charcoal (high density)	X	
Wood charcoal (low density)		X
Violet (*Viola* sp.)		X
Functional Criteria	**Wigwam**	**Longhouse**
Food refuse (high density)	X	
Food refuse (low density)		X

dwellings. If they were, their larger size should accommodate more people and correspondingly denser concentrations of materials. Since they do not, the structures may have served as public or communal structures.

In addition, the longhouses have significantly less wood charcoal than the wigwam structures, which is inconsistent with continuous occupation in the winter. If anything, the larger size and wider spacing of posts should require more fuel to maintain the heat of the longhouses, thereby producing more charcoal. However, this is not the case. The density of food remains also suggests a functional difference. Wigwam structures had more maize kernels, more total maize, and more nutshells. Moderately more wild rice was also present around the wigwam structures. The only food remains not present in much larger numbers around the wigwams was chenopodium. The low density of food remains and wood charcoal is inconsistent with interpreting the longhouses as habitation structures.

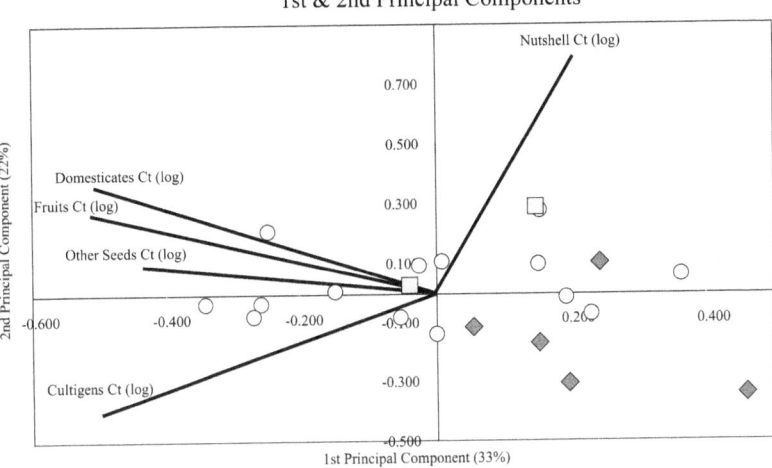

Figure 4.8. Principal components analysis: Structure association—first and second principal components

When analyzed by context, the PCA supports functional differences in structure types (fig. 4.8). Wigwam contexts are distributed across the graph, which is expected. As the locus of domestic activity, they should reflect a wide array of trash disposal patterns. Longhouses, in contrast, are clustered; they trend toward both the right and bottom sides of the PCA. In these contexts, most floral materials are generally absent or present only in relatively low densities. Floral materials are represented primarily by wild rice and/or chenopodium. These contexts come from a variety of features, ranging from small to large and about 100 to 2,000 liters in size. Because winter is typically a time of scarcity, these features should show evidence of increased reliance on easily stored resources, such as maize, wild rice, or acorns. Apart from a single feature, maize kernels are found in low densities. While proportionally important, wild rice is present in low to moderate densities. Nutshell is also found in low to moderate densities, which is inconsistent with a larger population of people aggregated under a single roof for long periods. Under these circumstances, food refuse should be equal or more concentrated than occurs with more dispersed households. So if the longhouses were used as habitations, the low firewood density indicates that they were summer structures. However, a warm season occupation is not supported by a high ubiquity of buds (about 80%). Therefore, it is likely that longhouses were special-purpose (i.e., nonhabitation) structures, though, the paleoethnobotanical data do not indicate what that function may have been. Ethnographically, the political and religious activities that would have taken place in such structures would have included fires and meals prepared elsewhere (e.g., Radin 1923; Skinner 1921). This special function may account for the presence of low quantities of domestic refuse and the presence of burials in two of the three identified longhouses (Jeske 2014; Jeske et al. 2017).

FIVE

Results of Isotopic Data Collection

According to Hart (1990), we should expect to see variation among Upper Mississippian agricultural systems. Since maize was an important aspect of all agricultural systems, that should include variation in maize reliance and therefore $\delta^{13}C$ values. For many years there have been two competing expectations for the relative importance of maize among Oneota and related groups. Traditional interpretations of Oneota suggest that their agriculture was less intensive than that of Middle Mississippians (e.g., Michalik 1982; Overstreet 1976). However, some scholars have argued that these Upper Mississippians were heavily reliant on the tropical domesticate (Gibbon 1972a). More recently, data from Langford sites support the latter argument (Edwards, Jeske, and Coltrain 2017; Emerson, Hedman, and Simon 2005; Emerson et al. 2010). The average $\delta^{13}C$ values of Langford sites are on par with Middle Mississippians. Left unanswered is whether Langford values are representative of their Oneota neighbors as well or if the differences noted between Langford and Oneota material culture and settlement (e.g., Jeske 1989, 2003b) also reflect significant differences in agricultural reliance.

We also have competing expectations for $\delta^{15}N$ values. As Middle Mississippians were a complex, hierarchical, and relatively urbanized

Table 5.1. Aggregated comparative isotopic data (*excludes anomalous value)

Archaeological Culture	Region	No. of Sites	n	Mean $\delta^{13}C$ (‰)	Mean $\delta^{15}N$ (‰)	Source
Middle Mississippian	American Bottom/Lower Illinois River valley	7	79	-12.95	9.21	Ambrose, Buikstra, and Krueger 2003; Hedman, Hargrave, and Ambrose 2002 2002
Late Woodland/ Middle Mississippian	Aztalan	1	8	-16.14	No data	Bender, Baerreis, and Steventon 1981
Oneota	Red Wing	1	5	-13.86	13.1 (9.43*)	Pratt 1994
Oneota	Riceford Creek	2	15	-13.36	10.29	Pratt 1994
Langford	Northern Illinois River valley	4	60	-12.24	9.73	Emerson et al. 2010

society without domesticated animals (except dog), it might be expected that individuals had less access to meat resources than their more rural Oneota neighbors and therefore lower $\delta^{15}N$ values (e.g., Hedman, Hargrave, and Ambrose 2002). However, if Theler and Boszhardt (2000, 2006) are correct and Oneota groups were faced with depleted deer populations, it would follow that $\delta^{15}N$ values may be as depressed as they were for Middle Mississippians. Even if Theler and Boszhardt's theory is only accurate in the La Crosse Locality, those samples should be lower than the Langford and eastern Oneota values. However, most researchers who have suggested shifts in Oneota hunting patterns have also suggested an increase in meat consumption through time. Gibbon (1972a, 1986) has argued that Oneota groups intensified hunting in the fourteenth century, and many authors (e.g., Boszhardt 1994) have suggested that people in the La Crosse area abandoned the locality to move west where bison was more plentiful.

Values from several relatively contemporaneous or culturally related sites were chosen for comparison (table 5.1). When some of the available cases could not be reliably tied to a specific context or time period, they were excluded from the comparative data set (e.g., Pratt 1994).

CANINE SURROGACY APPROACH ISOTOPIC RESULTS

Expectations

Based on the results of the human isotopic analyses, we can generate a series of expectations for the dog values. First, we should see moderate variation of both $\delta^{13}C$ and $\delta^{15}N$ values among samples from Upper Mississippian sites. It is likely that the variation within localities will be greater than between localities, creating a relatively homogeneous sample. If the dog bone values conform to the human bone values, the $\delta^{13}C$ values should range between -21‰ and -8‰ and $\delta^{15}N$ should range between 7‰ and 12‰. However, dog bone $\delta^{15}N$ values, in many regions around the world, including this one, are often slightly slower than their associated humans' values (Edwards, Jeske, and Coltrain 2017; Guiry 2012, 2013). The human bone values also suggest that the eastern Upper Mississippian $\delta^{15}N$ values should be slightly lower than the western Oneota (roughly 0.5‰) but the opposite should be true for $\delta^{13}C$ values (roughly 1.0‰). In other words, eastern Upper Mississippian values are expected to indicate that they ate more maize and less meat than western Oneota groups. The human bone values also suggest that overall Upper Mississippian values should have a narrower range than Middle Mississippian values.

Dog Isotopic Results

The summary results of the isotopic analysis are presented in table 5.2 (see also appendix B for the complete data set, e.g., C:N ratio). Each of the dogs has an accompanying AMS assay (table 5.3). The results from the Fisher and Nitschke Mounds were previously reported (Edwards et al. 2017) and were obtained using funding from the University of Wisconsin–Milwaukee's Preliminary Dissertation Grant. The remaining isotopes were obtained using funding from a National Science Foundation Dissertation Improvement Grant (Award no. 1640364).

Overall, the results conform to expectations. The radiocarbon assays align well with previously reported dates from each of the sites (see ch. 1). Where applicable, the dog bone values were generally in line with the associated human bone values (Edwards, Jeske, and Coltrain 2017). Upper Mississippian dogs consumed more maize than Late Woodland dogs, and dogs from collared ware sites consumed more maize than those from non-collared ware sites (i.e., Nitschke). In fact, the Nitschke dog appears to have eaten a very different suite of foods from that of all the other dogs.

The radiocarbon assays indicate that many of the dogs were relatively contemporaneous. One dog from Aztalan and the Nitschke dog clearly predate all the others. Two Aztalan dogs lived roughly at the time Middle Mississippians arrived. It is not known if they are associated with an exclusive Late Woodland or joint Late Woodland and Middle Mississippian occupation of the site. They are generally contemporaneous with both Crescent Bay dogs and one Diamond Bluff dog. While somewhat later, the remaining Diamond Bluff dog and the Fisher dogs still predate cal. AD 1300. The La Crosse dogs are the latest in the prehistoric sample, mostly postdating cal. AD 1300.

As predicted, the $\delta^{13}C$ analyses indicate moderate variation among the Upper Mississippian samples, along the lines predicted above. Upper Mississippian values were greater than the Late Woodland values, and eastern values were generally greater than western values. However, Red Wing values were more in line with eastern Upper Mississippian values than the La Crosse values. This finding suggests that La Crosse Locality individuals ate less maize than their neighbors, but all Upper Mississippians groups, as a whole, consumed more maize than Late Woodland groups. The Aztalan values, including the human values (Bender et al. 1981), are lower than even the La Crosse values.

Likewise, the $\delta^{15}N$ assays returned values within the expected ranges. As predicted, the dog bone values were slightly lower than the human values by roughly 0.5‰ (see ch. 3; Edwards, Jeske, and Coltrain 2017; Guiry 2013). The Late Woodland sample from Nitschke suggests that the inhabitants consumed the most meat of any represented in the sample. Early Upper Mississippian values tended to be lower than later Upper Mississippian values. The lowest values were present in the Crescent Bay and Aztalan samples.

Taken together, the data indicate that there were several different subsistence strategies in place during the Late Prehistoric of Wisconsin and northern Illinois. Statistical analysis is necessary to determine fine-grained differences within archaeological cultures, but the raw data do identify

Table 5.2. Canine isotopic results (for additional isotopic data, e.g., carbon nitrogen ratio see appendix B)

Locality	Site Number	Site Name	Context	δ13C vPDB	δ15N vAIR
Koshkonong	47JE904	CBHC	F10-14	-11.7	9.0
			F10-11	-13.7	8.1
Red Wing	47PI001	Diamond Bluff	Square G	-12.1	8.9
			square Z	-14.0	9.0
La Crosse	47LC34	Valley View	F99; Mandible 12	-11.6	9.4
			F106; Mandible 8	-13.8	8.8
	47LC61	Pammel Creek	F180; Mandible 2	-16.4	8.8
	47LC394	Sanford Complex	F59; Mandible 1	-13.6	9.0
			F516; Mandible 7	-14.9	8.7
			F37; Mandible 4	-14.0	9.3
	47LC0262	OT	F3; Level 10	-13.7	9.5
				-13.7	9.5
			F3; Level 12	-15.4	8.6
				-14.9	8.6
				-15.6	8.6
Langford	11CK4	Fisher*	Dog 1	-14.1	8.4
			Dog 2	-11.9	8.4
			Canid 3	-18.6	11.6
Late Woodland	47DO027	Nitschke*	Mound 21	-19.5	9.9
Middle Mississippian/ Late Woodland	47JE0001	Aztalan	Mandible 1	-15.1	8.3
			Mandible 2	-14.4	9.2
			Mandible 3	-16.2	8.2

* From Edwards et al. 2017.

broad differences among these larger groupings. First, Effigy Mound building people (and their dogs) ate a diet distinct from the Upper Mississippian pattern. The isotope values are concordant with a more mobile lifestyle, as argued by several authors (Salkin 2000; Stevenson et al. 1997). The Upper Mississippian values are in line with people who have shifted away from hunting and gathering and are heavily reliant on maize agriculture. However, the values also indicate variation in this general trend—with variable importance of both maize and meat. The Aztalan samples indicate an intermediate diet, one in which maize was a modestly important resource and animal resources were less important. Given these values, it is

Table 5.3. AMS results from *Canis lupus familiaris* samples

Locality	Site No.	Site Name	Context	Lab Code	Age BP	Error	1σ	%	2σ	%
Koshkonong	47JE904	CBHC	F10-14	3572	854	21	1169–1177	20	1156–1228	96
							1181–1214	80	1231–1247	4
			F10-11	3573	866	24	1162–1210	100	1050–1083	10
									1125–1136	1
									1150–1224	88
									1235–1241	1
Red Wing	47PI001	Diamond Bluff	Sq G	3574	870	19	1162–1194	80	1054–1077	6
							1196–1206	20	1153–1219	94
			Sq Z	3575	685	27	1278–1299	79	1270–1311	71
							1370–1379	21	1359–1387	29
La Crosse	47LC34	Midway	F99 Mand. 12	3759	485	22	1422–1439	100	1413–1445	100
			F106 Mand. 8	3760	437	19	1438–1452	100	1430–1467	100
	47LC34	Valley View	F180 Mand. 2	3761	543	20	1333–1336	6	1323–1346	22
							1398–1422	94	1393–1429	78
	47LC394	Sanford Complex	F59 Mand. 1	3762	540	21	1398–1424	100	1323–1346	19
									1393–1431	81
			F516 Mand. 7	3763	648	24	1290–1309	40	1283–1321	44
							1361–1386	60	1348–1392	56
			F37 Mand. 4	3764	466	21	1430–1444	100	1419–1450	100
	47LC0262	OT	Feature 3 Level 10	3765	415	19	1444–1465	100	1438–1487	100
									1605–1606	<1
				3766	305	27	1521–1575	74	1491–1602	75
							1625–1644	26	1614–1649	25

Table 5.3. AMS results from *Canis lupus familiaris* samples (*cont.*)

Locality	Site No.	Site Name	Context	Lab Code	Age BP	Error	1σ	%	2σ	%
	11CK4	Fisher*	Feature 3 Level 12	3767	418	19	1443–1464	100	1437–1486	100
				3768	250	20	1644–1663	100	1533–1536	1
									1636–1668	82
									1782–1797	17
									1948–1950	<1
				3769	361	19	1470–1517	65	1455–1524	56
							1594–1618	35	1559–1564	2
									1568–1631	42
Langford			Mandible 1	3029	745	29	1258–1282	100	1224–1239	9
									1240–1288	91
			Mandible 2	3030	760	25	1251–1279	100	1224–1281	100
			Mandible 3	3031	873	28	1059–1063	2	1045–1097	20
									1119–1142	5
							1154–1216	98	1146–1224	74
									1235–1241	1
Late Woodland	47DO027	Nitschke*	Mound 21	3033	1035	24	993–1019	100	973–1028	100
Middle Mississippian/ Late Woodland	47JE0001	Aztalan	Mandible 1	3791	942	24	1034–1050	20	1029–1154	100
							1082–1127	59		
							1135–1151	21		
			Mandible 2	3792	1049	26	985–1018	100	901–921	6
									955–956	<1
									960–1026	94
			Mandible 3	3793	976	31	1019–1047	48	999–1001	<1
							1089–1122	42	1013–1154	100
							1139–1148	10		

* From Edwards et al. 2017.

likely that nonmaize plant resources played a bigger role in their diet than at the other sites.

One anomalous sample was noted in the preliminary data set: Fisher Canid Mandible 3. Edwards, Jeske, and Coltrain (2017) argue that this may reflect one of four factors: (1) it is a wild canid, not a dog, that feeds on C_4 consuming animals; (2) it reflects earlier diets of the Fisher, not Langford, occupants of the site; (3) it reflects a change through time, with earlier populations consuming less maize and more meat; or (4) it reflects the overall range of diet at the site as it is still within the overall Mississippian dietary range. Because we cannot differentiate among these options, we must conservatively exclude it in the following discussion of isotopes.

INTEGRATING THE DATA SETS: A REGIONAL PERSPECTIVE

When dog isotopes are integrated into the human data sets, it is possible to make interregional and intercultural comparisons. To first determine if there are overall differences among Upper Mississippian populations, a series of Mann Whitney U tests were conducted on this non-normally distributed data set. The only Langford human samples that could be tested were from Material Service Quarry (MSQ), as the data from other sites were only provided as summary data (Emerson, Hedman, and Simon 2005). A regional comparison of isotope values was made between eastern (Koshkonong and Fisher dogs with MSQ humans) and western (Diamond Bluff and La Crosse dogs with Bryan humans) samples. The test confirmed the general trend noted above: groups in the east consumed more maize than those in the west (fig. 5.1). Such regional differences are expected based on Hart's (1990) expectation of variation among Upper Mississippian agricultural strategies.

In addition to geographic and synchronic differences, potential chronological shifts must be assessed. Gibbon's (1972a, 1986) grassland-fractionalized adaptation time line argues for reduced reliance on maize through time, so we should expect to see larger $\delta^{13}C$ values in earlier samples. However, Overstreet's (1997) chronology suggests that during the Classic Horizon (after AD 1350), the later samples should have greater $\delta^{13}C$ levels.

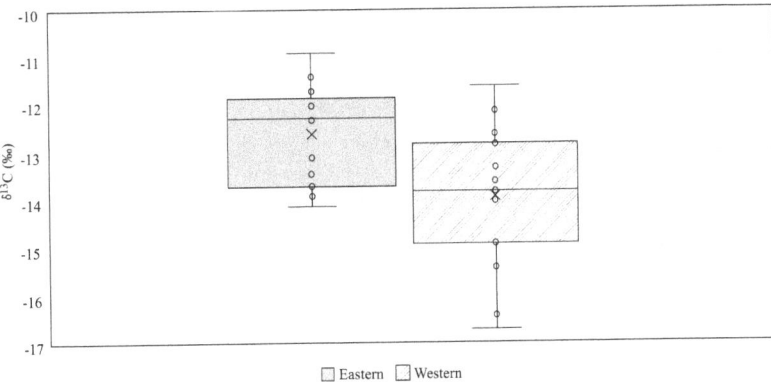

Figure 5.1. Box plot of aggregated δ¹³C values (‰) for eastern and western Upper Mississippian groups

While the earlier values were generally higher, the statistical tests paint a more complicated picture. When only Wisconsin sites are included (Red Wing and Koshkonong vs. La Crosse) there are no statistical differences (fig. 5.2). However, when all early samples are included (Red Wing, Koshkonong, and Langford vs. La Crosse) the differences become significant (fig. 5.3). So the first test appears to refute both Gibbon's and Overstreet's theories, as they both suggest no shift. The second test appears to support Gibbon's theory; early groups consumed greater amounts of maize than later groups. However, with the additional ten eastern samples, the increase in maize use values may just represent the geographic differences identified above. The data clearly indicate that the eastern samples have larger δ¹³C values than do western samples. Overall, δ¹³C values tend to decrease through time, but this trend is weak and is likely associated with multiple factors in addition to time.

To assess the idea that agriculture is associated with cultural complexity, comparisons of Middle and Upper Mississippian values were run. Because previous tests showed significant differences between eastern and western Upper Mississippian samples, each were independently compared to Middle Mississippian values. When Middle Mississippians were compared to eastern Upper Mississippian values, there were no statistical differences. However, when the western sites were compared to the Middle Mississippian samples, the results were significantly different. This finding indicates that eastern Upper Mississippian populations' maize consump-

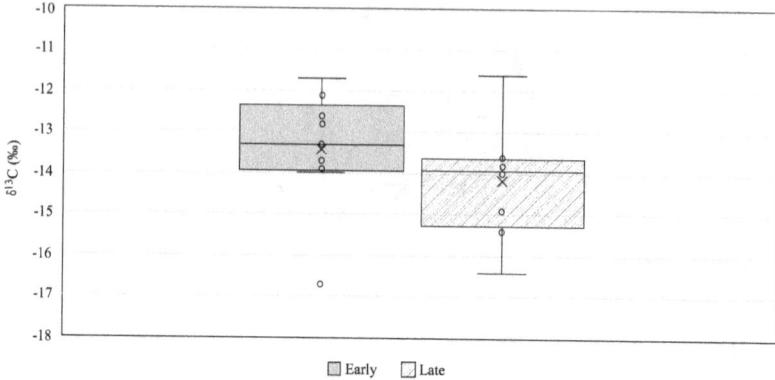

Figure 5.2. Box plot of aggregated $\delta^{13}C$ values (‰) for early and late Oneota groups

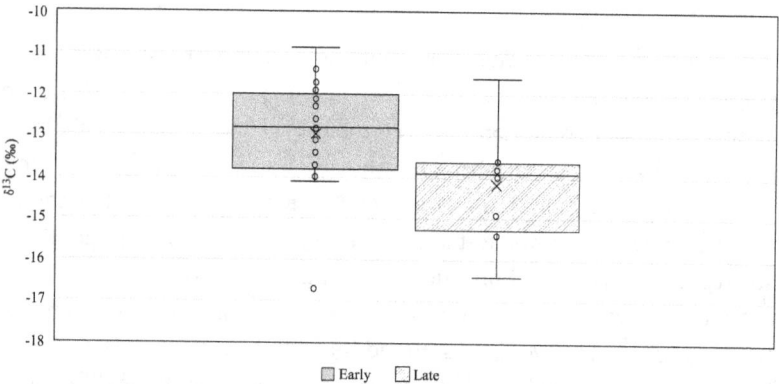

Figure 5.3. Box plot of aggregated $\delta^{13}C$ values (‰) for early and late Upper Mississippian groups

tion cannot be statistically differentiated from that of Middle Mississippians. However, the La Crosse inhabitants consumed significantly less maize than did American Bottom inhabitants (fig. 5.4).

The Late Woodland values were not used in the statistical comparison. Four samples are insufficient for statistical analysis. The fact that one of the specimens is from a non-collared ware site (Nitschke) further complicated the issue. It would be inappropriate to aggregate the Nitschke dog sample with the samples from Aztalan, a joint Middle Mississippian and collared ware site. However, it does appear that as a whole the Late Woodland samples indicate lower maize consumption. The bulk of the distribution is be-

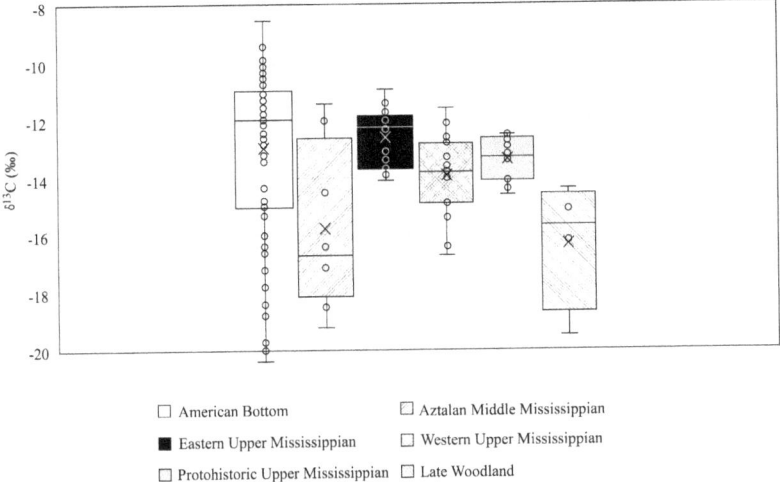

Figure 5.4. Box plot δ¹³C values (‰) among archaeological cultures and regions

yond the eastern Upper Mississippian range. However, the Aztalan samples are on par with many on the low end of the La Crosse range, and the Nitschke dog appears to have eaten as little maize as the Middle Mississippian elites.

For $\delta^{13}C$, it is also helpful to contextualize the isotope values in terms of total dietary contribution. Since collagen reflects protein consumption in well understood ways, it is possible to estimate maize's proportional contribution to the protein portion of the diet (see Hedman, Hargrave, and Ambrose 2002). The Middle Mississippians population's $\delta^{13}C$ values exhibit the widest range, accounting for 0% to 75% of total protein intake. The Upper Mississippian values, including the Langford sites with only summary data, have a narrower range, corresponding to 35% to 67% of protein intake. The Late Woodland values are the lowest, ranging between 3% and 35% of protein intake (table 5.4). The Middle Mississippian values emphasize the extreme diversity present in the hierarchically organized populations. The 95% confidence interval for all Middle Mississippians' maize consumption ranges from 2% to 82% of the protein intake. However, not all sites exhibit such a wide range. Sites like Schild A, Aztalan, and Cahokia exhibit extremely low $\delta^{13}C$ levels for a portion of their samples, indicating low maize consumption for at least one segment of the sites' populations (minimum values <15%). On the other hand, East

Table 5.4. Summary data for human and dog stable isotope data ($\delta^{13}C$)

Region	Site Name	n	δ13C				95% Confidence Interval		% Maize of Protein in Diet			95% Confidence Interval	
			μ	σ	Min	Max	Min	Max	μ	Min	Max	Min	Max
American Bottom	Cahokia	15	-16.8	1.9	-20.0	-13.3	-20.6	-13.0	20.6	-0.67	44.0	-4.6	45.8
	Corbin	13	-12.1	1.6	-15.0	-9.9	-15.3	-8.9	52.1	32.73	66.9	31.0	73.2
	ESLSQ	21	-11.0	1.1	-13.3	-8.5	-13.2	-8.8	59.6	44.20	75.9	44.9	74.3
	Florence	9	-11.2	1.0	-13.1	-10.1	-13.2	-9.3	57.7	45.27	65.2	45.0	70.5
	Hill Prairie	6	-14.6	3.9	-19.7	-10.2	-22.3	-6.8	35.5	1.33	64.7	-16.2	87.3
	Range	6	-11.4	1.5	-14.3	-10.3	-14.4	-8.4	56.9	37.07	64.0	36.8	76.9
	Schild A	9	-14.1	2.8	-20.4	-10.4	-19.	-8.5	38.4	-3.33	63.3	0.6	76.3
	Overall	79	-13.3	2.9	-20.4	-8.5	-19.1	-7.5	44.1	-3.33	75.9	5.7	82.6
Lake Mills	Aztalan	8	-15.8	2.9	-19.2	-11.4	-21.5	-10.0	27.6	4.67	56.7	-10.7	65.9
Overall Middle Mississippian		87	-13.5	3.0	-20.4	-8.5	-19.5	-7.6	42.6	-3.33	75.9	2.9	82.3
Koshkonong	CBHC	2	-12.7	1.4	-13.7	-11.7	-15.5	-9.9	48.0	41.33	54.7	29.1	66.9
La Crosse	Sanford	3	-14.2	0.7	-14.9	-13.6	-15.5	-12.8	38.2	33.33	42.0	29.3	47.1
	Valley View	1	-16.4	-	-16.4	-16.4	-	-	23.3	23.33	23.3	-	-
	Midway	2	-12.7	1.6	-13.8	-11.6	-15.8	-9.6	48.0	40.67	55.3	27.3	68.7
	OT	2	-14.6	1.2	-15.4	-13.7	-17.0	-12.2	35.7	30.00	41.3	19.6	51.7
	Overall	8	-14.2	1.4	-16.4	-11.6	-17.0	-11.3	38.2	23.33	55.3	19.1	57.3

Table 5.4. Summary data for human and dog stable isotope data (δ¹³C) (cont.)

		N											
Red Wing	Bryan	5	-13.9	1.7	-16.7	-12.6	-17.2	-10.5	40.3	21.33	48.7	18.1	62.5
	Diamond Bluff	2	-13.1	1.3	-14.0	-12.1	-15.7	-10.4	45.7	39.33	52.0	27.8	63.6
	Overall	7	-13.6	1.5	-16.7	-12.1	-16.7	-10.6	41.8	21.33	52.0	21.6	62.1
Upper Illinois	Gentleman Farm	10	-11.7	1.0	-14.4	-10.3	-13.7	-9.7	54.7	36.67	64.0	41.3	68.0
	Oakwood Mound	11	-12.6	1.2	-14.4	-10.2	-15.0	-10.2	48.7	36.67	64.7	32.7	64.7
	Fisher Overall	31	-12.3	1.2	-14.7	-9.8	-14.7	-9.8	51.0	34.67	67.3	34.7	67.3
	Fisher (humans)	29	-12.2	1.3	-14.7	-9.8	-14.8	-9.6	51.0	34.67	67.3	34.0	68.7
	Fisher (dogs)	2	-13.0	1.8	-14.1	-11.9	-16.5	-9.5	46.0	38.67	53.3	22.4	69.6
	MSQ	10	-12.5	1.0	-13.7	-10.9	-14.5	-10.5	49.4	41.33	60.0	36.2	62.6
	Overall Langford	62	-12.3	0.7	-14.7	-9.8	-13.6	-10.9	50.9	34.67	67.3	41.7	60.1
Overall Prehistoric Upper Mississippian		79	-12.6	0.6	-16.7	-9.8	-13.7	-11.4	48.7	21.33	67.3	41.0	56.4
Riceford Creek	Hogback	9	-13.2	0.7	-14.4	-12.5	-14.6	-11.9	44.6	36.67	49.3	35.5	53.7
	Wilsey	6	-13.6	0.9	-14.6	-12.5	-15.4	-11.8	42.1	35.33	49.3	30.3	53.9
	Overall	15	-13.4	0.8	-14.6	-12.5	-14.9	-11.8	43.6	35.33	49.3	33.4	53.8
Total Upper Mississippian		94	-12.7	0.5	-16.7	-9.8	-13.7	-11.7	47.9	21.33	67.3	41.3	54.6
Late Woodland	Nitschke	1	-	-	-19.5	-19.5	-	-	-	2.7	2.7	-	-
	Aztalan	3	-15.2	0.9	-16.2	-14.4	-17.1	-13.4	31.0	24.5	36.8	18.7	43.3
Overall Late Woodland		4	-16.3	2.3	-19.5	-14.4	-20.8	-11.8	23.9	2.7	36.8	-6.2	54.0

St. Louis Stone Quarry (ESLSQ) and Florence Street both have minimum values greater than 40% protein from maize. Hedman, Hargrave, and Ambrose (2002) note that these inter- and intrasite differences come from multiple sources, including geography, sex, and status. Generally, individuals from upland sites consumed more wild plants (e.g., acorn) and less maize. Males at some sites consumed more meat and less maize, and individuals of high status generally consumed significantly less maize and more meat (Ambrose, Buikstra, and Krueger 2003; Hedman, Hargrave, and Ambrose 2002).

The complex interplay of population movement, social hierarchies, and tiered settlement systems within the Mississippian populations leads to a wide range in maize consumption among individuals and sites. This finding stands in stark contrast to the Upper Mississippian samples. The variation, both among and within sites, is significantly less for the northern groups. The lowest recorded Upper Mississippian value represents a diet in which 20% of the protein came from maize. For the highest value, nearly 70% of the protein came from maize. While this represents a wide range (≈50% of protein), it is much smaller than the range of Middle Mississippians (≈75%). Furthermore, most Upper Mississippian values fall within a relatively narrow 16% range, at a 95% confidence interval. Much of the range can be accounted for by the variation among regions. The Langford samples are the most consistent and have the highest $\delta^{13}C$ values. The average Langford sample reflects a diet with more than 50% of the protein from maize. While the sample size is small, the Koshkonong dogs' values show a high proportion of protein from maize, on par with the Langford values (48% of protein). Western localities trend lower in averages (Red Wing, 45%; La Crosse, 40%; Riceford Creek, 45%).

The overall Late Woodland values appear to have a high degree of variation (95% confidence range = 0% to 54%). However, most of the range appears to be from intersite differences. Aztalan, a collared ware and Middle Mississippian site, has a relatively small amount of variation in the proportion of protein from maize (19% to 43% of protein at 95% confidence interval). The Late Woodland dog values from Aztalan trend lower than their Oneota neighbors at Koshkonong and elsewhere. The three Aztalan dogs ate more maize than some Upper Mississippians, particularly in the west (La Crosse and Red Wing), but even the high-end Aztalan samples are at the low end of the Upper Mississippian range. Nitschke, an Effigy Mound site, exhibits values on par with Middle Mississippian elites, as well as Middle Woodland people, a dog from the Richter site in Door County (Edwards, Jeske, and Coltrain 2017; Wellner 2006), and Late Archaic elites at the Jaco site in Jefferson County (Jeske et al. 2011; Romond et al. 2011). The single dog sampled appears to have consumed very little maize (<3% of protein). While the sample size is small, it conforms with previous expectations for Effigy Mound groups (see Edwards, Jeske, and Coltrain 2017 for a full discussion).

It should be noted that Fritz (2019) recently suggested that isotope values from the individuals buried in Mound 72 may not be an accurate proxy for agricultural reliance. Rather, they reflect a pre–AD 1200 American Bottom diet, a diet that included much less maize than the later Mississippian diet. She argues that these values correspond well with the relatively low maize macrobotanical densities at early Mississippian sites throughout the American Bottom, which indicates that this early diet was dominated by Eastern Agricultural Complex plants. Maize was present, but it was not the focus of the diet. If Fritz is correct, then the isotopic data cannot be used as a proxy measure for agricultural reliance in early Middle Mississippian contexts, as it would not be able to account for the significant role of EAC plants. In this case, the only measure of agricultural reliance is the macrobotanical data. While there are many issues inherent in intersite comparison, in this case it may still prove illuminating.

As Fritz notes, maize density values appear to correlate with the isotopic data. She notes that during the Lohman phase at the Range site (roughly contemporaneous with the Mound 72 burials), the maize density was 20.9 ct./10 liters of sediment (Fritz 2019, 96), whereas the contemporaneous density at KCV is more than three times greater (72 ct./10 liters). Range is thought to have been a local administrative (nodal) center. The overall density at CBHC is comparable (19 ct./10 liters) to Range, but the early CBHC sample is overrepresented by longhouse features. As noted above, longhouse features are not representative of domestic refuse. When only wigwam features are used, the density at CBHC is also more than three times greater (67 ct./10 liters). While it may not be possible to determine which group consumed more agricultural plants, we can argue that the Koshkonong residents relied more heavily on maize during this early time frame, the time frame when Cahokian elites had established their position in the Cahokian political system (e.g., Pauketat 1994).

However, even if we do not use the Mound 72 isotope values, it is unlikely to significantly affect the above interpretations. After removing the Mound 72 values, the American Bottom average remained relatively low (49% of protein contribution). Even removing the entire Cahokia sample, the average Middle Mississippian value is still less than 52% of protein contribution, not drastically higher than the Upper Mississippian values. And because Hedman's (Hedman, Hargrave, and Ambrose 2002) data set dates to the thirteenth century, after the spike in maize consumption, the values should be comparable.

Furthermore, the isotopic data indicate the Koshkonong residents were reliant on agriculture. Because there was no statistical difference between the early and late Koshkonong macrobotanical assemblages, the Koshkonong dog bone isotope values should be representative of the early diet. So if Fritz is correct, then the data indicate that maize-focused agriculture has earlier roots in the Oneota landscape than in the American Bottom. In either case, while both the American Bottom and Koshkonong diets were agriculturally based, the American Bottom diet was more variable and the Koshkonong diet was more uniform across the population and more focused.

An analysis of the $\delta^{15}N$ values also shows differences among archaeological cultures (fig. 5.5). However, there is less variation in $\delta^{15}N$ than $\delta^{13}C$. The data indicate that Middle Mississippian meat consumption was the most variable (7.6‰–11.9‰). The range for Upper Mississippians is smaller, 8.1‰–10.7‰. Late Woodland dogs had the smallest $\delta^{15}N$ range, 8.2‰–9.9‰ (table 5.5).

The Middle Mississippians with the highest $\delta^{15}N$ values consumed the most meat. Their values were higher than the highest prehistoric Upper Mississippians. Likewise, the Middle Mississippians at the low end of the spectrum consumed less meat than their Upper Mississippian counterparts. Because dog values trend 0.5‰ lower than humans, it may be necessary to calibrate the dog values to make them comparable to the human values (Edwards, Jeske, and Coltrain 2017; Guiry 2013). When dog $\delta^{15}N$ values are increased 0.5‰, the Upper Mississippian range increases marginally. This indicates that those Upper Mississippian humans who consumed the most meat may have eaten as much as Middle Mississippian elites. This increase indicates that almost all humans at Upper Mississippian sites ate more meat than the nonelites on Middle Mississippian sites.

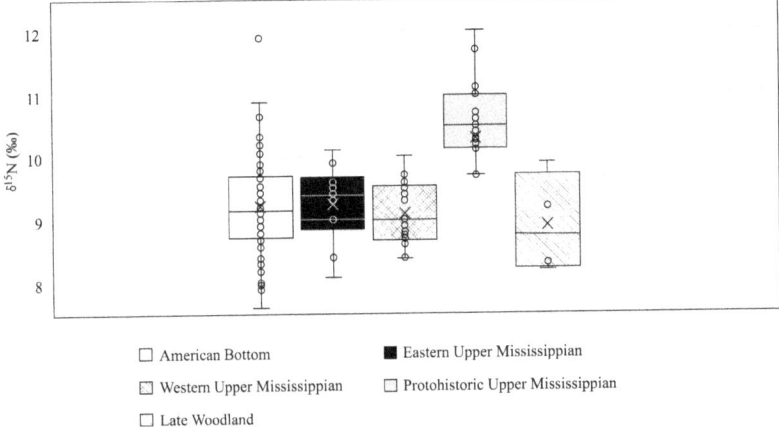

Figure 5.5. Box plot $\delta^{15}N$ values (‰) among archaeological cultures and regions

However, the isotopic samples cannot be statistically differentiated from eastern Upper Mississippian or western Oneota.

The chronological and geographic variation within the Upper Mississippian values must also be explored. Values from early and eastern sites (i.e., Langford sites and Crescent Bay) are more variable than the early western samples (i.e., Red Wing). Of these, Langford groups consumed the most meat. The Langford sample is also the largest (2 dogs and 60 humans), so the high end of meat consumption may be missing from the small samples at Crescent Bay (2 dogs) and Red Wing (2 dogs and 4 humans). At La Crosse (8 dogs), meat consumption is lower than in all the samples except Koshkonong. Koshkonong samples are lower than either Red Wing or La Crosse samples.

When the dog values are calibrated up 0.5‰, much of the variation disappears between localities. The Langford mean (9.7‰) is relatively unchanged because of the proportionally small number of dogs in the sample. However, the Red Wing sample shifts upward slightly (9.4‰). Because the samples are entirely comprised of dogs, the La Crosse (9.5‰) and Koshkonong (9.1‰) means increase the full 0.5‰. Therefore, after calibrating the dog $\delta^{15}N$ values, the interlocality variation becomes statistically insignificant. In other words, with calibration, most of the variation within the Upper Mississippian data set is between individuals within localities, not between localities (figs. 5.6, 5.7).

Table 5.5. Summary data for human and dog stable isotope data ($\delta^{15}N$)

Region	Site Name	n	μ	σ	Min	Max	95% Confidence Interval	
American Bottom	Cahokia	9	9.04	1.34	7.90	11.90	6.37	11.72
	Corbin	13	9.12	0.35	8.70	9.59	8.41	9.83
	ESLSQ	21	9.05	0.64	7.91	10.23	7.77	10.33
	Florence St.	9	9.87	0.44	9.02	10.33	8.99	10.75
	Hill Prairie	6	9.65	0.57	9.14	10.65	8.50	10.79
	Range	6	9.43	0.83	8.32	10.88	7.77	11.08
	Schild A	9	8.74	0.74	7.60	9.90	7.27	10.22
	Overall	73	9.21	0.77	7.60	11.90	7.66	10.75
Koshkonong	CBHC	2	8.55	0.64	8.10	9.00	7.28	9.82
La Crosse	Sanford	3	9.00	0.30	8.70	9.30	8.40	9.60
	Valley View	1	8.80	-	8.80	8.80	-	-
	Midway	2	8.90	0.71	8.40	9.40	7.49	10.31
	OT	2	9.05	0.64	8.60	9.50	7.78	10.32
	Overall	8	8.96	0.40	8.40	9.50	8.16	9.77
Red Wing	Bryan	4	9.43	0.70	8.40	10.00	8.02	10.83
	Diamond Bluff	2	8.95	0.07	8.90	9.00	8.81	9.09
	Overall	6	9.27	0.60	8.40	10.00	8.07	10.46
Upper Illinois	Gentleman Farm	10	9.50	1.00	8.70	10.20	7.50	11.50
	Oakwood Mound	11	9.90	1.20	9.50	10.50	7.50	12.30
	Fisher Overall	31	9.71	1.22	8.40	10.70	7.28	12.14
	Fisher (humans)	29	9.80	1.30	8.90	10.70	7.20	12.40
	Fisher (dogs)	2	8.40	0.00	8.40	8.40	8.40	8.40
	MSQ	10	9.56	0.33	9.00	10.10	8.91	10.21
	Overall Langford	62	9.69	0.67	8.40	10.70	8.36	11.02
Overall Prehistoric Upper Mississippian		79	9.43	0.53	8.10	10.70	8.37	10.49
Riceford Creek	Hogback	9	9.83	1.54	5.90	11.10	6.75	12.92
	Wilsey	6	10.98	0.73	10.20	12.00	9.53	12.44
	Overall	15	10.29	1.37	5.90	12.00	7.54	13.04
Total Upper Mississippian		94	9.57	0.49	5.90	12.00	8.58	10.56
Late Woodland	Nitschke	1	-	-	9.9	9.9	-	-
	Aztalan	3	8.5	0.55	8.2	9.2	7.44	9.66
Overall Late Woodland		4	8.89	0.81	8.2	9.9	7.26	10.51

The Late Woodland $\delta^{15}N$ values also vary between sites. The Nitschke dog consumed considerably more meat than its southern neighbors (its value is beyond the 95% confidence interval). Crescent Bay is the only site to have lower $\delta^{15}N$ than the Aztalan dogs. In fact, the CBHC dog $\delta^{15}N$ range closely mirrors the Aztalan range (0.1 lower at both limits of the range). Given the proximity of the sites, it is tempting to argue that deemphasized meat consumption is part of a long-standing local tradition, but a sample of five dogs from two sites in a relatively narrow time range makes

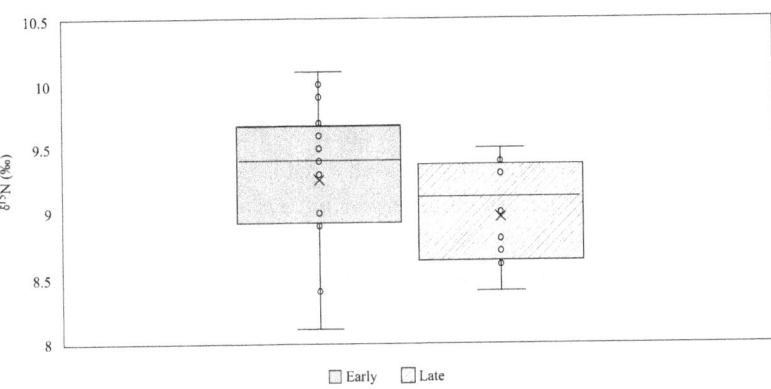

Figure 5.6. Box plot δ^{15}N values (‰) of Early and Late Prehistoric Upper Mississippian groups

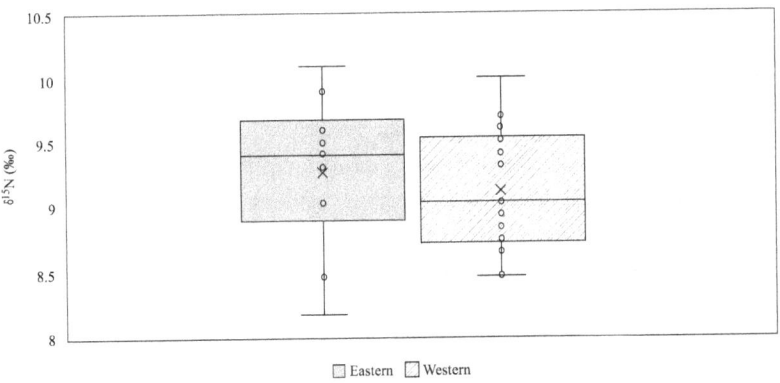

Figure 5.7. Box plot δ^{15}N values (‰) of eastern and western Upper Mississippian groups

this a tenuous assertion at best. The deemphasized consumption of meat may also be related to population packing, or the arrival of intrusive groups in the region, forcing a contraction of hunting territories. If there is competition over territory, hunters may remain closer to the villages to avoid ambushes by opposing groups, thereby reducing access to meat (see ch. 2). In such cases, some or all of the reduced meat may be replaced by plants, which would lower the δ^{15}N values.

The results of the isotopic analysis suggest that while there are some differences between Upper and Middle Mississippian populations, there is also a great deal of overlap. For Upper Mississippians, most of this overlap seems to be associated with regional variation (east vs. west). For Middle Mississippians, status and site type differences are the major sources of variation. Some general trends are apparent. Western Upper Mississippian groups tend to consume more meat than those in the east. Meat consumption is likely at the expense of maize, which trends lower than among their eastern counterparts (roughly 10% of total protein intake). Upper Mississippians consume, on average, slightly more maize than do their Middle Mississippian counterparts. However, this result is misleading and is largely due to the wide range of variation within Middle Mississippian populations. High-status individuals at Middle Mississippian sites show values indicating the least maize consumption (Ambrose, Buikstra, and Krueger 2003) of all samples. In addition, the residents of upland American Bottom sites show values associated with less maize than their low-status lowland counterparts. These lowland-dwelling, low-status Middle Mississippian individuals appear to have consumed more maize than all others sampled. This high maize consumption is largely at the expense of meat and wild plants, which accounts for a very small portion of the diet (<15% of protein for some individuals). The upland residents are not necessarily consuming more meat than the low-status lowland residents; rather, they are likely consuming more wild plants (Hedman, Hargrave, and Ambrose 2002).

SIX

The Koshkonong Diet

When both the macrobotanical and stable isotope data sets are combined, new inferences can be drawn, not just about the nature of the subsistence systems, but the inter- and intragroup dynamics that create and use them. To begin, we should address Brown's (1982) question of what kind of economy the Oneota had. There is a continuum of ideas concerning the nature of Oneota subsistence, with two extremes. For the first, maize was a minor resource and composed a small component of a diverse diet (e.g., Michalik 1982; Overstreet 1976, 1981). This idea was perhaps expressed most clearly by Overstreet.

> I submit that the adaptive pattern is one of intensive exploitation of the diverse resources found throughout the Eastern Ridges and Lowlands of Wisconsin. A heterogeneity of habitat occurs from site to site which in turn reflects a general pattern of adaptation. Based on the faunal and floral materials analyzed for Oneota sites, one can reconstruct a wide variety of resource zones which were utilized to varying degrees.... Oneota adaptation is characterized by a highly diffuse economy. The emergence of Oneota culture is directly linked to the elaboration and intensification of resources in zone 6, the horticultural zone. Through time, horticulture apparently becomes more and more intensive. However, focalization, in terms of Cleland's (1966) economic definition, never takes place. Thus, the model of adaptation for

Eastern Wisconsin Oneota populations is unique in the sense that aside from horticulture, which does intensify during later stages of development, a very broad range of wild flora and fauna continue as part of the exploitative pattern through the terminal stages of the Lake Winnebago Phase, which I would date to circa AD 1500 or later. The model employed here indicates that specificity of procurement such as that manifest in Middle Mississippian cultures or the Classic Plains Oneota cultures with a corn-bison tandem does not develop. The pattern is one of diverse resource utilization throughout the Oneota continuum in Eastern Wisconsin *with the general intensification of corn horticulture added to a mosaic or diffuse economic pattern.* (1981, 494; emphasis added)

Overstreet (1997, 290) later argued for a middle position, where maize was an economic cornerstone that acted as a stabilizing force for an overall mixed horticultural, hunting, and foraging economy (Overstreet 1997, 251). Some have wondered, suggested, or argued that the productivity of maize in the northern climate of Wisconsin, Minnesota, and northern Illinois may have been too marginal for staple-level crops to have been grown (e.g., Michalik 1982; for discussion of various models, see Brown 1982; Hart 1990). Brown (1982, 111–12), accounting for the concerns of population density and maize productivity, argued that "this economy owed as much to native food resources as it did corn agriculture." At the other extreme, authors like Gibbon (1986, 332) have argued "that corn dominated their diet and that the requirements of planting and growing corn were important factors in determining where they built their villages, [though] it is difficult to prove that this was so." Many other authors fall on the continuum between agriculture and horticulturally supplemented foraging.

Most authors seem to agree on one thing, namely, that the economies are locally adapted. Both Overstreet (1981, 1997) and Gibbon (1972a, 1986) argue that the economies in each locality are dependent on an adaptation to localized resources. Hart (1990, 575), using a microeconomic approach, argues that the general subsistence strategy, and particularly the agricultural system, should vary among and within regions. So we must ask, are Oneota diets diverse or focused, are they locally adapted, and are they agricultural or horticultural?

AGRICULTURAL OR HORTICULTURAL DIET?

Maize is found in nearly every context and in every feature. It is the densest and most ubiquitous plant in the macrobotanical assemblage. In addition to maize, the data show squash, beans, and chenopodium were also actively grown. Given the abundance of wild rice, it was likely cultivated as well (see discussion below). Our modern divisions between cultivated and fully domesticated plants probably meant little to the farmers who tended to both types. While the domesticated crops may have been grown over larger areas or may have been more reliant on human propagation and therefore required greater labor investment, both suites of plants would have required sowing, tending, and harvesting (Smith and Cowan 2003). This need for land and labor makes the separation of domesticated and cultivated plants, in this context, unnecessary and arbitrary. Because they were both grown at the same sites (or in the vicinity), they were part of the same subsistence system and more interconnected than they were with wild resources.

The placement of the sites adjacent to and directly on highly arable land also highlights the importance of agriculture for the people in the locality (Edwards 2010). Finally, the isotopic data indicate that both people and dogs at CBHC consumed large amounts of maize. Up to 55% of the protein in their diet came from the tropical plant. As it is a poor source of protein, maize likely accounted for an even greater portion of the overall diet. In the Koshkonong Locality, the two dogs' isotope levels indicate a diet in which 41% to 55% of the protein came from maize. While it is not possible to determine exactly how much maize was eaten relative to all other resources, the $\delta^{15}N$ ranged from 8.1‰ to 9.0‰, which is indicative of a relatively low meat diet. Even if the values are adjusted + 0.5‰ to account for the canine effect (see ch. 3), the CBHC values are still lower than most other Oneota samples. Therefore, it is likely that plants made up the bulk of the diet, and maize likely composed the bulk of the plants.

While the exact proportions of the various resources may be beyond our ability to know, it is possible to use these isotope values and modern nutrition information to generate bounds. According to the U.S. Department of Agriculture (USDA), uncooked maize contains 86 kilocalories (Kcal) and 3.27 grams of protein for every 100g serving (USDA 2017). We know that the diet included many species, including deer, wild rice, numerous types of fish, acorn, and goosefoot. The USDA provides nutritional information for

Table 6.1. Modern nutritional data of four food sources known in the prehistoric Koshkonong diet—all values for servings of 100 grams of raw food (USDA 2017)

	Maize	Wild Rice	Deer	Pike/Walleye	Goosefoot
Energy (Kcal)	86	357	120	93	43
Protein (g)	3.27	14.73	22.96	19.14	4.20

each of these resources (table 6.1). While it is not clear how representative modern varieties are of those used by the residents of the Koshkonong Locality, the USDA values can provide a proxy for model generation.

Using the ratio of calories to protein for each type of food, we can generate multiple models that fit the range of isotope values by adjusting the number of servings for each food type (fig. 6.1; table 6.2). The models were generated to examine several different scenarios, including small amounts of all nonmaize food types (low-diversity model) and high amounts of all nonmaize food types (high-diversity model), as well as a series of models where each individual resource was increased. For example, in the low-diversity model, chenopodium, acorn, fish, and meat are held to just half a serving (50g). Wild rice and maize levels are then adjusted until maize accounts for 41% of protein while maintaining a 2,000 Kcal diet. In this model, maize provides 49% of the calories. The model with the lowest caloric reliance on maize was the one with increased acorn consumption. The model that showed the greatest caloric reliance on maize was the high-meat diet. In this scenario, maize accounted for 67% of the calories and 41% of the protein. A final model was generated to estimate the highest possible caloric reliance on maize. This final model is a modified high-meat diet; it eliminates acorn and reduces meat to one serving each (deer and fish). At the high isotope level (55% of protein); maize accounted for 81% of the diet's calories.

No single model is necessarily correct. The composition of the diet undoubtedly varied among individuals based on age, gender, status, and kin group and membership in other social organizations. Also, the dietary compositions would have varied throughout the year. In the two dog samples maize accounted for 41% to 55% of the overall protein. This is an average over several years. So we can use these models to approximate the long-term significance of maize, likely between 45% and 75% of the overall diet (see

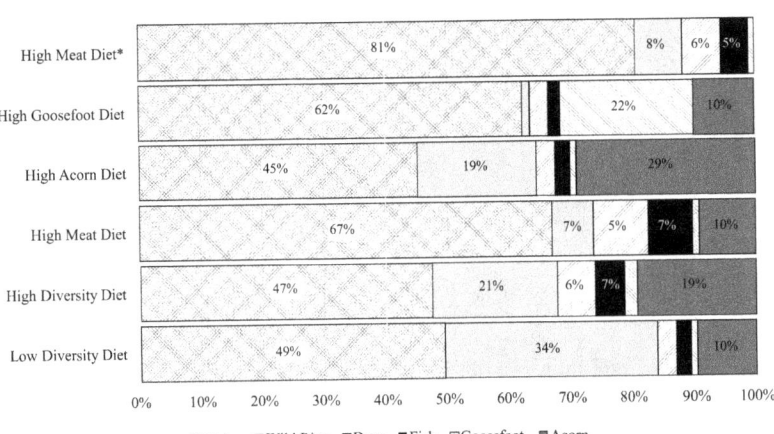

Figure 6.1. Caloric contributions of food sources to modeled diets

table 6.2). Even the low-end estimate indicates a diet primarily reliant on agriculture. If the caloric contributions of maize, wild rice, and chenopodium are totaled, then at minimum 65% of calories would be agricultural. In most models, agricultural reliance ranges between 75% and 93%.

DIVERSIFIED OR FOCUSED DIET?

The next question is whether this level of agricultural reliance should be considered diversified or focused. This question is deceptively complicated, and the answer depends on what part of the diet is examined and how one delineates diverse and focused. To some researchers, a diverse diet is one that includes many different foods. In short, the more taxa in a diet, the more diverse it is. However, as Lyman (2008) points out, the total number of resources (NTAXA) can be misleading. A diet may be dominated by a single source of food, which accounts for most calories, while still including many different taxa with minuscule dietary contributions. Is such a diet diverse? No. Conversely, what if ten taxa are evenly represented, or twenty?

To begin, it is necessary to identify the various resources and their relative significance. At this point, it is clear that maize was easily one of the most important resources, but it is unclear how other plants were used.

Table 6.2. Data from figure 6.1 depicting the total calorie and protein contributions of each food source in the model. Each serving is 100 grams. The column labeled 'P' is protein (measured in grams).

		Maize		Wild Rice		Deer		Fish		Goosefoot		Acorn	
		Kcal	P	Kcal	P	Kcal	P	Kcal	P	Kcal	P	Kcal	P
Amount per serving		86	3.27	357	14.73	120	22.96	93	19.14	43	4.2	387	6.15
low-diversity diet	servings	11.5		1.9		0.5		0.5		0.5		0.5	
	value	989	37.61	689.5	28.45	60	11.48	46.5	9.57	21.5	2.10	193.5	3.08
	% diet	49%	41%	34%	31%	3%	12%	2%	10%	1%	2%	10%	3%
high-diversity diet	servings	13.0		0.7		1.0		1.0		1.0		1.0	
	value	1118	42.5	239	9.89	120	22.96	93	19.14	43	4.20	387	6.15
	% diet	56%	41%	12%	9%	6%	22%	5%	18%	2%	4%	19%	6%
high meat diet	servings	15.5		0.4		1.5		1.5		0.5		0.5	
	value	1333	50.69	132.5	5.47	180	34.44	139.5	28.71	21.5	2.10	193.5	3.08
	% diet	67%	41%	7%	4%	9%	28%	7%	23%	1%	2%	10%	3%
high acorn diet	servings	10.5		1.1		0.5		0.5		0.5		1.5	
	value	903	34.34	388.5	16.03	60	11.48	46.5	9.57	21.5	2.10	580.5	9.23
	% diet	45%	41%	19%	19%	3%	14%	2%	12%	1%	3%	29%	11%
high goosefoot diet	servings	14.5		0.1		0.5		0.05		10		0.5	
	value	1247	57.42	23	15.18	60	11.48	46.5	9.57	430	42.00	193.5	3.08
	% diet	62%	41%	1%	14%	3%	14%	2%	12%	22%	37%	10%	3%
high meat (maize 55% protein) diet	servings	18.75		0.4		1		1		0.5		0	
	value	1612.5	61.31	153.0	6.31	120.0	22.96	93.0	19.14	21.5	2.10	0.0	0.00
	% diet	81%	55%	8%	6%	6%	21%	5%	17%	1%	2%	0%	0%

In addition to maize, wild rice and acorn were both highly ranked resources. Because the recovered nutshell represents waste from food preparation and the wild rice represents accidentally burned grains, it is not possible to determine which plant was the second-ranked resource and which was the third ranked. The diachronic and multivariate analyses show that acorn was intermittently a very important resource during the first two centuries that the sites were occupied. Wild rice was recovered and likely used in consistently high densities but never in the extreme densities of acorn. Sometime after AD 1200, acorn use declined significantly, but it remained an important resource. As acorn use declined, wild rice became more important and likely was the second-ranked resource.

It is not clear how wild rice was integrated into the subsistence system. Historically, many groups actively cultivated the plant (Jenks 1901; Vennum 1988). As its name implies, wild rice is not domesticated, though it is native to Wisconsin (Vennum 1988). Despite its indigeneity and lack of morphological changes, the plant is considered by many researchers to have been cultivated prehistorically (e.g., Arzigian 2000). Using the plausibility argument developed by Asch and Asch Sidell (Asch and Asch Sidell 1982, cited in Smith 1992, 108), a strong argument for its cultivated status can be made. Of the argument's seven parts, wild rice meets six criteria, and only six are applicable: (1) it is economically important (e.g., Arzigian 2000; ch. 4); (2) it is more economically important than in preceding time periods (see Arzigian 2000 and contrast ch. 4 above with Egan-Bruhy 2009; Egan 1993b); (3) it has few to no barriers to being artificially propagated (Jenks 1901; Vennum 1988); (4) there are ethnographic accounts of artificial propagation (Jenks 1901; Vennum 1988); (5) it is found in conjunction with other cultivars; and (6) its use increased prehistorically (see ch. 4 above). The final criterion, increase in population levels and cultural complexity, is not applicable as population levels are unclear, and the relationship between agricultural and cultural complexity is not absolute. Given that wild rice fits all the six applicable criteria, I argue that it should be treated as a cultivated plant.

Goosefoot appears to have been an important plant at CBHC and a consistent but lower-ranked resource at KCV. The botanical record may fail to capture the full importance of the plant, as its greens may have also been eaten, leaving few archaeologically visible traces. Olsen (2003) has shown that *Chenopodium berlandieri*, a southern variety of the plant, was grown at CBCH. It would not have survived without human intervention, so it would have been planted and tended as an agricultural plant.

Several other plants also follow this pattern. Maygrass, amaranth, knotweed, and little barley have all been found at KCV and/or CBHC (Olsen 2003). They are also either non-native to Wisconsin or only some species are native to Wisconsin (Asch and Hart 2004; Smith 1985, 1992). People in the Eastern Woodlands had been cultivating these crops for well over a thousand years (Smith 1992, 103). While the non-native variants were certainly cultivated (Asch and Asch Sidell 1982; Ford 1979), it is unclear where on the wild weed to domesticated continuum the wild varieties (or nondifferentiated seeds) lie (Smith 1992, 104–7). They may have been sown along with their cultivated counterparts. Or it is possible they were uncultivated but exploited in wild or disturbed habitats. In other analyses from CBCH, a small number of sunflower seeds were also recovered (Egan-Bruhy 2014).

Historically, bulrush (*Scirpus validus*), a wetland plant, was cultivated for use as a medicine by the Cherokee (Asch 1994). Seeds of the *Scirpus* genus have been recovered from one context at each site. It is therefore possible that the residents were managing a population of bulrush, though such an argument is tentative at best. Asch (1994) notes that where it was grown it was not intensively cultivated. So even if Koshkonong residents did grow bulrush, it was not likely a major labor investment, nor would it have used much space that could have been dedicated to other crops.

Beyond the cultigens, at least three domesticated species were grown for food: maize, beans, and squash. The presence of squash and beans in low ubiquities likely underrepresents their importance. It is likely that most of the evidence of their use did not preserve (Toll 1988). Furthermore, these agricultural products could help fix nitrogen back into the soils (Gallagher 1992; Hart 2008; Monaghan, Schilling, and Parker 2014; Mt. Pleasant 2010; Thorne 1979). This would have been extremely important given maize's reliance on nitrogen (Gallagher and Sasso 1987; Janick et al. 1974; Monaghan, Schilling, and Parker 2014). In addition, if maize was intercropped with the other two, further benefits could be attained. Maize stalks can act as scaffolds for the beans and as squash leaves spread across the ground, helping to prevent the growth of weeds and reducing labor requirements in midsummer (Gallagher 1992; Harwood 1979; Mt. Pleasant 2010; Mt. Pleasant and Burt 2010).

Quantifying the diversity of remains is a difficult task. Diversity indices can help determine, in a relative sense, how diverse a diet is. They have long been used in both zooarchaeological (Lyman 2008) and paleoethnobotanical studies (Popper 1988). Unfortunately, the data are rarely available in a sufficiently comparable manner to include both data sets in a single index, which in turn leads to another issue: what part of the diet is being examined—flora or fauna or both. Previous zooarchaeological analyses from Koshkonong relied on class-level data and number of identified specimens (NISP) values, so they are not particularly helpful for this scale of analysis (e.g., Hunter 2002). More detailed analyses of Koshkonong samples are currently under way. Preliminary results indicate that the number of faunal species (NTAXA) is large, and deer and fish predominate in the assemblage (R. McTavish, pers. comm.). Therefore, this discussion must focus on the floral portion of the diet. However, the nitrogen isotopes can allow for some additional inferences.

The NTAXA suggests that the diet at the sites is relatively diverse (CBHC = 36; KCV = 33). However, many of the taxa are represented by very few specimens or only a single specimen. Also, because the isotopes suggest that maize, a single taxon, constituted over half of the diet, the NTAXA may not be a good measure. Relative to KCV, CBHC is more diverse on most metrics. The Shannon index (table 6.3) measures both how rich (NTAXA) the assemblage is and how evenly distributed the resources are. However, high diversity values can be a result of reliance on many resources or on a very even distribution of a few resources. In both cases, no one resource dominates the assemblage. The Shannon index for CBHC is 1.89, compared to 1.42 for KCV. While CBHC shows greater diversity, the difference does not appear to be large. However, both are toward the low end of the potential diversity spectrum. In the case of these assemblages, the maximum values were 4.28 and 4.19, respectively. The Koshkonong values are roughly one-third as diverse as the maximum possible diversity score. The low diversity is likely caused by the heavy presence of maize, which dominates the assemblage.

The evenness scores are 0.53 for CBHC and 0.41 for KCV; this supports the maize effect, as CBHC is proportionally less dominated by maize and also shows a more even distribution. The importance of goosefoot at CBHC explains much of this shift. At KCV three plants (maize, acorn, and wild rice) dominate the assemblage. By adding a fourth important plant to the mix, the evenness is increased, thereby reducing the level of focus in the diet. Overall, the Shannon index suggests that the Koshkonong floral assemblage is relatively focused.

Simpson's index supports this assertion. CBHC has an index of 0.22 with an evenness of 4.47. KCV has an index of 0.33 and an evenness of

Table 6.3. Koshkonong Locality diversity indices

Site	NTAXA	H*	E**	Simpson's D	1/D
CBHC	36	1.89	0.53	0.22	3.01
KCV	33	1.42	0.41	0.33	4.47
KCV (excluding F12-26)	31	1.20	0.34	0.40	2.53
Hypothetical focused	2	0.66	0.95	0.53	1.88
Hypothetical diverse	36	0.08	0.02	0.01	71.00

*H= Shannon's index value.
**E= evenness derived from Shannon's index value.

3.01. These values become magnified if F12-26 (an extreme acorn outlier) is removed (D = 0.39, 1/D = 2.52) from the KCV sample. The diversity index indicates that KCV is less diverse and more dominated by maize and acorn. Simpson's index is not necessarily linear, so the fact that the values are closer to 0 (the most diverse possible value) does not necessarily indicate that the diets are not focused. For reference, two hypothetical assemblages were created, based on the CBHC assemblage. A hypothetical focused assemblage modifies the actual CBHC assemblage by removing all but the two most abundant taxa (acorn and maize). This exercise barely raises the Simpson's index to 0.5. A hypothetical diverse sample, with the same NTAXA as CBHC but evenly distributed (equal to the value of maize), would have a Simpson's index score of <0.03. The values from both sites more closely match the focused example. Because it is not possible to statistically compare the values, all that can be said is that the Koshkonong diet appears to be relatively focused but includes several minor resources.

Unfortunately, these indices include only the floral portion of the subsistence assemblages. However, both the $\delta^{13}C$ and the $\delta^{15}N$ values can be used to make inferences about the whole diet. The $\delta^{15}N$ values indicate that meat did not provide a large portion of the diet's protein, and the models (see fig. 6.1) never exceeded 16% of total calories. The $\delta^{13}C$ values indicate that the bulk of the protein came from maize. While the faunal assemblage includes many species, the total contribution was almost certainly less calorically important than maize. The data indicate that the Koshkonong Locality assemblage reflects an agriculturally focused diet. This degree of agricultural reliance and low diversity does not conform to the expectations of most scholars.

SEVEN

Regional Dietary Trends

Given that the Koshkonong diet does not conform to expectations, it is important to determine if the Koshkonong Locality is unique in the Upper Mississippian world, that is, in what ways it is similar and in what ways it is unique. Using the same strategies as those in the Koshkonong analysis (isotopic analysis; paleobotanical measures of density, ubiquity, and diversity), we can contextualize the Koshkonong sites' dietary patterns, including assessment of agricultural reliance, identification of nonagricultural resources, and quantification of dietary diversity. The other Upper Mississippian localities, as well as Late Woodland and Middle Mississippian samples, are discussed in relation to the patterns identified in Koshkonong. An initial examination of the data indicates a modest amount of variation within and among archaeological cultures, though a careful examination reveals several patterns that were not readily visible (tables 7.1–7.5).

UPPER MISSISSIPPIAN COMPARISONS

Upper Mississippian localities show variation across the board. There is no single subsistence strategy that fits all regions. While essentially every locality exhibits relatively high reliance on maize, there appears to be variation in agricultural output and reliance, and each region utilizes a unique suite of domesticated and wild resources to buffer maize. This results in variable isotopes, divergent ubiquity and density levels, and variable diversity indices.

Table 7.1. $\delta^{13}C$ and macrobotanical density data for all localities. Isotopic data are presented as the proportion of protein from C_4 plants. Macrobotanical data presented as count per 10 liters.

Locality	% Maize 2σ Min	% Maize 2σ Max	Density Domesticates Min	Density Domesticates Max	Density Cultigens Min	Density Cultigens Max	Density Nutshell Min	Density Nutshell Max	Density Fruits Min	Density Fruits Max	Density Other Seeds Min	Density Other Seeds Max
Koshkonong	29.14	68.86	13.32	48.61	11.43	14.59	8.86	9.16	0.54	0.66	1.16	1.58
La Crosse	19.09	57.25	1.4	13.21	2.66	45.02	0.56	23.79	0.05	9.17	0.92	2.38
Red Wing	21.56	62.06	84.99		11.83		0.88		0.54		49.81	
Langford	41.71	60.11	4.05	15.00	0.12	0.43	7.71	14.57	0.06	0.15	1.14	3.00
Middle Fox	—		2.81	33.55	0.57	2.9	3.09	331.29	0.20	0.32	0.23	5.16
Door	—		0.00	1.27	0.05	0.06	2.89	9.23	0.18	1.09	0.30	0.45
Fisher	—		78.66		4.81		34.62		7.42		13.7	
Waupaca	—		9.21	46.52	0.47	18.73	4.73	76.15	0.30	1.03	0.47	3.95
Late Woodland	2.67	54.01	0.14	6.36	0.00	0.27	0.27	105.96	0.00	0.62	0.00	0.24
Middle Mississippian	2.86	82.32	47.91	311.89	0.89	64.32	38.24	42.36	0.61	0.67	0.87	10.63

Table 7.2. Diversity indices for all study sites, ordered according to Simpson's index (largest to smallest)

Site Name	Region	Site Type	NTAXA	Shannon H	Shannon e	Simpson's D	Simpson's 1/D
Centra 53/54	Late Woodland	Warm season camp	10	2.01	0.87	0.14	7.31
Burley Brew	Waupaca	Village	18	2.09	0.72	0.15	6.46
Filler	La Crosse	Warm season village	21	2.09	0.69	0.17	5.84
Washington Irving	Langford	Village	24	1.96	0.61	0.20	5.09
CBHC	Koshkonong	Village	36	1.89	0.53	0.22	4.47
Citgo	Door	Cold season camp	9	1.60	0.72	0.24	4.15
Schrage	Middle Fox	Village	17	1.82	0.64	0.24	4.25
OT	La Crosse	Warm season village	17	1.70	0.60	0.31	3.25
Aztalan	Middle Mississippian	Village	17	1.29	0.45	0.31	3.22
KCV	Koshkonong	Village	33	1.42	0.41	0.33	3.01
Zimmerman	Langford	Village	19	1.37	0.46	0.37	2.72
Hoxie Farm	Fisher	Village	41	1.37	0.37	0.41	2.41
Pamperin Park	Door Peninsula	Cold season camp?	11	1.30	0.54	0.42	2.35
Blinded by the Light	Waupaca	Village	25	1.39	0.43	0.43	2.30
Aztalan	Late Woodland	Village	16	1.12	0.40	0.45	2.21
River Quarry	Late Woodland	Winter camp	6	0.90	0.50	0.48	2.04
Bryan	Red Wing	Village	33	0.97	0.28	0.62	1.62
Tremaine	La Crosse	Warm season village	19	1.23	0.41	0.67	1.47
Lundy	Middle Mississippian	Village	26	0.70	0.22	0.71	1.40
Dambrowski	Waupaca	Village	14	0.62	0.24	0.77	1.30
Soggy Oats	Middle Fox	Fall camp	14	0.43	0.16	0.86	1.17
Murphy	Late Woodland	Winter camp	11	0.23	0.10	0.91	1.10

Table 7.3. Ubiquity values of taxa categories for all comparative and study sites

Locality	Site	Domesticates	Cultigens	Nutshell	Fruits	Other	Maize
Koshkonong	KCV	95%	100%	79%	58%	95%	95%
	CBHC	100%	100%	100%	43%	95%	100%
Middle Fox	Soggy Oats	50%	50%	75%	25%	75%	50%
	Schrage	63%	23%	51%	17%	23%	63%
Waupaca	Burley Brew	60%	40%	70%	20%	40%	60%
	Dambrowski	77%	31%	65%	23%	23%	77%
	BBTL	60%	50%	78%	26%	76%	60%
Door	Citgo	0%	14%	71%	14%	29%	0%
	Pamperin Park	19%	4%	67%	52%	33%	19%
Langford	Washington Irving	89%	11%	100%	22%	30%	67%
	Zimmerman	92%	8%	67%	25%	43%	92%
Fisher	Hoxie	74%	71%	42%	32%	71%	72%
Red Wing	Bryan	75%	46%	14%	19%	45%	74%
La Crosse	OT	49%	10%	59%	70%	30%	40%
	Filler	60%	78%	62%	8%	70%	58%
	Tremaine	30%	40%	5%	20%	11%	29%
Late Woodland	Centra 53/54	6%	17%	17%	17%	6%	6%
	Murphy	71%	18%	65%	0%	35%	71%
	River Quarry	91%	0%	91%	9%	0%	91%
Middle Mississippian	Aztalan	83%	50%	83%	67%	50%	83%
	Lundy	92%	31%	76%	20%	24%	92%

Table 7.4. Presence of fruit genera by locality. An "x" indicates the presence of a member of that genera in the locality.

Archaeological Culture	Region	Locality	*Gaylussacia* (huckleberry)	*Crataegus* (hawthorn)	*Celastrus* (staff vine)	*Fragaria* (strawberry)	*Morus* (mulberry)	*Prunus* (cherry)	*Rhus* (sumac)	*Rubus* (raspberry)	*Solanum* (nightshade)	*Vaccinium* (blueberry)	*Cenchrus* (sandbur)	*Vitis* (grape)	*Viburnum* (haw)	Total
Langford		Fox–Des Plaines		x						x	x					3
		Upper Illinois River Valley														0
Oneota		Fisher	x			x				x	x	x				5
	Eastern Wisconsin	Koshkonong	x	x					x	x	x	x				6
		Middle Fox									x				x	2
		Green Bay								x	x			x		3
		Waupaca		x						x	x		x			4
	Western Wisconsin	Red Wing			x	x		x	x		x	x		x		7
		La Crosse	x			x	x	x			x	x		x		7
Late Woodland		Collared									x	x		x		3
		Non-collared									x	x				2
Middle Mississippian		Apple River		x						x	x	x		x		5
		Wisconsin							x	x	x					3
Total			3	4	1	3	1	4	6	6	11	4	1	5	1	

Koshkonong and Northern Illinois

Given its southern location, Koshkonong has long been thought to have had closer connections to Illinois groups than its northern neighbors did (e.g., Gibbon 1972a, 175). Schneider (2015) has noted some evidence of interaction between groups in the two regions; there are a few vessels in Koshkonong with Fisher-like traits but of local manufacture. If there is a stronger connection between the two regions, then it may be expressed in the subsistence data as well.

Langford isotope values suggest that they consumed as much and possibly somewhat more maize than their Koshkonong neighbors. However, with only two dogs sampled from Koshkonong, further research is needed. Also, all the isotopic samples, both human and dog, came from the Upper

Table 7.5. Distribution of nonfruits/domesticates/cultigens organized by taxonomic family. An "x" indicates presence of one or more undifferentiated members of that taxonomic family in the locality, the numbers indicate how many genera have been identified in that locality.

Archaeological Culture	Region	Locality	Amaranthaceae (amaranth)	Apiaceae (parsley)	Asteraceae (aster)	Brassicaceae (mustard)	Betulaceae (birch)	Caryophyllaceae (carnation)	Cyperaceae (sedge)	Euphorbiaceae (spurges)	Fabaceae (legume/pea)	Hydrocharitaceae (water nymph)	Hypoxidaceae (star grass)	Iridaceae (iris)	Lamiaceae (mint)	Myricaceae (sweet gale)	Nelumbonaceae (Indian lotus)	Orobanchaceae (boomrape)	Poaceae (grass)	Polygonaceae (knotweed)	Portulacaceae (purslane)	Rhamnaceae (buckthorn)	Rosaceae (rose)	Rubiaceae (madders)	Solanaceae (nightshade)	Typhaceae (cattail)	Verbenaceae (verbena)	Violaceae (violet)	Total
Langford		Fox–Des Plaines	1		1			1	1		1						1		x					1					8
		IL River Valley	1		1	x			1									1			1	1							7
Oneota	Fisher		1	x	1	x			2		1	1	1		x				2		1		1		x				15
	Eastern Wisconsin	Koshkonong	1		x	x		1	1	x	1	1	1		x				1	1						1		1	13
		Middle Fox			x				1	1	1					1			x	1			x						7
		Green Bay											1						x				x						3
		Wausau	1		x				1				1	1	1				x				x			1		1	10
	Western	Red Wing	1		2				1				1	1					3	1	1						1		10
	Western Wisconsin	La Crosse	1		x				x		x								x		1	1		1					7
Late Woodland	Collared		1			1	1																						4
	Non-collared					x	1									1			x				x	1					4
Middle Mississippian	Apple River							1	1				1						2				1						5
	Wisconsin		1																				1					2
Total			9	1	8	4	2	2	8	2	5	2	4	1	3	1	1	1	10	3	3	1	7	3	1	2	1	2	

Illinois River valley, so this trend may not extend to the other Langford localities. The macrobotanical assemblage at Zimmerman is consistent with a high reliance on domesticated crops (see tables 7.1, 7.3). Maize is ubiquitous, though it occurs in somewhat lower densities than at CBHC. Squash is present in one-third of the samples, more than twice the ubiquity or density of CBHC. The assemblage contains few cultigens, which is consistent with most other Langford sites (Egan 1988; Jeske 1990). Nut densities are also lower than in the Koshkonong Locality. There are no isotopic data from Zimmerman; however, it is close to sites with isotopic data, such as Gentleman Farm and MSQ. Given its proximity and the consistency of the Langford isotope values across four sites (Emerson, Hedman, and Simon 2005; Emerson et al. 2010), Zimmerman occupants likely consumed similar amounts of maize. The diversity values are very close to KCV, indicating that they were roughly as focused on agriculture, but the macrobotanical assemblage indicates that the nonmaize components of the Langford diet were very different. Given the lack of cultigens and the lower nut levels, the high-meat model described for Crescent Bay is likely a good fit with the Upper Illinois River subsistence strategy. The relatively high $\delta^{15}N$ values support this interpretation (μ = 9.69‰). Where Koshkonong groups used cultigens to buffer maize production, Upper Illinois Langford groups appear to have used meat and wild plants.

Like Zimmerman, Irving has a near-absence of cultigens. The site's diversity score is on par with Crescent Bay's. Relative to Koshkonong, nut densities are low. Like the Koshkonong sample, acorn is the densest nut type. Interestingly, acorn is absent at Zimmerman. Squash is present in one-fourth of the samples but at densities on par with CBHC. Maize is present in three-fourths of features, but kernel densities are lower than 1 kernel/10 liters. Densities are not always a faithful reflection of dietary contribution. However, with values this low, the importance of maize must be questioned, at least relative to other Langford sites. It is possible that hinterland groups, living in the Fox River valley, relied on maize to a lesser degree than those in the Illinois River valley. Additional research is required to test this inference. If it is so, Jeske's (1990, 232) assertion that Irving represents a horticultural base camp for a logistically mobile group is supported. Rather than rely heavily on agriculture, the residents may have heavily exploited local resources and expanded their catchment through satellite sites such as Cooke (Jeske 1990, 233).

Unfortunately, there are no published $\delta^{13}C$ isotope values from Fisher populations, so the Langford isotope values may not be representative of all Upper Mississippians in northern Illinois. The Hoxie Farm assemblage contains some of the densest floral deposits of any Upper Mississippian site. Domesticates are present in great densities (78.66 ct./10 liters, exceeded only by the Lundy site) and ubiquities (74%). Unlike their Langford neighbors, cultigens are present in high ubiquities (71%) and densities (34.62 ct./10 liters). Nuts are a common occurrence (42% ubiquity) at a modest density (4.81 ct./10 liters). Even with a single line of evidence, these values indicate a major reliance on agricultural foods. It would be unsurprising if future isotopic data demonstrate a reliance on maize that is similar to or greater than Langford groups. The cultigen assemblage is heavily dominated by goosefoot (85% of cultigen seeds recovered), though it is also supported by moderate levels of erect knotweed. There are one or two seeds of several other taxa but not in sufficient numbers to suggest that they made a serious dietary contribution. The diversity scores are between KCV and Crescent Bay values.

Koshkonong and Western Wisconsin

While the two-sigma range for Koshkonong $\delta^{13}C$ values overlap with La Crosse and Red Wing, Koshkonong averages about 10% higher than La Crosse and roughly 5% higher than Red Wing. Densities of domesticates are higher at both KCV and CBHC than at any of the La Crosse comparative sites. While the Bryan site in the Red Wing Locality has a domesticate density roughly twice that of KCV and roughly six times that of CBHC, the Koshkonong sample has greater ubiquity levels. In Koshkonong domesticate ubiquity (95%–100%) is marginally greater than Bryan (75%) and considerably greater than La Crosse (30%–60%). Taken together, the earlier localities (i.e., Red Wing and Koshkonong) are likely more reliant on domesticates than the La Crosse Locality. Integrating diversity indices and other floral data support this contention.

For example, while Koshkonong sites trend toward the diverse end of the spectrum, they are generally more focused than La Crosse samples. If the outlier feature T316 is excluded from the Tremaine sample, then both Filler and Tremaine diversity indices indicate a less focused diet than at Koshkonong. However, OT has an intermediate diversity, between CBHC and KCV. Each La Crosse floral assemblage is distinct, but the general pattern is of a diet reliant not only on domesticates but also a variable array of EAC plants. So the Koshkonong diet is relatively focused on maize, wild rice, and a small number of other resources, whereas the La Crosse diet relies on a wider variety of domesticated and otherwise cultivated resources. Both diets rely on farming, but Koshkonong is generally more focused on tropical domesticates, and the La Crosse diet relies on a more diverse suite of plants, particularly EAC cultigens.

This data set is a good reminder of the issues of intersite comparisons using macrobotanical remains (e.g., Hastorf and Popper 1988). Given the similarity of the isotope values at the CBHC and Red Wing sites and the large difference in density values, raw density values alone are clearly not good indicators of the relative importance of maize. In addition to issues of preservation and context, the time scale represented by the two lines of evidence must be considered. In most contexts, refuse pits contain trash from a relatively narrow range of time. Therefore, the density values are the result of short-term activities. Furthermore, according to the Schlep effect, the bulk of the pits' context is likely refuse, from activities in proximity to the pit itself. Isotope values, on the other hand, represent years of consumption as it takes many years before bone collagen totally turns over, roughly thirty years in humans (Harkness and Walton 1972; Libby et al. 1964; Stenhouse and Baxter 1977, 1979). For isotope values, the location in which food is eaten is irrelevant. Therefore, in most cases the isotopes are representative of long-term and wide-ranging human actions.

Conversely, an isotopic data point reflects the consumption patterns of a single individual, whereas most refuse pits reflect the consumption patterns of several people, perhaps a household, clan, or other social group. So each data set is simultaneously providing data on both a broader and more constrained set of human activities. Even if there were no issues of preservation or context, we should not expect a direct linear relationship between macrobotanical and isotopic data sets. Ubiquity levels, in this case, did follow the isotope values but did not indicate how different the assemblages were; that is, they provide ordinal-level data only.

Cultigen densities are similar in Koshkonong and Red Wing, though they are much more ubiquitous in Koshkonong samples (table 7.6). In La Crosse, cultigen values are highly diverse. OT and Filler densities are roughly half as high as Koshkonong, but Tremaine densities are three times greater.

Table 7.6. Comparison of cultigens among western Wisconsin and Koshkonong Locality sites: Little barley includes undifferentiated little barley/wild rice and values may overestimate its importance in the Koshkonong Locality.

Site	Measurement	Goosefoot	Sunflower	Wild Rice	Little Barley	Erect Knotweed	Barnyard Grass	May Grass
Bryan	Density (ct./10l)	9.97	1.05	0.30	0.39	0.10	-	-
	Ubiquity	43%	12%	7%	7%	3%	-	-
Tremaine	Density (ct./10l)	-	-	1.41	42.83	0.66	0.06	-
	Ubiquity	-	-	9%	33%	7%	3%	-
Filler	Density (ct./10l)	11.04	-	13.20	-	0.24	2.04	-
	Ubiquity	56%	-	52%	-	8%	16%	-
OT	Density (ct./10l)	2.32	-	2.85	0.18	-	0.06	0.06
	Ubiquity	6%	-	3%	3%	-	3%	1%
CBHC	Density (ct./10l)	3.85	-	9.13	0.09	0.04	0.01	-
	Ubiquity	76%	-	86%	19%	15%	5%	-
KCV	Density (ct./10l)	0.74	-	7.88	0.53	0.04	-	0.02
	Ubiquity	63%	-	89%	37%	5%	-	5%

Ubiquity levels are also variable, ranging from 10% to 78%, and the variation in ubiquity does not correspond with the density levels. In the Koshkonong Locality, wild rice dominates the cultigens, with modest levels of goosefoot at CBHC. All other cultigens appear to be minor inclusions. For Red Wing, goosefoot stands out with high densities and modest ubiquity values. Other cultigens have a minimal presence in the Bryan site's assemblage.

Despite the physical proximity of the La Crosse sites, there is a considerable amount of variation within the macrobotanical assemblages. The isotope values reflect some diversity in the diet, with $\delta^{13}C$ values ranging from -16.4‰ to -11.6‰ (23%–55% protein from maize). However, even the lowest values indicate a heavy reliance on maize. If the high-goosefoot model, discussed in the previous chapter for CBHC, is adjusted for La Crosse values we can estimate the role of maize in the western sites. When the high chenopodium model is set so that 23% of the protein is derived from maize, then maize would provide 35% of the calories. With this model, goosefoot would account for another 22% of the calories. If the goosefoot was actively cultivated, then these two alone would account for more than half the caloric intake. Filler also includes beans, squash, and several cultigens. So even if the residents relied on maize to a lesser extent than did the residents at CBHC, it does not necessarily mean that they relied on agriculture to a lesser extent. Rather, the La Crosse agricultural system appears to be more diverse, and either it included a wider suite of plants or at least the other taxa accounted for a larger proportion of the diet.

It is important to remember that the landscape in the La Crosse and Koshkonong Localities are very different. The settlement patterns are also very different while still highlighting the economic centrality of farming. Koshkonong is situated in the formerly glaciated portion of the state, while La Crosse is in the Driftless Area (Martin 1965). According to Sasso (1993, 327), "At the core of the [La Crosse] Oneota subsistence was the cultivation of maize, beans, squash in specially prepared fields or agricultural plots located in fertile bottomland soils, and in perhaps, sandy locations atop terraces." Several ridged agricultural sites have been identified in the La Crosse valley and surrounding region but represent only one aspect of a multitiered settlement system (Sasso 1989, 1993). Extending the agricultural potential model developed for Koshkonong (Edwards 2010), most of the arable lands were restricted to the bottomlands, and most of the terrace soils are excessively drained and do not hold sufficient water. Arable land in La Crosse is considerably rarer than in Koshkonong.

Sasso's (1989, 1993) settlement system model includes three types of relevant sites. Major villages were placed on terraces overlooking but with immediate access to the bottomland soils. Satellite hamlets were placed in analogous settings that allowed the interconnected communities to expand their access to arable land. And agricultural sites are most commonly ridged fields, which improved soil arability and harvest reliability (Gallagher 1992; Gallagher and Sasso 1987; Riley and Freimuth 1979; Sasso 2003b; Sasso and Brown 1987).

In Koshkonong, sites could be easily placed with access to arable land in diverse edaphic settings. If all the Koshkonong sites were concurrently occupied, then the network of villages would have magnified the amount and diversity of accessible arable soils. To accomplish this level of access in La Crosse, populations were distributed over a wider area and several sites and site types; that is, La Crosse inhabitants lived in villages and hamlets, spread across a much wider area than in the Koshkonong Locality. In both localities, fields were significantly modified to increase arability, and in some cases, ridged fields may have been constructed. While paleobotanical and isotopic measures of agricultural reliance may have varied between the localities, one of the major goals of site placement remained the same: to ensure access to significant amounts of arable land in a variety of settings. The relationship between major villages and arable land is similar in La Crosse and Red Wing. There was also a network of habitation sites that linked back to major villages such as Diamond Bluff and Bryan, though it is not clear if they functioned in fashion similar to the La Crosse hamlets (Fleming 2009).

Koshkonong and Eastern Wisconsin

There are no isotopic data for most localities in eastern Wisconsin. Therefore, the macrobotanical remains are more useful for understanding the role of agriculture in this region. The same issues of density and ubiquity discussed for the La Crosse comparison exist here, but without isotopic data from all localities, it is not possible to similarly counteract the issues.

As in western Wisconsin, there is a considerable amount of variation both within and between localities. The Door Peninsula–Green Bay region sites of the Wolf River Tradition appear to be the least focused on agriculture. One of the two sites has no domesticates, and the other has the lowest density of domesticates of any of the comparative Oneota sites. Both sites have the lowest densities of cultigens. Domesticates at CBHC are more than ten times greater. Because at least one of the sites has been definitively interpreted as a winter camp and the second is possibly a winter-only encampment, it is tempting to attribute the low density to seasonality. However, maize is highly storable, as are many cultigens. It does not seem logical to invest significant amounts of labor in agriculture and then not eat the food in any measurable quantity when it is cold outside. While nutshell density is modest, the levels are not sufficiently high to suggest that either site was a nut processing camp. The site reports do not suggest any special function for the sites, so it is unlikely that the dietary indicators are due to a restricted set of actions occurring on site.

Ubiquity levels of cultivated plants are also very low. At Pamperin Park, fewer than one in five features contained any domesticates, and fewer than one in twenty contain cultigens. Only one erect knotweed seed was found in a single context at Citgo. For these two sites, there is little data to suggest that cultivated plants were consumed to the same degree as in other localities.

However, diversity values at Green Bay sites generally indicate a somewhat more focused diet than that at Koshkonong, although an examination of the resources used indicates that it is not necessarily an agriculturally focused diet, so it is important to determine what is causing this low diversity score. Together, the sites indicate the use of three types of fruits and three types of other seeds. Koshkonong sites include the use of six types of fruit and thirteen other seeds. The narrow diet breadth contributes significantly to the low diversity indices and is likely affected greatly by the length of occupation and the range of activities that occurred on site. Because the data sets are not fully comparable, it is difficult to compare the diets of the Koshkonong and Door Peninsula Localities. To quantify how similar or different the localities are would require the inclusion of sufficient sites to represent the entire year. Despite this problem, the current comparison is informative. This analysis serves to highlight the differences in the overall subsistence settlement strategies used in the two regions. The focus in Koshkonong was on a small number of concentrated, long-term, year-round habitations, whereas people in and around the Door Peninsula seem to be more focused on mobility, using more sites across a wider range of territory (cf. Bruhy 2015).

In the Middle Fox Passage, domesticates and cultigens are more plentiful than in Green Bay. Among the Middle Fox Passage sites, domesticates are present in more than half the features and cultigens are present in a quarter of the features. Densities are also much higher in the Middle Fox than in Green Bay, but both the densities and the ubiquities are lower than either Crescent Bay or KCV.

While the macrobotanical remains at Schrage do not match those in the Koshkonong Locality, the region contains some of the most extensive sets of raised agricultural fields known (Peske 1966; Sasso 2001, 2003b). With the tremendous investment of labor required to create the ridged fields, it is hard to imagine a scenario in which agriculture was not a major component of the locality's diet. Furthermore, numerous hoes have been recovered from sites in the region. The number and distribution of the hoes underscores the importance of the agricultural pursuits (Sasso 2014). The ubiquity levels are also comparable or greater than at La Crosse sites, where maize contributed as much as 55% of the protein in the diet. It should be noted that the majority of agricultural sites in the Middle Fox are on the west side of Lake Winnebago, opposite Schrage (Sasso 2001, 2003b). The Schrage site is also relatively early (Schneider and Richards 2010). The agricultural sites are poorly dated, and the Middle Fox contains a late Oneota occupation (see Overstreet 1997). While there may have been some temporal or geographic variation within the locality, agriculture contributions were likely on par or greater in the Middle Fox than in La Crosse.

In the Waupaca Locality, domesticate and cultigen ubiquities are on par if not greater than at the Schrage site. Densities are also greater than at Schrage and are generally on par with the Koshkonong Locality. The cupule-to-kernel ratios at the sites are sufficiently different; Hamilton and colleagues (2010, 260) have suggested that agricultural fields were placed differently at the two sites. At BBTL, the ratio suggests that much of the maize processing occurred on site, and very little occurred at the Dambrowski site. Despite being farther from agricultural fields and showing little evidence of maize processing, Dambrowski has a higher ubiquity (76% vs. 60%) and density (41.8 vs. 10.4 ct./10 liters) of maize than BBTL. Squash is also important at all three sites.

Cultigens account for a very small portion of the Dambrowski assemblage, but goosefoot, barnyard grass, and erect knotweed are present in modest densities at Burley Brew and BBTL. Agriculture provided a significant amount of food to the residents' diet, though the agricultural system appears to be very different from that of the Koshkonong or Middle Fox Locality.

In sum, each locality seems to have had a different system of agricultural production. Koshkonong groups utilized fields in the immediate vicinity of their habitations, and available evidence suggests that they rarely created ridged fields. Processing occurred on site, and agricultural plants were recovered in great densities and ubiquities. Isotope values confirm that maize was a major component of the diet in the region. In the Waupaca and Middle Fox Localities, agriculture was also of great importance, though apparently there was no need to grow and process all the crops near the main villages.

In the Green Bay region, the comparative sites show little evidence that agriculture or even horticulture was a major aspect of the diet. Densities and ubiquities were very low, and access to arable land was likewise low. If only one variable was low, it would be insufficient to infer that agriculture was less important. However, all three lines of evidence point to that conclusion. This inference needs to be confirmed through analysis of larger villages in the region.

Not only did the method of farming vary, but so did the types of supplemental plants. While the Waupaca and Middle Fox sites do have wild rice, it is in small quantities that are not comparable to Koshkonong. Furthermore, these other sites seem to rely on other cultigens, such as barnyard grass, to a greater degree than Koshkonong. The one uniting cultigen is goosefoot. Only this plant is significantly present in all three localities.

CROSS-CULTURAL DIVERSITY COMPARISON

Koshkonong and Late Woodland

As Late Woodland groups are generally thought to be less reliant on agriculture, all things being equal, Late Woodland sites are expected to have the greatest floral diversity and the lowest maize levels and $\delta^{13}C$ levels but higher $\delta^{15}N$ values. However, questions of site function, seasonality, and group mobility complicate these simple expectations. Furthermore, collared and non-collared ware sites should have distinct floral assemblages. The comparative sample includes both types of Late Woodland sites. Three of the sites (pre–Middle Mississippian Aztalan, River Quarry, and Murphy) are collared ware sites, and Centra is a non-collared ware site. Given that non-collared-ware-producing populations are thought to have been more mobile and even less reliant on agriculture, if at all (Salkin 1986, 2000; Stevenson et al. 1997; Stoltman 2000), a foraging population should have even higher diversity indices, lower densities and ubiquities of maize and other cultivated resources, and isotope levels consistent with low to no maize and higher meat consumption (e.g., Winterhalder and Goland 1997).

However, the sites are not all directly comparable to each other or to the Oneota sites. With the exception of Aztalan, the two collared ware sites are interpreted as winter encampments, and the non-collared ware site is a summer camp. Given the seasonal differences, it is likely that the projected diversity differences should be magnified. The reduced availability of foods in the winter would lead to a less diverse diet relative to warm season sites where more wild foods are readily available.

Among Late Woodland sites, the diversity values fit expectations. Murphy has the highest diversity score, whereas Centra and River Quarry have the lowest. Aztalan, a year-round village, has slightly higher diversity scores than the winter camps. However, the scores are low for different reasons. The winter camps have low diversity because they have few taxa. Aztalan has many taxa, as we would expect from a site occupied in all seasons, but has low diversity because it is highly focused (i.e., uneven), with hickory making up more than 60% of the assemblage. Even though the Aztalan indices are derived from Picard (2013, 143), my values vary slightly. To make the results consistent with my other diversity indices, I discounted fungus (a nonfood taxa) and taxa not identified to at least family (i.e., unidentified [UNID] nutshell) and merged the tentatively identified taxa (cf.) with the securely identified taxa so that the NTAXA score was not artificially inflated.

The other macrobotanical and isotopic data from Madison ware–producing sites conform well to expectations. Centra contains a single maize kernel and only four cultigen seeds. The isotope values from Nitschke indicate very low maize intake (<3% of protein). Taken together, these data suggest that cultivated resources were relatively unimportant, which is consistent with the idea that these groups were relatively mobile and relied heavily on foraging (Stevenson et al. 1997). This non-collared ware pattern is decidedly distinct from the Koshkonong and general Upper Mississippian agricultural pattern.

The data from collared ware sites are somewhat less clear, as no single pattern can be identified. River Quarry and Murphy are both winter encampments, and both are collared ware sites. However, they show two very different patterns. At River Quarry, macrobotanicals are congruent with a maize- and nut-focused diet. Maize and nutshell are each present in 91% of contexts. Nutshell densities are more than 50% higher at River Quarry than at KCV. Maize is present in a modest density of 5.57 kernel fragments per 10 liters. While much lower than even CBHC, this density is higher than that at many Oneota sites, including La Crosse, where maize accounted for at least 20% of the protein. Both nuts and maize are easily stored, so it is logical to find them in a winter camp. There are few other taxa present but no cultigens, and there is a single fruit seed. Agricultural crops accounted for roughly half the assemblage and likely constituted a large portion of the residents' winter diet.

The Murphy macrobotanical assemblage is dominated by acorn, which accounts for 95% of the assemblage by count, is present in more than 60% of contexts, and has a density greater than 100 shell fragments per 10 liters. Maize is also present; alone, it would appear to have a significant presence (72% ubiquity, 4.46 ct./10 liters). But relative to acorn, maize is easily missed as a minor resource. Unlike River Quarry, the site has several cultigens (3 taxa, 18% ubiquity, 0.24 ct./10 liters). However, they appear unimportant in the assemblage relative to the amount of acorn.

The two sites have distinct subsistence signatures. The River Quarry diet consisted almost entirely of maize and nuts in relatively equal proportions. The bulk of the nuts were hickory, and no acorns were present. At Murphy, residents had small amounts of cultigens, modest amounts of maize, and massive quantities of acorn. As at the Koshkonong sites, Murphy residents appear to have turned to acorn as a buffer food. At both sites, maize likely contributed substantial calories to the diet, though the proportion is not currently known.

As a multiseason site, the Aztalan assemblage is most comparable to the Koshkonong sites. Like River Quarry, hickory was the most important nut resource, and it outnumbered maize by nearly two and a half times. Goosefoot was also an important resource and accounted for most of the cultivars in the exclusively Late Woodland component. Barnyard grass was also present. These plants indicate a strong reliance on agriculture, supplemented with foraging for nuts and other resources.

Even before the arrival of Middle Mississippians, agriculture was an important resource at Aztalan. The dogs sampled from Aztalan are all potentially from pre–Middle Mississippian contexts, though at least two are likely from the early portion of the joint occupation of the site. They indicate that maize provided between a quarter and a third of the dietary protein. The $\delta^{15}N$ values also indicate that meat consumption was relatively low (8.2‰–9.2‰). Even adjusting for the 0.5‰ dog-human differences noted in Langford samples (Edwards, Jeske, and Coltrain 2017), the values indicate relatively low meat consumption. Using the model developed for Koshkonong (see fig. 7.2), a low-meat diet should still reflect a modest caloric input from maize, which likely provided more than 25% of the calories for most if not all individuals.

Koshkonong and Middle Mississippian

Middle Mississippian diets are regularly thought of as primarily focused on maize, both within the American Bottom (e.g., Griffin 1967) and beyond (Goldstein and Freeman 1997). Isotopic studies have shown this to be true for many Middle Mississippian site residents, whose diets were composed of more than 50% maize (Emerson, Hedman, and Simon 2005; Hedman, Hargrave, and Ambrose 2002). The combined Middle Mississippian and Late Woodland component at Aztalan generally fits this trend. The diversity index is in the middle of the Oneota range, where we know from isotope values that maize was a significant part of the diet. Somewhat unexpectedly, the diversity score is higher than for the Late Woodland component. The evenness score and an examination of the data indicate that the relative high diversity is from a reduced focus on hickory. Hickory's proportional importance drops by 50%, from first to third place. The proportional importance of maize increases by roughly 25%, though it remains in second place. Finally, goosefoot jumps from obscurity to first place, accounting for nearly 40% of the assemblage. The end result is that the Middle Mississippian assemblage is dominated by three taxa with relatively equal representation (maize, chenopodium, hickory), whereas the Late Woodland assemblage is strongly dominated by just two taxa (maize and hickory). Furthermore, while the Middle Mississippian NTAXA may be larger by one, most species present are agricultural domesticates or cultivars. The higher diversity score indicates greater agricultural diversity and a diet more focused on cultivated foods.

Unsurprisingly, the Lundy site is one of the least diverse assemblages. The only sites with lower diversity indices are seasonal or special-purpose camps (Murphy and Soggy Oats) and the Oneota village site of Dambrowski. Both Dambrowski and Lundy have modest NTAXA (14 and 26, respectively) but are dominated by a single taxon, maize. Maize occurs in more than 85% of the assemblages at both sites. Furthermore, at Lundy and Dambrowski, nutshell accounts for roughly 10% of the assemblage, and cultigens make up the bulk of the rest. Excluding nuts, wild resources are only minor components of the assemblages.

All categories of plants, including both domesticates and cultigens, were highly ubiquitous. Domesticate densities at Aztalan are on par with KCV, while densities of both nutshell (47.91 ct./10 liters) and cultigens (64.32 ct./10 liters) were several times denser than at either Koshkonong site. It therefore appears that agriculture was likely just as if not more important at Aztalan as at Koshkonong, though less focused on maize. Given the relatively homogeneous environmental setting at Aztalan (Picard 2013) and the population's clear perception of a threat (e.g., defensive wall, evidence of violent deaths), it is not surprising that the residents would concentrate on aggregated and manageable resources that could be procured near the settlement (Barrett 1933; Goldstein and Freeman 1997; Goldstein and Richards 1991; Richards 1992; Rudolph 2009).

On many counts, the Lundy assemblage resembles the Aztalan assemblage. Domesticates (92% ubiquity, 311.89 ct./10 liters) and nutshell (76% ubiquity, 42.36 ct./10 liters) dominate. Unlike Aztalan, cultigens are only a minor component (31% ubiquity, <1 ct./10 liters), though small numbers of several cultivated taxa have been identified. The high ubiquity and extreme density of domesticates and Middle Mississippian isotope values at the site suggest maize was of great importance. However, essentially all the available isotope values are from sites much farther south. It is not clear how similar we should expect the diets in these two regions to be. However, Emerson, Millhouse, and Schroeder (2007) argue that the diet at Lundy is comparable to the Middle Mississippian diet in the Central Illinois River valley. And Buikstra, Rose, and Milner (1994) provide the mean $\delta^{13}C$ values from Dickson Mounds. The overall mean from 32 samples is -11.36‰, which is 57% of the protein in the diet. There are no standard deviations or other summary data provided, so the expected range of variation is unknown. However, given the variation in both Upper and Middle Mississippian populations, it seems likely that a significant portion of the population likely consumed maize far in excess of 57% of their protein intake.

To provide some context, the overall American Bottom mean of maize provided by protein is 44%. The means of four American Bottom site samples were close to the Dickson Mounds mean (52%–60%). The 95% confidence intervals for maize contributions ranged from 31% to 77% of protein. It is possible that the Dickson Mounds values had a much smaller standard deviation, but we do not have that information. Therefore, we can only make the tentative inference that maize provided as much as 71% of the protein.

There are also several human isotope values from Aztalan that are thought to date to this time period. However, the only ones from secure contexts come from mounds and are thought to represent high-status individuals (Bender, Baerreis, and Steventon 1981). Therefore, we should not expect them to be representative of the general population.

If the dietary contribution model generated for Koshkonong is modified, we provide some potential caloric bounds for maize. By removing wild rice, changing raw acorn to dried hickory (no raw values were provided by the USDA [2017]), and using deer as the proxy for meat, the model should roughly approximate the Lundy and Aztalan diets. Hickory acts as the filler variable (like wild rice in the Koshkonong example); its values are automatically adjusted to ensure a 2,000 Kcal diet. Goosefoot and venison are kept stable, and maize values are adjusted until the protein levels fit the data. Those eating a low-meat diet would likely be eating more maize, so this diet will be calibrated to achieve 71% of protein. This requires 17.5 servings of maize (75% of calories) and 0.6 serving of hickory. The individuals with high-meat diets were likely eating less maize. Therefore, the high-meat diet (2 servings of venison, 1 of goosefoot), when calibrated for maize providing 31% of protein, requires 9.25 servings of maize (40% of calories) and 1.4 servings of hickory. All other likely combinations resulted in caloric contributions between these two extremes. Overall, maize likely contributed 40% to 75% of the caloric intake for most of the population.

In summary, elements of Middle Mississippian populations may have relied on agriculture to a greater degree than did Langford and Wisconsin Oneota populations. Hickory was a common buffer resource for Middle Mississippian groups and even in small quantities could have provided a considerable number of calories. The importance of cultivars in the agricultural system varies among sites. However, at both sites, Middle Mississippian populations appear to be largely focused on terrestrial plant resources. Wild rice, while present, was insignificant to these people. Population size may explain the greater Middle Mississippian emphasis on agricultural production. If the populations were much larger at Aztalan or Lundy relative to Koshkonong, then the agricultural system would need to be intensified.

VARIATION OF LOW-RANKED FLORAL RESOURCES

Each of the localities and archaeological cultures seems to rely on a different but often overlapping suite of natural resources. The composition of fruit and seed assemblages vary, both by site and by region. Some fruits are quite ubiquitous and present in many localities (see table 7.4). For example, nightshade (*Solanum* sp.) is present in eleven localities. The two Langford sites are the only ones in this study that do not have any nightshade. Contrary to popular belief, not all varieties of nightshade are poisonous. For example, tomatoes (*Solanum lycoperiscum*) are in the nightshade genus.

Other fruits, like staff vine (*Celastrus* sp.) or mulberry (*Morus* sp.), are present in only a single locality (Red Wing and La Crosse, respectively). The number of fruits present in a locality's assemblage varies as well. The Zimmerman assemblage was devoid of fruits; however, their absence is likely the result of a sampling issue. Emerson and colleagues (2005, 88) argue that "the record for fleshy fruits is relatively robust." Late Woodland sites, both collared and non-collared ware, are otherwise at the low end of the spectrum, with only two (*Rubus* sp. and *Solanum* sp.). For Centra, this may be due to the small number of features available for analysis. The Middle Fox Locality also only has two fruit taxa (*Solanum* sp. and *Viburnum* sp.). Western Wisconsin sites appear to be the most diverse, with 7 genera in each locality, followed closely by Koshkonong (6) and both Fisher and Apple River (5).

Many of the fruit-bearing plants are naturally ubiquitous throughout the region, so environmental differences are not likely a major factor. Furthermore, there is considerable geographic overlap between some of the groups (e.g., Koshkonong and Aztalan or Langford and Fisher), but they used a different suite of fruits. Koshkonong groups used all three genera that their Aztalan contemporaries used but also included modest amounts of hawthorn (*Crataegus*) and raspberries (*Rubus*). Raspberries grow wild throughout the region, thrive along the forest edge, and were consumed by the Late Woodland residents prior to the arrival of their southern neighbors. There is no environmental reason that these berries would have been excluded from the Middle Mississippian diet. Perhaps it was a cultural idiosyncrasy or deforestation that drove the plant beyond the typical catchment.

The remaining wild specimens are divided across 28 taxonomic families and 41 genera. Table 7.5 shows the distribution of these other seeds bearing plants across families. An x indicates that at least one seed of that family was identified but not to genus. Numbers indicate the number of identified genera in the assemblage. The table shows that there is a great deal of diversity among localities; however, most families are represented by no more than one or two seeds per site. The grass family (*Poaceae*) is the second most abundant family and has the most ubiquitous natural distribution. This family is large and diverse, though its genera are often difficult to distinguish (Deloit 1970; Martin and Barkley 1961; Montgomery 1977). A total of six genera have been identified among the comparative sites, though 78% of the seeds were only identified to family. These seeds are most common in La Crosse, Red Wing, and Fisher contexts, possibly due in part to their location in the Prairie Peninsula. However, for the two Langford sites discussed here, *Poaceae* seeds were not plentiful, though given the site placement and geographic overlap of Langford and Fisher groups (Jeske 1989, 1990), the opposite pattern is expected.

Some other taxa of note are water nymph (*Najas* sp.) in the Koshkonong Locality, yellow star grass (*Hypoxis* sp.) found in several localities, and amaranths (*Amaranthus* sp.) in Red Wing. Members of the amaranth family are relatively ubiquitous in the sample. However, more than half the seeds were identified at the Bryan site. If this trend is present in other Red Wing sites, the substantial use of amaranth may be a local trait (sensu Egan-Bruhy 2014). Yellow star grass is present in several localities but is only common at Fisher and Waupaca Locality sites. Like amaranth, the use of this ubiquitous plant seems to represent a localized strategy. Water nymph was the most abundant seed in this "other seed" category, though every seed was from Koshkonong sites (primarily KCV). Most of these small seeds were clustered in the bottom of F12-01 and F12-06. It is not clear what use this plant had, but it is present in densities too great to be incidental inclusions. Rather than food, it is possible that the seeds represent the remains of a pit lining (Egan-Bruhy, pers. comm.). The large number of these seeds in Koshkonong and the total absence elsewhere is puzzling.

The single pattern that emerges is fruits and other seeds from wild plants are far less numerous than their agricultural, horticultural, or nut counterparts. While taphonomic and use or consumption patterns (e.g., whether a seed is generally exposed to fire during cooking) may play a role, they do not fully explain the significantly low densities and ubiquities of these seeds. Many species likely represent additions to the diet; others may have served nonsubsistence functions. Given how maize focused many of the diets are, these seeds that represent foods, particularly the fruits, likely served as seasonal sources of flavor and variety in an otherwise homogeneous diet. Which flavors, and in what proportions, varied among groups. Environmental differences played a role in plant availability. However, the range of environmental variation does not perfectly track with the dietary diversity (e.g., *Poaceae* between Langford and Fisher or Aztalan and Koshkonong differences). Local cultural preferences appear to have played a role in determining which plants were chosen for exploitation.

MULTIVARIATE ANALYSES OF LATE PREHISTORIC DIETS

The analyses above provide useful information about the similarities and differences among Koshkonong and other Late Prehistoric diets, but each examines only a small part of the overall picture. To understand the larger picture, a principal components analysis that included each of the sites was implemented. Like the Koshkonong-only PCA, variables included the density of each floral category. In addition, because sites rather than contexts were objects, it is also possible to include ubiquity values of each floral category as variables. The overall model explains 94% of the variation. The first three components, which provide the most useful information, explain 79% of the variation. By varying the combination of components depicted together, variation within and among localities can be highlighted, which allows for better identification of important trends in the data set.

The first principal component (38% of variation) does not provide a great deal of analytical clarity (fig. 7.1). Broadly, the first principal component separates those that have dense deposits (positive values) from assemblages that are less dense (negative values). It weights domesticates, cultigens, and nutshell relatively evenly, so those assemblages with high densities

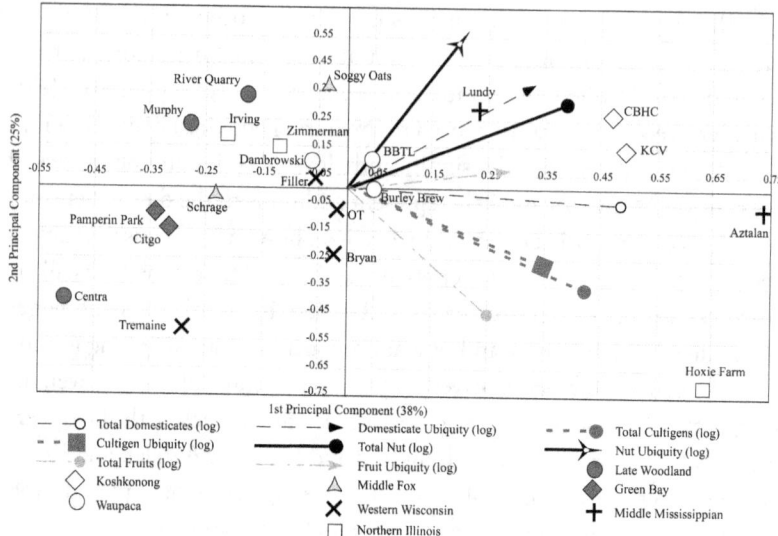

Figure 7.1. Principal components analysis: Interregional analysis, first and second principal components

of all three are ranked highest (e.g., Aztalan) while those that are high primarily in one (e.g., Lundy) still receive a relatively high rank but are shifted left in figure 7.1. Those with few materials overall (e.g., Centra) have highly negative scores. It is notable that most sites cluster with other sites in their locality. Despite the variation, the first component demonstrates that there are broadly shared patterns within each locality. Clear Upper Mississippian exceptions are Soggy Oats (a seasonal camp) and Tremaine.

The collared ware sites also cluster together, and the non-collared Centra stands separately. This result aligns well with the patterns noted in the univariate analysis and fits well with expectations. That is, these culturally distinct groups have demonstrably distinct subsistence patterns (Clauter 2010, 2012; Rosebrough 2010; Salkin 1987, 2000; Stoltman 2000). While these differences in density explain over a third of the data set's variation, the other components help to explain the differences with greater clarity. The second (25% of variation) and third (16% of variation) principal components are analytically more useful as they provide more nuanced indications of how the assemblages are different (fig. 7.2). Issues of equifinality require that the graphed values be interpreted carefully with the actual data on hand. Technically, the second principal component sep-

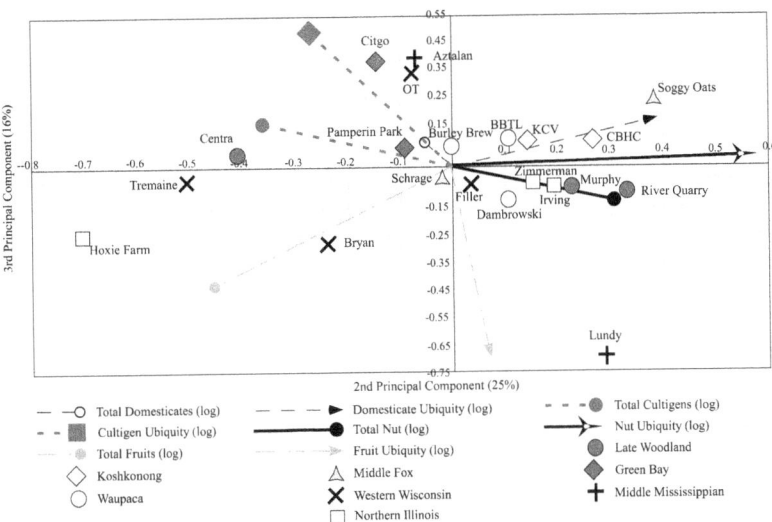

Figure 7.2. Principal components analysis: Interregional analysis, second and third principal components

arates sites with both high nutshell values (both density and ubiquity) and ubiquitous domesticates from those that have relatively high fruit densities and high cultigen values (both density and ubiquity). However, because maize is common in most samples, differences in nutshell and cultigen values dominate the overall structure of the axis. In other words, unless maize ubiquities are extremely low, maize plays little role in determining a site's position. Negative values indicate that cultigens and/or fruits outnumber nutshell. The Green Bay sites are the two exceptions; their very low domesticate ubiquities (0%–19%) pull them to the left side of figure 7.2, despite their proportionally high nutshell ubiquity.

The third principal component (fig. 7.2, y-axis) largely separates sites with higher fruit ubiquities from those with higher cultigen ubiquities, though cultigen and fruit density also play a large part. So sites where fruits are more ubiquitous tend to have negative scores (e.g., Langford sites). Sites where cultigens are more ubiquitous tend to have positive scores (e.g., Koshkonong). However, sites with very high cultigen densities but typical fruit densities can get pulled upward (e.g., Aztalan) and sites with high levels of both (e.g., Hoxie Farm) get pulled toward the center. In rare cases (i.e., Bryan), assemblages with extremely low nutshell ubiquities can be pulled downward. One important thing to consider here is that the domesticate density loading is low on both the second and third principal components. Put simply, the domesticate density is related to the overall density of an assemblage (i.e., when overall macrobotanicals are dense, domesticates are also dense). Beyond this, domesticate density offers little information about the nature of variation among Late Prehistoric subsistence trends.

Eastern Wisconsin Localities

In figure 7.2, most of the eastern Oneota sites are generally graphed near one another and apart from La Crosse sites. Oneota villages from the same locality tend to group together. Generally, eastern Wisconsin sites appear on the right side of the graph and follow the general patterns described above. Except for Green Bay sites, eastern sites all have a strong pull to the right side due to their propensity for maize and nutshell. Koshkonong sites have higher cultigen ubiquity than nutshell, but the combined ubiquity of nutshell and maize as well as the higher density of nutshell pull them well to the right of the origin. The high cultigen values keep the Koshkonong sites in the first quadrant. The modest fruit levels do little to affect the score. While maize is important in all Oneota localities (apart from Green Bay), Koshkonong stands out because of its high density and ubiquity of both nutshell and cultigens. However, as noted above, it is not likely that both were high at the same time. The high nutshell densities are largely from a handful of contexts that may represent times of scarcity, perhaps during the first half of the region's occupation. Most of the high cultigen density features are from the second half of the occupation. So Koshkonong is unique in that it uses both buffering techniques, though not at the same time.

Langford sites are similarly pulled to the right; however, the lack of cultigens at Langford sites also pulls them into the fourth quadrant. Langford sites stand out because of their lack of cultigens and, to a lesser degree, their modestly high nutshell ubiquities.

The Waupaca sites are all slightly left of the Koshkonong and Langford sites, though for slightly different reasons. BBTL and Burley Brew have relatively more nutshells than cultigens, pulling them to the right, but their low domesticate ubiquities (60%) pull them to the left. Dambrowski has a significantly lower nutshell density, but the nutshell and domesticate ubiquity relative to cultigen density or ubiquity helps pull it to the right.

Burley Brew is also pulled back to the left because it has a relatively high density of fruit seeds (third highest overall). The Waupaca sites group together because they represent variants on the same theme. They rely on both nutshell and cultigens, though the proportional emphasis is on nutshell. However, this does not necessarily mean that nut meats provided more food than cultigens; these scores are just relative to other sites.

The Middle Fox sites are poorly grouped, with Schrage on the far lower left side of the eastern Wisconsin group and Soggy Oats on the upper right. However, this pattern is not unexpected given the functional differences between the two sites. As a seasonal camp, the assemblage represents two things, food being brought to the site (likely domesticates) and food being processed (nutshell). This pulls the Soggy Oats site to the far right, and while cultigens may not have been plentiful in the assemblage, they outpace fruits, pulling it upward. Like Burley Brew and BBTL, Schrage has relatively low domesticate densities, though it is modestly ubiquitous. Schrage does not have as many nutshell fragments to pull it back to the right. Its cultigens are also quite low, which keeps the site near the origin on both axes. The general pattern noted for Schrage is generally like that seen for Burley Brew.

While technically in eastern Wisconsin, the Green Bay sites do not fit the pattern expressed by the other eastern groups. This can be seen graphically. These sites distinguish themselves with their high nutshell relative to everything else. Despite the high nutshell levels, their low to absent maize pulls them far to the left. The even ubiquity of cultigens and fruits at Pamperin Park keeps its y-axis score raised. So despite the relative proximity of Burley Brew and Pamperin Park to other eastern Oneota localities, both Green Bay sites represent a unique subsistence system, one where nutshell outrepresents all other taxa, domesticates included. These northern groups also stand out from their southern neighbors on many other levels, notably ceramics (i.e., the high proportion of grit-tempered Mero vessels) (Mason 1966; Overstreet 1997, 2010).

Hoxie Farm, the last eastern site, is at the opposite end of the x-axis. Despite the high ubiquity of domesticates, the cultigen levels are high, and the nutshell levels are low. The fruit density is also high (roughly five times greater than the second highest), which has a strong leftward pull. The Hoxie Farm occupants then used the opposite buffering strategy from that of Langford groups. Langford groups used nuts and not cultigens, with low densities of fruit seeds. The Fisher example has a high density of fruits and cultigens, with a high cultigen ubiquity as well.

The principal components analysis reinforces that despite the shared reliance on maize among most eastern Oneota groups, each locality developed a distinct and locally unique subsistence pattern. Furthermore, long-noted differences in ceramic traditions (e.g., Fisher vs. Langford, Mero vs. the rest of Wisconsin) correspond to differences in subsistence practices. Overall, nuts mark an important resource, one that appears increasingly important in the north. Conversely, maize values generally decrease with latitude.

Western Wisconsin Localities

Turning to western Wisconsin, the Bryan position and subsistence strategy appear similar to Koshkonong and many eastern localities. Like Hoxie, it has very high domesticate levels, but the cultigen levels are significantly higher than the nutshell, so it is pulled significantly to the left. Because the density of domesticates has little effect, the abnormally high maize densities do not pull Bryan or Hoxie toward the eastern sites. However, the modest fruit densities are much lower (7%) than at Hoxie, so it has a middle position between the Waupaca and Fisher sites. Like Fisher, Hoxie values represent a diet in which cultigens are relied on to a great degree and nut meats are only a minor resource.

The La Crosse sites are highly scattered. Filler groups closely with the eastern sites, particularly Schrage. Both sites have similar domesticate ubiquities, and both sites have greater nutshell densities than cultigen densities. However, cultigens at Filler appear to have been more important. OT represents a different pattern; domesticate ubiquity is low (<50%), cultigen density is high but ubiquity is low, and nutshell density and ubiquity is high. Tremaine has low maize ubiquities, which pulls the site far to the left. Its high density of cultigens and low nutshell density pulls it even farther left. The relatively high ratio of fruit ubiquity to cultigen ubiquity brings the y-axis value to near zero. So Tremaine is a site with little maize and even less nutshell. Cultigens appear to be the most important resource, but cultigen values are not as high as might be expected given the low values of everything else.

It is not clear why there is so much variability among western Wisconsin sites. It may be due to temporal shifts, sampling bias, or some other issue.

However, it should be noted that PCA highlighted the generally lower levels of maize among La Crosse sites, which is consistent with the isotopic data. It also highlights the relative importance of cultigens compared to nuts. This finding is consistent with Gallagher and Arzigian's (1994) assertion that La Crosse groups practiced a risk management strategy of intensification through diversification. Their agricultural strategy included a wider and more balanced array of plants. Also of note, despite their proximity, the La Crosse and Red Wing subsistence strategies are considerably different. The Red Wing subsistence strategy has more in common with groups much farther to the east than with their neighbors to the south.

Cross-Cultural Comparisons

Middle Mississippian sites do not cluster together. The PCA suggests that they are at opposite ends of a spectrum of high domesticate utilization. Both Aztalan and Lundy have high densities and ubiquities of domesticates and nutshell. However, Lundy's is a maize-focused subsistence system, with nutshell as a backup. Cultigens and fruits are rarely used (31% and 20% ubiquities, respectively) and are not used in large densities. While the density of fruit seeds is not high, the proportion of fruit seeds to cultigens is much greater than other sites, which is what places Lundy so low on the y-axis. Cultigens are proportionally so unimportant that even fruit seeds have comparable levels. However, at Aztalan, cultigens are fairly common (50% ubiquity) and present in higher densities than at any other site. So while both Middle Mississippian groups focused on maize-centered agriculture, those at Aztalan heavily exploited cultigens and nutshell to bolster their food supplies. Those at Lundy ate relatively large amounts of nuts but seem to have largely bypassed the cultigens.

The two collared ware Late Woodland sites group closely with the eastern Oneota and Langford village sites. The close grouping is largely a product of high nutshell and maize levels coupled with low cultigen levels. In short, the eastern Upper Mississippian diet is very similar to the winter Late Woodland diet. Centra is significantly farther away from the other Late Woodland sites on the far left side of the graph. The first principal component highlighted that it has far fewer materials than all the other sites. However, the first and second principal components indicate that the composition of the assemblage is also different. Like the Green Bay sites, the leftward position of Centra is largely due to the low domesticate ubiquity, but it is pushed even farther left because of the low nutshell levels and proportionally large fruit levels. However, the equal fruit and cultigen ubiquity help to moderate its y-axis score. The non-collared ware diet is truly diverse and unfocused. It is easily distinguished by its low levels of domesticates and relatively even levels of everything else.

TYING IT ALL TOGETHER

Without reservation, Koshkonong, Middle Mississippian, Fisher, and Langford sites should all be described as participating in agricultural economies. Based on the floral data, Lundy should be described simply as agricultural, without any modifiers. However, given the isotopic data from other Middle Mississippian sites, it is likely that there were substantial variations within the population. Elites likely had a diet heavily supplemented with meat and possibly cultigens or wild plants. The lowest-ranked members of society likely had a diet consisting of nearly all maize (see Ambrose, Buikstra, and Krueger 2003). Those with intermediate status likely consumed a greater variety of foods than the lowest-ranked members of society but still had a maize-focused diet. Because the Apple River valley had lower population densities than the American Bottom, it is likely that nuts and other wild plants were more widely available to more people than in the American Bottom proper.

Aztalan likely also had a great deal of diversity dependent on one's position in the social hierarchy. However, the high representation of both cultigens and nutshell suggests that overall there was greater diversity in the diet. Maize still constituted the bulk of the caloric intake, but various cultigens and hickory nuts were used as important secondary resources. The importance of meat at the site is not clear, but given the hierarchical nature of the site's social structure status and meat consumption were likely linked. Overall, the Aztalan diet looks to have been a diversified agricultural diet.

Koshkonong, Langford, and Fisher groups all appear to have been highly reliant on agriculture, and maize likely contributed similar proportions of the diet (inferred for Fisher because there are no isotopic data). However, each group supplemented its diet in unique ways. Early on, Koshkonong groups relied on a mixed support system. Cultigens, namely, chenopodium and wild rice, were regularly used as supplements. Acorn was also regularly used; typically, it was recovered in low densities and intermittently it was used in mass. The $\delta^{15}N$ levels indicate that these resources were used at the expense of meat in the diet. Meat likely composed only 5% to 10% of the calories consumed. Samples from later contexts show that acorn use decreased as wild rice use increased. It is not known if meat use changed over time. This later subsistence system should be described as cultigen supported.

Langford groups seem to have avoided the use of cultigens (Egan 1988; Jeske 1990), and based on the $\delta^{15}N$ levels, likely supplemented the maize-based diet with hunting and/or fishing. Both Zimmerman and Washington Irving also suggest that nuts were an important dietary supplement. Domesticate densities at Irving suggest that agriculture may have been less important in the northern Langford hinterlands, though more data are needed before this inference can be made with any confidence.

At Hoxie Farm, the high densities and ubiquities of both cultigens and domesticates suggest that the diet was heavily reliant on maize and substantially supplemented with cultigens. Nut meat provided a tertiary resource. Broadly, this subsistence strategy most closely resembles the late Koshkonong subsistence system, though the nature of the nondomesticate cultivation would have been substantially different. Koshkonong residents relied heavily on wild rice, a plant grown separately from other cultivated plants. Hoxie residents relied on a variety of cultivars, goosefoot most substantially, but erect knotweed was also a commonly used resource. It is not known if Hoxie is representative of other Fisher sites, but as the only one in this sample Fisher sites should tentatively be described as maize agricultural, supplemented with cultigens.

The Red Wing Locality appears to follow a similar pattern as Hoxie and late Koshkonong. Relative to Hoxie, Bryan has similar levels of domesticates, far less nuts, and moderately less cultigens. The $\delta^{15}N$ values indicate that meat was of greater importance than in Koshkonong but less than for Langford groups. The $\delta^{13}C$ levels indicate maize use was either on par with Koshkonong or slightly lower. Regardless, maize was clearly a major component of the diet and the Red Wing subsistence system was clearly centered on maize agriculture, supplemented with cultigens and hunting.

There is no isotopic data for the Middle Fox, Waupaca, and Green Bay Localities, so inferences are somewhat more tentative. Maize was clearly important in both the Waupaca and Middle Fox Localities. However, nuts also appear to have contributed significantly to the diet. Dambrowski is an exception: the diet there appears to be more mixed agriculture/foraging. Given the difficulties of comparing densities and ubiquities across sites, without isotopic data it is difficult to determine the relative importance of nuts and maize.

Since Soggy Oats is a nut processing camp, it is not considered representative of the general subsistence patterns in the Middle Fox. Given the regularity with which maize has been found without flotation (e.g., Gibbon 1969, 1971, 1972b; Overstreet 1976, 1981) and the large numbers of ridged fields in the region (e.g., Peske 1966; Sasso 2003a), it is difficult to not consider the subsistence system in the Middle Fox as maize agricultural. Based on Schrage, it was heavily supplemented with nuts. Given the importance of this region to Oneota groups and its long occupation span, additional macrobotanical research is needed. Furthermore, isotopic data are badly needed to contextualize any such future work so that the subsistence patterns can be described with greater confidence and supporting data. Until then, it will be unclear how important maize was relative to Koshkonong or other localities.

The Dambrowski site suggests that the Waupaca Locality subsistence system should be described as maize agricultural, supplemented primarily with nuts and small amounts of cultigens. Burley Brew and BBTL appear to be less focused on maize and with a more mixed strategy. However, given the interpretation of Schrage and Dambrowski, the Waupaca system should likely be interpreted as maize agricultural heavily supplemented with nuts.

The Green Bay sites appear to be less reliant on maize. Even with the difficulties of comparing assemblages across sites, it is difficult to envision the residents at Citgo or Pamperin Park growing maize to the same degree as noted for Middle Fox or Koshkonong groups given the results of this analysis. While it is possible that these sites are not representative of the locality, many other authors have posited that these northeastern groups were less reliant on maize. Overstreet (1997, 260) notes that maize kernels are often "lacking from Mero Complex sites." Given the long-standing contention that maize was less important in this region, there are no data to suggest that these sites are atypical of the Green Bay region.

The La Crosse assemblage is more difficult to interpret. Its macrobotanical assemblage exhibits greater variation than eastern assemblages, though the available isotopic data suggest relative uniformity. Perhaps future research that incorporates other La Crosse area sites will shed light on this issue. For now, what we can say is that $\delta^{13}C$ values indicate similar if slightly lower reliance on maize at La Crosse than at Koshkonong. The small samples make this inference tentative. The $\delta^{15}N$ values suggest that hunting and fishing were more important at La Crosse than at Koshkonong and likely approached the levels seen in Langford samples. The placement of sites relative to arable land and the construction of ridged fields emphasize the importance of agriculture (e.g., Gallagher and Arzigian 1994; Sasso 1989, 1993), even where the macrobotanical remains may not. The macrobotanical assemblage suggests that maize was heavily supplemented with cultigens and nut meats, supporting Gallagher and Arzigian's (1994) contention that La Crosse agriculture was intensified through diversification.

Both the isotopic and macrobotanical data support the common assertion that non-collared ware sites in eastern Wisconsin were primarily reliant on foraging, whereas collared ware sites were more sedentary and practiced either maize horticulture or agriculture (e.g., Salkin 2000; Stevenson et al. 1997; Stoltman 2000). Interpretations of these sites are hampered by their seasonality variability and the lack of isotopic data. However, the information at hand suggests a considerable reliance on maize, perhaps rivaling some Oneota groups. In winter, maize was heavily supplemented with nuts. Based on the pre-Mississippian assemblage at Aztalan and other sites not considered here (Picard 2013), a variety of cultigens were also used throughout the year.

EIGHT

Understanding the Implications of Agriculture

Identifying agricultural reliance is only a first step. It is more important to understand the implications of an agricultural economy for the people. At a very basic level, the chosen subsistence strategies require certain investments of time, energy, and organization of persons to be successful. It is through this understanding that it is possible to connect the material of the archaeological record to past systems of labor investment and social organization (e.g., Fowler 1983; Hastorf 1993). Because we know that agricultural crops were fundamental components of the diet, we can infer that the needs and the labor requirements to ensure successful harvests were likely a major consideration when deciding how to schedule tasks and organize labor parties. To estimate the timing of labor requirements, a firm understanding of the nature and type of the agricultural system is required.

AGRICULTURAL LABOR AND TIMING

Gallagher and Arzigian (1994) argue that the labor investments, or in their words "agricultural inputs," can be broken down into seven parts: construction of agricultural technology (e.g., digging sticks), field clearance, field construction, cultivation, soil improvement, harvest, and storage. The nature of the work and the labor requirements would depend heavily on the type of field system used. Referring to prehistoric British agricultural practices, Fowler (1983, 107) defined an agricultural system as delineated areas used regularly in a patterned way and with individual farmed plots as fields. If we use this as a working definition, the term "agricultural system" refers to all fields within the Koshkonong area and the ways in which the land there was regularly modified and used. Historically, Native American agricultural systems were typically described as using corn hills placed in and around villages, typically no more than a few miles away (for a summary, see Gallagher 1992; Sasso 2003b). A second type of raised field has been reported in archaeological contexts, particularly in Wisconsin and Michigan. The raised garden bed, or ridged field as it is also known, has been thoroughly described (e.g., Gallagher 1992; Gallagher and Sasso 1987; Sasso 2003a, 2003b; Peske 1966). It is unclear which type or types of agricultural fields were used in the Koshkonong Locality.

Raised Fields in the Koshkonong Locality

There are several agricultural sites reported within the Koshkonong Locality (table 8.1). Most are corn hills thought to be associated with the historic Ho Chunk village at Crab Apple Point. Two are raised garden beds and are of unknown association. They are often thought to be associated with the Oneota occupation of the region, though there is little data that can be used to address the issue. Both raised beds and corn hills may have been used in the Koshkonong Locality. It is possible that each of the villages had a series of raised garden beds; however, this may not have been necessary given the higher proportions of good-rated arable land and higher elevations near KCV and CBHC. Therefore, we must look to other, less direct indicators to infer the field types used at study sites.

Tilling Technology. Oneota agriculture is often associated with scapula hoe technology, particularly hoes made of bison scapulae (Gibbon 1972a; Michalik 1982; Overstreet 1981, 1997; Peske 1966; Sasso 2014; Tiffany 1979). Peske (1966) goes as far as to argue that the furrows between garden beds at the Eulrich site near Lake Winnebago were made with a scapula. He is not the only person to associate hoes with raised garden bed agriculture. However, not all Upper Mississippian societies in the region are associated with hoe technology. Jeske (1989) contrasted Oneota (Fisher and Huber)

Table 8.1. List of agricultural sites in the Koshkonong Locality

Site Name	Site Number	Site Type	Association	Reference
Crab Apple Point	47JE0093	Corn hills	Historic Ho-Chunk	Stout and Skavlem 1908
Bingham Corn Hills	47JE1158	Corn hills	Historic Ho-Chunk	Stout and Skavlem 1908
Saunders Corn Hills	47DA1201	Corn hills	Historic Ho-Chunk	Stout and Skavlem 1908
Messemer Garden Beds	47JE0092	Raised beds	Unknown	Brown 1909; Stout and Skavlem 1908
Loge Bay Cornfields	47JE0087	Raised beds	Unknown	Stout and Skavlem 1908

with Langford sites in northern Illinois. He notes that Oneota sites were generally found in lower elevations, where adjacent arable land would be wetter and where hoe technology would be most useful. He notes that hoes were common on Oneota sites. In contrast, Langford sites are found in upland settings, with drier soils, and are associated with digging sticks instead of hoes. He argues that Fisher and Langford groups utilized distinct agricultural systems and that the Langford groups probably only created corn hills in the upland settings.

Excavations at CBCH and KCV have not recovered a single artifact identifiable as a hoe, not shell, stone, or scapula. However, numerous digging sticks have been recovered from both sites, made from antler and bison horn (Edwards 2016). Given that KCV and CBHC are in an upland setting analogous to Langford and have digging sticks, the fields immediately near the sites likely included corn hills rather than garden beds. While the residents of the Koshkonong Locality may have constructed other types of raised fields, upland agriculture using corn hills seems to be the most likely field type in the immediate vicinity of the study sites.

Field Clearance

Ethnographic accounts provide the best means of approximating the agricultural labor investments. For example, the accounts of Maxi'diwiac (Buffalo Bird Woman), a Hidatsa woman, provide some of the most detailed descriptions of Native American agricultural practices (Wilson 1917). For the Hidatsa, the process began with burning the area. Maxi'diwiac says it helped make soils easy to till. Burning offered many other benefits, among them, increasing nutrient content (Fritz 2000; Gallagher and Arzigian 1994; Wagner 2003). Burning was widely recorded in the ethnohistorical record and sometimes occurred in a large radius around an entire village. It has been argued that this practice goes back as far as the Archaic, as it can also help manage plant communities and consequently animal populations (Wagner 2003).

Despite the lack of direct evidence, we can safely infer that burning took place in the Koshkonong Locality. Dorney and Dorney (1989) argue that the presence of oak savannahs like those reported in the Koshkonong Locality by the General Land Office surveyors (Brink 1835; Burnham 1836; Miller 1833) are a result of regular burning by Native American populations (see also Bowles, Jones, and McBride 2003; Gleason 1913; McLain and Elzinga 1994). This alone suggests that burning on a large scale was practiced. It is not clear how far back in time the practice would have extended, perhaps five thousand years (Griffin 1994; Nuzzo 1994). The fact that the Koshkonong groups were practicing agriculture would require them to manage the forests so that they could plant their gardens. Without iron axes, fire would be the only efficient way to clear trees. This also would have created a more attractive habitat for deer. Finally, fallowing and burning would be an ideal means of replenishing the soils' nutrients (Fritz 2000; Gallagher and Arzigian 1994).

Field Construction, Cultivation, and Maintenance

Once fields were cleared, either corn hills or garden beds would need to be constructed. Among the Hidatsa, the initial construction was separate from sowing, but in subsequent years hill maintenance occurred concurrently with sowing or weeding (Wilson 1917). While Maxi'diwiac and others of her generation used iron hoes, her grandmother would build corn hills with a digging stick. Maxi'diwiac said that this was the traditional practice. While we cannot claim that these accounts are a direct analogy to Koshkonong practices, given the similarity in technology and the available arable land near the sites, the general patterns are likely similar. This may be especially true for corn hills, given Gallagher's (1992) argument that the construction and use of corn hills was quite consistent throughout much of the eastern United States.

Ethnographic evidence indicates that planting occurred between April and June in northern latitudes (e.g., Doolittle 2002; Wilson 1917). Maxi'diwiac's account suggests that it could take roughly 250 to 350 person-hours to plant the maize in a single field. Other crops would likely take less time, as they were not planted in the same abundance. The number and size of fields varied among families. For Oneota groups without iron earth-breaking implements, the process would be slower than reported. This number may be further underestimated if the Koshkonong groups attempted to grow larger surpluses. While the Hidatsa grew maize sufficient to feed the population for one year, and to seed for two (Wilson 1917), other historic groups, such as the Huron, grew enough food for two to four years (Hurt 1987, 34). Larger surpluses would necessitate larger fields and more labor. Without population estimates, estimates of total area cultivated at a given time, and experimental data concerning the efficiency of digging sticks, it is not prudent to estimate precisely the amount of time spent preparing fields and planting. However, we can infer that women likely spent the bulk of their day from April through June planting the various crops. Men may have helped clear the fields in March or April, though they had likely turned their attention to nonagricultural pursuits during cultivation (Doolittle 2002; Hurt 1987; Wilson 1917).

Garden Maintenance

Once planting was done, maintenance of the fields would be necessary. In their description of input number 5: soil improvement, Gallagher and Arzigian (1994) argue that additional steps to improve the fertility of the soil were often taken. They cite the addition of charcoal and other cultural material (presumably some of which was nutrient-rich) to the soils to increase fertility at Sand Lake. Peske (1966) notes a similar pattern for raised ridges near Lake Winnebago. At what point in the year this material would have been added is unclear, but doing so could help decrease the frequency of field rotation.

Gallagher and Arzigian (1994) also cite the need to protect crops from competition and predators. Ethnographically and ethnohistorically, protection from competing weeds was largely accomplished by weeding with hoes or digging sticks. Often, this resulted in the mounding of dirt around the plants, so even if corn hills were not constructed prior to planting, they would often exist by the end of the growing season. Mounding also helped to support the weight of the growing maize stalks, which had short roots and could easily be blown or knocked over (Doolittle 2000; Hurt 1987; Wilson 1917). Birds were apparently one of the most significant animal threats. To protect the crops from animals, groups across the Eastern Woodlands and into the Plains built platforms where women and girls would sit and look after the fields (Doolittle 2000).

Harvesting and Processing

For the Hidatsa, preparation for harvest would need to begin in early August. By the middle of the month, squash would start to ripen and would continue ripening for some time. Shortly thereafter, an early harvest of green corn could commence. Later in the fall, ripe corn would be harvested. Beans ripened shortly after, and finally sunflowers would be harvested (Wilson 1917). The exact techniques used to dry, thresh, and winnow the crops varied among groups, but these processes were invariably labor-intensive (Wilson 1917). An important benefit of tropical domesticates (e.g., maize or beans) is that they were more easily harvested than EAC plants (Smith and Cowan 2003). By emphasizing domesticates, a significant amount of time is freed for other activities, such as foraging for berries and nuts or harvesting wild rice. However, little is known about the means of growing most EAC cultigens (Mueller et al. 2017).

Storage

The amount of food surplus varied, both by group and by circumstance, but ethnographic and ethnohistorical accounts place it between one and four years of surplus (Hurt 1978, 34; Wilson 1917). The process of filling the pits would not have been particularly time-consuming, though the process of digging the pits would have been labor-intensive. At KCV, roughly one-third of pits are regularly more than a meter deep and a meter or more wide (Edwards 2014a; Edwards and Spott 2012). Pits at CBHC are often of equal diameter, and many extend to similar depths, particularly when erosional patterns from modern agricultural practices are taken into consideration (Moss 2010). Houses at both sites are surrounded by pit features; in some cases they appear to be within structures, in other cases just outside. A palimpsest effect complicates the identification of relationships between pits and houses. The sites were occupied for four centuries, so pits and houses were often built and rebuilt in the same area, and even overlap. In some cases, features that are physically within a few meters of one another are on the opposite end of the temporal occupation span (e.g., KCV F12-01 and 12-06). Regardless, the number and size of features makes it clear that a considerable amount of food was stored at the site.

SEASONALITY OF LABOR INVESTMENT

Given the importance of agricultural resources, agricultural work would have accounted for a large amount of labor. Based on ethnographic and ethnohistorical accounts, this labor would have been conducted largely by women of the Koshkonong Locality and would have consumed much of their time from spring into fall. Particularly during planting and harvest, this would have left little time for other activities, though this work was hardly the only responsibility of the women of the village. Given the numerous competing time constraints, careful planning would have been essential at certain times of the year. Looking at the needs of the plants grown in the locality, we can make several inferences about the seasonal scheduling of labor, or at least an important aspect of women's labor and some aspects of men's labor.

Winter–Early Spring

Few indicators of cold season occupation exist, but several are present at both KCV and CBHC. The presence of buds indicates that firewood was gathered and burned during the late winter or the early spring. While lumber may have been stockpiled in the warmer months, at least some wood was collected year-round. Firewood collection was the most labor-intensive cold season activity indicated by the paleoethnobotanical assemblages. The gathering of firewood, from an unknown distance, across what was likely a snow-covered landscape would have required greater time and energy expenditures than in warmer months. Archaeologically, it is impossible to determine who would have been responsible for gathering the firewood, but at least some ethnographic accounts describe the task falling to women, sometimes with the help of dogs (Morey 2010, 92; Schwartz 1997, 51).

Until spring, there would be few to no wild plants available for harvest, and most fallen berries or nuts that may have been missed by wildlife would have been covered by snow (Arzigian 1993; Jochim 1976; Keene 1981). Therefore, during the winter months, any plants consumed would have been stored foods, and most labor requirements during the winter would have been related to meal preparation. During this time, it is possible that some of the agricultural implements were constructed or repaired. Because stored food would likely compose much of the diet, time that would otherwise be spent procuring the foods could be spent on other activities. If so, ensuring that equipment, needed in the spring, was built or repaired would appear to be an efficient use of time. Given that deer antlers are at their largest between fall and late winter and that deer are among the few available large fauna in winter, fall- and winter-hunted deer would produce antlers for use as digging sticks (Indiana Department of Natural Resources 2017). Deer and elk shed their antlers naturally in late winter, and these can be found on the ground in February and March. Antler tools have been found in abundance at KCV and CBHC (Edwards 2014a; Edwards and Spott 2012; Van de Pas, McTavish, and Klemmer 2015). However, it is not possible to determine when maintenance of such tools occurred with the available archaeological data (fig. 8.1).

As the snow and ice melted and spring began, most wild plant foods would still be unavailable. Aquatic tubers are among the few plants that are available in spring, edible, and archaeologically visible. They could have been collected to replenish diminishing food stocks or provide variety to the meal, or some combination thereof. Several features at both KCV and CBHC have aquatic tubers. Foraging parties would have been organized from these villages, to at least in part search for these early spring foods.

Late Spring–Summer

While some plants bear fruits in the spring, most of the plants identified in the assemblages are not available until late summer or fall. However, chenopodium and purslane produce copious edible leaves, and aquatic tubers are available as soon as the ice melts on water. Though in less quantities than in winter, firewood would have undoubtedly been needed. Even if it was not necessary for warmth, firewood would have been required for cooking.

Late summer is a time when many different types of fruits would start to ripen. This includes many tree- and bush-based berries, including rasp-

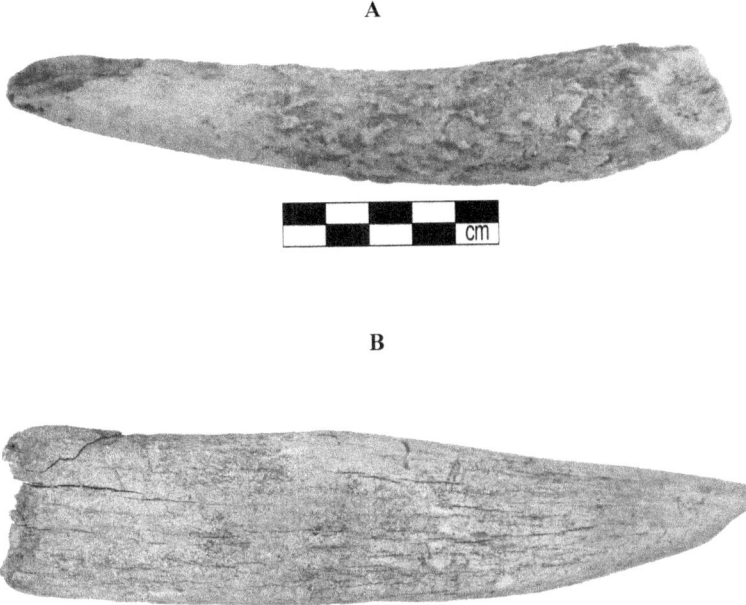

Figure 8.1. Digging sticks produced from faunal elements—A, Antler; B, Bison horn—identified by R. McTavish. Photo used with permission of the University of Wisconsin–Milwaukee Archaeological Research Laboratory, Program in Midwestern Archaeology.

berries, cherries, hawthorn, and strawberries in late spring through fall. The assemblage from both sites shows that these plants were consumed with some regularity (5%–35% ubiquity per taxon but 40%–60% ubiquity overall) but in relatively small quantities (<1 fruit seed per 10 liters of sediment). The ubiquity of the seeds suggests that they may have been systematically harvested. If so, then the most logical time to do so would be late summer, between the green corn harvest and the primary harvest of the other crops. The low densities are likely due to the mode of consumption and preparation. Wild fruits and berries can be eaten raw, which would limit the number entering the archaeological record. By harvesting the berries early, not only is labor conflict reduced, but it also limits the time for birds or other competitors to raid the patches. It is not possible to precisely determine the time of harvest; however, this is a logical explanation, and it better fits the archeological data. If fruits and berries were only harvested opportunistically, the ubiquities would likely be much lower. This is not to say that additional berries were not opportunistically harvested while collecting firewood or other resources when they were available. In fact, the wide availability of the fruits in the disturbed areas around the settlements would have made them ideal snacks while coming to or going from the villages.

Late Summer–Fall

Harvesting and processing the crops would have consumed a significant amount of time during the fall; however, we can see in the paleoethnobotanical assemblages that other activities occurred as well. Wild rice was collected in mass quantities and would have required significant amounts of labor to process for use and storage, including parching, threshing, and winnowing (Jenks 1901; Vennum 1988).

Numerous wild fruits that ripen in fall have also been identified. Like fruits and berries, nuts begin to ripen toward the end of summer and well into fall. Of the four genera in the assemblage, hazelnut ripens first in August and goes into September. Acorn is the next most available in September to October. Hickory and walnut are the latest to ripen, in October. The high ubiquity of nuts (100% at CBHC and 84% at KCV) indicates that nuts were an important resource; however, their importance varied by genera and site. At CBHC, density and ubiquity measures indicate acorn and hickory were the most important resource. At KCV, walnut and acorn were important, whereas hickory and hazelnut were quite unimportant.

While most of the contexts had at least some nuts, the distribution is decidedly clustered in a few contexts. The mean density of nuts was greater than 30 fragments per 10 liters, while the median density is roughly one-fifth. It is possible that these dense concentrations are simply remnants of processing or burning for fuel. However, nut meats are rare. If the nuts were collected for use as fuel, then the nut meats should have been burned with the shells. The lack of nut meats indicates that the nuts were processed and the edible portions removed prior to burning. Most of the contexts do not appear to be processing deposits. The contexts with the densest concentrations (KCV F12-26, CBHC F06-63B) do not look much different, in profile (morphology, soil color, texture, etc.) or otherwise, from similar contexts. During excavation, F12-26 did not stand out from other features, and there is no indication that the materials in the pit are from a primary context. Both F12-26 and F06-63B appear to be tertiary contexts like most of the others. The floral remains within then should be an aggregation of the waste from all the activities near the features and should reflect numerous activities. The high density of nutshell in these contexts may be the result of processing, but the nutshell is expected to be mixed in with the general food waste. However, these contexts have low densities of most other floral remains. They have among the lowest densities of maize, cultigens, and fruits. Essentially, the only plant of significance in these contexts is acorn. So if these contexts do not represent the use of nuts solely as fuel and they do not represent simply processing contexts, then what do they represent? I suggest that they are the result of acorns serving as a buffer or starvation resource. During times when other resources were scarce, nut use rises. The PCA highlights this finding (see ch. 4): the first principal component shows that nutshell is negatively correlated with all other values. When other food resources are scarce, the use of nutshell increases. This pattern is particularly strong in the early contexts where nutshell concentrations are most dense.

Implications of Seasonality

A better understanding of the timing and distribution of labor resources can provide the groundwork when trying to understand the gendered social dynamics both within and among Upper Mississippian societies. Benn (1995, 115) argues that "women almost certainly dominated the horticultural production process with their labor and knowledge, [but] we need to know about the relative importance of the total contribution by women to the subsistence base to develop assumptions about their social influence." Perhaps when connected with an updated analysis of houses (e.g., Hollinger and Benn 1995) and households (e.g., O'Gorman 2010) and sufficiently robust mortuary data, this line of inquiry may bear fruit. Gibbon (1995, 188, 189) rightly suggests that we still have little understanding of the basic social dynamics within any given Oneota group. He also suggests that "there may be gender-related symbolic and ritual aspects" to systems of exchange because (a) ethnohistorical accounts suggest that different types of items were exchanged by different genders; (b) exchange often worked through affinal or fictive kin networks; and (c) the goods exchanged were the result of someone's labor, often women's. While it is beyond the scope of this book to follow these issues, the data presented above are a preliminary step toward addressing some of them if incorporated with many other lines of evidence.

NINE

Risk Management in Oneota Economies

As discussed in chapter 2, risk management strategies are a necessary part of any subsistence system, but one size does not fit all (sensu Kipnis 2002). The nature and types of strategies used can be informative about the source and severity of the managed risks and the underlying cultural processes (Cashdan 1990a, 1990b; Halstead and O'Shea 1989a, 1989b; Hart 1993). Therefore, we must determine what types of risk management strategies were employed. It is necessary to identify the sources of risk in the Koshkonong Locality.

Environmental risks are ubiquitous and can range from hailstorms to droughts and from insect infestations to fungal infections. Moisture is a key factor. To borrow an astronomical term, crops require a Goldilocks zone, where moisture levels are just right, neither too much nor too little; and the last and first frosts each year must be sufficiently spaced (Doolittle 2002, 121). The upland farming practiced throughout much of the Koshkonong Locality would be threatened by drought and killing frosts, which is especially true for the lighter soils that are the easiest to turn with digging sticks (Heidenreich 1978, 375; O'Shea 1989, 64). While these factors could be mitigated, for example, by drainage ditches, irrigation, or ridged fields, it would be a labor-intensive proposition.

In addition to the normal variation, major climate shifts were in motion in the ninth and tenth centuries as the Medieval Warm Period shifted

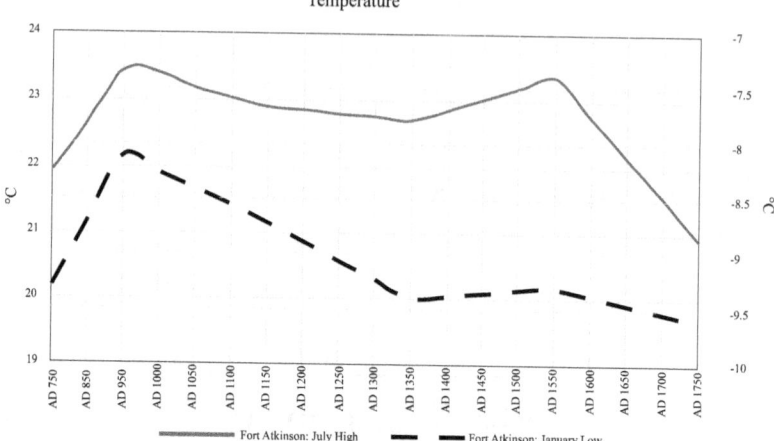

Figure 9.1. Modeled mean temperatures (° Celsius) for January and July in Fort Atkinson, Wisconsin (after McEaney and Bryson 2005)

into the Little Ice Age (Lamb 1982; Stahle and Cleavland 1994). In the Koshkonong Locality, temperatures peaked near AD 950 and cooled until AD 1350, near the end of the Oneota occupation of the region (fig. 9.1). July mean temperatures dropped nearly one degree Celsius before slowly climbing again until roughly AD 1550. January mean temperatures dropped even more, from -8.5°C to less than -9.5°C (McEnaney and Bryson 2005). For reference, global temperatures have risen 0.8°C since 1880 (Melillo, Richmond, and Yohe 2014). In addition to cooling temperatures, annual precipitation and evaporation rates varied widely, so the available precipitation fluctuated regularly.

This trend occurred throughout southeastern Wisconsin, though to varying degrees (fig. 9.2). Water was plentiful when Oneota groups began occupying the region, but the available water decreased. By approximately AD 1125, drought conditions were likely common. These dry conditions continued for roughly fifty years; water levels slowly began to rise through the first half of the sixteenth century (McEnaney and Bryson 2005). Long-term moisture fluctuations were not limited to southeastern Wisconsin and have been found in neighboring areas (e.g., Minnesota; Shuman et al. 2009).

It should be noted that these figures show long-term trends and miss the interannual variation, which was significant. Though figure 9.2 shows a fifty-year period with falling temperatures and negative rainfall, it does not

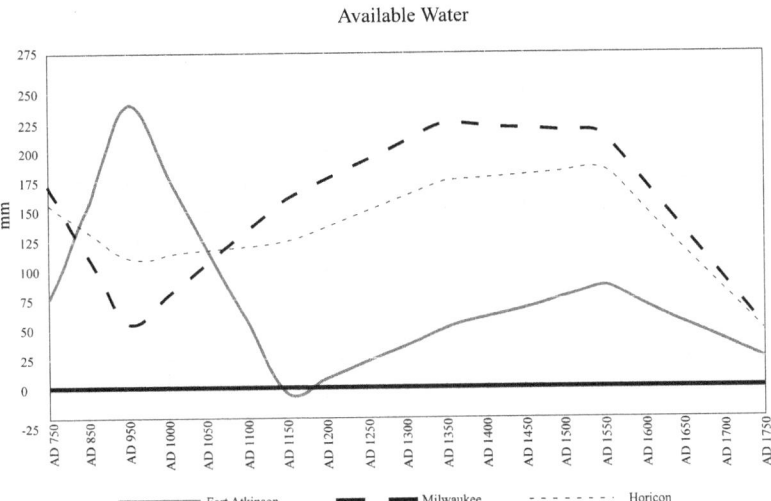

Figure 9.2. Modeled available water (mm) in Fort Atkinson, Milwaukee, and Horicon, Wisconsin (after McEaney and Bryson 2005)

mean that these conditions were present each year. Dry seasons could occur during wet phases, and the reverse; cold years could be mixed in warm-trending phases. These patterns should be seen as trends for that time period, not ubiquitous conditions. Environmental risks were not the only issue: the Koshkonong Locality was also subjected to social threats. For approximately the first two hundred years that Oneota groups lived in the region, the landscape of southeastern Wisconsin was shared with three other groups: widely spread non-collared ware producing peoples, scattered collared ware producing peoples, and one joint Middle Mississippian–Late Woodland group at Aztalan (Richards and Jeske 2002). Through time, the other groups disappeared from the landscape, and it seems that at least some of them may not have gone peacefully.

Relatively few formal burials have been uncovered in the Koshkonong Locality. However, at least one individual died after a violent attack. Isolated human remains are somewhat more common (Jeske 2014). One individual at CBHC was shot with an antler-tipped arrow, which chipped the iliac crest of the left innominate (fig. 9.3). The individual was also possibly stabbed several times in the chest. Another convincing example of violence also comes from CBHC. Multiple elements of an adult cranium were recovered from a refuse pit (Jeske and Sterner-Miller 2014). The cranium showed evidence that it was struck with a blunt object, possibly a war club (see fig. 9.3). These are the clearest two indicators of violence at the sites, but several other burials show evidence of blunt force trauma to the face or other critical areas. In some cases, the evidence of violence is partially obscured by poor preservation (Jeske 2014). Furthermore, prehistoric weapons could kill while leaving little to no trace on the skeleton (Milner 2005).

When compared to data from Aztalan (Rudolph 2009), the south (e.g., Emerson et al. 2010; Milner, Anderson, and Smith 1991), and the north (Karsten 2015), a pattern of regional violence emerges. There is no evidence to show who the Koshkonong Oneota were fighting, or how often, but violence was certainly a real threat, at least intermittently. Even in more peaceful times, they may have needed to take steps for protection or to minimize contact with hostile or opposing groups (Milner 2007; VanDerwarker and Wilson 2016).

The data clearly indicate that there were several risk factors for Koshkonong Oneota residents. The typical interannual environmental variation can require significant efforts to ameliorate (sensu Halstead and O'Shea 1989b). When magnified by the alteration of climatic episodes, the environment may have been even less predictable, and when combined with the threat of attack, groups living in southeastern Wisconsin would have faced considerable uncertainty and risk factors (Stephens and Charnov 1982). To successfully manage them, similarly extreme management strategies would be required. To understand how these factors affected and interacted with existing social structures and intergroup politics, it is essential to identify what strategies were employed.

EVIDENCE OF RISK MANAGEMENT STRATEGIES

Narrowing Diet Breadth

The data needed to compare Koshkonong and Late Woodland sites are somewhat ambiguous, largely due to seasonality issues. NTAXA at Koshkonong sites tends to be greater, but this may be due to the long occupation spans at the sites (multiple years and seasons vs. multiple single-season occupations).

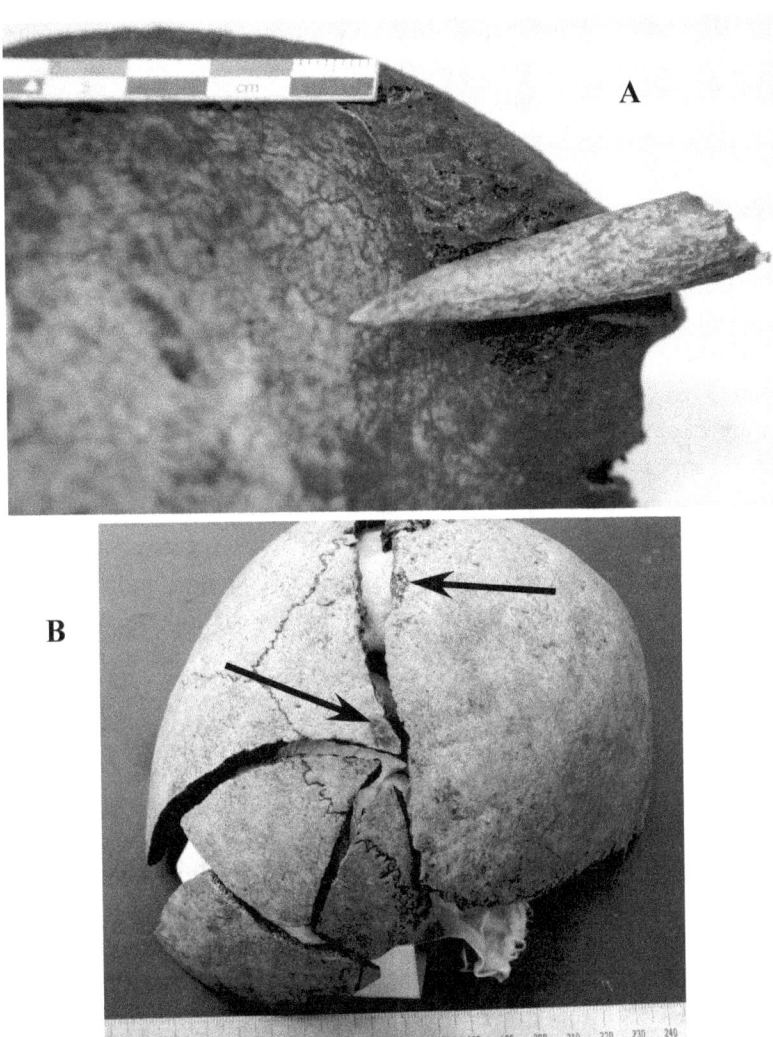

Figure 9.3. Examples of bioarchaeological evidence of violent trauma in the Koshkonong Locality: A, Iliac crest perforated by antler-tine projectile point; B, Cranial elements with evidence of blunt force trauma. Photo used with permission of the University of Wisconsin–Milwaukee Archaeological Research Laboratory, Program in Midwestern Archaeology.

Using diversity indices, Centra 53/54, the sole non-collared ware site, fits expectations. Its diversity indices are significantly higher. Koshkonong and all other groups assumed to be reliant on maize have a much more focused diet. River Quarry and Murphy both show more focused diets, though being occupied in winter, focused diets are expected. The Late Woodland component at Aztalan also has a diversity index that suggests a more focused diet; however, the diversity score is largely due to the proportionally large presence of hickory nutshell that depresses it. Setting aside nutshell, the diet does not appear to be nearly as focused as at Koshkonong. Conversely, Koshkonong's joint reliance on maize and a few buffer resources (e.g., wild rice, acorn, goosefoot) pushes its diversity indices higher. However, an examination of the full data set indicates that the Koshkonong groups appear to be more heavily focused on maize agriculture (i.e., based on density and ubiquity) and follow the expected intensification patterns.

Through time, the number of utilized resources increases, from 25 to 34. However, the importance of these new taxa is minimal, and the diversity indices show that the diet becomes more focused. Both the Simpson's (0.28 vs. 0.33) and Shannon (1.75 vs. 1.65) indices indicate that the diet was narrowed as a small number of taxa (maize and wild rice) became increasingly important in the diet. The corresponding reduction in acorn and increase in wild rice largely explain the shifting values. Furthermore, at least one of the new species, the domesticate bean, represents a greater focus on agricultural production.

The Aztalan and CBCH isotopic data support the interpretation that collared ware Late Woodland groups consumed less maize than their Oneota neighbors. One of the samples likely predates the Oneota occupation of Koshkonong (2σ cal. AD 901–1026), but two are contemporaneous with the early Oneota dates (2σ cal. AD 1013–1154) and are likely no more than a century older than the two CBHC dogs (2σ cal. AD 1050–1224 and 1156–1228). The highest maize value from Aztalan dogs is 5% of protein lower than the low CBHC dog (0.7‰). There is a roughly 30% of protein (5.1‰) difference between the minimum Aztalan dog and the maximum CBHC dog. The $\delta^{15}N$ values are very close between the two sites, so it does not appear that variation in animal protein should significantly alter the caloric importance of the two samples. While the sample size is small, the data generally support an increased focus on maize for Oneota groups.

The model predicts that maize-using groups will intensify and focus their diet on agricultural and/or locally aggregated resources. Relative to Late Woodland groups, Koshkonong sites appear to intensify both sets of resources. Koshkonong has much higher densities and ubiquities of maize and possibly cultigens. Even if goosefoot and wild rice are considered wild plants, they represent wild aggregated resources that were exploited more intensively. Through time, this process continues in the Koshkonong Locality: the reliance on aggregated nonmaize resources continues, and there is increased reliance on wild rice, which becomes more abundant (from 4.2 to 14.3 ct./10 liters) and a greater proportion of the macrobotanical assemblage.

The model also predicts that some highly ranked resources may become overexploited, that their rank will drop, and that high-ranked resources with large variances will be dropped in favor of lower variance resources. One highly ranked resource, acorn, did drastically drop in rank. Overall nutshell falls from an average of 38.2 ct./10 liters and 0.23g/10 liters to 4.45 ct.10/liters and 0.04g/10 liters. Acorn specifically falls from a mean of 27.42 ct./10 liters and 0.11g/10 liters to 1.78 ct./10 liters and 0.01g/10 liters.

It is unclear if acorn became less important because of an intentional choice to intensify wild rice harvests or because of resource depression (e.g., from deforestation). However, I find it likely that a combination of both factors came into play. Nuts and wild rice harvests can fluctuate from year to year, in some cases wildly (Gardner 1997; Vennum 1988). Given the size and range of available habitats in and around Lake Koshkonong and the historical prevalence of wild rice in the lake, it is probable that a portion of wild rice stands were productive in all but the worst years (Lapham 1855). It is also possible to cultivate larger and more productive stands. Methods could range from the relatively low labor-intensive practice of spreading seeds to the much more labor-intensive practice of tending the plants much like one would an agricultural field (Jenks 1908; Vennum 1988). So while wild rice may have had unpredictable variances, it may have been a manageable task to limit the degree of the interannual variability.

Conversely, oak husbandry, while possible, is much more labor-intensive and often less effective. It requires a great deal of time to implement and even more time for the labor to bear fruit, because many trees only produce nuts every few years. It requires clearing the competing flora around each oak tree to reduce competition. But humans have a limited ability to reduce the effects of fluctuating water levels or other issues that affect mast production. So without clearing around and protecting numerous oaks in multiple edaphic settings, it is unlikely that yields would increase significantly (Gardner 1997). If such a task is undertaken, it is possible that the productivity of other resources would be depressed. For example, if oaks are near the edge of a grove, clearing around them would reduce the availability of many berries that prefer forest edge habitats. Furthermore, if oak was used as a building material or for firewood, then over the centuries of occupation of the Koshkonong Locality the number of oak trees would decrease, which would reduce the number of available acorns for harvest. So acorn represents a resource that would have been prevalent in the area, but deforestation would have slowly increased the search time for the food and its variability would have made it a risky resource on which to depend.

Both wild rice and acorn would have had the additional risk of competition from animals. Historically, birds were often a threat to wild rice harvests (Vennum 1988). However, the wild rice could have acted as a bird lure for hunters. Simultaneous waterfowl population control and food procurement could have been advantageous bonuses to wild rice harvesting. While birds are not particularly plentiful in the Koshkonong assemblages (Agnew et al. 2016; Edwards 2013; Edwards and Pater 2011; Van de Pas, McTavish, and Klemmer 2015), most of the birds identified have been waterfowl (McTavish, pers. comm.). Squirrels, deer, and other animals often compete with humans for nuts, though acorn would not act as an aggregating draw to the same degree as wild rice (Gardner 1997). So as acorns fall, foragers would have needed to immediately harvest them, which could conflict with maize harvesting efforts.

Comparatively, wild rice harvests are more conveniently timed and therefore more forgiving to the crowded fall scheduling. Many stands of wild rice will ripen before the second (i.e., nongreen) harvest of maize and will continue to ripen over the course of several weeks. A single stalk will produce numerous seeds, which will take one and a half to two weeks to ripen, and the peak harvest time is the first half of September (WDNR 2016). Therefore, it may be possible to obtain large amounts of wild rice without sacrificing labor for the maize harvest. Furthermore, if labor is needed elsewhere for a day, or even a week, the wild rice stands will likely still be producing significant quantities of wild rice when labor is available once again.

The variance of the macrobotanical assemblage supports acorn as a riskier resource. In early contexts, the acorn count variance was over 3,400. The wild rice variance ranges from 20 to 250. While later contexts exhibit considerable wild rice variance, it is still a fraction of the acorn variance. Acorn density is quite low in later contexts, 7.2 ct./10 liters, but relative to the mean (VMR = 4.0) it is still variable, and acorn is present in low enough quantities that it may not represent intense harvesting but opportunistic gathering while obtaining firewood, checking traps, or doing other tasks in wooded areas.

Given the sharp drop in acorn levels and the corresponding rise in wild rice, I argue that two of the model's expectations are met. Due to deforestation (i.e., resource depletion) and inherent risk, Koshkonong groups chose to reduce their reliance on acorns and instead intensified their harvests of wild rice. This change may have corresponded with increased efforts to cultivate the plant, though this cannot be confirmed with archaeological data. The model predicts that resource depletion will lead to one or more high-ranked resources dropping in the resource ranking or out of the diet breadth. Acorn remains part of the diet breadth, but after AD 1200 it does not appear to have been a significant resource. Oak trees fit both the expected criteria for a dropped resource; they take many years to grow, and there are often years between substantial nut crops (slow regeneration), so acorn represents a risky food source (high variance).

The corresponding rise in wild rice also fits expectations that over time aggregated resources would rise in importance. Wild rice is a highly aggregated resource, and while its risk levels (variance) may not have been ideal, they were lower than noted for acorn and could have been mitigated by cultivation methods of various intensities.

The model also predicts that reliance on agriculture would increase through time. This expectation is not well supported. The bean is introduced, suggesting that a new item was added to the agricultural repertoire. However, given the poor preservation potential of beans, it is difficult to judge the importance of the single definitive specimen. It indicates greater agricultural diversity but not necessarily intensity. Goosefoot levels remain the same. Squash levels are too low to determine a baseline much less detect a change.

Maize is somewhat ambiguous. The densities of maize kernels in early and late contexts are statistically no different ($p = 0.35$ for count, $p = 0.2$ for weight). Generally, this finding would indicate that maize use

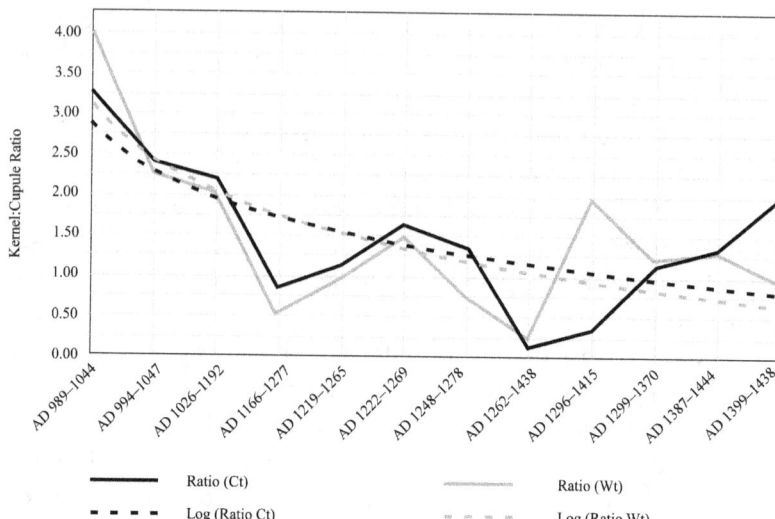

Figure 9.4. Maize kernel-to-cupule ratio through time in the Koshkonong Locality

did not increase through time. However, other changes are present. The proportional importance of maize increases from 46% to 54% of the assemblage. Later contexts have significantly more maize cupules (fig. 9.4). One potential cause is a shift in maize processing techniques. If so, it is possible that the new techniques resulted in the preservation of proportionally fewer maize kernels.

The diversity indices also suggest a narrowing of the diet breadth. It is not clear if this represents an actual increased production in maize relative to other plants or just a proportional rise with static production levels. The maize kernel to wood charcoal ratio, which assumes that the amount of wood burned is proportional to population size, suggests that there is no significant change (Miller 1988). The ratio for both early and late contexts is 0.013 gram of maize for every gram of charcoal. So the density of maize did not change through time. The ubiquity of maize also did not change through time, and we do not have appropriate isotopic data to investigate further. Currently, the data indicate that the importance of maize remained constant through time, while the overall focus on agriculture grew, at least modestly, with the addition of beans. The increased focus on wild rice narrowed the diet and can still be interpreted as increased reliance on cultivated plants. Overall, the expectation of localized intensification is met, though only partially.

Table 9.1. Summary data of excavation and feature count and size for study sites

	Excavated Area (m2)	Features				
		No Features	Total Area (m²)	Mean Area (m²)	Features: Excavation	% Area
CBHC	831.6	115	88.7	0.8	0.14	11
KCV	159.7	32	23.7	0.7	0.20	15
Total	991.3	147	112.4	0.8	0.15	11

Storage

Both Crescent Bay and KCV have numerous pit features, most of which are clustered near house structures. Between the two sites, a total of 147 pits have been identified, with approximately 1,000 m² excavated (table 9.1). Features account for 11% of the total area excavated. Feature depth varies significantly, from a few centimeters beneath the plow zone to over a meter. This likely represents only a fraction of the features present at the site; approximately 10% of Crescent Bay has been excavated and 0.3% of KCV. So there is considerable evidence that pits were regularly constructed, but it is not clear how many were used for storage or how many were used concurrently. Of the 147 pits, 25 were classified as shallow basins, that is, <10 cm below plow zone (Moss 2010). The size of these pits suggests that they were not used for storage, but their original depth is unknown. Some areas, particularly the northern portion of CBHC, have been truncated by plowing and subsequent erosion. Pits that appear shallow may have been moderately deep. Discounting shallow basins, there are 112 pit features that are large enough to have been used for storage. However, in each case, in the terminal stage of the pits' use life, they were either emptied or filled with refuse. Therefore, it is possible that at least some of these larger pits were never used for storage.

Estimating the importance of storage is also problematic. Based on ethnographic accounts, each family likely had more than one cache pit at a time. Based on Maxi'diwiac's recollections, each extended family household, of roughly fifteen people, had four storage pits. In total, they contained roughly one year's worth of food and were used for many years (Wilson 1917). So we should expect several pits associated with each house. The number can be expected to grow if the house area was used for longer than a feature's use life, so it is difficult to set a baseline for the number or sizes of features. In Koshkonong, it is unclear how large households were, so the number and size of features cannot be easily compared to ethnographic examples. The features are often superimposed, creating a difficult palimpsest to untangle. Further complicating the issue, neighboring features can be separated by several hundred years. Given these factors, it is unclear how many storage pits were in use at a given time, and it is difficult to determine the total amount of storage available to each household. Given the ubiquity, number, and size of features, storage was important; however, it cannot be further quantified.

EVIDENCE FOR OTHER RISK MANAGEMENT STRATEGIES

The data support interpreting the physical and political environments in the Koshkonong Locality as risky. Thus far, several predicted risk management strategies have been identified: intensification, storage, exchange, and raiding. Rather than broaden the diet breadth through diversification, Koshkonong groups focused on agriculture, wild rice, and acorn. These aggregated resources were stored in large cache pits. There is evidence of limited interaction with other Oneota groups and possibly some Late Woodland ones. However, this interaction does not appear to have been regular or significant. Evidence also suggests that intergroup violence was a reality to the Koshkonong population, though it is unclear who attacked them or which group was the aggressor. The evidence does not directly indicate that they raided others. However, the cyclical nature of warfare in the Late Prehistoric suggests that if attacked. Koshkonong groups would have retaliated (Dye and King 2007; Emerson 2007; Milner 2007; Snow 2007). Even if warfare was a poor buffering strategy—that is, it did not bolster food reserves (sensu Halstead and O'Shea 1989b)—its cyclical nature would have limited the viability of other risk management strategies (Hart 1993).

Mobility

As noted in chapter 3, an examination of mobility patterns should provide insight into the nature of relative risk severity. An examination of the settlement subsistence data supports social risk aversion as the primary threat in the Koshkonong Locality. The Koshkonong settlement system is the flattest (i.e., it has the fewest numbers of site types) and most physically constrained of any Oneota locality examined. Neighboring groups to the south (Langford), west (La Crosse and Red Wing), and northeast (Green Bay) used seasonal mobility and special-purpose camp sites and other types of camps to increase catchment ranges or otherwise expand their presence or control of the landscape.

Taking La Crosse as an example, the use of hamlets to expand access to arable land, the use of inland extractive camps to procure resources, and the relocation of villages to more sheltered regions in the cold season indicate a high degree of logistical mobility and a modest degree of residential mobility. In times of intergroup conflict or resource scarcity, each trip to a logistical camp represents an opportunity to be ambushed by opposing groups. Each hamlet represents a vulnerable target where people can be more easily killed and resources more easily stolen or destroyed. The fact that the La Crosse groups were willing and able to take such risks indicates that the risk level was acceptably low. Researchers have demonstrated that when there is a significant and persistent threat of attack, people tend to constrict their catchment ranges and take defensive postures, even when it has negative impacts on health and social relationships (for worldwide archaeological, historical, and ethnographic accounts, see VanDerwarker and Wilson 2016). Regionally, such actions are most evident in the Central Illinois River valley, where both Middle Mississippian and Oneota populations severely altered subsistence practices and landscape use patterns with serious health consequences (Milner 2007; Milner, Anderson, and Smith 1991; VanDerwarker and Wilson 2016).

The dispersed nature of the La Crosse settlement system should not be conflated with low risk of intergroup hostilities. The evidence clearly indicates there was hostility. The construction of palisades throughout the region is a solid indicator that the people were concerned about attacks (Sasso 1989; Stevenson 1985). Skeletal remains indicate that conflict resulted in severe injury, death, and dismemberment of numerous individuals (Blaine 1979; Holtz-Leith 2006). Sasso (1989, 283) suggests that the aggregation of population near La Crosse was a response to the risk of attack. Strength in numbers was an important aspect of the defensive strategy. Perhaps the large numbers of people in the La Crosse Locality, which based on site density was several times larger than Koshkonong (WHS 2011), provided a sense of safety to work parties venturing to extractive camps and those living in hamlets. And it may have been a sufficient deterrent to justify the sense of security.

It is also important to note that most of La Crosse's occupation span is post–AD 1400. As noted in chapter 1, at or just after AD 1400 most Oneota localities were abandoned, the Middle Mississippian occupation at Cahokia was abandoned, and Late Woodland groups had vanished from the landscape. Populations were largely aggregated in La Crosse, Middle Fox, and near the Chicago/Calumet area. These large buffer zones may have provided sufficient additional security to justify the broader settlement system. When regional conflicts flared, populations could retreat to the more defended village locations and return to their dispersed pattern when it ebbed (Brown and Sasso 2001).

In contrast, the Koshkonong groups were clustered on the landscape and surrounded by three different cultural groups. Compared to La Crosse, these neighbors were physically close. Even if populations were smaller, the presence of so many groups would have increased competition for land and resources. This competition could easily breed hostilities in lean times (Halstead and O'Shea 1989b; Keeley 2016; Wilson and VanDerwarker 2016). Such competition likely accounts for the relatively small number of Oneota sites in the region, the placement of villages on defensible locations, and the placement of many extractive sites between rather than beyond the main villages. If each Oneota village at KCV, at Carcajou Point, and on the CBCH ridge (either CBHC, Schmeling, or Crab Apple Point) were simultaneously occupied, it would create a defensive perimeter around the highly productive lands between the sites, thereby minimizing risk and territorial footprint while maximizing subsistence potential. Trips outside this perimeter were apparently few or very short, as there are only four potential logistical camps outside of the core Oneota territory (see fig. 2.4). Koshkonong residents did not travel away from their villages or establish small-scale habitations in the same way that La Crosse, Langford, and Red Wing groups did (Fleming 2009). While the risk of an ambush or raid was real in each area, the Koshkonong groups appear to have reacted the most strongly. Of the expected responses to raiding (table 9.2), Koshkonong exhibits nearly all the predicted responses that can be readily seen in the archaeological record. Clear palisades are the only exception: Carcajou Point is the only site that has shown any potential evidence of a palisade (Overstreet 1978). While Koshkonong does

Table 9.2. List of common responses to raiding present in the Koshkonong Locality

Responses to Raiding	Present
Palisades, especially with redoubts	?
Settlements in defensive locations	x
Aggregated populations	x
Restricted movement on landscape	x
Seasonal scheduling of labor for defense	?
Increased evidence of weaponry	?
Fleeing region from enemy	?

not show clear evidence of redoubts, ditches, or other characteristics that could clearly indicate the features were defensive (Keeley, Fontana, and Quick 2007), the locality does show evidence of population aggregation in defensive locations and restricted movement on the landscape (see also McTavish 2016). Unfortunately, it is not possible to see seasonal shifts in labor, increased weaponry, or flight from enemies with the available archaeological data.

The distinctness of Koshkonong remains true when compared to all the Oneota regions in this study. While groups to the north of Koshkonong (i.e., Waupaca and Middle Fox) may not have moved villages seasonally, their settlement networks are more diverse and far reaching. In the Middle Fox, numerous site types (e.g., nut processing sites like Soggy Oats) have been identified throughout the region; many are far from the apparent core habitation area near the major lakes. Either the greater number of people in the region (based on site density) or their relationship with neighbors made the Middle Fox residents feel sufficiently safe to venture away from their main villages (WHS 2011).

The Waupaca system is less clear but shows the same pattern. The village sites are located away from arable land and major lakes or wetlands. This site distribution suggests a willingness on the part of the Waupaca Locality residents to travel farther from home to obtain resources than did Koshkonong groups. Given the high levels of maize, it appears that the resources were being exploited to a similar degree. This required farmers to travel longer distances from villages. The site distribution is also more dispersed than in Koshkonong. Nearly 6 km as the crow flies separate Burley Brew from Blinded by the Light. This does not include other sites in the locality for which we do not have comparative floral data, which are even more dispersed. On the other hand, Carcajou Point is separated from Crab Apple Point by less than 3.5 km, with Crescent Bay, Schmeling, and Purnell in between.

In short, the Koshkonong groups appear to have limited mobility, even by Oneota standards. While other Oneota groups used dynamic settlement systems, the Koshkonong system was relatively flat, with much of the labor occurring at or near the main village sites. For example, there are several small sites (e.g., Blue Heron) located between the blufftop sites (e.g., Crescent Bay and Schmeling) and the wetland shores of Koshkonong (Hunter 2003). These sites have yielded low densities of Oneota sherds and no evidence for features. They likely represent small work sites or short-term camps.

The only example that appears more extreme is Aztalan. Unlike Koshkonong or other hinterland Middle Mississippian localities, no network of allied villages has been established for this Middle Mississippian site. The only other site with appreciable numbers of sherds is Bethesda Lutheran Home (47JE0201), located 15 km away, which consists of a series of features with approximately ten Lohmann phase vessels (Hendrickson 1996). Like Koshkonong, subsistence resources appear to have been heavily exploited in the area immediately surrounding the site. While Koshkonong had a flat settlement system of several sites, Aztalan's apparently consisted of a single large, heavily fortified village. The two samples with the most extreme violence avoidance settlement systems are very close. Their proximity and corresponding defensive postures are not likely a coincidence. The lack of trade goods between these two close neighbors is striking. The prevalence of trauma on skeletons in both areas is notable. The lack of exchange suggests that these were people in disconnected social networks. If the populations of the sites were interconnected, then there should be some evidence of interaction (trade, marriage, fictive kin). And despite decades of research in both localities, nothing suggesting trade has been reported. While there is some symbolic overlap (Schneider 2015), the designs are distinct and are more likely to represent different ideas about how to portray regional ideologies (Edwards and Jeske 2015).

Intermarriage or shared ceremonies should have greater similarities (e.g., Hart et al. 2016; Stone and Downum 1999). In these dissociated conditions, even if no blows were exchanged between these two groups, the presence of the other would have been a significant risk. Add mobile foragers and semisedentary farmers to the list, and both groups would have had ample risk of developing boundary disputes if they utilized the same settlement systems as other Oneota groups (Allen 1996; O'Shea and McHale Milner 2002; Stone and Downum 1999).

However, other Woodland groups were present throughout eastern Wisconsin in the eleventh through thirteenth centuries (Stevenson et al. 1997). Aztalan is the one variable that Middle Fox, Waupaca, and Green Bay groups would not have had to contend with, at least not to the same degree. The extreme behavior must have begun in large part from the Middle Mississippian complex on the Crawfish. However, the pattern continues into the fourteenth century after the abandonment of Aztalan and the disappearance of Late Woodland groups from the landscape. It is possible that those in Koshkonong felt threatened by other Upper Mississippian groups for the entire occupational span. Research by Jeske and colleagues (2016, 2017) has demonstrated that the Koshkonong Locality is physically the most isolated Upper Mississippian group in Wisconsin or northern Illinois. In Wisconsin, all Oneota localities are connected to all other Oneota localities at the 30 km level. That is, the boundaries of each locality are either within 30 km of one another or there are intervening sites separated by no more than 30 km. The Koshkonong Locality sites are each farther than 30 km from any other Upper Mississippian sites, including those in northern Illinois. Even a series of potential Oneota sites along the Wisconsin River connects La Crosse and Red Wing sites with the eastern localities.

To summarize, the identified settlement system in the Koshkonong Locality indicates that the residents felt the threat of an enemy attack was greater than the threats posed by environmental risks. They apparently felt threatened more than most other groups examined as they restricted mobility to a significant degree. This threat is visible for the entire occupational span of the region. It is unclear if other Upper Mississippian groups were consistently seen as a threat and what role Aztalan and Late Woodland groups played in creating the stress-induced responses on the part of the Koshkonong residents. It is likely that the political situation in the region evolved through time, and the Koshkonong residents' political networks shifted. However, the perception of a threat was ubiquitous, so even in times when violence levels were low, the Koshkonong settlement system remained unchanged.

Diversification

While the Koshkonong risk management repertoire does not include the most obvious form of diversification, an increase in diet breadth, it does include several diversification strategies, primarily agricultural ones. Spatial diversification is one means of reducing interannual variance (Marston 2011, 192–93). Often referred to as field distribution or scattering, it is among the most reliable diversification methods (e.g., Goland 1993; Marston 2011; McCloskey 1972, 1991; Winterhalder 1990).

Crop Diversification. Agricultural diversification was also achieved through crop diversification, a common practice worldwide (e.g., Marston 2011). During the early period of Oneota occupation of the Koshkonong Locality, both maize and squash were grown. These crops have different growing lengths and nutritional requirements, so the loss of one would not necessarily lead to the loss of the other. Radiocarbon dates confirm that beans were added to the ensemble by no later than AD 1400. Using all three crops could provide additional calories, and the squash and beans would have provided a needed variety of nutrients to a largely maize-based diet. For example, beans could provide necessary amino acids that are lacking in maize (Kaplan 1965, 360), in addition to the well-documented benefits of growing all three plants in the same field (Gallagher 1992; Gallagher and Sasso 1987; Hart 2008; Harwood 1979; Monaghan, Schilling, and Parker 2014; Mt. Pleasant 2010; Mt. Pleasant and Burt 2010).

It is impossible to know specifically how the three plants were grown together in the Koshkonong Locality—whether they were grown in the same field (intercropped) or grown separately but rotated through the same fields (sequentially cropped) or whether there was no overlap. However, the intercropping and sequential cropping account for the bulk of historical and ethnographic accounts; when sufficiently detailed, historical accounts of intercropping is nearly unanimous, though ethnographic accounts from the Plains are less consistent. There, beans and maize were often grown together, but squash was separated (Doolittle 2002, 144–45, 156–57). Given the ubiquity of the two systems and the benefits they engendered, it is likely that one of the two systems was used prehistorically.

According to Doolittle (2000, 145), intercropping two or three plants is not an easy task. It requires effective timing given the variation in growing season. The need to stagger either planting or harvest and work around the growing crops can increase labor requirements up to threefold. If Doolittle's assessment is accurate, this was a costly system, but given its historical ubiquity, it likely paid for itself through greater crop yields. If so, it would have reduced the need for field fallowing, allowing for larger plantings and larger harvests for longer periods. These harvests would apparently include healthier crops and a more nutritionally diverse diet. Given the proportionally large role of maize, the long occupation of the locality, and the stability of maize in the diet, such a system would have been essential. In fact, intercropping or some level of crop rotation would almost certainly have been necessary in order to maintain high maize yields for the roughly four-hundred-year occupation span.

It also appears that diversification was achieved by diversifying the maize itself. Historically, many types of maize were grown in the Eastern Woodlands (Cutler and Blake 1969; Doolittle 2000; Fritz 1992; Hart 1999; Hurt 1987; King 1994). Based on the angle of maize cupules, it is possible to differentiate the number of rows and at least approximate some of the different types of maize grown. While charring affects the angle, it typically does so in a predictable manner (King 1994). Because of the overlap in the number of rows in various maize breeds (see Cutler and Blake 1969; King 1994) in the Midwest, they are generally divided into two types: low-row flint with northeastern origins and high-row pop with southern origins (e.g., Fritz 1992). Both high-row and low-row varieties have been identified at both KCV and CBHC, confirming that this diversification strategy was used. However, because the specific breed cannot be determined, I am wary of making any more specific claims about the merits of either type or the proportions in which they were grown.

Classification of Diversification Strategies

When we examine the risk management categories, diversification, mobility, storage, exchange, raiding, and intensification, there is solid evidence for several. Mobility is the least established by the evidence. Those with the strongest evidence appear to have been part of what O'Shea (1989) referred to as simple management systems because they do not include outside groups. It includes the regular variant (i.e., it occurred regularly) such as storage or intensive agriculture. It also includes simple episodic strategies or those that occur when agricultural outputs are insufficient.

Simple Strategies. For example, diversification through field scattering and intercropping would have occurred regularly. Low-level diversification through the consumption of berries and other minor components would have been an annual affair. Higher-level diversification, such as including fish, acorns, and wild rice in the diet, may have been regularly practiced but episodically intensified. In the case of the latter two, acorn harvesting begins as episodic and ends as a regular strategy, whereas wild rice harvesting begins as a regular strategy and ends as episodic. While the plants are used as a regular buffering mechanism, they are consumed in relatively lower amounts than during their episodic peaks. During these low times, variance is low, indicating that they were a consistent part of the diet. During the episodic phase, variance jumps to levels at least fifty times greater. In short, the plants have baseline use levels, but from time to time the amount spikes. At this time, I cannot conclusively demonstrate that high acorn or wild rice values are directly correlated with low amounts of maize, but the PCA generally supports this pattern. In most cases when maize levels are low, nutshell or wild rice levels tend to increase.

Conversely, it appears that storage was consistently a regular strategy. Storage pits would have been used to store surplus all year. Additional stores may have been held within the houses themselves. Intralocality exchange was likely regular, though it likely would have intensified in times of need so long as the resource failure did not affect everyone in the locality.

Complex Strategies. Two types of complex strategies are defined, intergroup trade and raiding. The evidence for both is limited, and it is unclear how often either system was used. While the threat of raids apparently elicited a significant response, it is unknown if they occurred often. Given the large quantities of agricultural materials recovered, they did not prevent people from completing their essential tasks (Stone and Downum 1999, 123). Even if Koshkonong groups were raiding regularly, it seems unlikely that they could successfully steal and transport significant quantities of food. The evidence of exchange is also limited; while it is notoriously difficult to archaeologically assess the success of trade on buffering, there is little to indicate that it was substantial.

Whatever trade existed is of an unknown nature. According to Gibbon (1995), we should expect local trade to include pottery, nets, and storable foods. Of these, nets are unlikely to survive, and the traded food would be indistinguishable from the local. A total of 30 sherds, less than

0.1% of the 43,000 sherds examined from the Oneota sites at Koshkonong, are identified as Woodland, making up a total of seven vessels (Schneider 2015). Of those, one is a surface find at the multicomponent Schmeling site, and one is from shallow contexts at KCV, near the base of the plow zone. Of the remaining vessels, recovered from solid contexts, two are from Crescent Bay and four are from Schmeling, hardly enough to suggest any significant trade or interaction. Neither Aztalan nor any Koshkonong sites have any ceramics from the other. Fisher-inspired ceramics are present in Schneider's (2015) assemblage but are almost as rare as Late Woodland sherds.

The presence of Oneota pottery at a Late Woodland site in the Madison lakes and Yahara River region 25 km west of Crescent Bay suggests a low degree of interaction between Koshkonong and Late Woodland groups, or a later expansion from Koshkonong to the Yahara River (see fig. 2.4). Regionally, Gibbon (1995) argues that manufactured goods or raw materials are also common trade items. The ceramic similarities with Oneota groups to the north also suggests some degree of interaction. The similarities suggest at least low-level interaction but not necessarily what would be expected if the exchange was a major facet of a subsistence strategy. Other manufactured items might include stone tools. However, at CBHC 75% of the stone tools, made from identifiable material, are from local stone (Sterner 2012). At KCV, the values are even more biased toward local production, 96% (Wilson 2016). A number of copper artifacts have been recovered from excavations at CBHC, Schmeling, Carcajou Point, and KCV, and copious amounts have been collected through metal detection at the Crab Apple Point site (Pozza 2016, 2019). These may represent long-distance procurement or trade with groups in northeastern Wisconsin, based on laser ablation inductively coupled plasma mass spectrometry (Hill and Jeske 2011). Alternatively, some or all may have been made from float copper, carried down by glaciers and left in glacial till. Regardless, the totality of the materials recovered suggests that very limited exchange took place between Koshkonong and outside groups. The final type of trade item in the Koshkonong Locality is galena cubes, which would have come from the southwest, near the modern borders of Illinois, Iowa, and Wisconsin. Galena cubes have been identified during several field seasons at CBHC (Schneider 2015, 126), and one cube was identified in the 2017 season at KCV. There is little reason to think that the trade for copper or galena was an important aspect of a complex buffering strategy.

The sum of the risk management strategies indicate that the Koshkonong subsistence system was locally focused. Plants like wild rice and maize were available in the immediate vicinity of the sites, and their productivity could be heavily influenced by human action and account for the bulk of the diet. Resources that were less available decreased in importance. For example, as larger tracts of land were deforested, hunting of large game such as elk would be pushed farther from habitation sites and hunting them would become both costlier and more dangerous. Isotopic analyses appear to confirm this, as $\delta^{15}N$ levels indicate relatively low levels of meat consumption by cal. AD 1150. Floral resources such as acorn that would decrease with reduction in forested land also became more scarce.

IMPLICATIONS OF THE KOSHKONONG RISK MANAGEMENT SYSTEM

Taken together, the data begin to point in a single direction. The Koshkonong Oneota were relatively isolated. This seclusion was part of a reinforcing cycle. The isolation required simple risk management strategies. Simple strategies can encourage isolation because they are only possible when a group maintains territorial integrity (O'Shea 1989; Stone and Downum 1999). This need placed a feedback loop into the cycle that encouraged the continuance of the isolationist system. This resulted in profound impacts on intralocality organization, interlocality interaction, and the subsistence settlement system.

Territorial Integrity

By definition, simple systems require a high degree of self-sufficiency. That is, simple systems do not include outside groups, so the bulk of necessary resources must be provided directly by the group's members (O'Shea 1989). This self-sufficiency provides a larger measure of stability and flexibility because the group does not rely on the cooperation of outside forces and can adjust practices from year to year. However, it has limited ability to buffer against severe or sustained localized issues. The strength of a simple system comes from its ability to control or significantly manipulate the local conditions. If other groups are granted or create access to the territory, then that control is lost. If groups cannot protect their farm fields, rice beds, populations, and so on, then their ability to influence their production and harvest level is compromised. If other groups enter at will, to take or destroy resources, risk management strategies fail. Agricultural intensification fails if crops are destroyed; diversification fails if foragers are harassed or foods are stolen. Storage fails if harvests are destroyed or caches are looted.

Therefore, boundary security would have been essential for survival in the Koshkonong Locality, but physical security needed to be balanced with food security. Site placement reflects these dual requirements. Physical security could be achieved by multiple means, often total population aggregation. Milner (2007) notes that Iroquoian and proto-Iroquoian groups who were subjected to intense warfare deployed some of the most elaborate and substantial stockades in the Great Lakes region. Historically, each tribe was concentrated in one or possibly two villages (Allen 1996; Bamann et al. 1992). In both circumstances, the reaction to outside threats was to aggregate on a central position on the landscape. This was often coupled with sizable buffer zones ($\geq$ 30 km) separating one group from another (Lambert 2002; Milner 2007). By aggregating in a single large village, the population attained strength in numbers and deterrence from attack (Stone and Downum 1999).

The Koshkonong group used an alternative approach; their villages, as many as six, were spread across a 10 km^2 area. So why do some groups aggregate on the landscape and others spread across several sites? I suggest that the nature of the Koshkonong risk management strategy necessitated a different tactic. While the single-settlement system increased physical security, it also increased the risk of catastrophic crop failure or destruction at the hands of an enemy (O'Shea 1989). A single site may be good for defending the people and stores within, but its ability to control the landscape around the site is reduced. By concentrating everyone in a central location, the ability to spot or quickly respond to an attack is diminished.

Koshkonong's isolation induced a dual need for boundary control and adequate subsistence; dispersing settlements across the core territory could do both simultaneously. This safety is derived from the distribution of the population. Dispersed sites increase visibility of the surrounding region by giving the occupants clear lines of sight (McTavish 2016). These clear sight lines can discourage small-scale attacks and decrease response times if the enemy is spotted. However, it leaves each site more susceptible to a large-scale attack.

The region that would most benefit from this site distribution is the area between them. I argue that this region was the core subsistence area for the locality. I do not argue that the area beyond was not hunted, farmed, fished, and so on. Rather, distribution of sites created dual resource rings. The outer ring represented a greater risk, in terms of both physical safety for the people and the likelihood of resource destruction. The inner ring represented a safe zone, a core region where resources could be better protected, which is essentially another form of risk buffering, or at least a system that could enable more efficient risk buffering. Because of the additional security, the inner ring could be utilized more intensively at lower risk. For example, agricultural fields could be concentrated here. The sites' placement would allow for fields to be established on diverse soils, which would help maintain yields. The outer ring could still host fields or act as a wild resource catchment area.

By maintaining security, the system could have added increased dietary stability, but this would create a need to maintain this settlement system. So long as the risk of a large-scale catastrophic attack remained sufficiently low, each village would have been relatively safe. A central breadbasket would have routinely provided a strong subsistence base. But any deviation from this would have increased risk. Further spreading of villages would make them easier targets; further concentration would reduce the collective group's ability to diversify and make their fields more vulnerable to attack. Such a system would have necessitated considerable intralocality communication, coordination, and cooperation.

RISK MANAGEMENT STRATEGY AND SUBSISTENCE SHIFTS

One strength of simple risk management systems is their flexibility (O'Shea 1989). As environmental conditions shift, so too can the subsistence practices. However, the regular use of certain risk management strategies can also increase the importance of the social institutions that house them, leading to yet other changes (Halstead and O'Shea 1989b). Following this assertion, if reciprocal familial exchange did become an important aspect of the intralocality exchange, then there should be a shift in the importance of extended kin networks.

Subsistence System Shifts

The above-noted shift from acorn to wild rice as a primary buffer is the biggest example of a subsistence shift, which is expected given the local-focused risk management strategy. If the residents were following efficiency models, the deforestation noted above should occur most intensively near the villages (Lee 1969; Vita-Finzi and Higgs 1970), not just because the firewood would be easiest to gather from there but also because agricultural fields placed near the sites (for efficiency and/or defense) would necessitate tree clearance from much of the area around the sites. The inner ring would receive a greater proportion of these activities, both because it is a safer area and because it is closer to all sites (i.e., more efficient), whereas the outer rings are only near one site. This would lead to increased rates of deforestation than in the outer regions. As an aquatic resource, there would be no competition over space between wild rice and agriculture. So if no actions were taken, the efficiency of wild rice should remain the same while the efficiency of mast resources should decrease. Because wild rice output can be intensified with relatively minimal effort, it is even more advantageous. That is, harvests can be increased without significantly expanding foraging range, not only increasing the marginal efficiency of the plant, but also its safety factor.

The shift in the maize cupule:kernel ratio and increased density of maize cupules, coupled with the consistent maize kernel density, may indicate that this pattern shifted after AD 1200 (see fig. 9.4). The increased cupules indicate that a greater amount of maize was processed on site. While the model predicted an increase in agricultural production, there are several functional reasons that this may not have been feasible. In the Central Illinois River valley, maize production remained stable even as warfare forced groups to withdraw from territories away from major villages (VanDerwarker and Wilson 2016). There it is thought that all the available arable land within a safe distance of the village was in use, so intensification was not possible. In fact, if field areas cannot be expanded then some researchers have suggested that we should not expect to see an increase in intensity. Jones, for example, states:

> Finally, the history of agriculture should not be seen as an inexorable linear progression of increasing intensity: if the earliest agriculture was

itself labour intensive, further intensification in later periods is unlikely, and any increased production is likely to have been through other processes, such as expansion and/or extensification. The direction, as well as the rate, of change may have varied, depending on the prevailing economic and cultural conditions at different times and places, and the possibility of reversals in the direction of change should be entertained, with agriculture becoming more or less intensive depending on local circumstances. (2005, 174)

So if the threats, or perceived threats, to safety in the Koshkonong Locality did not diminish after the abandonment of Aztalan, then there is little reason to expect an increase in maize output. According to Jones (2005, 174), intensification without physical expansion of fields may have been too labor intensive. Benn (1995, 120) indicates that the increase in labor investment took place during the Late Woodland, with the adoption of maize. Without significantly larger populations or a drastic reorganization, increased labor investments may not have been feasible. VanDerwalker and Wilson (2016) suggest that Middle Mississippian groups in the Central Illinois River valley may have had to increase labor to maintain productivity, otherwise the minimal fallowing periods would have reduced the overall productivity. In Koshkonong, shifting labor from the fields to the rice beds may have been the better choice. The marginal return on increased labor investment for wild rice would have been relatively high (Jenks 1988) and could reduce wild rice variance. So if food production could be intensified more efficiently by shifting to wild rice, then there is no reason to expect that maize would be intensified.

The shift in kernel:cupule ratio appears more extreme than it is (table 9.3). Overall, in the early dated contexts, maize cupules are relatively rare, accounting for less than 25% of maize recovered. Cupules become much more common in later contexts, accounting for roughly half of the identified maize. However, this distinction is in large part due to KCV F12-01, which has a large sample and therefore a strong impact on the overall early ratio. When all of the samples with radiocarbon dates are plotted, a general negative trend can be seen, but it is not as extreme as the dichotomous view suggests (fig. 9.4). The change may simply be related to deforestation. As firewood became increasingly scarce, maize cobs could be used as a partial fuel substitute. However, maize cobs are much less dense than wood and

Table 9.3. Maize kernel-to-cupule ratio through time

Time Period	Kernel Count	Cupule Count	Ratio (ct.)	Kernel Weight (g)	Cupule Weight (g)	Ratio (wt.)
Overall	9,749	8,147	1.20	84.13	74.30	1.13
Early	4,241	1,661	2.55	35.58	13.50	2.64
Late	3,229	2,711	1.19	28.47	22.60	1.26

are unlikely to have a significant impact on the required firewood volume. The second possible explanation is related to increasing hostilities. If violence was increasing, then the farmers may have reduced the amount of time spent away from the protection of the village. Processing the maize at home would help to do this.

Little is known about the nature of violence trends in the Koshkonong Locality. It is unclear when violence started, if it became more severe through time, if it fluctuated, or if it dissipated. However, there are some basic indicators that can be used to draw inferences. For example, Aztalan is occupied by Middle Mississippians from roughly AD 1100 until shortly after AD 1200 (Picard 2013; Richards and Jeske 2002; Zych 2013). Given that the palisade was burned multiple times and the skeletons show evidence of violent trauma, it is likely that escalating violence was a contributing factor to the site's abandonment (Goldstein and Freeman 1997; Rudolph 2009). To the south, Milner, Anderson, and Smith (1991) indicate that major violence began at roughly AD 1300 with the regional movement of Oneota populations. Finally, the entire Koshkonong Locality was abandoned soon after AD 1400, and it is unlikely that the root causes sprang up overnight. Rather, their roots are likely in the preceding century or even centuries. So there appears to be a general trend toward increasing violence, with potential flare-ups around AD 1100 when Middle Mississippians arrive and potentially again in AD 1200 when they depart. An uptick in violence may also have been seen in AD 1300 as people to the south began to move about the landscape, though it is unclear what impact this would have had as far north as the Koshkonong Locality.

While the kernel-to-cupule ratio trends downward, it also fluctuates. Several of these fluctuations do seem to align with the times of expected jumps in violence; however, we cannot definitively associate these two. First, the vagaries of the radiocarbon record make it difficult to determine the actual order of pit usage; many have considerable overlap at the two-sigma level. Second, there are several reasons for the potential shifts, which can include seasonal variation and pit function, among others. For example, KCV F12-01 is likely the earliest dated pit in the Koshkonong Locality. It has the highest ratio of kernels to cupules (3.3 ct., 4.0 wt.); but individual zones within the pit vary, from Zone M with a ratio of 0.7 by weight to Zone L with a ratio of 8.1 by weight. Therefore, I limit my interpretations to overall tends. The proportion of cupules tends to increase through time; this indicates that people processed more maize on site, which possibly reflects increased perceptions of threat in the region.

The three shifts indicated above suggest that the general practice of local resource reliance, boundary maintenance, and minimizing travel away from village sites increased over time. While maize agriculture did not increase, wild rice use did, which is indicative of greater reliance on aggregated resources (rice over acorn) and may indicate that maize levels could not be realistically increased without increasing the distance between villages and fields or that it required an unrealistic increase in labor output. The ratio of kernels to cupules also indicates that people were engaging in more activities at the villages, which is consistent with responses to increasing violence. While these practices would help to maintain physical safety and could minimize interannual production variance, they increased the chances that a regional climatic episode could have devastating effects. In short, the emphasis on local resource procurement enhanced physical safety, but a severe drought or large-scale hailstorm could have devastating impacts. In such situations, only significant storage and a well-developed social network could help to ameliorate the effects.

Social Shifts. Halstead and O'Shea (1989b) have asserted that social institutions with embedded risk management strategies are subject to change. If reliance on the strategies increase, so too does the reliance on the institution(s). If subsistence strategies need to be altered, it will require alterations to the social institutions for the subsistence shifts to take place. As described above, the kin networks were heavily integrated into subsistence and risk management systems.

Households were crucial in organizing labor pools, particularly during planting and harvests. Intralocality exchange would have proceeded through extended kin networks. Households would have managed surplus. Essentially, kin networks were integrated with the subsistence and risk management strategies at almost every level. Therefore, it is likely that Koshkonong kin networks underwent alterations or transformations as subsistence systems shifted and risk management techniques were altered. Many such shifts are potentially visible archaeologically, though our ability to recognize them in the archaeological record may be limited.

One common area of speculation is that of gender relations. Given the gendered nature of the subsistence system, Oneota researchers have often argued that the rising role of agriculture would have increased the status of women in society (e.g., Hollinger and Benn 1995; O'Gorman 2010; Overstreet 1981). As agriculture (women's labor) became increasingly important relative to hunting (men's labor), the role of women shifted in society, potentially even resulting in a shift in matrilineal/matrilocal residence patterns.

Others, such as Benn (1995), have argued that Oneota marks a shift in the other direction. In the Late Woodland, there was relative gender balance, but women's influence began to wane as territorial disputes led to increasing warfare. He argues that violence was in part present because warfare was codified in the male role. Snow (2007) makes a similar point about Iroquoian groups to the east. For Snow, warfare was the primary form of male social currency. For a man to raise his station or earn the right to marry, he first had to prove his capabilities as a warrior.

There is insufficient data to determine the relative roles of men and women within the Koshkonong Locality. However, the locally focused intense settlement system would have created a new gender dynamic. The increasingly important role of women in the economic sphere could have raised their status, particularly if they were able to control access to the agricultural surplus, as did Iroquoian women (Heidenreich 1978). However, the social and economic importance of physical security, likely provided by men, may have offset any gains. In addition to warfare, hunting may have become a form of costly social signaling for men (e.g., Bliege Bird and Smith 2005, 226; Gmelch 1992; Hawkes 1990). Ethnographically, hunting was not only considered a male activity; it was often tied to male status (e.g., Radin 1923; Skinner 1921). In the case of the Koshkonong Locality, overhunting of animals within the core area could have happened relatively quickly, which means that some hunting expeditions would have to occur at a distance from habitation sites. Given the distance and the threat of attack, a successful hunt could have performed a role similar to that of a war party in generating social capital (e.g., Snow 2007). It is beyond the scope of this research to follow this line of inquiry any further, but it should be noted that the subsistence practices did not operate in a vacuum. They would have affected and in return been affected by intragroup power dynamics.

If intragroup exchange was a significant factor, then it should be reflected in the importance of extended kin networks. Carpiaux (2018) has noted that F12-06, a late feature (ca. AD 1400), has more very large vessels (>40 cm orifice diameter). These very large vessels are also found in earlier features, though not with the same frequency. Orifice diameter is often thought to be associated with the number of people being fed, so increases in vessel size is either associated with larger households where more mouths are being fed on a regular basis or with feasting where large numbers of people are being fed intermittently (Betts 2006; Blitz 1993; Turner and Lofgren 1966). The increasing number of large pots at KCV may be associated with larger households; however, the feature also contains many examples of more typically sized pots (<35 cm orifice diameter), suggesting that much of the cooking was for a single household but larger pots were occasionally needed to cook for a bigger group, such as for a feast (Carpiaux 2018).

The ceramic data suggest that feasting may have increased in importance through time, though additional research is necessary to confirm this. If this is the case, it supports my contention that feasting served as a mechanism to encourage overproduction of food and maintenance of intralocality kinship networks. Through time, the accumulation of shortages would reinforce the need for intersite food sharing, labor pooling, and overproduction whenever possible. Therefore, feasting may have occurred more often to reinforce the social bonds that facilitated these actions, or feasting may have included larger groups of people (e.g., the entire moiety instead of only the clan) to increase the efficiency of such cooperative networks. The movement of pottery among sites is another example of intralocality exchange. While petrographic data show movement, the data cannot demonstrate if its intensity changed through time (Schneider, Scheutz, and Ahlrichs 2012).

TEN

Assessing the Relationship between Agriculture and Political Complexity in the Midcontinent

Despite the long-held belief, a relationship between agriculture and cultural complexity is not supported by the data. The macrobotanical and isotopic data agree that Oneota groups ubiquitously grew substantial amounts of agricultural crops and subsisted heavily on maize. Maize likely constituted between 45% and 75% of the caloric intake of Koshkonong residents. By any reasonable metric, they were agriculturalists. Yet their social organization shows no evidence of measurable hierarchy: leaders appear to have influence rather than power, and settlements are not organized into chiefly networks. Furthermore, there is no evidence of monumental architecture or large population densities.

In a systematic analysis of burials from eastern Wisconsin Oneota and Langford sites, Foley Winkler (2011, 170–71) argues that they "have a relatively egalitarian socio-political structure" and continues to assert that differences among burials are the result of horizontal social differences, not vertical ones, "representing an egalitarian system with achieved social status." She argues that corporate group membership (e.g., clan or lineage) likely crosscut all other identities and accounts for much of the variation in the burial data. Brown (1967) also argues that larger corporate identity affected burial characteristics and suggests that a phratry or moiety system is evidenced in

Langford burial practices. So burials provide evidence for the importance of extended family networks and corporate level control, but nothing suggests that one corporate group has greater control than all the others.

With regard to monumental architecture, the closest example is burial mounds, such as those at Walker Hooper, which were morphologically no different from conical Woodland-era mounds (Gibbon 1972b; Jeske 1927). Langford sites are often associated with mounds (e.g., Brown 1967; Fowler 1940; Griffin 1948; Langford 1927), though there is nothing to suggest any serious level of centralized social control. Certainly there is nothing at the scale present in Middle Mississippian contexts (Emerson 1991, 1992, 1999; Goldstein and Freeman 1997; Green 1997; Griffin 1967; Pauketat 1994, 2004; Young and Fowler 2000).

Settlement systems also show marked difference in levels of political stratification. Middle Mississippian sites show highly hierarchical multi-tiered settlements, with differing levels of political control and access to religious infrastructures at each tier (Emerson 1992; Fowler 1978). While some Oneota settlement systems are complex and multifaceted, they do not contain this embedded hierarchical power structure. In La Crosse, hamlets appear to be associated with major villages (Sasso 1989), but there is no evidence that the settlement system was established in a manner that would allow for the control of people, ceremony, and labor through it. While simpler relative to the American Bottom, even most hinterland Middle Mississippian localities (e.g., the Central Illinois River valley and Apple River) use a version of this system (Emerson 1991). Oneota localities are often at the opposite end of the power continuum; for example, in the Koshkonong Locality, it appears that the settlement system was more heterarchical than hierarchical. There is no evidence that one site had more political or religious control than the others.

The total weight of the evidence demonstrates that Oneota represents a lifeway or series of lifeways that emphasizes achieved over ascribed status. Political power is dispersed among multiple corporate groups rather than funneled through one. These are views shared by many researchers (e.g., Benn 1989; Gallagher and Arzigian 1994). And yet Oneota groups are maize agriculturalists, with domesticates accounting for at least half their diet. When cultigens are included, that proportion rises precipitously. While possibly never reaching peak Middle Mississippian levels, many members of Oneota societies consumed as much maize as or more than a large portion of people in Middle Mississippian societies. To grow sufficient maize would have required the mobilization of large segments of the labor force. Every spring and fall, essentially every able-bodied woman would need to be at work in the fields for long hours each day. Every time a new field would be cleared, male labor was likely included. With such agriculturally reliant diets and agriculturally focused subsistence systems, the egalitarian nature of these groups appears to contradict the commonly assumed relationship between agriculture and cultural complexity.

INTRALOCALITY PRODUCTION AND EXCHANGE

The only way that many of the diversification strategies would work is if people and food were moving among the sites, which is supported by some data. KCV residents had access to backwater and creek resources (Edwards 2010) but still consumed large quantities of fish that came from the lake (McTavish and Edwards 2014). Occupants of Crescent Bay, Schmeling, Purnell, and Carcajou Point could have kept them from gaining access to the lake—both overland or via the creek—but they did not. Some mechanism allowed KCV inhabitants access to lake fish.

In addition, the distinct soils among sites would have buffered loss only if people in the areas that produced more shared with people in the areas that produced less, which would require food moving among the sites. The defensive strategy would work only if the people at each site cooperated with one another. So we must ask, what social mechanisms allowed for the food to move from one site to the other, and what long-term effects could this generate? Understanding the means of production is key. Households were likely the basis of subsistence production in the Koshkonong Locality.

Given the physical scale and intensity of the agricultural system, household-level production is sensible and cross-culturally common (Bogaard 2005). Global ethnographic accounts of foragers suggest that large packages of food (e.g., meat) brought in by men are more likely to be shared than small packages of plants foraged by women (Kohler 1993). In short, when agriculture is the domain of women, household production is the norm (Flannery 2002). In the Eastern Woodlands and Great Plains, the bulk of ethnohistorical and ethnographic accounts suggest or imply that household production was the norm for agriculturalists (e.g., Doolittle 2000; Wilson 1917). Most cases where supra-household groups directed subsistence activities were in ranked societies with chiefly leaders. In these cases, households controlled a portion of the fields, and another portion was communal; the surpluses from the shared field were stored in communal structures (Scarry and Scarry 2005). The archaeological evidence also supports household production going back to the prehistoric period. There is no evidence of a communal storage facility at KCV, CBHC, or any other Koshkonong site, which indicates that larger political or corporate groups did not control production. Rather, storage pits tend to cluster around habitation structures. Household storage is consistent with household-scale production and risk pooling. Societies that practice group-level production and risk pooling, even those with noncommunal housing, tend to have a shared storage system so that supplies and distribution can be accessed by everyone (Weissner 1982, 174). The clustering of storage facilities around Koshkonong structures is consistent with household production and storage.

Therefore, food and other goods needed to be exchanged among Koshkonong sites to take full advantage of the diversification practices. If household-level production was the norm, then households themselves would have to be integrated into the intralocality exchange network. Again, ceramics are a good place to start (e.g., Gibbon 1995; Schneider 2015). The stylistic ceramic data suggest close ties among the sites' occupants (Carpiaux 2015, 2018; Schneider 2015). Compositional data indicate that a portion of the pots moved from one site to others (Schneider et al. 2012). Schneider (2015, 360) has suggested that such intralocality exchange should be expected to flow through kinship lines (real and fictive) via reciprocal exchange, and Carpiaux (2018) demonstrates that there existed a series of very large cooking vessels indicative of large-group cooking, which could be part of Schneider's proposed exchange systems.

Despite field scattering, variation among household output is to be expected, which would leave some households with less food. In particularly poor years, food supplies may be insufficient. Reciprocal exchange within extended families can help balance these issues. If families at different sites are connected through kinship, then the full power of the risk management strategies could be utilized. Halstead and O'Shea (1989b) also argue that such an internal exchange (sensu Gibbon 1995) between sites can only be reliable if embedded in permanent social structures. Otherwise, risk management systems are "prone to fall into disuse because of the infrequency with which they are activated ... [so] there is a strong selective pressure for them to become increasingly embedded within more regular cultural practices" (Halstead and O'Shea 1989b, 5). The costlier the risk management strategy (in terms of lost efficiency), the more embedding of the strategies is necessary. The Koshkonong system came with costs associated with time management and maintaining interhousehold cooperation.

To maintain intralocality distribution networks, the exchange would necessarily occur with and without subsistence shortfalls. The kinship lines would need to be embedded with a degree of mutual obligation that would bind the members together and create an expectation of generosity (Mauss 1990). Acts such as regular feasting can ensure that overproduction is maintained and routinize the idea of sharing with extended kin (e.g., extended families, clans, or moieties).

The ethnographic and ethnohistorical accounts are filled with descriptions of feasts, which extended family groups, often clans, were mandated to hold, either annually or for certain occasions (Blair 1911; Densmore 1979; Keesing 1987; Kohl 1985; Lurie 1966, 1978; Radin 1923; Skinner 1921). For example, Radin (1923) recounts several annual Ho Chunk feasts for renewing war bundles and medicine bundles, as well as numerous other occasions of clan-held feasts.

Typically, each clan had its own feasting traditions, so not only would they serve to bond the members partaking in them, but they could also serve to symbolically separate those from other feasting networks. Other ceremonies, such as the Thunderer chief's health ceremony, included people from all clans. In each of the ceremonies, the responsibility for hosting was typically held by an individual, but his relatives each had responsibilities for providing certain types of support. The end result was that extended families were expected to sit down, engage with one another face-to-face, and, in the process, reaffirm the reciprocal bonds that they held with each other, which is evidenced in the KCV ceramics (see Carpiaux 2018).

DEFINING AGRICULTURE AND ITS EFFECTS

If reliance on agriculture is not a good measure of cultural complexity, what is the relationship between them? Price and Bar-Yosef (2011, S171) argue that agriculture involves "changes in the structure and organization of societies" and that it is "a totally new relationship with the environment. Humans truly begin to harness the earth.... [F]armers utilize the landscape intensively and create a milieu that suits their needs." Price and Bar-Yosef (2011, S172) continue to identify factors that they see as important to the development of agriculture; these include sedentism, population density, resource abundance, constraints of movement (social or geographic), processing and storage technology, and wealth accumulation. They argue that competition would often lead to wealth and status differentiation at the individual or household level. Their description of agriculture fits the situation in the Late Prehistoric Midcontinent well. Social groups reorganized, from the mobile hunter-forager system of the Effigy Mound builders to the somewhat more nucleated collared ware producers and the much more sedentary and nucleated Upper Mississippian groups (Richards and Jeske 2002). This would have required a shift in labor organization to accommodate the changes in resource availability and the greater sedentism (Benn 1989, 1995).

It also represents a new relationship with the environment. People were no longer moving across the landscape regularly. Some of the first year-round sites in the region were occupied during this transition. Landscapes had to be cleared, burned, and modified to a degree that was never previously needed (Wagner 2003). So why do Middle Mississippians and groups in the Near East and elsewhere so often develop social inequality (Price 1995)? The one variable missing in the Oneota sites is evidence of wealth accumulation. For some reason, it appears that Oneota groups do not allow, or outside factors prevent, any single household or lineage from obtaining a greater level of wealth or power. This difference is reflected in the isotopic variances. An examination of the standard deviations shows that Oneota groups consumed maize and meat at much more equal levels. The Oneota samples with the lowest $\delta^{13}C$ values received roughly 20% less protein from maize than those with the highest $\delta^{13}C$ values. This pattern is consistent among most Oneota localities.

And while a 20% difference is not insignificant, it is only a fraction of what is typically seen within any single Middle Mississippian site. Mississippian elites were able to control access to meat and other alternatives to maize. As a result, the nonelites in major sites like Cahokia and their lowland farming hamlets had access to few other resources (Ambrose, Buikstra, and Krueger 2003). The nonelites in the hinterland sites fared somewhat better, as their distance from the major towns afforded them greater access to nuts, berries, and other wild resources (Hedman, Hargrave, and Ambrose 2002).

Maize is present and important in both Wisconsin and northern Illinois and the American Bottom prior to the development of this complex system or the appearance of Oneota groups on the landscape. Late Woodland groups in both areas ate maize extensively (Clauter 2012; Egan-Bruhy 2009; Emerson and Titelbaum 2000; Green and Nolan 2000; Jeske 1992; Johannessen 1993; Kelly 2002; Munson 1987; Rindos and Johannessen 2000; Salkin 2000; Theler and Boszhardt 2000). Both groups were undergoing the transition to a maize-based subsistence system concurrently, yet developed distinct forms of surplus management and political leadership. So the transition to a maize-based economy cannot be the driving factor. Perhaps different population densities or ideologies were at work.

Perhaps one of the reasons we do not see the expected ramifications of such a monumental shift is because we are oversimplifying the transition and reducing it to a dichotomous agricultural or nonagricultural system (Smith 2001). Smith (2001, 3–4) states that because of this dichotomous approach, "scholars will attempt to categorically relegate or displace to one side or the other any anomalous in-between societies." When societies are grouped in such ways, it can mask variation within patterns and trends. A great deal of research has been conducted to understand what Smith (2001) calls the middle ground, the continuum between those who rely entirely on wild foods and those who rely entirely on domesticated ones. But even recognizing that there is a middle ground does not necessarily eliminate our biases. For example, Harris (1989) developed an evolutionary framework to understand the transition from foraging to agriculture (fig. 10.1). However, the assumption that agriculture requires social ranking or stratification is built into the model.

A comparison of Oneota agricultural practices with the model belies this assumption. The first criterion of Harris's level three is that land clearance results in altered vegetation compositions. Clearance of the oak savannahs surrounding most eastern Oneota sites would have been required. Wagner's (2003) research indicates that clearance by means of fire may have been occurring since the Archaic, and Dorney and Dorney (1989) suggest that the oak savannahs actually may have been the product of regular fires. The second criterion is that systematic soil tillage modifies soil

	Level 1 Low Energy Expenditure	Level 2 Moderate Energy Expenditure	Level 3 High Energy Expenditure		
			Cultivation (systematic tillage)	Agriculture	Specialized agricultural systems
Food Procurement Strategy	Foraging (wild food procurement)	Interventionist foraging (wild plant production - minimal tillage)			
Food Procurement Techniques	- Burning vegetation - Collecting/gathering - Protective tending	- Replacement planting - Transplanting - Tending (e.g., weeding) - Harvesting - Storage - Drainage/irrigation	- Land clearance - Systematic soil tillage - Cultivation of domesticated crops - Production/proportion of multiple domesticates/domesticate varieties		
Select Ecological Effects	- Reduces natural competition - Increases soil fertility - Selection of habitat - Synchronizes plant life cycles	- Maintains minimum population threshold in the wild - Broadens range/habitats through anthropogenic seed dispersal -- Soil modification -- Reduces competition -- Increases soil productivity - Selection for desired dispersal mechanism - Selection for/redistribution of propagules w/ desired traits	- Creation of new vegetation composition & structure - Modification of soil results in -- New soil texture -- Soil structure -- Increased fertility - Establishment of agroecosystems		

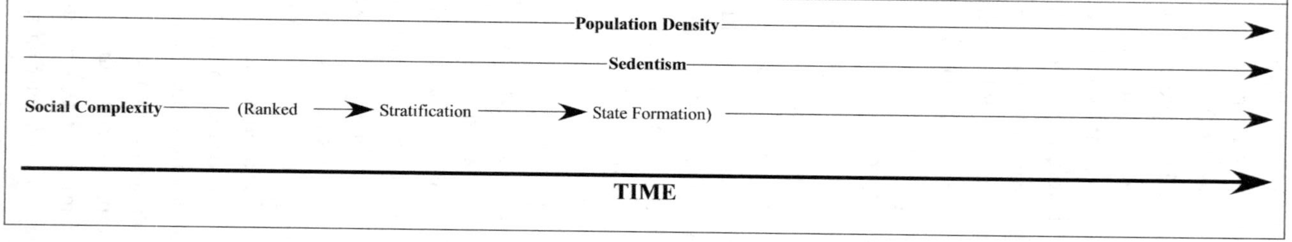

→ Population Density
→ Sedentism
Social Complexity ——— (Ranked ——→ Stratification ——→ State Formation)

TIME →

Figure 10.1. People-plant interactions within domestication continuum (after Harris 1989, 17)

texture, structure, and fertility. The construction of corn hills is assumed to have occurred in many locations. This is accomplished by a tilling-like action and has many of the same benefits but with reduced effort (Doolittle 2000; Hurt 1987). Other Oneota groups went to the next level and constructed ridged fields. These large features certainly modified the soils and provided numerous benefits in terms of fertility (Gallagher and Sasso 1987; Gallagher et al. 1985, 1987; Riley and Freimuth 1979). The third criterion, agriculture, is distinguished from cultivation by the production of domesticated crops, especially the production of different varieties of domesticated crops. Oneota groups, and even their Late Woodland ancestors, produced at least two varieties of maize. In the pre-Mississippian occupation of Aztalan, both high- and low-row maize variants have been identified (Picard 2013). Using other definitions of agriculture produces the same result: Oneota groups were agricultural. As developed by Zvelebl (1996), agriculture is any system where domesticates and cultigens together account for more than half the diet. And Ford (1985) states that agriculture is a combination of field techniques and use of domesticates.

Oneota groups meet all the criteria to be considered fully agricultural, yet they do not contain any of the listed markers of increased cultural complexity given by Harris (1989) and assumed or implied by many others. The question becomes, why? Clearly, there is an issue with some of the models. While moving away from the false dichotomous systems, elements of the old unilinear evolution paradigms (e.g., Buckland 1878; Morgan 1877; Tylor 1881) were revived with a processual twist. The Oneota examples show that such models need to be multilinear; they need to allow for divergent choices and outcomes. Gallagher and Arzigian (1994, 184) move toward this perspective. They suggest that the lack of agricultural specialization in Oneota contexts is the distinguishing factor. Specialized programs emphasize one or two resources at the expense of others. This, they argue, is associated with increasing cultural complexity. They suggest that Oneota groups used an alternative approach, intensified agriculture with diversification. This distinction, they felt, was associated with more egalitarian practices, slower population growth, and lower incidences of malnutrition.

However, this argument does not fully capture the patterns described in this study. For example, Aztalan and Koshkonong sites exhibit similar levels of specialization (i.e., similar diversity indices, densities, ubiquities, etc.). In fact, by the second half of the occupation span, the focus on wild rice and maize could be construed as a significant specialization. Yet Aztalan exhibits evidence for considerable social stratification not present in any Oneota groups (Birmingham and Goldstein 2005; Goldstein and Freeman 1997). There are currently insufficient data to come to any clear conclusions. The answers likely lie much earlier than the appearance of shell-tempered pottery and the appearance of Upper and Middle Mississippian groups in the archaeological record. This line of inquiry requires a fuller understanding of the long-term cultural trajectories that Oneota and Middle Mississippian ancestral groups traveled.

Regardless of why there are no markers of increased cultural complexity, the data presented above are clear: agriculture is not necessarily associated with cultural complexity or social inequality. Egalitarian groups are fully capable of modifying their environment, taking a highly active role in their subsistence system, and producing significant quantities of agricultural goods. On a per capita basis, egalitarian groups appear to be capable of producing similar amounts of food. The difference in their agricultural system is one of distribution, not of production. While it could be argued that lower population densities among Oneota groups means that agriculture was not as intensive, I take issue with this on two points. First, essentially anything a larger group of people do is going to appear more intensive. Just because twenty people can do twice the work of ten, it does not mean that the smaller group is less invested or reliant on the products of that labor. Second, if agriculture is to be measured in total output, then perhaps population density is the key factor in determining cultural complexity, not subsistence practices (e.g., scales of economy in Winterhalder and Kennett 2009). If so, then I would argue that agriculture arises when people have a need (real or perceived) and the means (technological, social, and environmental) to produce more food than their natural environment can support. In many cases, it is associated with increasing population densities. Then traditional arguments and assumptions may apply. Here the increased population may necessitate greater levels of cooperation to manage land and resources. This may foster situations that allows one group to eventually obtain the upper hand and exert power over others. In other cases, it can occur in groups with small population densities. In the low population density scenarios, there is no reason to assume that the adoption of agriculture will be followed by increasing levels of social inequality, monumental architecture, or other traditional markers of cultural complexity.

ELEVEN

Conclusions

THE KOSHKONONG LOCALITY

The groups living in the Koshkonong Locality were faced with many threats, but the perceived risk of attack was among the greatest. Responses to perceived threats are strongly reflected in the subsistence and settlement systems. Numerous risk management strategies were employed, most centered on intensive resource acquisition.

Agriculture was used intensively, to a greater degree than was practiced by contemporaneous Late Woodland groups and apparently nearly on par with Middle Mississippian neighbors. Regardless of the definition used, both lines of data support the interpretation that the residents of the Koshkonong Locality were maize agriculturalists (Ford 1985; Harris 1989; Zvelebl 1996). This resource was the densest and most ubiquitous in Koshkonong's macrobotanical assemblages. Isotope values suggest that it accounted for 40% or more of the protein intake and as much as 75% of the caloric intake. In addition to maize, squash, beans (in later contexts), and goosefoot were grown in the locality (Olsen 2003). Wild rice was consumed to a significant degree and was likely cultivated by the locality residents. In the various models, these cultivated crops accounted for as much as 85% of the calories in the diet and likely accounted for at least 70%, except possibly in rare instances such as famine. Meat resources likely accounted for no more than 15% of the diet, and wild plants likely accounted for no more than 10% to 20%, depending on the model.

The planting, tending, and harvesting activities would have required tremendous amounts of labor, particularly in spring and fall. Women likely were the ones who did most of this work. While there is no direct evidence, men's economic labor was likely centered on hunting, defense, and retaliatory war raids. Both men and women likely took part in craft production, ritual activities, and a variety of nonsubsistence activities, but these are beyond the scope of this project.

Despite differences within the sites' assemblages, the macrobotanical remains typically clustered closer together on multivariate tests than with sites in other localities, suggesting that the residents shared a similar mental template for how to get food and what foods to eat. They likely also shared food with each other, creating a tightly knit social network. This network of sites would have relied on one another to a significant degree, not only for subsistence aid, but also for defense. Such close connections were almost certainly maintained through reciprocal relations, which would be reaffirmed in feasts, marriages, and other structured social obligations. This intralocality network also appears to be the largest social group within the primary risk-buffering network, indicating that they used a simple buffering system (i.e., one society).

The use of a simple risk management system and local network reliance are also reflected in the settlement system, which is small and flat. The locality consists of several village sites that likely acted as base camps for most activities. The small number and geographic range of the ephemeral camps indicate that when the day's work was done people typically returned to the villages rather than making multiday trips to procure food or resources. The evidence of exchange is also minimal. This system necessitates maintaining territorial integrity. This was enabled by the distribution of sites, which were situated where they could effectively maintain territorial integrity while maximizing spatial diversity. The space between the sites would be a safer territory where much of their agricultural activities likely took place. Over time, work was increasingly done at the village sites. Remains of maize cobs suggest that in later contexts, processing of agricultural goods took place more often on site than in the fields. So it is likely that as intergroup tensions increased, people did not rely solely on the safety of this core territory and took further steps to increase security of both the people and their harvests.

The data suggest ways that the social interactions may have been affected by these risks and mitigation strategies. However, there are few strong indicators of the nature of social interactions and social institutions that would have been at work in the locality. Gender dynamics were likely in flux, with the value of each gender's labors providing complementary value. Kinship networks would have been essential to maintain the social integrity of the locality, but little data are available to interpret how the networks were organized or how they operated. To date, the most we can say is that the locality represents a close-knit and relatively (but not totally) closed social system.

REGIONAL TRENDS

On a basic level, the Koshkonong Locality is representative of most contemporaneous Oneota localities. The data indicate that Waupaca, Middle Fox, Langford, Red Wing, and Fisher groups were all highly agricultural and concerned with both defense and climatic threats. There is variation among these groups; each followed a version of this basic Oneota template. Much like each group followed a basic template for ceramics but had their own local and unique style (Schneider 2015), this was the case with subsistence. Most groups appear to have consumed as much maize as those living in Koshkonong, though they hunted to a somewhat greater degree. Each group used its own blend of wild plants as buffering resources. For example, Langford groups did not use cultivated starchy and oily seeds (Egan 1988, 1993a; Jeske and Hart 1988). Fisher and northern Wisconsin sites (Waupaca and Green Bay) stand out for their use of yellow star grass (Egan-Bruhy 2001b, 2010b, 2012; Egan-Bruhy and Nelson 2013). Koshkonong sites exemplify the general trends most strongly: their focus on local resource acquisition is the most extreme, and the settlement pattern supports it. They appear to be the most defensive and insular of the contemporaneous Oneota groups examined.

The Wolf River Tradition sites near Green Bay do not seem to follow the general model. These sites' assemblages do not suggest that maize was particularly important. The slightly later La Crosse sites appear to rely on maize to a slightly lower degree and on hunting and fishing more than in Koshkonong. This may be a result of a shift toward greater mobility to allow for increased bison hunting (e.g., Boszhardt 2000; Gibbon 1972a). La Crosse sites appear to fit well with the description of intensification through diversification argued by Gallagher and Arzigian (1994), whereas Koshkonong exemplifies intensification through focalization.

Late Woodland groups appear to have consumed less maize than did Oneota groups. The limited data here support the contention that non-collared ware groups were more mobile and relied more on hunting and gathering than on horticulture or agriculture. The groups living on collared ware sites, excluding Aztalan, were more seasonally mobile than noted for most Oneota groups and definitely more than for Koshkonong. Agriculture (or horticulture?) was important but less important than for Oneota groups, except possibly for Wolf River sites (at least those near Green Bay). Maize was a significant resource, providing as much as half the calories for some individuals.

The Middle Mississippian sites clearly were occupied by maize agriculturalists. The assemblages consistently had some of the highest maize ubiquities and showed the highest densities. However, there was regional variation in buffering resources and techniques. It is difficult to quantify their maize reliance relative to Oneota groups. The isotopic data from the American Bottom suggest that low-status urban individuals consumed more maize than any Oneota individuals. However, high-status Middle Mississippians consumed little maize and significantly greater quantities of meat (Ambrose, Buikstra, and Krueger 2003). Everyone living in outlying sites consumed a wider array of plant foods (Hedman, Hargrave, and Ambrose 2002). Given the position of Lundy and Aztalan in the hinterland and the floral diversity in the assemblages, particularly at Aztalan, it seems likely that most of those living at the hinterland sites did not eat the extreme levels of maize seen in the American Bottom. However, on average, they may have consumed slightly more maize than most people living at Oneota sites.

Middle Mississippian groups are known for developing complex social hierarchies, constructing monumental mounds, instituting ranked settlement systems (except Aztalan), and congregating in dense population centers (Smith 1978). All are common markers for political complexity. However, there are no indications that the contemporaneous development of agriculture within the Oneota world was linked to such traits. Therefore, I argue that Oneota represents an exception to the tendency for groups to develop more complex forms of political organization as they begin to rely more on agriculture (e.g., Harris 1989). It is not clear why Middle Mississippian and Oneota populations developed such distinct social institutions and forms of political organization. Initial population density and several other social and economic factors are likely at play. However, maize agriculture does not seem to be the key catalyst (sensu Fritz 1992), nor does agriculture require such complexity or hierarchy to develop.

IMPLICATIONS OF THIS RESEARCH

This research makes significant contributions in four ways. First, it is the first application of the canine surrogacy approach in the western Great Lakes (see Edwards et al. 2017). This approach allows for the acquisition of important dietary data without the destructive testing of human remains. Destruction of human remains is a growing ethical concern among archaeologists (Wilson 2008), particularly when invested communities, such as descendant Native American groups, are opposed to such treatment. CSA offers a means to avoid such destruction without sacrificing research goals. Second, this project is a rare combination of dietary isotope and macrobotanical data, thus allowing for stronger and more holistic inferences (sensu Wylie 2000). Third, the isotopic data provide the first regionwide measure of Upper Mississippian maize consumption and marks a major step toward understanding Upper Mississippian subsistence systems and variation in maize consumption and hunting practices. Fourth, the application of isotopic, botanical, and settlement data calls attention to important aspects of social interaction within the Koshkonong Locality.

APPENDIX A

Macrobotanical Data

Context Information and Charcoal

Feature #	Zone	FXN	Liters	% sorted Lt.	% sorted Hvy.	Wood Charcoal ct.	Wood Charcoal wt.	Bark Charcoal ct.	Bark Charcoal wt.
Koshkonong Creek Village									
FF12-01	E	Both	101	25	25	12722	129.93	216	5.200
FF12-01	I	Both	211	12.5, 6.25	3.125	30863	443.221	344	10.024
FF12-01	L	Both	10	100	100	1175	19.151	37	0.463
FF12-01	M	Both	7	100	100	2755	17.201	46	0.0813
FF12-01	P	Both	81	25	25	12454	126.438	78	1.519
FF12-06	A2	Both	143	25	12.5	19788	241.408	160	19.88
FF12-06	B	Both	284	12.5	12.5	52518	632.32	400	2.080
FF12-06	D	Both	4	100	100	542	4.273	12	0.070
FF12-06	E	Lt	2	100		388	2.420	15	0.088
FF12-06	G	Both	16	100	100	1720	33.957	32	0.256
FF12-06	I	Both	6	100	100	1054	9.245	0	0
FF12-06	L	Both	22	100, 50	100, 50	5480	86.182	67	1.557
FF12-06	O	Both	28	50	50	8480	100.752	79	96.886
FF12-06	Q	Both	7	100	100	2546	28.998	21	0.319
FF12-06	R	Both	16	100	100	6142	51.056	140	1.565
FF12-06	S	Both	1	100	100	18	0.083	2	0.01
FF12-06	V	Both	68.5	100, 50	25	6822	110.722	51	0.869
FF12-06	W	Both	18	100	50	4516	55.34	13	0.435
FF12-26	n/a	Both	79	50	100, 12.5	6870	76.362	118	1.218

Appendix A: Macrobotanical Data 219

Context Information and Charcoal (cont.)

Feature #	Zone	FXN	Liters	% sorted Lt.	% sorted Hvy.	Wood Charcoal ct.	Wood Charcoal wt.	Bark Charcoal ct.	Bark Charcoal wt.
Crescent Bay Hunt Club									
FF00-11		Both	304	x	x	4710	57.340	7	0.030
FF00-11	B	Both	126.5	x	x	1283	15.620	1882	10.880
FF00-26	B	Both	189.5	x	x	5604	68.230	0	0.000
FF02-25	x	Both	57	25	100	3046	43.830	32	0.230
FF04-03		Both	27	100	50	2510	15.490	7	0.044
FF04-14	1	Both	42	50	25	6433	84.183	0	0.000
FF04-14	2	Both	38	x	x	8260	118.120	208	2.680
FF04-14	3N	Both	10	100	100	2287	27.736	1	0.042
FF04-14	4	Both	54	25	25	15320	203.036	56	1.092
FF04-14	5	Lt	50	50		3130	35.324	26	0.164
FF04-14	6N	Both	7	100	x	2909	28.800	96	0.560
FF04-15	A	Both	174	12.5	6.125	21040	235.120	32	0.280
FF04-15	C	Both	105	100, 10	100	6126	748.200	91	0.450
F04-22	x	Both	950	16.5	33	43346	640.550	662	1.002
FF06-63	A	Both	145	10	7.5	7210	80.500	180	1.800
FF06-63	B	Both	32	10	7.5	3040	39.700	450	2.500
FF06-63	C	Both	33	10, 100	100	333	4.130	59	0.430
F10-14	n/a	Both	300	12.5	100	15879	167.466	304	2.592
F10-19	n/a	Both	110	50	50	6250	95.696	18	0.142
F10-29	n/a	Both	375	6.25	100	18273	221.038	1	0.001
F10-98	n/a	Both	88	25	25 100	6794	76.117	72	0.496

Note: Italicized figures indicate estimated counts; values are extrapolated from raw subsample values.

220 *Appendix A: Macrobotanical Data*

Nutshell

Feature #	Zone	Nutshell total ct.	Nutshell total wt.	Carya ct.	Carya wt.	Corylus ct.	Corylus wt.	Juglans ct.	Juglans wt.	Juglandaceae ct.	Juglandaceae wt.	Quercus ct.	Quercus wt.
Koshkonong Creek Village													
FF12-01	E	117	0.804	17	0.388	0	0	0	0	0	0	100	0.416
FF12-01	I	664	4.053	72	0.744	0	0	0	0	0	0	592	3.309
FF12-01	L	6	0.014	0	0	0	0	0	0	0	0	6	0.014
FF12-01	M	3	0.016	0	0	0	0	0	0	0	0	3	0.016
FF12-01	P	102	1.274	62	1.046	0	0	0	0	0	0	40	0.228
FF12-06	A2	243	2.318	89	1.884	0	0	0	0	0	0	154	0.434
FF12-06	B	369	4.871	304	4.784	1	0.039	0	0	0	0	64	0.048
FF12-06	D	0	0	0	0	0	0	0	0	0	0	0	0
FF12-06	E	0	0	0	0	0	0	0	0	0	0	0	0
FF12-06	G	14	0.197	13	0.167	0	0	0	0	1	0.03	0	0
FF12-06	I	2	0	0	0	0	0	1	0	0	0	1	0
FF12-06	L	11	0.099	0	0	0	0	0	0	7	0.098	4	0.001
FF12-06	O	16	0.15	0	0	0	0	0	0	0	0	16	0.15
FF12-06	Q	2	0.008	0	0	0	0	0	0	0	0	2	0.008
FF12-06	R	1	0.004	0	0	0	0	0	0	0	0	1	0.004
FF12-06	S	0	0	0	0	0	0	0	0	0	0	0	0
FF12-06	V	5	0.048	0	0	0	0	0	0	0	0	5	0.048
FF12-06	W	3	0.008	0	0	0	0	0	0	0	0	3	0.008
FF12-26	n/a	4334	19.315	53	1.445	0	0	0	0	0	0	4281	17.87

Nutshell (cont.)

Feature #	Zone	Nutshell total ct.	Nutshell total wt.	Carya ct.	Carya wt.	Corylus ct.	Corylus wt.	Juglans ct.	Juglans wt.	Juglandaceae ct.	Juglandaceae wt.	Quercus ct.	Quercus wt.
Crescent Bay Hunt Club													
FF00-11		61	0.66	33	0.46	1	0.01	10	0.09	0	0	17	0.1
FF00-11	B	74	0.58	15	0.28	3	0.05	1	0.04	23	0.1	32	0.11
FF00-26	B	9	0.045	1	0.01	0	0	0	0	7	0.03	1	0.005
FF02-25	x	12	0.14	0	0	3	0.05	0	0	9	0.09	0	0
FF04-03		567	2.781	66	0.66	53	0.277	13	0.065	0	0	435	1.779
FF04-14	1	112	0.418	70	0.216	4	0.02	0	0	0	0	38	0.182
FF04-14	2	28	0.175	0	0	3	0.02	22	0.15	0	0	3	0.005
FF04-14	3N	13	0.057	0	0	1	0.007	1	0.008	0	0	11	0.042
FF04-14	4	16	0.42	16	0.42	0	0	0	0	0	0	0	0
FF04-14	5	6	0.04	0	0	6	0.04	0	0	0	0	0	0
FF04-14	6N	4	0.02	0	0	0	0	4	0.02	0	0	0	0
FF04-15	A	108	0.464	0	0	0	0	0	0	0	0	108	0.464
FF04-15	C	54	0.335	0	0	1	0.005	35	0.22	0	0	18	0.11
F04-22	x	261	2.2	35	1.38	0	0	0	0	104	0.36	122	0.46
FF06-63	A	340	2.5	70	0.7	0	0	10	0.4	0	0	260	1.4
FF06-63	B	950	5.3	110	1.8	0	0	0	0	190	1.2	650	2.3
FF06-63	C	66	0.38	1	0.01	0	0	0	0	5	0.04	60	0.33
F10-14	n/a	396	1.873	19	0.223	2	0.011	0	0	0	0	375	1.639
F10-19	n/a	72	0.526	8	0.256	0	0	0	0	0	0	64	0.27
F10-29	n/a	464	2.381	66	0.92	0	0	15	0.317	0	0	383	1.144
F10-98	n/a	65	0.399	21	0.219	0	0	8	0.064	0	0	36	0.116

Maize

Feature #	Zone	Zea mays Total ct.	Zea mays Total wt.	Zea mays Kernel Fragments ct.	Zea mays Kernel Fragments wt.	cf. Kernel Fragment ct.	cf. Kernel Fragment wt.	Cupule/ Glume ct.	Cupule/ Glume wt.	cf. Cupule/ Glume ct.	cf. Cupule Glume wt.	Cob Fragment ct.	Cob Fragment wt.
Koshkonong Creek Village													
FF12-01	E	1295	9.997	1017	7.848	0	0	278	2.149	0	0	0	0
FF12-01	I	856	7.561	650	6.184	0	0	200	1.184	0	0	6	0.193
FF12-01	L	61	0.1787	32	0.159	0	0	29	0.0197	0	0	0	0
FF12-01	M	50	0.289	24	0.117	0	0	26	0.172	0	0	0	0
FF12-01	P	708	6.725	556	5.501	0	0	152	1.224	0	0	0	0
FF12-06	A2	1158	7.66	821	5.136	0	0	337	2.524	0	0	0	0
FF12-06	B	2896	26.408	1534	14.416	0	0	1346	11.704	0	0	16	0.288
FF12-06	D	74	0.439	31	0.194	0	0	43	0.245	0	0	0	0
FF12-06	E	49	0.553	5	0.1	0	0	41	0.357	0	0	3	0.096
FF12-06	G	157	1.617	100	1.33	0	0	57	0.287	0	0	0	0
FF12-06	I	22	0.211	7	0.106	0	0	15	0.105	0	0	0	0
FF12-06	L	182	1.943	115	0.911	6	0.026	50	0.292	0	0	11	0.714
FF12-06	O	96	0.68	32	0.176	0	0	64	0.504	0	0	0	0
FF12-06	Q	130	0.733	38	0.175	0	0	92	0.558	0	0	0	0
FF12-06	R	107	0.776	67	0.453	0	0	40	0.323	0	0	0	0
FF12-06	S	0	0	0	0	0	0	0	0	0	0	0	0
FF12-06	V	244	2.106	147	1.013	0	0	84	0.701	0	0	13	0.392
FF12-06	W	95	0.511	69	0.36	0	0	25	0.145	0	0	1	0.006
FF12-26	n/a	276	3.268	108	1.136	0	0	166	1.67	0	0	2	0.462

Appendix A: Macrobotanical Data   223

Maize (cont.)

Feature #	Zone	Zea mays Total ct.	Zea mays Total wt.	Zea mays Kernel Fragments ct.	Zea mays Kernel Fragments wt.	cf. Kernel Fragment ct.	cf. Kernel Fragment wt.	Cupule/ Glume ct.	Cupule/ Glume wt.	cf. Cupule/ Glume ct.	cf. Cupule/ Glume wt.	Cob Fragment ct.	Cob Fragment wt.
Crescent Bay Hunt Club													
FF00-11		151	1.82	77	1.32	0	0	74	0.5	0	0	0	0
FF00-11	B	102	0.96	54	0.65	0	0	48	0.31	0	0	0	0
FF00-26	B	260	2.23	34	0.41	0	0	224	1.81	0	0	2	0.01
FF02-25	x	149	1.57	140	1.46	0	0	9	0.11	0	0	0	0
FF04-03		87	0.488	54	0.29	0	0	33	0.198	0	0	0	0
FF04-14	1	392	3.111	296	2.375	0	0	92	0.706	0	0	4	0.03
FF04-14	2	156	2.05	34	1.09	6	0.26	101	0.63	0	0	0	0
FF04-14	3N	108	1.247	67	0.803	0	0	41	0.444	15	0.07	0	0
FF04-14	4	744	10.15	556	4.604	0	0	188	5.546	0	0	0	0
FF04-14	5	156	1.444	78	0.796	0	0	74	0.62	0	0	4	0.028
FF04-14	6N	61	0.37	33	0.28	19	0.06	9	0.03	0	0	0	0
FF04-15	A	1160	9.224	912	6.8	0	0	232	1.856	0	0	16	0.568
FF04-15	C	366	2.76	135	1.2	0	0	231	1.56	0	0	0	0
F04-22	x	1091	10.15	627	6.39	144	0.64	300	2.12	0	0	20	1
FF06-63	A	280	2	120	0.6	0	0	160	1.4	0	0	0	0
FF06-63	B	20	0.1	10	0.05	0	0	10	0.05	0	0	0	0
FF06-63	C	15	0.095	14	0.09	0	0	1	0.005	0	0	0	0
F10-14	n/a	2262	15.645	366	2.672	0	0	1847	10.959	0	0	49	2.014
F10-19	n/a	946	10.54	94	1.128	0	0	820	8.27	0	0	32	1.142
F10-29	n/a	548	6.832	314	2.882	0	0	234	3.95	0	0	0	0
F10-98	n/a	386	3.931	206	1.927	0	0	156	1.104	0	0	24	0.9

224 *Appendix A: Macrobotanical Data*

Other Domesticates

Feature #	Zone	C. pepo Rind ct.	C. pepo Rind wt.	C. pepo Seed ct.	C. pepo Seed wt.	P. vulgaris ct.	P. vulgaris wt.	Nicotiana ct.
Koshkonong Creek Village								
FF12-01	E	0	0	4	0.096	0	0	0
FF12-01	I	0	0	0	0	0	0	0
FF12-01	L	0	0	0	0	0	0	0
FF12-01	M	0	0	0	0	0	0	0
FF12-01	P	0	0	0	0	0	0	0
FF12-06	A2	0	0	0	0	0	0	12
FF12-06	B	0	0	0	0	0	0	0
FF12-06	D	0	0	0	0	0	0	0
FF12-06	E	0	0	0	0	0	0	0
FF12-06	G	0	0	0	0	0	0	0
FF12-06	I	0	0	0	0	0	0	0
FF12-06	L	0	0	3	0.025	2	0.081	0
FF12-06	O	0	0	0	0	0	0	0
FF12-06	Q	0	0	0	0	0	0	0
FF12-06	R	0	0	0	0	0	0	0
FF12-06	S	0	0	0	0	0	0	0
FF12-06	V	0	0	0	0	1	0.05	2
FF12-06	W	5	0.006	0	0	1	0.57	0
FF12-26	n/a	0	0	0	0	0	0	0

Other Domesticates (cont.)

Feature #	Zone	C. pepo Rind ct.	C. pepo Rind wt.	C. pepo Seed ct.	C. pepo Seed wt.	P. vulgaris ct.	P. vulgaris wt.	Nicotiana ct.
Crescent Bay Hunt Club								
FF00-11	B	0	0	0	0	0	0	0
FF00-11	B	1	0	0	0	0	0	8
FF00-26	B	0	0	0	0	0	0	12
FF02-25	x	0	0	0	0	0	0	0
FF04-03		0	0	0	0	1	0.02	0
FF04-14	1	0	0	0	0	0	0	0
FF04-14	2	0	0	0	0	0	0	0
FF04-14	3N	0	0	0	0	0	0	0
FF04-14	4	0	0	0	0	0	0	0
FF04-14	5	0	0	0	0	0	0	0
FF04-14	6N	0	0	0	0	0	0	0
FF04-15	A	0	0	0	0	0	0	0
FF04-15	C	0	0	0	0	0	0	0
F04-22	x	13	1.03	0	0	0	0	0
FF06-63	A	0	0	0	0	0	0	0
FF06-63	B	0	0	0	0	0	0	0
FF06-63	C	0	0	0	0.04	0	0	0
F10-14	n/a	8	0.112	32	0.04	0	0	0
F10-19	n/a	0	0	0	0	0	0	0
F10-29	n/a	0	0	0	0	0	0	0
F10-98	n/a	0	0	8	0.092	0	0	0

226 *Appendix A: Macrobotanical Data*

Cultigens

Feature #	Zone	Chenopodium	cf. Chenopod	Echinochloa	Hordeum pusillum	Hordeum/ Zizania	Phalaris caroliniana	Polygonum sp.	Polygonum erectum	Zizania Aquatica	cf. Zizania aquatica
Koshkonong Creek Village											
FF12-01	E	0	4	0	4	0	0	4	0	16	0
FF12-01	I	16	0	0	0	0	0	0	0	96	32
FF12-01	L	1	0	0	0	0	0	0	0	3	0
FF12-01	M	2	0	0	0	0	0	0	0	4	0
FF12-01	P	8	0	0	0	0	0	0	0	28	0
FF12-06	A2	0	0	0	4	32	0	0	0	152	0
FF12-06	B	0	0	0	0	0	0	0	0	248	5
FF12-06	D	0	0	0	0	0	0	0	0	9	4
FF12-06	E	0	0	0	0	0	0	0	0	0	2
FF12-06	G	0	0	0	0	0	0	0	0	6	0
FF12-06	I	0	0	0	0	0	0	0	0	1	0
FF12-06	L	23	0	0	0	0	0	0	0	65	0
FF12-06	O	2	0	0	0	0	0	0	0	0	0
FF12-06	Q	1	0	0	1	0	2	0	0	16	0
FF12-06	R	4	1	0	1	0	0	0	0	13	0
FF12-06	S	0	0	0	0	0	0	0	0	0	0
FF12-06	V	7	0	0	0	6	0	0	0	105	0
FF12-06	W	11	0	0	0	8	0	0	0	10	0
FF12-26	n/a	2	0	0	0	2	0	0	0	22	0

Cultigens (*cont.*)

Feature #	Zone	Chenopodium	cf. Chenopod	Echinochloa	Hordeum pusillum	Hordeum/Zizania	Phalaris caroliniana	Polygonum sp.	Polygonum erectum	Zizania Aquatica	cf. Zizania aquatica
Crescent Bay Hunt Club											
FF00-11	B	174	0	0	0	0	0	0	0	0	0
FF00-11	B	0	27	0	0	0	0	4	0	145	0
FF00-26	B	68	0	0	0	0	0	0	0	0	1
FF02-25	x	0	0	0	0	0	0	0	0	1	0
FF04-03		6	0	0	0	0	0	1	0	8	0
FF04-14	1	0	0	0	0	12	0	0	0	50	0
FF04-14	2	16	0	0	0	0	0	0	0	121	92
FF04-14	3N	7	0	0	0	0	0	0	0	2	0
FF04-14	4	24	0	0	0	4	0	0	0	216	0
FF04-14	5	10	0	0	0	2	0	0	0	14	0
FF04-14	6N	0	0	2	0	0	0	0	0	28	0
FF04-15	A	160	0	0	0	0	0	0	0	136	0
FF04-15	C	0	0	0	10	0	0	0	0	160	0
F04-22	x	546	0	0	0	0	0	0	0	43	0
FF06-63	A	50	0	0	0	0	0	0	0	0	0
FF06-63	B	0	0	0	0	0	0	0	0	0	10
FF06-63	C	3	0	0	0	0	0	0	0	0	0
F10-14	n/a	32	0	0	0	0	0	0	8	409	0
F10-19	n/a	40	0	0	0	0	0	0	0	30	0
F10-29	n/a	64	0	0	0	0	0	0	0	176	0
F10-98	n/a	12	0	0	0	0	0	0	0	24	0

228 *Appendix A: Macrobotanical Data*

Fruits

Feature #	Zone	Crataegus	Frageria	cf. Gaylussacia baccata	Prunus pensylvanica	Prunus nigra	Rhus	cf. Rhus	Rubus	Sambucus	Solanum
Koshkonong Creek Village											
FF12-01	E	0	0	0	0	0	0	4	0	0	0
FF12-01	I	0	0	0	0	16	0	0	0	0	0
FF12-01	L	0	0	0	0	0	0	0	0	0	0
FF12-01	M	0	0	0	0	0	0	4	0	0	0
FF12-01	P	0	0	0	0	0	0	4	0	8	0
FF12-06	A2	0	0	0	0	0	0	0	0	0	0
FF12-06	B	0	0	0	0	0	0	0	0	0	0
FF12-06	D	0	0	0	0	0	0	0	0	0	0
FF12-06	E	0	0	0	0	1	0	0	0	1	0
FF12-06	G	0	0	0	0	0	0	0	0	1	0
FF12-06	I	0	0	0	0	0	0	0	0	0	2
FF12-06	L	0	0	0	0	0	0	0	0	4	0
FF12-06	O	0	2	0	0	0	0	0	0	0	0
FF12-06	Q	0	1	0	0	2	2	0	0	6	0
FF12-06	R	0	0	0	0	0	0	0	0	0	0
FF12-06	S	0	0	0	0	2	0	0	0	2	0
FF12-06	V	0	0	0	0	0	0	0	0	0	0
FF12-06	W	0	0	0	0	0	0	0	0	0	0
FF12-26	n/a	2	0	0	0	0	0	2	0	0	0

Appendix A: Macrobotanical Data 229

Fruits (cont.)

Feature #	Zone	Crataegus	Frageria	cf. Gaylussacia baccata	Prunus pensylvanica	Prunus nigra	Rhus	cf. Rhus	Rubus	Sambucus	Solanum
Crescent Bay Hunt Club											
FF00-11	-	0	0	0	0	1	0	0	0	0	0
FF00-11	B	0	0	0	1	0	0	0	4	0	0
FF00-26	B	0	0	0	0	0	0	0	0	0	0
FF02-25	X	0	0	0	0	0	0	0	0	0	0
FF04-03		0	0	0	0	0	0	0	0	0	0
FF04-14	1	0	0	0	0	0	0	0	14	0	0
FF04-14	2	0	0	0	0	0	0	0	0	0	20
FF04-14	3N	0	0	0	0	0	0	0	0	0	0
FF04-14	4	4	0	0	0	0	0	0	0	0	0
FF04-14	5	0	0	0	0	0	0	0	0	0	0
FF04-14	6N	0	0	0	0	0	0	0	0	0	0
FF04-15	A	0	0	0	0	0	0	0	0	0	0
FF04-15	C	0	0	0	0	0	0	0	0	0	32
F04-22	x	32	0	0	0	0	0	0	0	0	0
FF06-63	A	0	0	0	0	0	0	0	0	0	0
FF06-63	B	0	0	1	0	0	0	0	0	0	0
FF06-63	C	0	0	0	1	0	0	0	0	0	0
F10-14	n/a	8	0	0	0	0	0	0	24	0	24
F10-19	n/a	0	0	0	0	0	0	0	0	0	0
F10-29	n/a	0	0	0	0	0	0	0	0	0	0
F10-98	n/a	0	0	0	0	0	0	0	24	0	24

Other Seeds: Part 1

Koshkonong Creek Village

Feature #	Zone	Acalypha	Amaranthus	cf. Amaranthus	Apiaceae	Asteraceae	cf. Asteraceae	Brassicaceae	Brasenia schreberi	Moehringia	Cyperaceae	Euphorbiaceae	Ipomea	Lamium	Najas	Panicum	cf. Panicum	Poaceae	Potentilla
FF12-01	E	0	0	4	0	0	0	0	0	0	0	0	0	0	#	0	4	0	0
FF12-01	I	0	16	16	0	0	0	0	0	0	32	0	0	0	96	0	0	0	0
FF12-01	L	0	1	0	0	0	0	0	0	0	0	0	0	0	0	0	0	1	0
FF12-01	M	0	1	0	0	0	0	0	0	0	1	0	0	0	1	0	0	1	0
FF12-01	P	0	0	0	0	8	0	0	0	0	0	0	0	0	0	0	0	0	4
FF12-06	A2	0	0	0	0	0	0	0	4	0	0	0	0	0	20	0	0	8	0
FF12-06	B	0	0	0	0	0	0	0	8	0	0	0	0	0	0	0	0	0	0
FF12-06	D	0	0	0	0	0	0	0	0	0	0	0	0	0	1	0	0	0	0
FF12-06	E	0	0	0	0	6	0	0	0	0	0	0	0	0	1	0	0	0	0
FF12-06	G	0	0	0	0	0	2	0	0	0	0	0	0	0	1	4	0	0	0
FF12-06	I	0	0	0	0	0	0	0	0	0	0	0	0	0	3	4	0	2	0
FF12-06	L	0	0	0	0	0	0	0	0	0	0	0	0	0	4	0	0	6	0
FF12-06	O	0	0	0	0	2	0	1	0	0	0	0	0	0	10	0	0	0	0
FF12-06	Q	0	0	0	0	0	0	0	0	0	0	0	0	0	0	2	0	3	0
FF12-06	R	0	2	0	0	0	0	0	1	0	3	0	0	0	0	0	0	0	0
FF12-06	S	0	0	0	0	0	0	0	0	0	0	0	0	0	0	0	0	0	0
FF12-06	V	0	0	0	0	0	0	0	0	0	0	0	0	0	#	0	0	0	0
FF12-06	W	0	0	0	0	0	0	0	0	0	0	0	0	0	10	0	0	0	0
FF12-26	n/a	0	0	2	0	0	0	0	0	0	0	0	0	0	0	0	0	0	0

Appendix A: Macrobotanical Data   231

Other Seeds: Part 1 (cont.)

Feature #	Zone	Acalypha	Amaranthus	cf. Amaranthus	Apiaceae	Asteraceae	cf. Asteraceae	Brassicaceae	Brasenia schreberi	Moehringia	Cyperaceae	Euphorbiaceae	Ipomea	Lamium	Najas	Panicum	cf. Panicum	Poaceae	Potentilla
Crescent Bay Hunt Club																			
FF00-11	B	1	0	0	0	0	0	10	0	0	0	0	0	0	0	0	0	1	0
FF00-11	B	0	0	0	0	0	0	4	0	0	0	1	0	0	0	0	0	28	8
FF00-26	x	0	0	13	0	0	0	0	0	0	0	0	0	0	0	0	4	4	0
FF02-25		0	0	0	0	0	0	0	0	0	0	0	4	0	0	0	0	0	0
FF04-03	1	0	0	1	0	0	0	0	0	0	0	0	0	0	0	0	0	0	0
FF04-14	2	0	0	0	0	0	8	0	0	1	0	4	0	1	8	0	0	0	0
FF04-14	3N	0	0	0	0	0	0	0	0	0	0	0	0	0	56	0	0	0	0
FF04-14	4	0	0	0	4	0	0	0	0	0	0	0	0	0	4	0	0	2	0
FF04-14	5	0	0	0	0	0	0	0	0	0	0	2	0	0	0	0	0	0	0
FF04-14	6N	0	0	0	0	0	0	0	0	0	0	0	0	0	0	10	0	10	0
FF04-15	A	0	0	0	0	0	10	0	0	0	0	0	0	0	0	0	0	20	0
FF04-15	C	0	0	0	0	0	0	0	0	0	0	0	0	0	0	0	0	0	0
F04-22	x	0	0	66	0	0	0	0	0	0	0	0	0	0	0	0	0	30	0
FF06-63	A	0	0	0	0	0	0	0	0	0	0	0	0	0	0	0	0	2	0
FF06-63	B	0	0	0	0	0	0	0	0	0	0	0	0	0	0	0	0	0	0
FF06-63	C	0	0	8	0	0	0	0	0	0	0	0	0	0	0	0	0	0	0
F10-14	n/a	0	0	0	0	0	0	0	0	0	0	0	0	0	0	0	0	0	2
F10-19	n/a	0	0	0	0	0	0	0	0	0	0	0	0	0	0	0	0	0	0
F10-29	n/a	0	0	0	0	0	0	0	0	0	0	0	0	0	0	0	0	0	0
F10-98	n/a	0	0	0	0	0	0	0	0	0	0	0	0	0	0	0	0	0	0

Other Seeds: Part 2

Feature #	Zone	Rosaceae	cf. Rosaceae	Scirpus	Setaria	Silene	Strophostyles helvoela	cf. Strophostyles helvoela	Viola	Verbena	Unidentified Seed Type	Unidentifiable
Koshkonong Creek Village												
FF12-01	E	4	4	0	0	0	0	0	0	0	8	0
FF12-01	I	0	0	0	0	0	0	0	0	0	0	48
FF12-01	L	0	0	0	1	0	0	0	0	0	0	1
FF12-01	M	4	0	0	0	0	0	0	0	0	0	0
FF12-01	P	4	0	0	0	0	0	0	0	0	8	8
FF12-06	A2	0	0	0	0	0	4	0	0	0	0	0
FF12-06	B	0	0	0	0	0	0	0	0	0	0	0
FF12-06	D	1	0	0	0	0	0	0	0	0	0	0
FF12-06	E	0	0	0	0	0	0	0	0	0	0	0
FF12-06	G	1	0	0	0	0	0	0	0	0	0	0
FF12-06	I	0	0	0	0	0	0	0	0	0	0	6
FF12-06	L	0	0	0	0	0	0	0	0	0	0	4
FF12-06	O	2	0	4	0	0	0	0	0	0	0	5
FF12-06	Q	0	0	0	1	0	0	0	0	0	0	0
FF12-06	R	2	0	0	0	0	0	0	0	0	2	10
FF12-06	S	0	0	0	0	0	0	0	0	0	0	0
FF12-06	V	0	0	0	0	0	0	0	0	0	0	4
FF12-06	W	0	0	0	0	0	0	0	0	0	0	10
FF12-26	n/a	0	0	0	0	2	0	0	2	0	0	0

Appendix A: Macrobotanical Data 233

Other Seeds: Part 2 (cont.)

Feature #	Zone	Rosaceae	cf. Rosaceae	Scirpus	Seteria	Silene	Strophostyles helveola	cf. Strophostyles helveola	Viola	Verbena	Unidentified Seed Type	Unidentifiable
Crescent Bay Hunt Club												
FF00-11	B	0	0	0	0	0	0	0	0	0	0	20
FF00-11	B	0	0	0	0	0	0	0	0	0	0	8
FF00-26	B	0	0	0	0	0	0	0	0	0	4	0
FF02-25	x	0	0	0	0	0	0	0	0	0	0	4
FF04-03		0	0	0	0	0	0	0	0	0	2	0
FF04-14	1	0	0	0	0	0	0	0	0	0	4	12
FF04-14	2	8	0	0	0	0	4	10	0	4	2	0
FF04-14	3N	0	0	0	0	0	0	0	0	0	0	0
FF04-14	4	4	0	0	0	0	0	0	0	0	0	16
FF04-14	5	0	0	0	2	0	0	0	0	0	12	0
FF04-14	6N	0	0	0	0	0	0	2	0	0	0	0
FF04-15	A	0	0	0	0	0	0	0	0	0	64	8
FF04-15	C	10	0	0	0	0	0	0	20	0	2	10
F04-22	x	40	0	0	0	0	0	0	0	0	6	#
FF06-63	A	0	0	0	0	0	0	0	0	0	0	20
FF06-63	B	0	0	0	0	0	0	0	0	0	0	20
FF06-63	C	0	0	0	0	0	0	0	0	0	0	10
F10-14	n/a	0	0	0	0	0	0	0	0	0	8	34
F10-19	n/a	0	0	0	0	0	0	0	0	0	0	0
F10-29	n/a	0	0	16	0	0	0	0	0	0	0	0
F10-98	n/a	0	0	0	0	0	0	0	0	0	0	2

234 *Appendix A: Macrobotanical Data*

Other Floral Remains: Part 1

Feature #	Zone	Bud ct.	Bud wt.	Fungus ct.	Fungus wt.	Herbaceous Stem ct.	Herbaceous wt.	Monocot Stem ct.	Monocot Stem wt.	Peduncle ct.	Peduncle wt.	Pine Scales ct.	Pine Scales wt.
Koshkonong Creek Village													
FF12-01	E	0	0	337	1	0	0	0	0	8	0	0	0
FF12-01	I	0	0	738	2	0	0	0	0	0	0	0	0
FF12-01	L	0	0	13	0	1	0.001	0	0	0	0	0	0
FF12-01	M	0	0	31	0	0	0	0	0	0	0	0	0
FF12-01	P	0	0	56	1	4	0.001	0	0	0	0	0	0
FF12-06	A2	0	0	292	0	0	0	0	0	0	0	0	0
FF12-06	B	0	0	1785	6	16	1.136	0	0	0	0	0	0
FF12-06	D	1	0	1	0	0	0	0	0	0	0	0	0
FF12-06	E	0	0	0	0	0	0	0	0	0	0	0	0
FF12-06	G	0	0	31	0	0	0	0	0	0	0	0	0
FF12-06	I	0	0	14	0	0	0	0	0	0	0	0	0
FF12-06	L	1	0	23	0	1	0	0	0	1	0	0	0
FF12-06	O	0	0	108	0	0	0	0	0	0	0	0	0
FF12-06	Q	0	0	64	0	0	0	3	0	0	0	0	0
FF12-06	R	0	0	7	0	0	0	2	0	0	0	0	0
FF12-06	S	0	0	0	0	0	0	0	0	0	0	0	0
FF12-06	V	0	0	4	0	0	0	0	0	0	0	0	0
FF12-06	W	1	0	45	0	0	0	0	0	0	0	0	0
FF12-26	n/a	0	0	53	0	0	0	0	0	98	1	0	0

Other Floral Remains: Part 1 (cont.)

Feature #	Zone	Bud ct.	Bud wt.	Fungus ct.	Fungus wt.	Herbaceous Stem ct.	Herbaceous wt.	Monocot Stem ct.	Monocot Stem wt.	Peduncle ct.	Peduncle wt.	Pine Scales ct.	Pine Scales wt.
Crescent Bay Hunt Club													
FF00-11	B	0	0	16	0	25	0.07	0	0	0	0	0	0
FF00-11	B	4	0	6	0	0	0	28	0	0	0	0	0
FF00-26	B	1	0	1	0	0	0	0	0	0	0	0	0
FF02-25	x	0	0	27	0	0	0	4	0	0	0	0	0
FF04-03		0	0	0	0	0	0	0	0	0	0	5	0
FF04-14	1	0	0	29	0	0	0	0	0	1	0	0	0
FF04-14	2	0	0	38	0	0	0	0	0	1	0	0	0
FF04-14	3N	0	0	2	0	0	0	0	0	0	0	0	0
FF04-14	4	0	0	156	0	0	0	0	0	0	0	0	0
FF04-14	5	0	0	2	0	0	0	0	0	0	0	0	0
FF04-14	6N	0	0	29	0	0	0	0	0	0	0	0	0
FF04-15	A	0	0	328	1	0	0	0	0	0	0	0	0
FF04-15	C	0	0	42	0	0	0	0	0	40	0	0	0
F04-22	x	20	0	107	0	0	0	120	0	0	0	0	0
FF06-63	A	0	0	20	0	0	0	0	0	0	0	0	0
FF06-63	B	0	0	0	0	0	0	2	0	0	0	0	0
FF06-63	C	0	0	0	0	0	0	3	0	0	0	0	0
F10-14	n/a	8	0	18	0	0	0	0	0	8	0	40	0
F10-19	n/a	0	0	84	0	0	0	0	0	0	0	2	0
F10-29	n/a	0	0	93	0	0	0	2	0	0	0	0	0
F10-98	n/a	0	0	36	0	0	0	0	0	0	0	0	0

236 *Appendix A: Macrobotanical Data*

Other Floral Remains: Part 2

Feature #	Zone	Rhizome ct.	Rhizome wt.	Tuber (Aquatic) ct.	Tuber (Aquatic) wt.	Tuber (Terrestrial) ct.	Tuber (Terrestrial) wt.	Twig ct.	Twig wt.	Poaceae Stem ct.	Poaceae Stem wt.	UNID Organic ct.	UNID organic wt.
Koshkonong Creek Village													
FF12-01	E	0	0	0	0	0	0	0	0	0	0	10	1
FF12-01	I	0	0	0	0	0	0	0	0	0	0	16	0
FF12-01	L	0	0	0	0	0	0	0	0	0	0	0	0
FF12-01	M	1	0	0	0	0	0	0	0	0	0	5	0
FF12-01	P	0	0	0	0	0	0	0	0	0	0	8	0
FF12-06	A2	0	0	8	0	0	0	0	0	0	0	56	1
FF12-06	B	0	0	0	0	0	0	0	0	0	0	32	1
FF12-06	D	0	0	0	0	0	0	0	0	0	0	1	0
FF12-06	E	0	0	0	0	0	0	0	0	0	0	0	0
FF12-06	G	0	0	0	0	0	0	0	0	0	0	3	0
FF12-06	I	0	0	1	0	0	0	2	0	0	0	0	0
FF12-06	L	0	0	8	0	0	0	0	0	0	0	12	0
FF12-06	O	0	0	0	0	0	0	0	0	1	0	24	0
FF12-06	Q	0	0	0	0	0	0	0	0	0	0	0	0
FF12-06	R	0	0	0	0	0	0	0	0	0	0	6	0
FF12-06	S	0	0	0	0	0	0	0	0	0	0	0	0
FF12-06	V	0	0	1	0	0	0	0	0	0	0	16	0
FF12-06	W	0	0	0	0	0	0	0	0	0	0	7	0
FF12-26	n/a	0	0	0	0	0	0	0	0	4	0	8	0

Other Floral Remains: Part 2 (cont.)

Feature #	Zone	Rhizome ct.	Rhizome wt.	Tuber (Aquatic) ct.	Tuber (Aquatic) wt.	Tuber (Terrestrial) ct.	Tuber (Terrestrial) wt.	Twig ct.	Twig wt.	Poaceae Stem ct.	Poaceae Stem wt.	UNID Organic ct.	UNID organic wt.
Crescent Bay Hunt Club													
FF00-11	B	0	0	0	0	0	0	0	0	0	0	0	0
FF00-11	B	0	0	0	0	0	0	0	0	63	0	0	0
FF00-26	B	0	0	0	0	0	0	0	0	0	0	0	0
FF02-25	x	0	0	0	0	0	0	0	0	32	0	0	0
FF04-03		0	0	0	0	0	0	0	0	14	0	0	0
FF04-14	1	0	0	0	0	4	0	0	0	0	0	0	0
FF04-14	2	0	0	0	0	0	0	0	0	0	0	0	0
FF04-14	3N	0	0	0	0	0	0	0	0	1	0	0	0
FF04-14	4	0	0	0	0	16	1	0	0	48	0	0	0
FF04-14	5	0	0	0	0	0	0	0	0	14	0	0	0
FF04-14	6N	0	0	0	0	0	0	0	0	0	0	0	0
FF04-15	A	0	0	0	0	24	2	0	0	24	1	0	0
FF04-15	C	0	0	11	0	1	0	0	0	161	1	0	0
F04-22	x	0	0	0	0	0	0	0	0	72	2	0	0
FF06-63	A	0	0	0	0	0	0	0	0	120	0	0	0
FF06-63	B	0	0	5	0	0	0	0	0	150	1	0	0
FF06-63	C	0	0	3	0	0	0	0	0	16	0	0	0
F10-14	n/a	0	0	0	0	8	0	0	0	64	0	8	0
F10-19	n/a	0	0	0	0	0	0	0	0	12	0	0	0
F10-29	n/a	0	0	0	0	0	0	0	0	1	0	0	0
F10-98	n/a	0	0	0	0	0	0	0	0	0	0	4	0

APPENDIX B

CSA Isotopic Data

ACRF	Site	Context/Lot No.	Taxon	Skeletal Element
3572	CBHC, 47JE904	F10-14	*C. familiaris*	left rib
3573	CBHC, 47JE904	F10-11	*C. familiaris*	zygomatic
3574	Diamond Bluff, 47PI2	Sq. G	*C. familiaris*	left mandible
3575	Diamond Bluff, 47PI2	Sq. Z	*C. familiaris*	left mandible
3759	Valley View, 47LC34	1979.1852.0 F99	*C. familiaris*	mandible frag
3760	Valley View, 47LC34	1979.942.463 F106	*C. familiaris*	mandible frag
3761	Pammel Creek 47LC61	1984.1637.41 F180	*C. familiaris*	mandible frag
3762	Sanford, 47LC394	1991.1658 F59	*C. familiaris*	mandible frag
3763	Sanford, 47LC394	1991.2321 F516	*C. familiaris*	mandible frag

Duplicate Run

ACRF	Site	Context/Lot No.	Taxon	Skeletal Element
3764	Sanford, 47LC394	99.1504.01 F37	*C. familiaris*	mandible frag
3765	OT, 47LC0262	1988.56.1219.2 F3	*C. familiaris*	skull frag
3766	OT, 47LC0262	1988.56.1219.1 F3	*C. familiaris*	mandible frag
3767	OT, 47LC0262	1988.56.909.3 F3	*C. familiaris*	skull frag
3768	OT, 47LC0262	1988.56.909.1 F3	*C. familiaris*	skull frag
3769	OT, 47LC0262	1988.56.909.2 F3	*C. familiaris*	skull frag
3791	Aztalan, 47JE1	Specimen 1	*C. familiaris*	left mandible
3792	Aztalan, 47JE1	Specimen 2	*C. familiaris*	right mandible
3793	Aztalan, 47JE1	Specimen 3	*C. familiaris*	left mandible

ACRF	$\delta^{13}C$ ‰ vPDB	$\delta^{15}N$ ‰ vAIR	Weight % C	Weight % N	C:N Ratio	Atomic C:N	Wt % Collagen
3572	-11.7	9.0	41.3	15.2	2.7	3.2	6.5
3573	-13.7	8.1	42.6	15.4	2.8	3.2	4.1
3574	-12.1	8.9	40.1	14.6	2.7	3.2	5.8
3575	-14.0	9.0	41.9	15.2	2.8	3.2	7.5
3759	-11.6	9.4	40.8	14.8	2.8	3.2	7.2
3760	-13.8	8.8	40.8	14.8	2.8	3.2	12.6
3761	-16.4	8.8	42.2	15.4	2.7	3.2	4.5
3762	-13.6	9.0	45.6	16.3	2.8	3.3	16.3
3763	-14.9	8.7	39.4	14.1	2.8	3.3	3.1
3763	-14.9	8.6	38.6	13.8	2.8	3.3	
3764	-14.0	9.3	42.3	15.0	2.8	3.3	5.3
3765	-13.7	9.5	43.9	15.6	2.8	3.3	6.3
3766	-13.7	9.5	38.9	13.4	2.9	3.4	3.3
3767	-15.4	8.6	37.2	13.2	2.8	3.3	3.4
3768	-14.9	8.6	40.8	14.8	2.8	3.2	4.1
3769	-15.6	8.6	40.5	14.8	2.7	3.2	6.5
3791	-15.1	8.3	43.2	15.6	2.8	3.2	4.6
3792	-14.4	9.2	40.8	14.9	2.7	3.2	5.8
3793	-16.2	8.2	42.4	15.5	2.7	3.2	7.2

Appendix B: CSA Isotopic Data 241

ACRF	AMS Lab Code	¹⁴C Age	1σ Error	Cal 2σ Age Range AD	Confidence Interval Median
3572	D-AMS021779	854	21	1156–1228	1191
3573	D-AMS021780	866	24	1050–1224	1182
3574	D-AMS021781	870	19	1054–1219	1180
3575	D-AMS021782	685	27	1270–1387	1292
3759	D-AMS021787	485	22	1413–1445	1429
3760	D-AMS021783	437	19	1430–1467	1445
3761	D-AMS021784	543	20	1323–1429	1406
3762	D-AMS021785	540	21	1323–1431	1407
3763	D-AMS021786	648	24	1283–1392	1355
3764	D-AMS021788	466	21	1419–1450	1435
3765	D-AMS021789	415	19	1438–1487	1455
3766	D-AMS021790	305	27	1491–1649	1561
3767	D-AMS021791	418	19	1437–1486	1453
3768	D-AMS021792	250	20	1636–1797	1654
3769	D-AMS021793	361	19	1455–1631	1515
3791	D-AMS021794	942	24	1029–1154	1097
3792	D-AMS021795	1049	26	901–1026	996
3793	D-AMS021796	976	31	1013–1154	1084

REFERENCES CITED

Agnew, Drew, AmySue Greiff, Rachel C. McTavish, and Amy Klemmer. 2016. "Investigations of Risk Management and Cultural Continuity: Oneota Faunal Patterns in the Lake Koshkonong Locality." Paper presented at the Midwest Archaeological Conference, Iowa City, IA.

Alex, Robert. n.d. "47PI2 Diamond Bluff Site, Pierce County, Wisconsin." Unpublished field notes in possession of the author.

Allen, Kathleen M. S. 1996. "Iroquoian Landscapes: People, Environments, and the GIS Context." In *New Methods, Old Problems: Geographic Information Systems in Modern Archaeological Research*, edited by H. D. G. Maschner, 198–222. Carbondale: Center for Archaeological Investigations, Southern Illinois University at Carbondale.

Allitt, Sharon, R. Michael Stewart, and Timothy Messner. 2008. "The Utility of Dog Bone (*Canis familiaris*) in Stable Isotope Studies for Investigating the Presence of Prehistoric Maize (*Zea mays* ssp. mays): A Preliminary Study." *North American Archaeologist* 29: 343–67.

Ambrose, Stanley H. 1987. "Chemical Isotopic Techniques of Diet Reconstruction in Eastern North America." In *Emergent Horticultural Economies of the Eastern Woodlands*, edited by W. F. Keegan, 87–109. Carbondale: Center for Archaeological investigations, Southern Illinois University at Carbondale.

Ambrose, Stanley H., Jane Buikstra, and Harold W. Krueger. 2003. "Status and Gender Differences in Diet at Mound 72, Cahokia, Revealed by Isotopic Analysis of Bones." *Journal of Anthropological Archaeology* 22: 217–26.

Ambrose, Stanley H., and Michael J. DeNiro. 1986. "The Isotopic Ecology of East African Mammals." *Oceologia* 69: 395–406.

Ambrose, Stanley H., and Lynette Norr. 1993. "Introduction: Are You What You Eat?" In *Prehistoric Human Bone: Archaeology at the Molecular Level*, edited by J. B. Lambert and G. Grupe, 1–37. New York: Springer-Verlag.

Arzigian, Constance. 1989. "The Pammel Creek Site Floral Remains." *Wisconsin Archeologist* 70: 111–56.

———. 1993. "Analysis of Prehistoric Subsistence Strategies: A Case Study from Southwestern Wisconsin." PhD dissertation, University of Wisconsin–Madison.

———. 2000. "Middle Woodland and Oneota Contexts for Wild Rice Exploitation in Southwestern Wisconsin." *Midcontinental Journal of Archaeology* 25: 245–67.

Arzigian, Constance, and Robert F. Boszhardt. 1989. "Introduction: Environmental Setting and History of Investigations at the Pammel Creek Site." *Wisconsin Archeologist* 70: 1–40.

Arzigian, Constance, Robert F. Boszhardt, Holly P. Halverson, and James L. Theler. 1994. "The Gunderson Site: An Oneota Village and Cemetery in La Crosse, Wisconsin." *Journal of the Iowa Archaeological Society* 41: 3–75.

Arzigian, Constance, James L. Theler, Robert F. Boszhardt, Roland L. Rodell, and Michael Scott. 1989. "Summary of the Pammel Creek Site Analysis and a Proposed Oneota Seasonal Round." *Wisconsin Archeologist* 70: 273–80.

Asch, David L. 1994. "Aboriginal Specialty-Plant Cultivation in Eastern North America: Illinois Prehistory and a Post-Contact Perspective." In *Agricultural Origins and Development in the Midcontinent*, edited by W. Green, 25–83. Iowa City, IA: Office of the State Archaeologist.

Asch, David L., and John P. Hart. 2004. "Crop Domestication in Prehistoric Eastern North America." In *Encyclopedia of Plant and Crop Science*, edited by R. M. Goodman, 314–19. New York: Marcel Dekker.

Asch, David L., and Nancy Asch Sidell. 1982. "A Chronological Development of Prehistoric Agriculture in West-Central Illinois." Paper presented at the 47th Annual Meeting of the Society for American Archaeology, Minneapolis.

Baerreis, David A., and R. A. Bryson. 1965. "Climatic Episodes and the Dating of the Mississippian Cultures." *Wisconsin Archeologist* 46: 203–20.

Baerreis, David Albert, Reid A. Bryson, and John E. Kutzbach. 1976. "Climate and Culture in the Western Great Lakes Region." *Midcontinental Journal of Archaeology* 1: 39–57.

Bamann, Susan, Robert Kuhn, James Molnar, and Dean R. Snow. 1992. "Iroquoian Archaeology." *Annual Review of Anthropology* 21: 435–60.

Bar-Yosef, Ofer. 2000. "The Context of Animal Domestication in Southwestern Asia in Mashkour." In *Archaeozoology of the Near East IV A: Proceedings of the 4th International Symposium on the Archaeozoology of Southwestern Asia and Adjacent Areas*, edited by M. Choyke and F. Poplin, 184–94. Groningen: Rijksuniversiteit Center for Archaeological Research and Consultancy and Groningen Institute for Archaeology.

Barrett, Samuel A. 1933. *Ancient Aztalan*. Bulletin of the Public Museum of the City of Milwaukee 13. Milwaukee, WI: Milwaukee Public Museum.

Benchley, Elizabeth D., Melvin L. Fowler, Harold Hassen, and Gregory James. 1979. *Final Report to the State Historical Society of Wisconsin for Archaeological*

Investigations in Milwaukee County, Wisconsin, 1980–1981. Report of Investigations 31. Milwaukee: University of Wisconsin–Milwaukee Archaeological Research Laboratory.

Bender, Barbara. 1978. "Gatherer-Hunter to Farmer: A Social Perspective." *World Archaeology* 10: 204–22.

Bender, Margaret M., David A. Baerreis, and Raymond L. Steventon. 1981. "Further Light on Carbon Isotopes and Hopewell Agriculture." *American Antiquity* 46: 346–53.

Benn, David W. 1989. "Hawks, Serpents, and Bird-Men: Emergence of the Oneota Mode of Production." *Plains Anthropologist* 34: 233–60.

———. 1995. "Woodland People and the Roots of the Oneota." In *Oneota Archaeology Past, Present, and Future*, edited by W. Green, 91–140. Iowa City, IA: Office of the State Archaeologist.

Berres, Thomas Edward. 2001. *Power and Gender in Oneota Culture: A Study of a Late Prehistoric People*. DeKalb: Northern Illinois University Press.

Betts, Colin. 2006. "The Identification of Protohistoric Epidemics in the Upper Mississippi Valley." *American Antiquity* 71: 233–59.

Binford, Lewis R. 1980. "Willow Smoke and Dogs' Tails: Hunter-Gatherer Settlement Systems and Archaeological Site Formation." *American Antiquity* 45: 4–20.

Bird, Catherine M. 1997. "Langford Tradition Settlement System and the Role of Material Culture in the Maintenance of Social Boundaries." PhD dissertation, University of Wisconsin–Milwaukee.

Bird, Robert. 1970. "Maize and Its Natural and Cultural Environment in the Sierra Huánuco, Peru." PhD dissertation, University of California, Berkeley.

Birmingham, Robert A. 1975. "The Langford Tradition and Its Environmental Context in the Rock River Valley, Illinois." Master's thesis, University of Wisconsin–Milwaukee.

Birmingham, Robert A., and Lynne Goldstein. 2005. *Aztalan: Mysteries of an Ancient Indian Town*. Madison: Wisconsin Historical Society Press.

Blaine, Martha Royce. 1979. *The Ioway Indians*. Civilization of the American Indian 151. Norman: University of Oklahoma Press.

Blair, Emma Hellen. 1911. *The Indian Tribes of the Upper Mississippi Valley and Region of the Great Lakes as described by Nicolas Perrot, French commandant in the Northwest; Bacqueville de la Potherie, French royal commissioner to Canada; Morrell Marston, American army officer, and Thomas Forsyth, United States agent at Fort Armstrong*. Cleveland, OH: Arthur H. Clark.

Bliege Bird, Rebecca, and Eric Alden Smith. 2005. "Signaling Theory, Symbolic Interaction, and Social Capital." *Current Anthropology* 46: 221–48.

Blitz, John H. 1993. "Big Pots for Big Shots: Feasting and Storage in a Mississippian Community." *American Antiquity* 58: 80–86.

Bluhm, Elaine A., and Allen Liss. 1961. "The Anker Site." In *Chicago Area Archaeology*, edited by E. A. Bluhm, 89–137. Urbana: Illinois Archaeological Survey.

Bochrens, Herve, Marjan Mashkour, Dorothee G. Druker, Issam Moussa, and Daniel Billiou. 2006. "Stable Isotope Evidence for Paleodiets in Southern Turkmenistan during Historical Period and Iron Age." *Journal of Archaeological Science* 33, no. 2: 253–64.

Bogaard, Amy. 2005. "'Garden Agriculture' and the Nature of Early Farming in Europe and the Near East." *World Archaeology* 37: 177–96.

Boszhardt, Robert F. 1989. "Ceramic Analysis and Site Chronology of the Pammel Creek Site." *Wisconsin Archeologist* 70: 41–94.

———. 1994. "Oneota Group Continuity at La Crosse: The Brice Prairie, Pammel Creek, and Valley View Phases." *Wisconsin Archeologist* 75: 173–236.

———. 1998. "Oneota Horizons: A La Crosse Perspective." *Wisconsin Archeologist* 79: 196–226.

———. 2000. "Turquoise, Rasps, and Heartlines: The Oneota Bison Pull." In *Mounds, Modoc, and Mesoamerica*, edited by S. R. Ahler, 361–73. Illinois State Museum Scientific Papers Series, vol. 38. Springfield: Illinois State Museum.

———. 2004. "Blind Dates and Blind Faith: The Timeless Story of the 'Emergent' Oneota McKern Phase." *Wisconsin Archeologist* 85: 3–30.

Bowles, Marlin L., Michael D. Jones, and Jenny L. Mc Bride. 2003. "Twenty-Year Changes in Burned and Unburned Sand Prairie Remnants in Northwestern Illinois and Implications for Management." *American Midland Naturalist* 149: 35–45.

Brink, John. 1835. "General Land Office Survey Notes for the Interior Sections of Township 5 North, Range 13 East, 4th Meridian, 1835." Electronic document, available at http://digicoll.library.wisc.edu/SurveyNotesHome.html; accessed September 2016.

Brown, Charles E. 1909. "Additions to the Record of Wisconsin Antiquities III." *Wisconsin Archeologist* 8: 113–38.

Brown, James A. 1961. *The Zimmerman Site: A Report on the Excavations at the Grand Village of the Kaskaskia*. Report of Investigations No. 9. Springfield: Illinois State Museum.

———. 1965. "The Prairie Peninsula: An Interaction Area in the Eastern United States." PhD dissertation, University of Chicago.

———. 1967. *The Gentleman Farm Site, La Salle County, Illinois*. Report of Investigations No. 12. Springfield: Illinois State Museum.

———. 1982. "What Kind of Economy Did the Oneota Have?" In *Oneota Studies*, edited by G. E. Gibbon, 107–12. University of Minnesota Publications in Anthropology No. 1. Minneapolis: University of Minnesota.

———. 1990. "The Oak Forest Site: Investigations into Oneota Subsistence-Settlement in the Cal-Sag Area of Cook County, Illinois." In *At the Edge of Prehistory: Huber Phase Archaeology in the Chicago Area*, edited by J. A. Brown and P. O'Brien. Kampsville, IL: Center for American Archaeology Press.

Brown, James A., and Patricia J. O'Brien, eds. 1990. *At the Edge of Prehistory: Huber Phase Archaeology in the Chicago Area*. Kampsville, IL: Center for American Archaeology Press.

Brown, James A., and Robert F. Sasso. 2001. "Prelude to History on the Eastern Prairies." In *Societies in Eclipse*, edited by D. S. Brose, C. W. Cowan, and R. C. Mainfort Jr., 205–28. Washington, DC: Smithsonian Institution Press.

Brown, Margaret Kimball. 1975. *The Zimmerman Site: Further Excavation at the Grand Village of Kaskaskia*. Reports of Investigations 32. Springfield: Illinois State Museum.

Buckland, A. W. 1878. "Primitive Agriculture." *Journal of the Anthropological Institute of Great Britain and Ireland* 7, no. 2: 2–20.

Buckmaster, Marla M. 1979. "Woodland and Oneota Settlement and Subsistence Systems in the Menominee River Watershed." PhD dissertation, Michigan State University.

Buikstra, Jane E., Jerome C. Rose, and George R. Milner. 1994. "A Carbon Isotopic Perspective on Dietary Variation in Late Prehistoric Western Illinois." In *Agricultural Origins and Development in the Midcontinent*, edited by W. Green, 155–67. Report 19. Iowa City: Office of the State Archaeologist, University of Iowa.

Burleigh, Richard, and Don Brothwell. 1978. "Studies on Amerindian Dogs, 1: Carbon Isotopes in Relation to Maize in the diet of Domestic Dogs from Early Peru and Ecuador." *Journal of Archaeological Science* 26, no. 4: 399–407.

Burnham, H. 1863. "Town 5, Range 13 East, 4th Meridian Northwest Territory." Electronic document, available at http://digicoll.library.wisc.edu/SurveyNotesHome.html; accessed September 2016.

Burton, Robert K., and Paul L. Koch. 1999. "Isotopic Tracking of Foraging and Long-Distance Migration in Northeastern Pacific Pinnipeds." *Oceologia* 119: 578–85.

Byers, David A. L., Susan Henrikson, and Ryan P. Breslawski. "Holocene Cold Storage Practices on the Eastern Snake River Plain: A Risk Mitigation Strategy for Lean Times." *Journal of Anthropological Archaeology* 43: 56–68.

Cancian, Frank. 1980. "Risk and Uncertainty in Agricultural Decision Making." In *Agricultural Decision Making: Anthropological Contributions to Rural Development*, edited by P. F. Bartlett, 161–76. Orlando, FL: Academic Press.

Cannon, Aubrey, Henry P. Schwarcz, and Martin Knyf. 1999. "Marine-Based Subsistence Trends and Stable Isotope Analysis of Dog Bones from Namu, British Columbia." *Journal of Archaeological Science* 26, no. 4: 399–407.

Carpiaux, Natalie C. 2015. "Oneota Ceramics from Lake Koshkonong: An Example from the Koshkonong Creek Village Site." Paper presented at the Midwest Archaeological Conference, Milwaukee, WI.

———. 2018. "The Koshkonong Creek Village Site (47JE349): Ceramic Production, Function, and Deposition at an Oneota Occupation in Southeastern Wisconsin." Master's thesis, University of Wisconsin–Milwaukee.

Carpiaux, Natalie C., and Richard W. Edwards IV. 2017. "Pits, Pots, and Paleobot: Feature Analysis at the Koshkonong Creek Village." Paper presented at the Midwest Archaeological Conference, Indianapolis, IN.

Cashdan, Elizabeth. 1990a. Introduction to *Risk and Uncertainty in Tribal and Peasant Economies*, edited by E. Cashden, 1–16. Boulder, CO: Westview Press.

———, ed. 1990b. *Risk and Uncertainty in Tribal and Peasant Economies*. Boulder, CO: Westview Press.

Chacon, Richard J., and Ruben G. Mendoza, eds. 2007. *North American Indigenous Warfare and Ritual Violence*. Tucson: University of Arizona Press.

Childe, V. Gordon. 2003. *Man Makes Himself*. 4th ed. London: Spokesman.

Clauter, Jody. 2003. "Late Woodland Cultural Complexity in Southeastern Wisconsin: A Ceramic Analysis from the Klug (47OZ26) and Klug Island (47OZ67) Sites." Master's thesis, University of Wisconsin–Milwaukee.

———. 2010. "Same Vessel, Different Mound: Ceramic Analysis from the Nitschke Mound Group (47DO27) and Nitschke Garden Beds (47DO518)." Paper presented at the Annual Meeting of the Society for American Archaeology, St. Louis, MO.

———. 2012. "Effigy Mounds, Social Identity, and Ceramic Technology: Decorative Style, Clay Composition, and Petrography of Wisconsin Late Woodland Vessels." PhD dissertation, University of Wisconsin–Milwaukee.

Clelland, C. E. 1966. *The Prehistoric Animal Ecology of the Upper Great Lakes Region*. Anthropological Papers. Ann Arbor: Museum of Anthropology, University of Michigan.

Clutton-Brock, Juliet, and Nanna Noe-Nygaard. 1990. "New Osteological and C-Isotope Evidence on Mesolithic Dogs: Companions to Hunters and Fishers at Star Carr, Seamer Carr, and Kongemose." *Journal of Archaeological Science* 17: 643–53.

Colson, E. 1979. "In Good Years and Bad: Food Strategies of Self-Reliant Societies." *Journal of Anthropological Research* 35: 18–29.

Cowell, Shannon H., Eric J. Scheutz, and Seth A. Schneider. 2008. "The Oneota Component at the Twin Knolls Site (47JE379)." Paper presented at the 54th Annual Midwest Archaeological Conference, Milwaukee, WI.

Creel, Scott, David Christianson, and John A. Winnie. 2007. "Predation Risk Affects Reproductive Physiology and Demography of Elk." *Science* 315: 960.

Cremin, William M. 1996. "The Berrien Phase of Southwest Michigan: Proto-Potawatomi?" In *Investigating the Archaeological Record of the Great Lake State*, edited by Margaret B. Holman, Janet G. Brashler, and Kathryn E. Parker, 383–414. Kalamazoo, MI: New Issues Press.

Cross, Paula, and Robert J. Jeske. 1988. "La Salle County Home (11-Ls-14) Faunal Analysis." In *Report on Test Excavations at Four Sites in the Illinois and Michigan Canal National Heritage Corridor, La Salle and Grundy Counties, Illinois*, edited by Robert J. Jeske and John P. Hart, 127–28. Contributions, vol. 6. Evanston, IL: Northwestern Archaeological Center.

Curtis, J. T. 1959. *The Vegetation of Wisconsin*. Madison: University of Wisconsin Press.

Cutler, H. C., and L. W. Blake. 1969. "Corn from Cahokia Sites." In *Explorations into Cahokia Archaeology*, edited by M. L. Fowler, 122–36. Bulletin 7. Urbana: Illinois Archaeological Survey.

Deloit, Richard J. 1970. *Illustrated Taxonomy Manual of Weed Seeds*. River Falls, WI: Agronomy Publications.

Densmore, Frances. 1979. *Chippewa Customs*. St. Paul: Minnesota Historical Society Press.

DIVA-GISI. 2013. "United States Administrative Area." Electronic document, available at http://www.diva-gis.org/datadown; accessed November 12, 2013.

Dobbs, Clark A. 1984. "Oneota Settlement Patterns in the Blue Earth River Valley, Minnesota." PhD dissertation, University of Minnesota.

Dobbs, Clark A., and Orrin C. Shane III. 1982. "Oneota Settlement Patterns in the Blue Earth River Valley, Minnesota." In *Oneota Studies*, edited by G. E. Gibbon, 5–68. University of Minnesota Publications in Anthropology, No. 1. Minneapolis: University of Minnesota.

Doolittle, William E. 2000. *Cultivated Landscapes of Native North America*. New York: Oxford University Press.

Dorney, Cheryl H., and John R. Dorney. 1989. "An Unusual Oak Savannah in Northeastern Wisconsin: The Effect of Indian-Caused Fire." *American Midland Naturalist* 122: 103–13.

Drennan, Robert D., and Dale W. Quattrin. 1995. "Social Inequality and Agricultural Resources in the Valle de la Plata, Columbia." In *Foundations of Social Inequality*, edited by T. D. Price and G. M. Feinman, 207–34. New York: Plenum Press.

Dye, David H., and Adam King. 2007. "Desecrating the Sacred Ancestor Temples: Chiefly Conflict and Violence in the American Southeast." In *North American Indigenous Warfare and Ritual Violence*, edited by R. J. Chacon and R. G. Mendoza, 160–81. Tucson: University of Arizona Press.

Edwards IV, Richard W. 2010. "Oneota Settlement Patterns around Lake Koshkonong in Southeast Wisconsin: An Environmental Catchment Analysis Using GIS Modeling." Master's thesis, University of Wisconsin–Milwaukee.

———. 2013. "Wisconsin Oneota Faunal Exploitation: A Case Study from the Crescent Bay Hunt Club (47JE904), Lake Koshkonong, Southeastern Wisconsin." Paper presented at the Annual Meeting of the Society for American Archaeology, Honolulu, HI.

———. 2014a. "Digging Deep for Answers: 2014 Excavations at the Koshkonong Creek Village (47JE379)." Paper presented at the Midwest Archaeological Conference, Urbana, IL.

———. 2014b. "An Examination of Canid Remains from the Crescent Bay Hunt Club." Paper presented at the Annual Meeting of the Society for American Archaeology, Austin, TX.

———. 2016. "Oneota Agricultural Systems of the Koshkonong Locality." Paper presented at the Annual Meeting of the Midwest Archaeological Conference, Iowa City, IA.

———. 2018. *Remnant Corn Hills at Carroll University: 47WK225*. Report of Investigations 476. Milwaukee: University of Wisconsin–Milwaukee Archaeology Research Laboratory.

Edwards IV, Richard W., and Robert Jeske. 2015. "Lake Koshkonong Locality's Place in the Oneota Cultural Landscape of the Lake Michigan Basin." Paper presented at the Midwest Archaeological Conference, Milwaukee, WI.

Edwards IV, Richard W., Robert Jeske, and Joan Coltrain. 2017. "Preliminary Evidence for the Efficacy of the Canine Surrogacy Approach in the Great Lakes." *Journal of Archaeological Science: Reports* 13: 516–25.

Edwards IV, Richard W., and Rachel C. McTavish. 2012. "A Tail of Two Fishes: Oneota Fish Exploitation at the Koshkonong Creek Village Site (47JE379) and the Crescent Bay Hunt Club (47JE904)." Paper presented at the Midwest Archaeological Conference, East Lansing, MI.

Edwards IV, Richard W., and Kimberly Pater. 2011. "What's on the Menu: An Updated Analysis of Subsistence at the Crescent Bay Hunt Club (47JE904)." Paper presented at the Midwest Archaeological Conference, La Crosse, WI.

Edwards IV, Richard W., and Elizabeth K. Spott. 2012. "An Oneota Village in an Upland Setting: 2012 Excavations at the Koshkonong Creek Village Site (47JE379)." Paper presented at the Midwest Archaeological Conference, East Lansing, MI.

Egan, Kathryn C. 1988. "Jehalo Site (11Gr96) Archaeobotanical Analysis." In *Report on Test Excavations at Four Sites in the Illinois and Michigan Canal National Heritage Corridor, La Salle and Grundy Counties, Illinois*, edited by R. Jeske and J. P. Hart. Evanston, IL: Northwestern Archaeological Center.

———. 1993a. "Floral Analysis: 1991 Excavations at the Zimmerman Site (11LS13D) LaSalle County, Illinois." Manuscript in possession of the author.

———. 1993b. *Phase II Evaluation and Phase III Mitigation at the Centra 53/54 Site, Washington County, Wisconsin*. Report of Investigations, R-0134. Jackson, WI: Commonwealth Cultural Heritage Group.

Egan-Bruhy, Kathryn C. 2001a. "Crescent Bay Hunt Clun Floral Analysis." In *Program in Midwestern Archaeology (Southeastern Wisconsin Archaeology Program): 2000–2001*, edited by R. Jeske, 57–61. Report of Investigations 148. Milwaukee: University of Wisconsin–Milwaukee.

———. 2001b. "Floral Analysis: Jimmy Junk (47WN-581), Muddy Meadows (47WN-618), Skeleton Bridge (47WN-126), Overton Annex (47WN-769), Overton Acres (47WN-588) and Soggy Oats (47WN-595), Winnebago County, Wisconsin." In *Archaeological Investigations along STH 110, USH 41 to CTH G*, vol. 126, edited by K. Dickerson, K. Krause, A. Marshall, M. L. Meinholz, and P. Ladwig. Madison: Museum Archaeology Program, Wisconsin Historical Society.

———. 2009. "Late Woodland Subsistence Patterns as Reflected (47DA736) at the Murphy and River Quarry Sites (47DA768), Dane County, Wisconsin." In *The Murphy (47DA736) and River Quarry (47DA768) Sites: Two Multi-Component Sites in Dane County, Wisconsin*, edited by M. Hawley, 243–55. Archaeological Research Series 8. Madison: Museum Archaeology Program, Wisconsin Historical Society.

———. 2010a. "Floral Analysis." In *Final Report: Archaeological Monitoring and Recovery of Sub-Roadbed Deposits at the Schrage Site, Calumetville, Wisconsin*, edited by S. A. Schneider and J. D. Richards, 225–46. Report of Investigations 180. Milwaukee: Historic Resource Management Services, University of Wisconsin–Milwaukee Archaeological Research Laboratory.

———. 2010b. "Floral Analysis: Burley Brew (47PT159), Dambrowski (47PT160) and Blinded by the Light (47PT191)." In *Phase III Data Recovery at Oneota Villages along the Waupaca/Tomorrow River in Portage County, Wisconsin: The Blinded by the Light (47PT191/BPT-0134) and Dambrowski (47PT160/47BPT137)*, edited by K. Hamilton, S. R. Kuehn, R. Riggs, and J. M. Kennedy, 146–51. Archaeological Research Series. Madison: Wisconsin Historical Society.

———. 2012. "Floral Analysis: Pamperin Park North (47BR0389)." Manuscript in possession of the author.

———. 2014. "Ethnicity as Evidence in Subsistence Patterns of Late Prehistoric Upper Great Lakes Populations." *Midcontinental Journal of Archaeology Occasional Papers* 1: 53–72.

Egan-Bruhy, Kathryn C., and Jean Nelson. 2013. "Floral Analysis." In *The Hoxie Farm Site Fortified Village: Late Fisher Phase Occupation and Fortification in South Chicago*, edited by D. K. Jackson and T. E. Emerson, 433–46. Illinois

State Archaeological Research Report 27. Urbana-Champaign: Illinois State Archaeological Survey.

Emerson, Kjersti E., and Thomas E. Emerson. 2015. "Ethnic Identity and Interaction in Late Prehistoric Northeastern Illinois." Paper presented at the Midwest Archaeological Conference, Milwaukee.

Emerson, Thomas E. 1991. "The Apple River Mississippian Culture of Northwestern Illinois." In *Cahokia and the Hinterlands*, edited by T. E. Emerson and R. B. Lewis, 164–82. Urbana: University of Illinois Press.

———. 1992. "The Mississippian Dispersed Village as a Social and Environmental Strategy." In *Late Prehistoric Agriculture: Observations from the Midwest*, edited by W. I. Woods, 198–216. Studies in Illinois Archaeology. Springfield: Illinois Historic Preservation Agency.

———. 1999. "The Langford Tradition and the Process of Tribalization on the Middle Mississippian Borders." *Midcontinental Journal of Archaeology* 24: 3–56.

———. 2007. "Cahokia and the Evidence for Late Pre-Columbian War in the North American Midcontinent." In *North American Indigenous Warfare and Ritual Violence*, edited by R. J. Chacon and R. G. Mendoza, 129–48. Tucson: University of Arizona Press.

Emerson, Thomas E., Kristin M. Hedman, and Mary L. Simon. 2005. "Marginal Horticulturalists or Maize Agriculturalists? Archaeobotanical, Paleopathological, and Isotopic Evidence Relating to Langford Tradition Maize Consumption." *Midcontinental Journal of Archaeology* 30: 67–118.

Emerson, Thomas E., Kristin M. Hedman, Robert E. Warren, and Mary L. Simon. 2010. "Langford Mortuary Patterns as Reflected in the Material Service Quarry Site in the Upper Illinois River Valley." *Wisconsin Archeologist* 91: 1–77.

Emerson, Thomas E., Robert Jeske, and Leighann Calentine. 2006. "A New Radiocarbon Date from a Langford Tradition House at the Fisher Site (11WI5)." *Illinois Archaeology* 17: 168–72.

Emerson, Thomas E., Phillip G. Millhouse, and Majorie Schroeder. 2007. "The Lundy Site and the Mississippian Presence in the Apple River Valley." *Wisconsin Archeologist* 88: 1–123.

Emerson, Thomas E., and Anne R. Titelbaum. 2000. "The Des Plaines Complex and the Late Woodland Stage of Northern Illinois." In *Late Woodland Societies: Tradition and Transformation across the Midcontinent*, edited by T. E. Emerson, D. L. McElrath, and A. C. Fortier, 413–28. Lincoln: University of Nebraska Press.

Faulkner, Charles. 1972. *The Late Prehistoric Occupation of Northwestern Indiana: A Study of the Upper Mississippian Cultures of the Kankakee Valley*. Prehistoric Research Series 5(1). Indianapolis: Indiana Historical Society.

Fischer, Anders, Jesper Olsen, Mike Richards, Jan Heinmeier, and Arny E. Sveinbjornsdottir. 2007. "Coast-Inland Mobility and Diet in the Danish Mesolithic and Neolithic: Evidence from Stable Isotope Values of Humans and Dogs." *Journal of Archaeological Science* 34: 2125–50.

Fitzhugh, Ben. 2001. "Risk and Invention in Human Technological Evolution." *Journal of Anthropological Archaeology* 20: 125–67.

Flannery, Kent V. 2002. "The Origins of the Village Revisited: From Nuclear to Extended Families." *American Antiquity* 67: 417–33.

Fleisher, B. *Agricultural Risk Management*. Boulder, CO: Lynne Reinner.

Fleming, Edward Paul. 2009. "Community and Aggregation in the Upper Mississippi River Valley: The Red Wing Locality." PhD dissertation, University of Minnesota.

Foley Winkler, Kathleen M. 2011. "Oneota and Langford Mortuary Practices from Eastern Wisconsin and Northeast Illinois" PhD dissertation, University of Wisconsin–Milwaukee.

Ford, Richard I. 1979. "Paleoethnobotany in American Archaeology." In *Advances in Archaeological Method and Theory*, vol. 2, edited by M. B. Schiffer, 285–336. New York: Academic Press.

———. 1985. "The Processes of Plant Food Production in Prehistoric North America." In *Prehistoric Food Production in North America*, edited by R. I. Ford, 1–18. Anthropological Paper No. 75. Ann Arbor: Museum of Anthropology, University of Michigan.

Fowler, Melvin L. 1940. "The Robinson Reserve Component: Its Cultural Affiliation and Significance." Master's thesis, University of Chicago.

———. 1978. "Cahokia and the American Bottom: Settlement Archaeology." In *Mississippian Settlement Patterns*, edited by B. D. Smith, 455–78. New York: Academic Press.

Fowler, Peter J. 1983. *The Farming of Prehistoric Britain*. Cambridge: Cambridge University Press.

Fritz, Gayle J. 1992. "'Newer,' 'Better' Maize and the Mississippian Emergence: A Critique of Prime Mover Explanations." In *Late Prehistoric Agriculture: Observations from the Midwest*, edited by W. I. Woods, 19–43. Studies in Illinois Archaeology. Springfield: Illinois Historic Preservation Agency.

———. 2000. "Native Farming Systems and Ecosystems in the Mississippi River Valley." In *Imperfect Balance: Landscape Transformations in the Pre-Columbian Americas*, edited by D. L. Lentz, 224–49. New York: Columbia University Press.

———. 2019. *Feeding Cahokia: Early Agriculture in the North American Heartland*. Tuscaloosa: University of Alabama Press.

Fuller, Dorian Q., Chris Stevens, and Meriel McClatchie. 2014. "Routine Activities, Tertiary Refuse, and Labor Organization: Social Inferences from

Everyday Archaeobotany." In *Ancient Plants and People: Contemporary Trends in Archaeobotany*, edited by M. Madella, C. Lancelotti, and M. Savard, 174–217. Tucson: University of Arizona Press.

Gallagher, Daphne E. 2014. "Formation Processes of the Macrobotanical Record." In *Method and Theory in Paleoethnobotany*, edited by J. M. Marston, J. D. A. Guedes, and C. Warinner, 19–34. Boulder: University Press of Colorado.

Gallagher, James P. 1992. "Prehistoric Field Systems in the Upper Midwest." In *Late Prehistoric Agriculture: Observations from the Midwest*, edited by W. I. Woods, 95–135. Studies in Illinois Archaeology. Springfield: Illinois Historic Preservation Agency.

Gallagher, James P., and Constance Arzigian. 1994. "A New Perspective on Late Prehistoric Agricultural Intensification in the Upper Mississippi River Valley." In *Agricultural Origins and Development in the Midcontinent*, edited by W. Green, 171–88. Report 19. Iowa City: Office of the State Archaeologist, the University of Iowa.

Gallagher, James P., Robert F. Boszhardt, Robert F. Sasso, and Katherine Stevenson. 1985. "Oneota Ridged Field Agriculture in Southwestern Wisconsin." *American Antiquity* 50: 605–12.

———. 1987. "Floodplain Agriculture in the Driftless Area: A Reply to Overstreet." *American Antiquity* 52: 398–404.

Gallagher, James P., and Robert F. Sasso. 1987. "Investigations into Oneota Ridged Field Agriculture on the Northern Margin of the Prairie Peninsula." *Plains Anthropologist* 32, no. 116: 141–51.

Gallagher, James P., and Katherine Stevenson. 1982. "Oneota Subsistence and Settlement in Southwestern Wisconsin." In *Oneota Studies*, edited by G. E. Gibbons, 15–28. University of Minnesota Publications in Anthropology No. 1. Minneapolis: University of Minnesota.

Gardner, Paul S. 1997. "The Ecological Structure and Behavioral Implications of Mast Exploitation Strategies." In *People, Plants, and Landscapes Studies in Paleoethnobotany*, edited by K. J. Gremillion, 161–78. Tuscaloosa: University of Alabama Press.

Gardner, Robert, and Karl G. Heider. 1969. *Gardens of War: Life and Death in the New Guinea Stone Age*. New York: Random House.

Garnsey, P., and I. Morris. 1989. "Risk and the Polis: The Evolution of Institutionalized Responses to Food Supply Problems and the Ancient Greek State." In *Bad Year Economics: Cultural Responses to Risk and Uncertainty*, edited by P. Halstead and J. M. O'Shea, 98–105. New Directions in Archaeology. New York: Cambridge University Press.

Gauch, Hugh G. 1982. *Multivariate Analysis in Community Ecology*. Cambridge: Cambridge University Press.

Gibbon, Guy. 1969. "The Walker Hooper and Bornick Sites." PhD dissertation, University of Wisconsin–Madison.

———. 1971. "The Bornick Site: A Grand River Phase Oneota Site in Marquette County." *Wisconsin Archeologist* 52: 85–137.

———. 1972a. "Cultural Dynamics and the Development of the Oneota Life-Way in Wisconsin." *American Antiquity* 37: 166–85.

———. 1972b. "The Walker-Hooper Site: A Grand River Oneota Site in Green Lake County." *Wisconsin Archeologist* 53: 149–290.

———, ed. 1982. *Oneota Studies*. Minneapolis: University of Minnesota.

———. 1986. "The Mississippian Tradition: Oneota Culture." *Wisconsin Archeologist* 67: 314–38.

———. 1995. "Oneota at the Periphery: Trade, Political Power and Ethnicity in Northern Minnesota and on the Northeastern Plains in the Late Prehistoric Period." In *Oneota Archaeology: Past, Present, and Future*, edited by W. Green, 175–99. Report 20. Iowa City: Office of the State Archaeologist, University of Iowa.

———. n.d. "Je 244: The Crescent Bay Hunt Club Site." Manuscript in possession of the author.

Gibbon, Guy, and Clark A. Dobbs. 1991. "The Mississippian Presence in the Red Wing Area, Minnesota." In *New Perspectives on Cahokia*, edited by J. B. Stoltman, 281–306. Madison, WI: Prehistory Press.

Gilmore, Melvin Randolph. 1919. *Use of Plants by the Indians of the Missouri River Region*. Thirty-third Annual Report to the Bureau of American Ethnology. Washington, DC: Smithsonian Institution, Government Printing Office.

Gladwin, Christina H. 1980. "A Theory of Real-Life Choice: Applications to Agricultural Decisions." In *Agricultural Decision Making: Anthropological Contributions to Rural Development*, edited by P. F. Barlett, 45–86. New York: Academic Press.

Gleason, H. A. 1913. "The Relation of Forest Distribution and Prairie Fires in the Middle West." *Torreya* 13: 173–81.

Gmelch, George. 1992. "Baseball Magic." *Elysian Fields* 11, no. 3: 25–35.

Goette, Susan, Michele Williams, Sissel Johannessen, and Christine A. Hastorf. 1990. "Experiments in Maize Charring." *Journal of Ethnobiology* 14: 1–21.

Goland, Carol. 1993. "Field Scattering as Agricultural Risk Management: A Case Study from Cuyo Cuyo, Department of Puno, Peru." *Mountain Research and Development* 13: 317–38.

Goldstein, Lynne, and Joan Freeman. 1997. "Aztalan—A Middle Mississippian Village." *Wisconsin Archeologist* 78: 223–49.

Goldstein, Lynne, and John D. Richards. 1991. "Ancient Aztalan: The Cultural and Ecological Context of a Late Prehistoric Site in the Midwest." In *Cahokia and the Hinterlands*, edited by T. E. Emerson and R. B. Lewis, 193–206. Urbana: University of Illinois Press.

Grantham, Larry. 1993. "The Illini Village of the Marquette and Jolliet Voyage of 1673." *Missouri Archaeologist* 54: 1–20.

Green, William. 1997. "Middle Mississippian Peoples." *Wisconsin Archeologist* 78: 202–22.

———. 2014. "Identity, Ideology and the Effigy Mound-Oneota Transformation." *Wisconsin Archeologist* 95: 44–72.

Green, William, and David J. Nolan. 2000. "Late Woodland People in West-Central Illinois." In *Late Woodland Societies: Tradition and Transformation across the Midcontinent*, edited by T. E. Emerson, D. L. McElrath, and A. C. Fortier, 345–86. Lincoln: University of Nebraska Press.

Greenacre, Michael. 1984. *Theory and Applications of Correspondence Analysis*. Orlando, FL: Academic Press.

Griffin, Duane. 1994. "Pollen Analog Dates for the Upper Midwest Oak Savannas." In *Living in the Edge: Proceedings of the North American Conference on Savannas and Barrens*, edited by James Fralish, 91–96. Normal, IL: United States Environmental Protection Agency.

Griffin, James B. 1937. "The Archaeological Remains of the Chiwere Sioux." *American Antiquity* 2: 180–81.

———. 1952. *The Archaeology of the Eastern United States*. Chicago: University of Chicago Press.

———. 1960. "Climatic Change: A Contributory Cause of the Growth and Decline of Northern Hopewellian Culture." *Wisconsin Archeologist* 41: 22–33.

———. 1967. "Eastern North American Archaeology: A Summary." *Science* 156: 175–91.

Griffin, John Wallace. 1946. "The Upper Mississippian Occupations of the Fisher Site, Will County, Illinois." Master's thesis, University of Chicago.

———. 1948. "Upper Mississippi at the Fisher Site." *American Antiquity* 4: 125–26.

Guiry, Eric J. 2012. "Dogs as Analogs in Stable Isotope-Based Human Paleodietary Reconstructions: A Review and Considerations for Future Use." *Journal of Archaeological Method and Theory* 19: 354–76.

———. 2013. "A Canine Surrogacy Approach to Human Paleodietary Bone Chemistry: Past Development and Future Direction." *Archaeobiological and Anthropological Sciences* 5: 275–86.

Gurven, Michael. 2004. "Reciprocal Altruism and Food Sharing Decisions among Hiwi and Ache Hunter-Gatherers." *Behavioral Ecology and Social Biology* 56: 366–80.

———. 2006. "The Evolution of Contingent Cooperation." *Current Anthropology* 47: 185–92.

Haas, Jennifer R., Jennifer L. Picard, and Catherine Jones. 2017. *Skeletal Analysis for Sites 47DA0464 (BDA-0625) and 47DA1428 (BDA-0622) for the Lower Yahara River Trail Phase I Improvements, Dane County, Wisconsin.* Report of Investigations 444. Milwaukee: University of Wisconsin–Milwaukee Archaeological Research Laboratory.

Hall, Robert L. 1962. *The Archaeology of Carcajou Point: With an Interpretation of the Development of Oneota Culture in Wisconsin.* 2 vols. Madison: University of Wisconsin Press.

———. 1991. "Cahokia Identity and Interaction Models of Cahokia Mississippian." In *Cahokia and the Hinterlands*, edited by T. E. Emerson and R. B. Lewis, 3–34. Urbana: University of Illinois Press.

———. 1993. "Red Banks." *Wisconsin Archeologist* 74: 10–79.

———. 1995. "Relating the Big Fish and the Big Stone: The Archaeological Identity and Habitat of the Winnebago in 1634." In *Oneota Archaeology: Past, Present and Future*, edited by W. Green. Iowa City: University of Iowa Press.

———. 1997. *An Archaeology of the Soul: North American Indian Belief and Ritual.* Urbana: University of Illinois Press.

Halstead, Paul, and John M. O'Shea, eds. 1989a. *Bad Year Economics: Cultural Responses to Risk and Uncertainty.* New York: Cambridge University Press.

———. 1989b. "Cultural Responses to Risk and Uncertainty." In *Bad Year Economics: Cultural Responses to Risk and Uncertainty*, edited by P. Halstead and J. M. O'Shea, 1–7. New Directions in Archaeology. New York: Cambridge University Press.

Hames, Raymond. 1990. "Sharing among the Yanomamo: Part I, The Effects of Risk." In *Risk and Uncertainty in Tribal and Peasant Economies*, edited by E. Cashdan, 89–106. Boulder, CO: Westview Press.

Hamilton, Kelly, Rodney Riggs, Jason M. Kennedy, and Steven R. Kuehn. 2010. *The Blinded by the Light (47PT191/BPT-0134) and Dambrowski (47PT160/0137) Sites, Phase III Data Recovery at Oneota Villages along the Waupaca/Tomorrow River in Portage County, Wisconsin.* Madison: Museum Archaeology Program.

Harkness, D. D., and A. Walton. 1972. "Further Investigations of the Transfer of Bomb ^{14}C to Man." *Nature* 240: 302–3.

Harris, David R. 1989. "An Evolutionary Continuum of People-Plant Interaction." In *Foraging and Farming: The Evolution of Plant Exploitation*, edited by D. R. Harris and G. C. Hillman, 11–26. New York: Routledge Taylor & Francis Group.

Hart, John P. 1990. "Modeling Oneota Agricultural Production: A Cross-Cultural Evaluation." *Current Anthropology* 31, no. 5: 569–77.

———. 1993. "Monongahela Subsistence-Settlement Change: The Late Prehistoric Period in the Upper Ohio River Valley." *Journal of World Prehistory* 7: 71–120.

———. 1999. "Maize Agriculture Evolution in the Eastern Woodlands of North America: A Darwinian Perspective." *Journal of Archaeological Method and Theory* 6: 137–80.

———. 2008. "Evolving the Three Sisters: The Changing Histories of Maize, Bean, and Squash in New York and the Greater Northeast." In *Current Northeast Paleoethnobotany II*, edited by J. P. Hart, 87–100. New York State Museum Bulletin 512. Albany: State University of New York.

Hart, John P., and Robert Jeske. 1987. *Report on a Systematic Archaeological Survey of Portions of the Illinois-Michigan Canal National Heritage Corridor, in Cook, Will, Du Page, Grundy and La Salle Counties, Illinois*. Contributions No. 5. Evanston, IL: Northwestern Archaeological Center.

Hart, John P., Termeh Shafie, Jennifer Birch, Susan Dermarkar, and Ronald F. Williamson. 2016. "Nation Building and Social Signaling in Southern Ontario: AD 1350-1650." *PLoS ONE* 11, no. 5: e0156178. doi:0156110.0151371/journal.pone.0156178.

Harwood, Richard R. 1979. *Small Farm Development: Understanding and Improving Farming Systems in the Humid Tropics*. Boulder, CO: Westview Press.

Hastorf, Christine A. 1993. *Agriculture and the Onset of Political Inequality before the Inka*. New York: Cambridge University Press.

Hastorf, Christine A., and Virginia S. Popper, eds. 1988. *Current Paleoethnobotany: Analytical Methods and Cultural Interpretations of Plant Remains*. Chicago: University of Chicago Press.

Hawkes, Kristen. 1990. "Why do Men Hunt? Benefits for Risky Choices." In *Risk and Uncertainty in Tribal and Peasant Economies*, edited by E. Cashdan, 145–66. Boulder, CO: Westview Press.

Hawley, Marlin F. 2011. *The Murphy and River Quarry Sites: Two Multi-Component, Native American Sites in Dane County, Wisconsin*. Archaeology Research Series, No. 8. Madison: Museum Archaeology Program, Wisconsin Historical Society.

Hedman, Kristin M., Eve A. Hargrave, and Stanley H. Ambrose. 2002. "Late Mississippian Diet in the American Bottom: Stable Isotope Analyses of Bone Collagen and Apatite." *Midcontinental Journal of Archaeology* 27: 237–71.

Heidenreich, C. E. 1978. "Huron." In *The Handbook of North American Indians*, vol. 15, edited by B. G. Trigger, 368–88. Washington, DC: Smithsonian Institution Press.

Heider, Karl. 1996. *Grand Valley Dani: Peaceful Warrior*. Belmont, CA: Thomson Wadsworth.

Hendrickson, Carl F. 1996. "Late Woodland and Middle Mississippian Interaction at the Bethesda Lutheran Home Site (47 Je 201), Jefferson County, Wisconsin." *Wisconsin Archeologist* 77: 11–35.

Henning, Dale R. 1998a. "Western Manifestations." *Wisconsin Archeologist* 79: 238–47.

———. 1998b. "Managing Oneota: A Reiteration and Testing of Contemporary Archaeological Taxonomy." *Wisconsin Archeologist* 79: 9–28.

Hill, Mark, and Robert J. Jeske. 2011. "Laser Sourcing of Copper from Late Archaic and Late Prehistoric Sites near Lake Koshkonong, Southeastern Wisconsin." Paper presented at the 58th Annual Meeting of the Midwest Archaeological Conference, La Crosse, WI.

Hodge, Fredrick Webb, ed. 1910, *Handbook of American Indians North of Mexico*. Washington, DC: Government Printing Office.

Hollinger, R. Eric, and David W. Benn. 1995. "Residence Patterns and Oneota Cultural Dynamics." In *Oneota Archaeology: Past, Present and Future*, edited by W. Green, 141–74. Office of the State Archaeologist Report, No. 20. Iowa City: University of Iowa.

Holtz-Leith, Wendy K. 2006. *Archaeological Investigations at the Oneota Village in the Heart of La Crosse, Wisconsin: Data Recovery at the Seventh Street Interchange, USH 14-61, South Avenue, within the Sanford Archaeological District, La Crosse, Wisconsin*. ROI no. 438. La Crosse: Mississippi Valley Archaeology Center at the University of Wisconsin–La Crosse.

———. 2011. *Data Recovery Results for a Portion of 47LC394, the Sanford Archaeological District, for the Reconstruction of USH 14/61, Jackson to Farnam Streets, in the City of La Crosse County, Wisconsin*. ROI 705. La Crosse: Mississippi Valley Archaeological Center at the University of Wisconsin–La Crosse.

Horner, George R. 1947. "An Upper-Mississippi House-Pit from the Fisher Village Site: Further Evidence." *Transactions of the Illinois State Academy of Sciences* 40: 26–29.

Hunter, Andrea A., and Caryn M. Berg. 1993. "Analysis of Floral Remains." In *The OT Site, (47LC262)*, edited by J. O'Gorman, vol. 1, 117–40. Madison: State Historical Society of Wisconsin.

Hunter, Chrisie L. 2002. "Understanding Upper Mississippian Subsistence and Settlement through the Use of Catchment Analysis: An Oneota and Langford Perspective." *Wisconsin Archeologist* 83: 76–97.

———. 2003. "Blue Heron Site (47JE1001): 2003 Investigations." In *Lake 2002/2003: Archaeological Investigations at Three Sites in Jefferson County, Wisconsin*, edited by R. J. Jeske, 164–82. Report of Investigations 153. Milwaukee: Archaeological Research Laboratory, University of Wisconsin–Milwaukee.

Hurt, Douglas J. 1987. *Indian Agriculture in America*. Lawrence: University of Kansas Press.

Indiana Department of Natural Resources. 2017. "Indiana Deer Biology." www.in.gov/dnr/fishwild/3359.htm. Accessed August 2017.

Janick, Jules, Robert W. Schery, Frank W. Woods, and Vernon W. Ruttan. 1974. *Plant Science: An Introduction to World Crops*. San Francisco: W. H. Freeman.

Jackson, Douglas K., ed. 2017. *The Hoxie Farm Site Main Occupationi Area: Late Fisher and Huber Phase Components in South Chicago*. Research Report 40. Urbana-Champaign: Illinois State Archaeological Survey.

Jackson, Douglas K., and Thomas E. Emerson, eds. 2013. *The Hoxie Farm Site Fortified Village: Late Fisher Phase Occupation and Fortification in South Chicago*. Research Report 27. Urbana-Champaign: Illinois State Archaeological Survey.

Jenks, Albert E. 1901. *The Wild Rice Gatherers of the Upper Lakes: A Study in American Primitive Economics*. Washington, DC: U.S. Government Printing Office.

Jeske, John A. 1927. "The Grand River Mound Group and Camp Site." *Bulletin of the Public Museum of the City of Milwaukee* 3, no. 2.

Jeske, Robert J. 1989. "Horticultural Technology and Social Interaction at the Edge of the Prairie Peninsula." *Illinois Archaeology* 1: 103–20.

———. 1990. "Langford Tradition Subsistence, Settlement, and Technology." *Midcontinental Journal of Archaeology* 15: 221–49.

———. 1992. "Environment, Ethnicity, and Subsistence Change: The Late Woodland to Mississippian Tradition in the Upper Midwest." *Michigan Archaeologist* 38: 55–71.

———. 2000a. *Southeastern Wisconsin Archaeology Program: 1999–2000*. Report of Investigations 145. Milwaukee: University of Wisconsin–Milwaukee.

———. 2000b. "The Washington Irving Site: Langford Tradition Adaptations in Northern Illinois." In *Mounds, Modoc, and Mesoamerica*, edited by S. R. Ahler, 265–94. Illinois State Museum Scientific Papers Series. vol. 28. Springfield: Illinois State Museum.

———. 2002. "The Langford Occupation at the LaSalle County Home Site (11LS14) in the Upper Illinois River Valley." *Wisconsin Archeologist* 83: 78–122.

———. 2003a. *Lake Koshkonong 2002/2003: Archaeological Investigations at Three Sites in Jefferson County Wisconsin*. Report of Investigations 153. Milwaukee: Archaeological Research Laboratory, University of Wisconsin–Milwaukee.

———. 2003b. "Langford and Fisher Ceramic Traditions: Moiety, Ethnicity or Power Relations in the Upper Midwest?" *Wisconsin Archeologist* 84: 165–80.

———. 2010. "Structures and Function at an Oneota Village." Paper presented at the Midwest Archaeological Conference, Bloomington, IN.

———. 2014. "Violence in the Wisconsin Oneota World: New Evidence from Lake Koshkonong." Paper presented at the Midwest Archaeological Conference, Urbana, IL.

Jeske, Robert J., and Richard W. Edwards IV. 2012. "Differential Land Use Patterns in the Rock River Watershed: Horicon Marsh versus Lake Koshkonong." Paper presented at the Annual Meeting of the Society for American Archaeology, Memphis, TN.

———. 2015. "Oneota of the Western Lake Michigan Basin: The Deep Periphery." Paper presented at the Midwest Archaeological Conference, Milwaukee, WI.

Jeske, Robert J., Richard W. Edwards IV, Katherine M. Sterner-Miller, and Robert Ahlrichs. 2015. "Archaeology around Wisconsin: University of Wisconsin–Milwaukee Program in Midwestern Archaeology." *Wisconsin Archeologist* 96: 123–25.

Jeske, Robert J., Kathleen M. Foley Winkler, and Louise C. Lambert. 2003. "Continuing Investigations at the Crescent Bay Hunt Club Site (47Je904), Jefferson County, Wisconsin." In *Lake Koshkonong 2002/2003: Archaeological Investigations at Three Sites in Jefferson County, Wisconsin*, edited by R. Jeske, 6–94. Report of Investigations 153. Milwaukee: Archaeological Research Laboratory, University of Wisconsin–Milwaukee.

Jeske, Robert J., Kathleen M. Foley Winkler, Daniel M. Winkler, and Richard W. Edwards. 2011. *Human Skeletal Remains and Material Culture Recovered from the Jaco Site (47JE1192) in Jefferson County, Wisconsin*. Report of Investigations 172. Milwaukee: Archaeological Research Laboratory, University of Wisconsin–Milwaukee.

Jeske, Robert J., and John P. Hart. 1988. *Report on Test Excavations at Four Sites in the Illinois and Michigan Canal National Heritage Corridor, La Salle and Grundy Counties, Illinois*. Contribution No. 6. Evanston, IL: Northwestern Archaeological Center.

Jeske, Robert J., Seth A. Schneider, Richard W. Edwards IV, Katherine M. Sterner, and Rachel C. McTavish. 2016. "Strangers in a Strange Land: The Lake Koshkonong Oneota Locality in Context." Paper presented at the Midwest Archaeological Conference, Iowa City, IA.

Jeske, Robert J., Seth A. Schneider, Elizabeth K. Spott, and Richard W. Edwards IV. 2013. "Archaeology around Wisconsin: University of Wisconsin–PIMA." *Wisconsin Archeologist* 94: 280–81.

Jeske, Robert J., and Katherine M. Sterner-Miller. 2014. *Report on the Discovery of Human Remains at the Crescent Bay Hunt Club Site (47 Je 904), Jefferson County, Wisconsin*. Report of Investigations 248. Milwaukee: Archaeological Research Laboratory, University of Wisconsin–Milwaukee.

Jeske, Robert, Katherine M. Sterner, Richard W. Edwards IV, Hannah Blija, Tania Milosavljevic, and Samantha Bomkamp. 2017. "Ten Seasons Later: The Crescent Bay Hunt Club Site and Wisconsin Oneota Lifeways." Paper presented at the Midwest Archaeological Conference, Indianapolis, IN.

Jochim, Michael. 1976. *Hunter-Gatherer Subsistence and Settlement: A Predictive Model*. New York: Academic Press.

Johannessen, Sissel. 1993. "Farmers of the Late Woodland." In *Foraging and Farming in the Eastern Woodlands*, edited by C. M. Scarry, 55–77. Gainesville: University of Florida Press.

Jones, Glynis. 2005. "Garden Cultivation of Staple Crops and Its Implications for Settlement Locations and Continuity." *World Archaeology* 37: 164–76.

Kaplan, Hillard, and Kim Hill. 1985. "Food Sharing among Ache Foragers: Tests of Explanatory Hypotheses." *Current Anthropology* 26: 223–46.

Kaplan, Hillard, Kim Hill, and A. Magdalena Hurtado. 1990. "Risk, Foraging and Food Sharing among the Ache." In *Risk and Uncertainty in Tribal and Peasant Economies*, edited by E. Cashdan, 107–44. Boulder, CO: Westview Press.

Kaplan, Lawrence. 1965. "Archaeology and Domestication in American Phaseolus (Beans)." *Economic Botany* 19: 358–68.

Karsten, Jordan. 2015. "Troubled Times in Late Prehistoric Central Wisconsin: Violent Skeletal Trauma among the Winnebago Phase Oneota." Paper presented at the Midwest Archaeological Conference, Milwaukee, WI.

Katzenberg, M. Anne. 1989. "Stable Isotope Analysis of Archaeological Faunal Remains from Southern Ontario." *Journal of Archaeological Science* 16: 319–29.

———. 1993. "Age Differences and Population Variation in Stable Isotope Values from Ontario, Canada." In *Prehistoric Human Bone: Archaeology at the Molecular Level*, edited by J. B. Lambert and G. Grupe, 39–62. New York: Springer-Verlag.

Kaufmann, Kira. 2005. "Effigy Mound Sites as Cultural Landscapes: A Geophysical Spatial Analysis of Two Late Woodland Sites in Southeastern Wisconsin." PhD dissertation, University of Wisconsin–Milwaukee.

Keegan, William F., and Brian M. Butler. 1987. "The Microeconomic Logic of Horticultural Intensification in the Eastern Woodlands." In *Emergent Horticultural Economies of the Eastern Woodlands*, edited by W. F. Keegan, 109–27. Occasional Papers No. 7. Carbondale: Center for Archaeological Investigations, Southern Illinois University.

Keeley, Lawrence. 1996. "War before Civilization: The Myth of the Peaceful Savage." Oxford: Oxford University Press.

———. 2016. "Food for War, War for Food, and War on Food." In *The Archaeology of Food and Warfare: Food Insecurity in Prehistory*, edited by A. M. VanDerwarker and G. D. Wilson, 291–302. New York: Springer.

Keeley, Lawrence H., Marisa Fontana, and Russel Quick. 2007. "Baffles and Bastions: The Universal Features of Fortifications." *Journal of Archaeological Research* 15: 55–95.

Keene, Arthur S. 1981. *Prehistoric Foraging in a Temperate Forest: A Linear Programming Model*. New York: Academic Press.

Keesing, Felix. 1987. *The Menominee Indians of Wisconsin: A Study of Three Centuries of Culture Contact and Change*. Madison: University of Wisconsin Press.

Kelly, John E. 1992. "The Impact of Maize on the Development of Nucleated Settlements: An American Bottom Example." In *Late Prehistoric Agriculture:*

Observations from the Midwest, edited by W. I. Woods, 167–97. Studies in Illinois Archaeology. Springfield: Illinois Historic Preservation Agency.

Kelly, John M. 2002. "Delineating the Spatial and Temporal Boundaries of Late Woodland Collared Wares from Wisconsin and Illinois." Master's thesis, University of Wisconsin–Milwaukee.

Keyes, Charles Reuben. 1929. "Some Methods and Results of the Iowa Archaeological Survey." *Wisconsin Archeologist* 8: 135–43.

King, Frances B. 1994. "Variability in Cob and Kernel Characteristics of North American Maize Cultivars." In *Corn and Culture in the Prehistoric New World*, edited by S. Johannessen and C. A. Hastorf, 35–53. Boulder, CO: Westview Press.

Kipnis, Renato. 2002. "Long-term Land Tenure Systems in Central Brazil: Evolutionary Ecology, Risk-Management, and Social Geography." In *Beyond Foraging and Collecting: Evolutionary Change in Hunter-Gatherer Settlement Systems*, edited by B. Fitzhugh and J. Habu, 181–230. Fundamental Issues in Archaeology. New York: Spring Science & Business Media.

Kohl, Johann Georg. 1985. *Kitchi-Gami: Life among the Lake Superior Ojibway*. Translated by L. Wraxall. St. Paul: Minnesota Historical Society Press.

Kohler, Timothy A. 1993. "News from Northern American Southwest: Prehistory on the Edge of Chaos." *Journal of Archaeological Research* 1: 267–321.

Kuijt, Ian. 2009. "What Do We Really Know about Food Storage, Surplus, and Feasting in Preagricultural Communities?" *Current Anthropology* 50: 641–44.

Kuznar, Lawrence. 2002. "On Risk-Prone Peasants: Cultural Transmission or Sigmoid Utility Maximization." *Current Anthropology* 43: 787–88.

Lamb, H. H. 1982. *Climate, History, and the Modern World*. New York: Methuen.

Lambert, Patricia M. 2002. "The Archaeology of War: A North American Perspective." *Journal of Archaeological Research* 10: 207–41.

Langford, George. 1927. "The Fisher Mound Group, Successive Aboriginal Occupations Near the Mouth of the Illinois River." *American Anthropologist* 29, no. 3: 153–205.

Lapham, Increase A. 1855. *Antiquities of Wisconsin: As Surveyed and Described*. Washington, DC: Smithsonian Institution.

Lawshe, Fred E. 1947. "The Mero-Site Diamond Bluff, Pierce County, Wisconsin." *Minnesota Archaeologist* 13, no. 4: 74–95.

Lee, Richard B. 1969. "!Kung Bushman Subsistence: An Input-Output Analysis." In *Environment and Cultural Behavior*, edited by A. P. Vayda, 47–79. Garden City, NY: Natural History Press.

Libby, Willard F., Rainer Berger, James F. Mead, George V. Alexander, and Joseph F. Ross. 1964. "Replacement Rates for Human Tissue from Atmospheric Radiocarbon." *Science* 146: 1170–72.

Logan, Brad. 1998. "Oneota Far West: The White Rock Phase." *Wisconsin Archeologist* 79: 246–67.

Lopinot, Neal H. 1992. "Spatial Temporal Variability in Mississippian Subsistence: The Archaeobotanical Record." In *Late Prehistoric Agriculture: Observations from the Midwest*, edited by W. I. Woods, 44–94. Studies in Illinois Archaeology. Springfield: Illinois Historic Preservation Agency.

———. 1994. "A New Crop of Data on the Cahokian Polity." In *Agricultural Origins and Development in the Midcontinent*, edited by W. Green, 127–53. Iowa City, IA: Office of the State Archaeologist.

Low, Bobbi S. 1990. "Human Responses to Environmental Extremeness and Uncertainty: A Cross-Cultural Perspective." In *Risk and Uncertainty in Tribal and Peasant Economies*, edited by E. A. Cashdan, 229–55. Boulder, CO: Westview Press.

Lyman, R. Lee. 2008. *Quantitative Paleozoology*. Cambridge Manuals in Archaeology. New York: Cambridge University Press.

Lynott, Mark J., Thomas W. Boutton, James E. Price, and Dwight E. Nelson. 1986. "Carbon Isotopic Evidence for Maize Agriculture in Southeast Missouri and Northeast Arkansas." *American Antiquity* 51: 51–65.

Lurie, Nancy Oestreich, ed. 1966. *Mountain Wolf Woman, Sister of Crashing Thunder: The Autobiography of a Winnebago Indian*. Ann Arbor: University of Michigan Press.

———. 1978. "Winnebago." In *Northeast*, edited by B. G. Trigger, 690–707. Handbook of North American Indians, vol. 15. Washington, DC: Smithsonian Institution Press.

Marston, John M. 2010. "Evaluating Risk, Sustainability, and Decision Making in Agricultural Land-Use Strategies at Ancient Gordion." PhD dissertation, University of California, Los Angeles.

———. 2011. "Archaeological Markers of Agricultural Risk Management." *Journal of Anthropological Archaeology* 30: 190–205.

———. 2014. "Ratios and Simple Statistics in Paleoethnobotanical Analysis: Data Exploration and Hypothesis Testing." In *Method and Theory in Paleoethnobotany*, edited by J. M. Marston, J. D. A. Guedes, and C. Warinner, 163–80. Boulder: University Press of Colorado.

Marston, John M., Jade D'Alpoim Guedes, and Christina Warinner. 2014. "Paleoethnobotanical Method and Theory in the Twenty-First Century." In *Method and Theory in Paleoethnobotany*, edited by J. M. Marston, J. D'Alpoim Guedes and C. Warinner, 1–18. Boulder: University Press of Colorado.

Martin, Alexander C., and William D. Barkley. 1961. *Seed Identification Manual*. Berkeley: University of California Press.

Martin, Lawrence. 1965. *The Physical Geography of Wisconsin*. Madison: University of Wisconsin Press.

Martin, Terrance J. 2002. "Faunal Analysis: The Langford Occupation at the Lasalle County Home Site in the Upper Illinois River Valley." *Wisconsin Archeologist* 83: 114.

———. 2013. "Animal Remains from the Fortified Village." In *The Hoxie Farm Site Fortified Village: Late Fisher Phase Occupation and Fortification in South Chicago*, edited by D. K. Jackson and T. E. Emerson, 447–50. Illinois State Archaeological Report 27. Urbana-Champaign: Illinois State Archaeological Survey.

Maschner, Herbert D. G., and Katherine L. Reedy-Maschner. 1998. "Raid, Retreat, Defend (Repeat): The Archaeology and Ethnohistory of Warfare on the North Pacific Rim." *Journal of Anthropological Archaeology* 17: 19–51.

Mason, Ronald J. 1966. *Two Stratified Sites on the Door Peninsula of Wisconsin*. Anthropological Papers. Ann Arbor: Museum of Anthropology, University of Michigan.

———. 1993. "Oneota and Winnebago Ethnogenesis." *Wisconsin Archeologist* 74: 400–421.

Mauss, Marcel. 1990. *The Gift: The Form and Exchange in Archaic Societies*. Translated by W. D. Halls. New York: Norton.

Maxwell, Moreau S. 1950. "A Change in the Interpretation of Wisconsin's Prehistory." *Wisconsin Magazine of History* 33: 427–43.

McCloskey, Donald N. 1972. "The Enclosure of Open Fields: Preface to a Study of Its Impacts on the Efficiency of English Agriculture in the Eighteenth Century." *Journal of Economic History* 32: 15–35.

———. 1991. "The Prudent Peasant: New Findings on Open Fields." *Journal of Economic History* 51: 343–55.

McEnaney, Katie, and Reid A. Bryson. 2005. *Archaeoclimactic Models for the Milwaukee, Horicon, and Fort Atkinson Areas*. Madison, WI: Archaeoclimactology Laboratory, Center for Climate Research.

McKern, William C. 1930. "The Kletzien and Nitschke Mound Groups." *Bulletin of the Public Museum of the City of Milwaukee* 3, no. 4: 417–572.

———. 1931. "Wisconsin Pottery." *American Anthropologist* 33, no. 3: 383–90.

———. 1943. "Regarding Midwestern Archaeological Taxonomy." *American Anthropologist* 45: 313–15.

———. 1945. "Preliminary Report on the Upper Mississippi Phase in Wisconsin." *Bulletin of the Public Museum of the City of Milwaukee* 16, no. 3: 109–285.

McLain, W. E., and S. L. Elzinga. 1994. "The Occurrence of Prairie and Forest Fires in Illinois and Other Midwestern States, 1670 to 1854." *Erigenia* 13: 79–90.

McTavish, Rachel C. 2013. "Evaluating the Aztalan Palimpsest: Faunal Analysis of a Mixed Late Woodland and Middle Mississippian Context." Paper Presented at the Society for American Archaeology Conference, Honolulu, HI.

———. 2015. "Life and Stress at a Langford Village Site: A Zooarchaeological Case Study at the Robinson Reserve Site (11CK2)." Paper presented at the Midwest Archaeological Conference, Milwaukee, WI.

———. 2016. "Viewshed Analyses for the Oneota Lake Koshkonong Locality: Defensibility as a Critical Variable in Settlement Studies." Paper presented at the Annual Meeting of the Midwest Archaeological Conference, Iowa City, IA.

———. 2019. "Foodways and a Violent Landscape: A Comparative Study of Oneota and Langford Human-Animal-Environmental Relationships." PhD dissertation, University of Wisconsin–Milwaukee.

McTavish, Rachel C., and Richard W. Edwards IV. 2014. "An Analysis of Variation in Oneota Watershed Exploitation in the Lake Koshkonong Locality." Paper presented at the Midwest Archaeological Conference, Urbana, IL.

Melillo, Jerry, Terese Richmond, and Gary Yohe. 2014. *Global Climate Change Impacts in the United States: The Third National Climate Assessment*. Washington, DC: U.S. Government Printing Office and U.S. Global Change Research Program.

Meyer, Alfred H. 1952. "Fundament Vegetation of the Calumet Region, Northwest Indiana–Northeast Illinois." *Papers of the Michigan Academy of Science, Arts and Letters* 36: 177–82.

Michalik, Laura K. 1982. "An Ecological Perspective on the Huber Phase Subsistence-Settlement System." In *Oneota Studies*, edited by G. E. Gibbon, 29–54. University of Minnesota Publications in Anthropology No. 1. Minneapolis: University of Minnesota.

Miller, Lorin. 1833. "General Land Office Survey Notes for the Interior Sections of Township 5 North, Range 12 East, 4th Meridian, 1833." Electronic document, available at http://digicoll.library.wisc.edu/SurveyNotesHome.html; accessed September 2016.

Miller, Naomi F. 1988. "Ratios in Paleoethnobotanical Analysis." In *Current Paleoethnobotany: Analytical Methods and Cultural Interpretations of Plant Remains*, edited by C. A. Hastorf and V. S. Popper, 72–85. Prehistoric Archaeology and Ecology Series. Chicago: University of Chicago Press.

Milner, George R. 1992. "Morbidity, Mortality and the Adaptive Success of an Oneota Population from West-Central Illinois." In *Late Prehistoric Agriculture: Observations from the Midwest*, edited by W. I. Woods, 136–66. Studies in Illinois Archaeology Springfield: Illinois Historic Preservation Agency.

———. 2005. "Nineteenth-Century Arrow Wounds and Perceptions of Prehistoric Warfare." *American Antiquity* 70: 144–56.

———. 2007. "Warfare, Population, and Food Production in Prehistoric Eastern North America." In *North American Indigenous Warfare and Ritual Violence*, edited by R. J. Chacon and R. G. Mendoza, 182–201. Tucson: University of Arizona Press.

Milner, George R., Eve Anderson, and Virginia G. Smith. 1991. "Warfare in Late-Prehistoric West Central Illinois." *American Antiquity* 56: 581–603.

Minnis, Paul E. 1985. *Social Adaptation to Food Stress: A Prehistoric Southwestern Example*. Prehistoric Archaeology and Ecology Series. Chicago: University of Chicago Press.

Monaghan, G. William, Timothy M. Schilling, and Kathryn E. Parker. 2014. "The Age and Distribution of Domesticated Beans (*Phaseolus vulgaris*) in Eastern North America: Implications for Agricultural Practices and Group Interaction." *Midcontinental Journal of Archaeology Occasional Papers* 1: 33–52.

Montgomery, Frederick H. 1977. *Seeds and Fruits of Plants of Eastern Canada and Northeastern United States*. Toronto: University of Toronto Press.

Morey, Darcy F. 2006. "Burying Key Evidence: The Social Bond between Dogs and People." *Journal of Archaeological Science* 33: 158–75.

———. 2010. *Dogs: Domestication and the Development of a Social Bond*. New York: Cambridge University Press.

Morgan, Lewis H. 1877. *Ancient Society: Or Researches in the Lines of Human Progress from Savagery through Barbarism to Civilization*. New York: Henry Holt and Co.

Morrison, Kathleen D., Gary M. Feinman, Linda M. Nicholls, Thegn N. Ladefoged, Eva Myrda-Runebjer, Glen Davis Stone, and Richard Wilk. 1996. "Typological Schemes and Agricultural Change: Beyond Boserup in Precolonial South India." *Current Anthropology* 37: 583–608.

Moss, James D. 2010. "Intrasite Feature Analysis of the Crescent Bay Hunt Club Site (47JE904), an Oneota Site in Southeastern Wisconsin." Master's thesis, University of Wisconsin–Milwaukee.

Mt. Pleasant, Jane. 2010. "The Science behind the Three Sisters Mound System: An Agronomic Assessment of an Indigenous Agricultural System in the Northeast." In *Histories of Maize: Multidisciplinary Approaches to the Prehistory, Linguistics, Biogeography, Domestication, and Evolution of Maize*, edited by J. Staller, R. Tykot and B. Benz, 529–38. Walnut Creek, CA: Left Coast Press.

Mt. Pleasant, Jane, and Robert F. Burt. 2010. "Estimating Productivity of Traditional Iroquoian Cropping System from Field Experiments and Historical Literature." *Journal of Ethnobiology* 30: 52–79.

Mueller, Natale G., Gayle J. Fritz, Paul Patton, Stephen Carmody, and Elizabeth T. Horton. 2017. "Growing the Lost Crops of Eastern North America's Original Agricultural System." *Nature Plants* 3: 1–5.

Mueller, Jon, and Jeanette E. Stephens. 1991. "Mississippian Sociocultural Adaptation." In *Cahokia and the Hinterlands*, edited by T. E. Emerson and R. B. Lewis, 297–310. Urbana: University of Illinois Press.

Munson, Patrick J. 1987. "Late Woodland Settlement and Subsistence in Temporal Perspective." In *Interpretations of Culture Change in the Eastern Woodlands during the Late Woodland Period*, edited by R. Yerkes, 6–15. Columbus: Department of Anthropology, Ohio State University.

Musil, Jennifer L. 1987. "The Lake Koshkonong Region: Survey and Effigy Mound Research." In *The Southeast Wisconsin Archaeology Project: 1986-87 & Project Summary*, edited by L. Goldstein, 122–50. Milwaukee: Archaeology Research Laboratory, University of Wisconsin–Milwaukee.

Nesper, Larry. 2002. *The Walleye War: The Struggle for Ojibwe Spearfishing and Treaty Rights*. Lincoln: University of Nebraska Press.

Newberry Library. 2016. "Atlas of Historical County Boundaries." Electronic document, available at https://publications.newberry.org/ahcbp/downloads/states.html; accessed March 2016.

Noe-Nygaard, Nanna. 1988. "$\delta^{13}C$ Values of Dog Bones Reveal the Nature of Changes in Man's Food Resources at the Mesolithic-Neolithic Transition, Denmark." *Isotope Geoscience* 73: 87–96.

Nuzzo, Victoria A. 1994. "Extent and Status of Midwest Oak Savanna: Presettlement and 1985." In *Living in the Edge: Proceedings of the North American Conference on Savannas and Barrens*, edited by James Fralish, 1–24. Normal, IL: U.S. Environmental Protection Agency.

O'Gorman, Jodie A., ed. 1993. *The Tremaine Site Complex: Oneota Occupation in the La Crosse Locality Wisconsin*, vol. 1: *The OT Site (47 Lc-262)*. Madison: State Historical Society of Wisconsin.

———. 1994. *The Tremaine Site Complex: Oneota Occupation in the La Crosse Locality Wisconsin*, vol. 2: *The Filler Site (47Lc-149)*. Madison: Museum Archaeology Program.

———. 1995. *The Tremaine Site Complex: Oneota Occupation in the La Crosse Locality Wisconsin*, vol. 3: *The Tremaine Site (47 LC-95)*. Madison: State Historical Society of Wisconsin.

———. 2010. "Exploring the Longhouse and Community in Tribal Society." *American Antiquity* 75: 571–98.

Olsen, M. Lee. 2003. "Agriculture, Domestication and Oneota Subsistence in Southern Wisconsin: The Crescent Bay Hunt Club Site." Master's thesis, University of Wisconsin–Milwaukee.

O'Shea, John M. 1989. "The Role of Wild Resources in Small-Scale Agricultural Systems: Tales from the Lakes and the Plains." In *Bad Year Economics: Cultural Responses to Risk and Uncertainty*, edited by P. Halstead and J. M. O'Shea. New York: Cambridge University Press.

O'Shea, John M. and Claire McHale Milner. 2002. "Material Indicators of Territory, Identity, and Interaction in a Prehistoric Tribal System." *Archaeology of Tribal Systems* 15: 200–226.

Overstreet, David F. 1976. "The Grand River, Lake Koshkonong, Green Bay, and Lake Winnebago Phases: Eight Hundred Years of Oneota Prehistory in Eastern Wisconsin." PhD dissertation, University of Wisconsin–Milwaukee.

———. 1978. "Oneota Settlement Patterns in Eastern Wisconsin: Some Considerations of Time and Space." In *Mississippian Settlement Patterns*, edited by B. D. Smith, 21–52. New York: Academic Press.

———. 1981. "Investigations at the Pipe Site (47FD10): Some Perspectives on Eastern Wisconsin Oneota Prehistory." *Wisconsin Archeologist* 62: 365–535.

———. 1989. *Oneota Tradition, Culture History: New Data from the Old Spring Site (47Wn350)*. Report of Investigations 219. Milwaukee, WI: Great Lakes Archaeological Research Center.

———. 1993. "McCauley, Astor, and Hanson: Candidates for the Provisional Dandy Phase." *The Wisconsin Archeologist* 74:120-196.

———. 1995. "The Eastern Wisconsin Oneota Regional Continuity." In *Oneota Archaeology: Past, Present, and Future*, edited by W. Green, 33–64. Report 20. Iowa City, IA: Office of the State Archaeologist.

———. 1997. "Oneota Prehistory and History." *Wisconsin Archeologist* 78: 250–97.

———. 1998. "East and West Expressions of the Emergent Oneota Horizon: Perceptual Problems and Empirical Realities." *Wisconsin Archeologist* 79: 29–37.

———. 2000. "Cultural Dynamics of the Later Prehistory in Southern Wisconsin." In *Mounds, Modoc, and Mesoamerica: Papers in Honor of Melvin L. Fowler*, edited by S. R. Ahler, 405–38. Illinois State Museum Scientific Papers 28. Springfield: Illinois State Museum.

———. 2001. "Dreaded Dolostone and Old Smudge Stories: Response to Critiques of Emergent Horizon Oneota ^{14}C Dates from Eastern Wisconsin." *Wisconsin Archeologist* 82: 33–86.

———. 2009. "The Mero Complex and the Menominee Tribe: Prospects for a Territorial Ethnicity." *Wisconsin Archeologist* 90: 179–224.

Park, Sung Woo. 2010. "Subsistence Change and Lithic Technological Response by Late Prehistoric and Historic Occupants of the Zimmerman Site (11ls13) in the Upper Illinois River Valley of Northern Illinois." *Wisconsin Archeologist* 91: 81–102.

Parmalee, Paul W. 1962. "The Faunal Complex of the Fisher Site, Illinois." *American Midland Naturalist* 68(2): 399–408.

Pater, Kimberly, Richard W. Edwards IV, and Elizabeth K. Spott. 2010. "An Updated Interpretation of the Koshkonong Creek Village Site." Paper presented at the Midwest Archaeological Conference, Bloomington, IN.

Pauketat, Timothy R. 1994. *The Ascent of Chiefs: Cahokia and Mississippian in Native North America.* Tuscaloosa: University of Alabama Press.

———. 2004. *Ancient Cahokia and the Mississippians.* Case Studies in Early Societies. New York: Cambridge University Press.

———. 2009. "Wars, Rumors of Wars, and the Production of Violence." In *Warfare in a Cultural Context: Practice, Agency, and the Archaeology of Violence,* edited by A. Nielsen and W. Walker, 244–62. Tucson: University of Arizona Press.

Pauketat, Timothy R., and Neal H. Lopinot. 1997. "Cahokian Population Dynamics." In *Cahokia: Domination and Ideology in the Mississippian World,* edited by T. R. Pauketat and T. E. Emerson, 103–23. Lincoln: University of Nebraska Press.

Pearsall, Deborah M. 1983. "Evaluating the Stability of Subsistence Strategies by Use of Paleoethnobotanical Data." *Journal of Ethnobiology* 3: 121–37.

———. 1988. "Interpreting the Meaning of Macroremain Abundance: The Impact of Source and Context." In *Current Paleoethnobotany: Analytical Methods and Cultural Interpretations of Plant Remains,* edited by C. A. Hastorf and V. S. Popper, 97–118. Prehistoric Archaeology and Ecology Series. Chicago: University of Chicago Press.

———. 2009. "Investigating the Transition to Agriculture." *Current Anthropology* 50: 609–13.

———. 2010. *Paleoethnobotany.* 2nd ed. Walnut Creek, CA: Left Coast Press.

Peres, Tanya M. 2010. "Methodological Issues in Zooarchaeology." In *Integrating Zooarchaeology and Paleoethnobotany: A Consideration of Issues, Methods, and Cases,* edited by A. M. VanDerwarker and T. M. Peres, 15–36. New York: Springer.

Peske, G. Richard. 1966. "Oneota Settlement Patterns and Agricultural Patterns in Winnebago County." *Wisconsin Archeologist* 47: 188–95.

Picard, Jennifer. 2013. "Northern Flint, Southern Roots: A Diachronic Analysis of Paleoethnobotanial Remains and Maize Race at the Aztalan Site (47JE0001)." Master's thesis, University of Wisconsin–Milwaukee.

Picard, Jennifer, and Rachel C. McTavish. 2015. "Ecology, Culture, Conflict and Diet: Comparisons of Two Late Prehistoric Sites in Wisconsin." Paper presented at the Society for American Archaeology, San Francisco, CA.

Popper, Virginia S. 1988. "Selecting Quantitative Measurements in Paleoethnobotany." In *Current Paleoethnobotany: Analytical Methods and Cultural Interpretations of Plant Remains,* edited by C. A. Hastorf and V. S. Popper, 53–71. Prehistoric Archaeology and Ecology Series. Chicago: University of Chicago Press.

Pozza, Jacqueline M. 2016. "Investigating the Functions of Copper Material Culture from Four Oneota sites in the Lake Koshkonong Locality of Wisconsin." Master's thesis, University of Wisconsin–Milwaukee.

———. 2019. "Approaching a Vast and Varied Copper Collection: An Analysis of Oneota Copper Artifacts of the Lake Koshkonong Region in Southeastern Wisconsin." *Journal of Archaeological Science: Reports* 25: 632–47.

Pratt, Daniel R. 1994. "A Carbon Isotope Analysis of Fifty-Nine Burials from the Upper Mississippi River Valley." Master's thesis, University of Minnesota.

Price, T. Douglas. 1995. "Agricultural Origins and Social Inequality." In *Foundations of Social Inequality*, edited by T. D. Price and G. M. Feinman, 129–51. New York: Plenum Press.

Price, T. Douglas, and Ofer Bar-Yosef. 2011. "The Origins of Agriculture: New Data, New Ideas: An Introduction to Supplement 4." *Current Anthropology* 52, no. S4: S163–S174.

Radin, Paul. 1923. *The Winnebago Tribe*. Thirty-Seventh Annual Report of the Bureau of American Ethnology. Washington, DC: Smithsonian Institute.

Rice, Glen, and Steven A. LeBlanc. 2001. *Deadly Landscapes: Case Studies in Prehistoric Southwestern Warfare*. Salt Lake City: University of Utah Press.

Richards, John D. 1992. "Ceramics and Culture at Aztalan, a Late Prehistoric Village in Southeast Wisconsin." PhD dissertation, University of Wisconsin–Milwaukee.

Richards, John D., and Robert Jeske. 2002. "Location, Location, Location: The Temporal and Cultural Context of Late Prehistoric Settlement in Southeast Wisconsin." *Wisconsin Archeologist* 83: 32–54.

———. 2015. *Preliminary Results of Accelerator Mass Spectrometry Dating of Food Residues on Prehistoric Ceramics from the Western Great Lakes and Prairie Peninsula Regions of the Midcontinent*. Report of Investigations 370. Milwaukee: Archaeological Research Laboratory, University of Wisconsin–Milwaukee.

Richards, John D., Patricia B. Richards, and Brian D. Nicholls. 1998. *Archaeological Investigations in the Carcajou Point Locale, Sumner Township, Jefferson County Wisconsin*. Report of Investigations 129. Milwaukee: Historic Resource Management Services, Archaeological Research Laboratory, University of Wisconsin–Milwaukee.

Richards, Patricia B. 1993. "Winnebago Subsistence." *Wisconsin Archeologist* 74: 272–89.

Riley, Thomas J., and Glen Freimuth. 1979. "Field Systems and Frost Drainage in the Prehistoric Agriculture of the Upper Great Lakes." *American Antiquity* 44: 271–85.

Rindos, David, and Sissel Johannessen. 2000. "Human-Plant Interactions and Cultural Change in the American Bottom." In *Late Woodland Societies: Tradition and Transformation Across the Midcontinent*, edited by T. E. Emerson, D. McElrath, and A. C. Fortier, 35–45. Lincoln: University of Nebraska Press.

Rodell, Roland L. 1984. "A Survey of Oneota Sites in the Lake Koshkonong Area." In *Southeast Wisconsin Archaeology Project: 1983–1984*, edited by L. Goldstein, 144–66. Report of Investigations 77. Milwaukee: University of Wisconsin–Milwaukee Archaeology Research Laboratory.

———. 1991. "The Diamond Bluff Complex and the Cahokia Influence in the Red Wing Locality." In *New Perspectives on Cahokia*, edited by J. B. Stoltman, 253–80. Madison, WI: Prehistory Press.

———. 1997. "The Diamond Bluff Site Complex: Time and Tradition in the Northern Mississippi Valley." PhD dissertation, University of Wisconsin–Milwaukee.

Romond, Sara, Kathleen M. Foley Winkler, Robert J. Jeske, Daniel M. Winkler, Kristin Hedman, Phil Slater, and Matthew Fort. 2011. "Late Archaic Lifeways in Southeastern Wisconsin: Evidence from the Jaco Site (47JE1192)." Paper presented at the 58th Annual Meeting of the Midwest Archaeological Conference, La Crosse, WI.

Rudolph, Katie Zejdlik. 2009. "A Taphonomic Analysis of Human Skeletal Material from Aztalan: Cannibalism, Hostility and Mortuary Variability." Master's thesis, University of Wisconsin–Milwaukee.

Salkin, Philip H. 2000. "The Horicon and Kekoskee Cultural Complexes in the Late Woodland Stage in Southeastern Wisconsin." In *Late Woodland Societies: Tradition and Transformation across the Midcontinent*, edited by T. E. Emerson, D. McElrath, and A. C. Fortier, 525–42. Lincoln: University of Nebraska Press.

Sampson, Kurt A. 2008. "Getting to the Point: Typology, Morphology, and Lithic Material Variation in the Milwaukee Public Museum Projectile Point Collection from the Aztalan Site." Master's thesis, University of Wisconsin–Milwaukee.

Sasso, Robert F. 1989. "Oneota Settlement Practices in the La Crosse Region: An Analysis of the Coon Creek Drainage in the Driftless Area of Western Wisconsin." PhD dissertation, Northwestern University, Evanston, IL.

———. 1993. "La Crosse Region Oneota Adaptations: Changing Late Prehistoric Subsistence and Settlement Patterns in the Upper Mississippi Valley." *Wisconsin Archeologist* 74: 324–69.

———. 1998. *Native American Agricultural Sites in Southeastern Wisconsin*. Report of Archaeological Investigations No. 2. Kenosha: University of Wisconsin–Parkside Lillian Traeger Anthropology Laboratory.

———. 2001. "Observations on the Oneota Cultivation Sites in Winnebago County." *Wisconsin Archeologist* 82: 125–38.

———. 2003a. "Agricultural Places and the Oneota Lifeway in Wisconsin." In *Theory, Method, and Practice in Modern Archaeology*, edited by R. Jeske and D. K. Charles, 252–65. Westport, CT: Praeger.

———. 2003b. "Vestiges of Ancient Cultivation: The Antiquity of Garden Beds and Corn Hills in Wisconsin." *Midcontinental Journal of Archaeology* 48: 195–231.
———. 2014. "Review of Bison Remains at Wisconsin Oneota Sites." *Wisconsin Archeologist* 95: 173–87.
Sasso, Robert F., and James A. Brown. 1987. "Land, Fields, and Maize: A Perspective on Oneota Agriculture." Paper presented at the Annual Meeting of the American Anthropological Association, Chicago.
Scarry, C. Margaret. 2003. "Patterns of Wild Plant Utilization in the Prehistoric Eastern Woodlands." In *People and Plants in Ancient Eastern North America*, edited by P. E. Minnis, 50–104. Washington, DC: Smithsonian Institution Press.
Scarry, C. Margaret, and John F. Scarry. 2005. "North American 'Garden Agriculture' in Southeastern North America." *World Archaeology* 37: 259–74.
Schirmer, Ronald C. 2002. "Plant-use Systems and Late Prehistoric Culture Change in the Red Wing Locality." PhD dissertation, University of Minnesota.
Schneider, Seth A. 2015. "Oneota Ceramic Production and Exchange: Social, Economic, and Political Interactions in Eastern Wisconsin between AD 1050–1400." PhD dissertation, University of Wisconsin–Milwaukee.
Schneider, Seth A., and John D. Richards. 2010. *Final Report: Archaeological Monitoring and Recovery of Sub-Roadbed Deposits at the Schrage Site, Calumetville, Wisconsin*. Report of Investigations 180. Milwaukee: Historical Resource Management Services, University of Wisconsin–Milwaukee Archaeological Research Laboratory.
Schneider, Seth A., Eric J. Scheutz, and Robert E. Ahlrichs. 2012. "Intraregional Social Interaction in Late Prehistory: Paste Compositional Analysis of Oneota Pottery Vessels in the Lake Koshkonong Region." *Field Notes: A Journal of Collegiate Anthropology* 4: 192–215.
Schoeller, Dale A. 1999. "Isotope Fractionation: Why Aren't We What We Eat?" *Journal of Archaeological Science* 26: 667–73.
Schurr, Mark R. 1998. "Using Stable Nitrogen-Isotopes to Study Weaning Behavior in Past Populations." *World Archaeology* 30: 327–42.
Schwartz, Marion. 1997. *A History of Dogs in the Early Americas*. New Haven, CT: Yale University Press.
Shennan, Stephan. 1997. *Quantifying Archaeology*. Edinburgh: Edinburgh University Press.
Shuman, Bryan, Anna K. Henderson, Colin Plank, Ivanka Stefanova, and Susy S. Ziegler. 2009. "Woodland-to-Forest Transition during Prolonged Drought in Minnesota after ca. AD 1300." *Ecology* 90, no. 10: 2792–2807.
Simon, Mary L. 1999. "Plant Remains from the Keeshin Farm Site." In *Keeshin Farm Site and the Rock River Langford Tradition in Northeastern Illinois*, edited by T. E. Emerson, 153–85. Research Report 58. Urbana: Illinois Transportation Archaeological Research Program, University of Illinois at Urbana-Champaign.

———. 2014. "Reevaluating the Introduction of Maize into the American Bottom and Western Illinois." *Midwest Archaeological Conference: Occasional Papers* 1: 97–134.

Skinner, Alanson. 1921. *Material Culture of the Menominee*. Indian Notes and Monographs. New York: Museum of the American Indian Heye Foundation.

Smith, Alexia. 2014. "The Use of Multivariate Statistics within Archaeobotany." In *Method and Theory in Paleoethnobotany*, edited by J. M. Marston, J. D'Alpoim Guedes, and C. Warinner, 181–204. Boulder, CO: University Press of Colorado.

Smith, Bruce D., ed. 1978. *Mississippian Settlement Patterns*. New York: Academic Press.

———. 1985. "Role of *Chenopodium* as a Domesticate in Pre-Maize Garden Systems of the Eastern United States." *Southeastern Archaeology* 4: 51–72.

———. 1992. *Rivers of Change: Essays on Early Agriculture in Eastern North America*. Washington, DC: Smithsonian Institution Press.

———. 2001. "Low-Level Food Production." *Journal of Archaeological Research* 9, no. 1: 1–43.

———. 2011. "The Cultural Context of Plant Domestication in Eastern North America." *Current Anthropology* 52, no. S4: S471–S484.

Smith, Bruce D., and C. Wesley Cowan. 2003. "Domesticated Crop Plants and Evolution of Food Production Economics in Eastern North America." In *People and Plants in Ancient Eastern North America*, edited by P. E. Minnis, 105–26. Washington, DC: Smithsonian Institution Press.

Smith, Eric Alden, and Robert Boyd. 1990. "Risk and Reciprocity: Hunter-Gatherer Socioecology and the Problem and Collective Action." In *Risk and Uncertainty in Tribal and Peasant Economies*, edited by E. Cashdan, 167–92. Boulder, CO: Westview Press.

Snow, Dean R. 2007. "Iroquois-Huron Warfare." In *North American Indigenous Warfare and Ritual Violence*, edited by R. J. Chacon and R. G. Mendoza, 149–59. Tucson: University of Arizona Press.

Spector, Janet. 1975. "Crabapple Point (Je-93), a Historic Winnebago Village Site in Jefferson County." *Wisconsin Archeologist* 56: 270–345.

Springer, James Warren, and Stanley R. Witkowski. 1982. "Siouan Historical Linguistics and Oneota Archaeology." In *Oneota Studies*, edited by G. E. Gibbon, 69–84. University of Minnesota Publications in Anthropology No. 1. Minneapolis: University of Minnesota.

Stahle, David W., and Malcolm K. Cleavland. 1994. "Tree-Ring Reconstructed Rainfall over the Southeastern U.S.A. during the Medieval Warm Period and Little Ice Age." In *The Medieval Warm Period*, edited by M. K. Hughes and H. F. Diaz, 199–212. New York: Springer.

Stelle, L. J., C. L. Rohrbaugh, J. A. Brown, T. E. Emerson, and R. Jeske. 1993. "Deciphering the Grand Village of the Illinois: A Preliminary Assessment of the Grand Village Research Project." *Illinois Archaeology* 5: 508–16.

Stenhouse, M. J., and M. S. Baxter. 1977. "Bomb ^{14}C as a Biological Tracer." *Nature* 267: 828–32.

———. 1979. "The Uptake of Bomb ^{14}C in Humans." In *Radiocarbon Dating*, edited by R. Berger and H. E. Suess, 324–41. Berkeley: University of California Press.

Stephens, D. W., and Eric L. Charnov. 1982. "Optimal Foraging: Some Simple Stochastic Models." *Behavioral Ecology and Sociobiology* 10, no. 4: 251–63.

Sterner, Katherine M. 2012. "Oneota Lithics: A Use-Wear Analysis of the Crescent Bay Hunt Club Assemblage from the 2004 Excavations." Master's thesis, University of Wisconsin–Milwaukee.

———. 2018. "Stone Tools and Agricultural Communities: Economic, Microwear, and Residue Analyses of Wisconsin Oneota Lithic Assemblages." PhD dissertation, University of Wisconsin–Milwaukee.

Sterner-Miller, Katherine M. 2014. *Another Piece of the Puzzle*. Paper presented at the Midwest Archaeological Conference, Urbana, IL.

Stevenson, Katherine. 1985. "Oneota Subsistence-Related Behavior in the Driftless Area: A Study of the Valley View Site Near La Crosse, Wisconsin." PhD dissertation, University of Wisconsin–Madison.

———. 1994. "Chronological and Settlement Aspects of the Valley View Site (47LC34)." *Wisconsin Archeologist* 75: 237–94.

Stevenson, Katherine P., Robert F. Boszhardt, Charles R. Moffat, Phillip H. Salkin, Thomas C. Pleger, James L. Theler, and Constance M. Arzigian. 1997. "The Woodland Tradition." *Wisconsin Archeologist* 78: 140–201.

Stoltman, James B. 2000. "A Reconsideration of the Cultural Processes Linking Cahokia to Its Northern Hinterlands during the Period AD 1000–1200." In *Mounds, Modoc, and Mesoamerica: Papers in Honor of Melvin L. Fowler*, edited by S. R. Ahler, 439–54. Illinois State Museum Scientific Papers, vol. 28. Springfield: Illinois State Museum.

Stone, Glenn Davis, and Christian E. Downum. 1999. "Non-Boserupian Ecology and Agricultural Risk: Ethnic Politics and Land Control in the Arid Southwest." *American Anthropologist* 101: 113–29.

Stout, A. B., and H. T. Skavlem. 1908. "The Archaeology of the Lake Koshkonong Region." *Wisconsin Archeologist* 7: 47–102.

Strezewski, Michael. 2006. "Patterns of Interpersonal Violence at the Fisher Site." *Midcontinental Journal of Archaeology* 31: 249–80.

Strezewski, Michael, Kristin M. Hedman, and Thomas E. Emerson. 2012. "Oakwood Mound: A Langford Mortuary Site in Will County, Illinois." *Wisconsin Archeologist* 93: 3–107.

Tankersley, K. B., and J. M. Koster. 2009. "Sources of Stable Isotope Variation in Archaeological Dog Remains." *North American Archaeologist* 30: 361–75.

ter Braak, Cajo J. F. 1995. "Ordination." In *Data Analysis in Community and Landscape Ecology*, edited by R. H. G. Jongman, C. J. F. ter Braak, and O. F. R. van Tongeren, 91–173. Cambridge: Cambridge University Press.

Theler, James L. 1989. "The Pammel Creek Site Faunal Remains." *Wisconsin Archeologist* 70: 157–242.

———. 1994. "Oneota Faunal Remains from Seven Sites in the La Crosse, Wisconsin, Area." *Wisconsin Archeologist* 75: 343–92.

Theler, James L., and Robert F. Boszhardt. 2000. "The End of the Effigy Mound Culture: The Late Woodland to Oneota Transition in Southwestern Wisconsin." *Midcontinental Journal of Archaeology* 25: 289–312.

———. 2006. "Collapse of Crucial Resources and Culture Change: A Model for the Woodland to Oneota Transformation in the Upper Midwest." *American Antiquity* 71: 433–72.

Thorne, D. Wynne. 1979. "Soil Organic Matter, Microorganisms, and Crop Production." In *Soil, Water, and Crop Production*, edited by D. W. Thorne and M. D. Thorne, 82–95. Westport, CT: AVI Publishing.

Tiffany, Joseph A. 1979. "An Overview of Oneota Sites in Southeast Iowa: A Perspective from the Ceramic Analysis of the Schmeiser Site, 13DM101, Des Moines County, Iowa." *Proceedings of the Iowa Academy of Science* 86: 89–101.

———. 1982. "Site Catchment Analysis of Southeast Iowa Oneota Sites." In *Oneota Studies*, edited by G. E. Gibbons, 1–14. University of Minnesota Publications in Anthropology No. 1. Minneapolis: University of Minnesota.

Toll, Mollie S. 1988. "Flotation Sampling: Problems and Some Solutions, with Examples from the American Southwest." In *Current Paleoethnobotany: Analytical Methods and Cultural Interpretations of Plant Remains*, edited by C. A. Hastorf and V. S. Popper, 36–52. Prehistoric Archaeology and Ecology Series. Chicago: University of Chicago Press.

Tubbs, Ryan M., and Jodie A. O'Gorman. 2005. "Assessing Oneota Diet and Health: A Community and Lifeway Perspective." *Midcontinental Journal of Archaeology* 30: 119–63.

Tung, Tiffany A. 2012. *Violence Ritual and the Wari Empire*. Gainesville: University Press of Florida.

Turner, Christy G., and Laurel Lofgren. 1966. "Household Size of Prehistoric Western Pueblo." *Southwestern Journal of Anthropology* 22: 117–32.

Tylor, Edward B. 1881. *Anthropology: An Introduction to Man and Civilization*. London: Macmillan and Co.

U.S. Department of Agriculture, Agriculture Research Service. 2017. "USDA National Nutrient Database for Standard Reference." Electronic document, available at www.ars.usda.gov/nutrientdata; accessed August 2017.

Van de Pas, Lucienne, Rachel C. McTavish, and Amy Klemmer. 2015. "The Role of Animals in Oneota Subsistence and Agricultural Technology: A Case Study from the Lake Koshkonong Locality." Paper presented at the Midwest Archaeological Conference, Milwaukee, WI.

VanDerwarker, Amber M. 2010. "Simple Measures for Integrating Plant and Animal Remains." In *Integrating Zooarchaeology and Paleoethnobotany: A Consideration of Issues, Methods, and Cases*, edited by A. M. VanDerwarker and T. M. Peres, 65–74. New York: Springer.

VanDerwarker, Amber M., and Gregory D. Wilson. 2016. "War, Food, and Structural Violence in Mississippian Central Illinois Valley." In *The Archaeology of Food and Warfare: Food Insecurity in Prehistory*, edited by A. M. VanDerwarker and G. D. Wilson, 75–105. New York: Springer.

Vennum, Thomas, Jr. 1988. *Wild Rice and the Ojibway People*. St. Paul: Minnesota Historical Society Press.

Vita-Finzi, Claudio, and E. Higgs. 1970. "Prehistoric Economy in the Mount Carmel Area of Palestine: Site Catchment Analysis." *Prehistoric Society* 36: 1–337.

Wagner, Gail E. 2003. "Eastern Woodlands Anthropogenic Ecology." In *People and Plants in Ancient Eastern North America*, edited by P. E. Minnis, 126–71. Washington, DC: Smithsonian Institution Press.

Walker, Phillip L. 2008. "Bioarchaeological Ethics: A Historical Perspective on the Value of Human Remains." In *Biological Anthropology of the Human Skeleton*, edited by M. A. Katzenberg and S. R. Saunders, 3–40. New York: Wiley-Liss.

Wedel, Mildred Mott. 1959. "Oneota Sites on the Upper Iowa River." *Missouri Archaeologist* 21, no. 2–4: 181.

———. 1976. "Ethnohistory: Its Payoffs and Pitfalls for Iowa Archaeologists." *Journal of the Iowa Archeological Society* 23: 1–44.

———. 1981. "The Ioway, Oto, and Omaha Indians in 1700." *Journal of the Iowa Archeological Society* 28: 1–13.

———. 1986. "Peering at the Ioway Indians through the Mist of Time: 1650–circa 1700." *Journal of the Iowa Archaeological Society* 33: 1–74.

Weissner, Polly. 1982. "Beyond Willow Smoke and Dogs' Tails: A Comment on Binford's Analysis of Hunter-Gatherer Settlement Systems." *American Antiquity* 47: 171–78.

Wellner, Kari L. 2006. "An Analysis of the Human Remains from the Richter Site (47DR80): Diet and Health at a North Bay Phase, Middle Woodland Site in Door County, Wisconsin." Master's thesis, University of Wisconsin–Milwaukee.

Wendrich, Willeke, and Hans Barnard. 2008. The Archaeology of Mobility: Definitions and Research Approaches. In *The Archaeology of Mobility: Old World and New World Nomadism*, 1-24. Los Angeles: Costen Institute of Archaeology, University of California, Los Angeles.

Wetterstrom, Wilma. 1978. "Cognitive Systems, Food Patterns, and Paleoethnobotany." In *The Nature and Status of Ethnobotany*, edited by R. I. Ford, 91–95. Anthropological Papers, no. 67. Ann Arbor: Museum of Anthropology, University of Michigan.

White, Christine D., Mary E. D. Pohl, Henry P. Schwarcz, and Fred J. Longstaffe. 2001. "Isotopic Evidence for Maya Patterns of Deer and Dog Use at Pre-Classic Colha." *Journal of Archaeological Science* 28: 89–107.

———. 2004. "Feast, Field, and Forest: Deer and Dog Diets in Lagartero, Tikal and Copan." In *Maya Zooarchaeology: New Directions in Method and Theory*, edited by K. F. Emery, 141–58. Monograph 51. Los Angeles: Costen Institute of Archaeology, University of California, Los Angeles.

Wilson, Gilbert Livingstone. 1917. *Agriculture of the Hidatsa Indians: An Indian Interpretation*. Studies in the Social Sciences, no. 9. Minneapolis: University of Minnesota.

Wilson, Gregory D., and Amber M. VanDerwarker. 2016. "Toward an Archaeology of Food and Warfare." In *The Archaeology of Food and Warfare: Food Insecurity in Prehistory*, edited by A. M. VanDerwarker and G. D. Wilson, 1–12. New York: Springer.

Wilson, Stephen. 2016. "Late Prehistoric Lithic Economies in the Prairie Peninsula: A Comparison of Oneota and Langford in Southern Wisconsin and Northern Illinois." Master's thesis, University of Wisconsin–Milwaukee.

Winterhalder, Bruce. 1986. "Diet Choice, Risk, and Food Sharing in a Stochastic Environment." *Journal of Anthropological Archaeology* 5: 369–92.

———. 1990. "Open Field, Common Pot: Harvest Variability and Risk Avoidance in Agricultural and Foraging Societies." In *Risk and Uncertainty in Tribal and Peasant Economies*, edited by E. Cashden, 67–88. Boulder, CO: Westview Press.

Winterhalder, Bruce, and Carol Goland. 1997. "An Evolutionary Ecology Perspective on Diet Choice, Risk, and Plant Domestication." In *People, Plants, and Landscapes: Studies in Paleoethnobotany*, edited by K. J. Gremillion, 123–60. Tuscaloosa: University of Alabama Press.

Winterhalder, Bruce, and Douglas J. Kennett. 2009. "Four Neglected Concepts with a Role to Play in Explaining the Origins of Agriculture." *Current Anthropology* 50: 645–48.

Winterhalder, Bruce, Flora Lu, and Brian Tucker. 1999. "Risk Sensitive Adaptive Tactics: Models and Evidence from Subsistence Studies in Biology and Anthropology." *Journal of Archaeological Research* 7: 301–48.

Wisconsin Department of Natural Resources (WDNR). 2015. "Indexes and PLSS." Electronic document, available at https://data-wi-dnr.opendata.arcgis.com/datasets?t=index; accessed March 2018.

——— 2016. "Harvesting Wild Rice in Wisconsin." Electronic document, available at http://dnr.wi.gov/topic/outdoorrecreation/activities/rice.html; accessed September 2016.

Wisconsin Historical Society (WHS). 2011. "Wisconsin Archaeological Site Inventory." Electronic document, www.wisahrd.org/ASI/Welcome.aspx; accessed January 2011.

Wright, Patti J. 2010. "Methodological Issues in Paleoethnobotany: A Consideration of Issues, Methods, and Cases." In *Integrating Zooarchaeology and Paleoethnobotany: A Consideration of Issues, Methods, and Cases*, edited by A. M. VanDerwarker and T. M. Peres, 37–64. New York: Springer.

Wylie, Alison. 2000. "Questions of Evidence, Legitimacy, and the (Dis)Unity of Science." *American Antiquity* 65: 227–37.

Young, Biloine Whiting, and Melvin L. Fowler. 2000. *Cahokia: The Great Native American Metropolis*. Urbana: University of Illinois Press.

Zvelebl, M. 1996. "The Agricultural Frontier and the Transition to Farm in in the Circum-Baltic Region." In *The Origins and Spread of Agriculture and Pastoralism in Eurasia*, edited by D. R. Harris, 323–45. Washington, DC: Smithsonian Institution Press.

Zych, Thomas. 2013. "The Construction of a Mound and a New Community: An Analysis of the Ceramic and Feature Assemblages from the Northeast Mound at the Aztalan Site." Master's thesis, University of Wisconsin–Milwaukee.

INDEX

The letter *t* following a page number denotes a table.

acorn
  as aggregated resource, 67, 85
  collection, 178
  consumption, 118, 120t, 121, 131, 141
  as dietary supplement, 83, 90, 155, 169
  recovered at Koshkonong, 87, 168, 177, 179
agriculture
  definition, 205–10
  gendered labor, 199, 203
  labor investment, 61, 159–65
  relationship to cultural complexity, 62–63, 201–3, 214–15
  risk management strategies, 57–59, 195
  seasonal labor variation, 165–69
American Bottom, 106t, 109–14, 142, 144, 214
antler tools, 161, 166, 167, 173, 175
Aztalan, 5, 47, 78t, 106t, 107t, 108, 127–28, 140–41, 154, 186, 197
  dog sample, 96, 98–99, 101t, 112, 176
  maize varieties, 209

bear, 76
burial, 76, 173–74, 201–2
  dog burial, 46, 76
  in longhouse, 94
  mound, 44
  Mound 72, 109

Cahokia, 2, 105–6, 112, 206
canine surrogacy approach, 79–80, 97
Carcajou Point, 31–35, 184, 191
chronology, 14, 16, 18–19, 25, 30–35, 75–76, 89, 102
corn hills, 65, 160–63, 209
Crab Apple Point, 25, 35, 160–61, 191
Crescent Bay Hunt Club/Crescent Bay (CBHC)
  background, 26–28
  Eastern Agricultural Complex (EAC) use, 68, 121–22, 134t
  floral diversity, 123–24, 127
  isotope data, 99t, 100t, 106t, 112, 117
  macrobotanical data, 84–88, 128
  mortuary data, 173–74
  sampling, 75–76, 77t, 78t, 83
  seasonality, 165–66

281

Crescent Bay Hunt Club/Crescent
    Bay (CBHC) (*cont.*)
  storage, 164, 181
  structure differences, 92–94
  trade and exchange, 191, 203–5

diet breadth, 53, 66, 180
diversity
  indices, 81, 122–24, 127, 140, 142,
    176
  risk management strategy, 52–53,
    57–59
Door Peninsula, 15, 127, 136–37

elites, 2, 105, 109, 110, 154, 206

Fisher
  archaeological culture, 4, 16, 18–19,
    146, 152, 154–55, 161, 213
  archaeological site, 37t, 44, 78t, 99,
    101t, 102, 107t, 112, 126t, 127t,
    128t, 129t, 130t
Fort Ancient, 13

garden bed, 65, 160–62
garden plot, 68

Hall, Robert, 25
household, 169, 181, 198, 200, 203–6
Huber, 16, 18–19, 25

Koshkonong Creek Village (KCV)
  background, 27, 29–31, 32t, 33t, 35t
  Eastern Agricultural Complex
    (EAC) cultigen use, 121–22, 134t
  floral diversity, 123–24, 127
  macrobotanical data, 84–87, 128
  sampling, 75–76, 77t, 78t, 83
  seasonality, 165–66
  storage, 164, 181
  trade and exchange, 191, 203–4

Koshkonong Locality
  agricultural sites, 65, 160–61, 171
  chronology, 30–35, 197
  climate, 172
  economy, 21, 67, 80–82, 124, 177,
    188–89
  excavation history, 25–26
  external relationships, 4–6, 73, 90, 191
  intergroup violence, 23, 173, 175,
    184–87
  landscape management, 162
  location, 2–3, 27
  maize consumption, 117–18,
    177–78, 197

Langford, 16–18, 25
localities, definition, 14
longhouse. *See* structures

Madison points, 14
Madison-ware ceramics, 46
Madison-ware sites, 140, 191
Material Service Quarry (MSQ), 44,
  102, 107t, 112

networks
  exchange, 51, 55, 186, 204
  kin, 51, 169, 194, 198–201, 213
  village, 136, 205, 212
Nitschke, 46, 98–99, 101t, 107t, 112

Oliver Phase, 13
Oneota
  definition, 13–14
  economy, 20–22
  historical connections, 24–25
  intergroup violence, 22–24
  origins, 17–18

Prairie Peninsula, 14, 146
Purnell, 27, 186, 203

risk, 6–7, 49–51
   definition, 51–52, 54
   environmental, 171–73
   management, 52, 60, 62–63, 192, 194, 212
   non-normative, 74
   social, 173–74

Schmeling, 26, 31, 33t, 191
Schrage, 36, 37t, 78t, 127t, 128t, 151
settlement system, 41, 60, 70, 108, 135–36, 182–83, 186–87, 193–94, 199, 202
Skavlem, H. T., 29
Soggy Oats, 37t, 38, 127–28, 156
storage, 6, 52–54, 56–57, 164–65, 181–82, 204
Stout, A. B. *See* Skavlem, H. T.
structures, 29, 41, 44–45, 61, 164–65
   function and seasonality, 90–94, 109
   household storage, 181–82, 190
   longhouse, 26
   non-house structures, 27
   sampling, 76, 77t
   seasonality, 169
   wigwam, 26, 109

Upper Mississippian, 13

violence
   at Koshkonong, 5, 173–74, 182, 197
   in Oneota societies, 22–23, 72
   relative to risk management, 7, 74, 186
   skeletal evidence, 23
   status, 199

Walker Hooper, 202
wigwam. *See* structures

Zimmerman, 25, 37t, 43–44, 78t, 127–28, 131, 145, 155

RICHARD W. EDWARDS IV
is a project archaeologist for Commonwealth Heritage Group.

www.ingramcontent.com/pod-product-compliance
Lightning Source LLC
Chambersburg PA
CBHW071403300426
44114CB00016B/2163